Using Race and Culture in Counseling and Psychotherapy:
Theory and Process

Janet E. Helms
University of Maryland, College Park

Donelda A. Cook
Loyola College in Maryland

Allyn and Bacon

Boston ▪ London ▪ Toronto ▪ Sydney ▪ Tokyo ▪ Singapore

Editor-in-Chief, Social Sciences: *Sean W. Wakely*
Series Editorial Assistant: *Susan Hutchinson*
Marketing Manager: *Joyce Nilsen*
Composition and Prepress Buyer: *Linda Cox*
Manufacturing Buyer: *Suzanne Lareau*
Cover Administrator: *Jenny Hart*
Editorial-Production Service: *Shepherd, Inc.*

Library of Congress Cataloging-in-Publication Data

Helms, Janet E., 1947–
    Using race and culture in counseling and psychotherapy : theory
and process / Janet E. Helms and Donelda A. Cook.
        p.   cm.
    Includes bibliographical references and index.
    ISBN 0-205-28565-1 (alk. paper)
    1. Minorities—Mental health.   2. Psychotherapy—Cross-cultural
studies.   3. Cross-cultural counseling.   I. Cook, Donelda A.
(Donelda Ann), 1955–   . II. Title.
    RC451.5.A2H45   1999
    616.89'14—dc21   98-36029
                                                      CIP

Printed in the United States of America

10 9 8 7 6 5   04 05 06 07 08

CONTENTS

List of Exercises   v
List of Insights   vi
List of Tables   vii
Preface   ix

1 Introduction   1

PART ONE   Who Enters the Process?   5

2 Becoming a Race- and
Culture-Sensitive Therapist   7

3 Applications of Racial and Cultural Terminology
to Therapy   15

4 The Sociopolitical Histories of the Original
Socioracial Groups   34

5 The Sociopolitical Histories of the Culture-Based
Socioracial Groups   55

6 Models of Racial Oppression and Sociorace   69

7 Aspects of Culture in Personhood   101

PART TWO   The Process   131

8 The Therapy Process:
Theoretical Orientations   133

9 Beginning the Therapy Process   158

10 Racial and Cultural Nuances in the
Psychotherapy Process   173

11 Racial and Cultural Themes
in Career Counseling   200

12 Racial and Cultural Dynamics
of Group Interventions   226

13 Collaborating with Indigenous Healers
and Helpers   254

PART THREE   Observing the Process   275

14 Using Race and Culture
in Therapy Supervision   277

15 Race and Culture in Therapy Research   299

16 Answers to Questions We've Been Asked   316

Appendix A: Ethical Principles of Psychologists and Code
of Conduct   327

Appendix B: Guidelines for Providers of Psychological Services
to Ethnic, Linguistic, and Culturally Diverse Populations   357

Index   363

EXERCISES

1 . 1   Some Rules We Live By   3

2 . 1   Who Are You?   12

2 . 2   The Meaning of Your Sociorace   13

3 . 1   Recognizing the Different Meanings of *Race*   18

3 . 2   Terminology Quiz   31

4 . 1   A New Racial World Order   36

4 . 2   African American History Quiz   53

5 . 1   Learning about American People   66

5 . 2   Do You Suffer from "Racial Oppression Syndrome"?   67

7 . 1   Thinking about Your Value Orientations   103

7 . 2   What Remains of Your Ethnic Culture?   125

8 . 1   Understanding Cultural Dynamics   144

9 . 1   Self-Assessing Your Racial and Cultural Biases in the Therapy Relationship   165

10 . 1   Practice in Assessing Your Multicultural Competencies   177

11 . 1   How to Get a Job   218

11 . 2   Evaluating Career Development Measures for Racial or Cultural Bias   219

12 . 1   An Inclusion Experience   232

12 . 2   Draw Your Culture   233

13 . 1   Identifying Your "Indigenous" Healers and Helpers   271

13 . 2   Making a Cross-Cultural Referral   272

14 . 1   Assessing Your Cultural Style in the Supervisory Process   293

INSIGHTS

4.1 A Personal Account of Being Caught between Two Races   47

6.1 A Proud American   94

7.1 Native American Children Speak   111

7.2 A Quest for Religious Freedom   121

7.3 African Cultural Principles   122

8.1 Tashi Enters Psychotherapy   135

8.2 Use of Person-Centered Therapy with an Asian Woman Client   151

9.1 Skin Color Commentaries   163

10.1 Ignoring the Client's System   186

11.1 "Career Choice" When There Is No Choice   206

11.2 A View of Work through Non-Middle-Class Eyes   207

11.3 What Is Education Good For?   221

13.1 The Origin of Morita or Personal-Experience Therapy   261

13.2 NTU Therapy: A Spiritual Psychotherapy   263

15.1 Some Research Approaches We Like   311

TABLES

2.1   Some Examples of Psychoracial and Psychocultural Factors in the Therapy Process   10

2.2   Some Examples of Sociocultural, Socioracial, and Class Factors in the Therapy Process   11

3.1   Summary of Potential Social Class Psychological (Proximal) Characteristics   25

4.1   Some Moments in Native American and European American Intergroup History   46

4.2   Some Moments in African American and European American Intergroup History   51

5.1   Moments in Spanish/Mexican and Anglo History   59

5.2   Moments in Asian/Pacific Islander and White American History   63

6.1   Selected Summary of Visible Racial or "Ethnic" Group (VREG)   82

6.2   Summary of Common Ego Status Themes in Helms's Racial Identity Models   85

6.3   Summary of ALANA Racial Identity Ego Statuses, Examples, and Information Processing Strategies (IPS)   87

6.4   Summary of White Racial Identity Ego Statuses, Examples, and Information Processing Strategies (IPS)   90

7.1   A Comparison of Individualistic and Collectivistic Cultural Cognitions, Emotions, and Behaviors   105

7.2   Some of Katz's (1985) White Cultural Components and Dimensions of Therapy   110

7.3   Landrine and Klonoff's (1994) Dimensions of Indigenous African American Culture   115

7.4   Some Dimensions of Helms's (1994) People of Color (and Black) Racial Identity   116

7.5   Acculturation Models for Native, Asian, and Latino/Latin American Socioracial and Ethnic Groups   119

8.1   Description and Racial and Cultural Examples of Freud's Defense Mechanisms   139

9.1   Race-Related Counseling Process Relationship Types When the Counselor Is Race-Avoidant   170

10.1   Summary of Sue et al.'s (1982) Characteristics of Culturally Skilled Counselors   176

10.2   An Adaptation of Worthington's (1989) Guidelines for Assessing Clients' Religion or Spirituality   192

11.1   A Summary of Super's Developmental Tasks and Some Relevant ALANA and White Racial Identity Vocational Themes   205

1 1 . 2   Occupation Distribution (%) of the Employed Civilian Labor Force by Gender and (Socio)race: 1991–1992   211

1 ? 1   A Segment of a Race-Explicit Discussion   247

1 4 . 1   Summary of Subscale and Process Items on which Supervisees, Individual Supervisors, and Group Supervisors Evaluated VREG Supervisees Differently   279

1 4 . 2   Summary of Subscale and Process Items on Which Supervisees, Individual Supervisors, and Group Supervisors Evaluated White Supervisees Differently   280

1 4 . 3   Summary of Visible Racial or Ethnic Group (VREG) and White Racial Identity Ego Statuses and Potential Approaches to Racial Issues in Supervision (PARI)   289

1 5 . 1   Summary of the Influence of White Identity on White Researchers' Cross-Cultural Scholarship   301

PREFACE

We intend this book to be the book that we wished for as graduate students and continued to wish for as mental health professionals, charged with the dual responsibilities of helping our clients function better and mentoring graduate students to be racially and culturally responsive mental health professionals. We intend it to be a book that acknowledges the diversities of people with respect to race and culture. However, for us, acknowledgement means more than giving lip service to the concepts. Rather, we are interested in exploring ourselves and encouraging others to explore the complex ways that race and culture influence their everyday lives in general and in the psychotherapy process in particular.

Moreover, we have attempted to communicate what we know about conducting therapy in a racially and culturally responsive manner. Much of what we discuss in the book we learned from our former clients who forced us to adapt our traditionally trained selves to respond to their cultural nuances. In addition, our conversations with graduate students and professionals led us to believe that there was a need for a book that would give therapists and therapists-in-training permission to step outside the bounds of traditional therapy approaches and to follow their cultural instincts.

More generally, we intend this book to be our contribution to a new movement in culturally and racially responsive counseling and psychotherapy. This movement is evolving from a position of merely recognizing that race and culture have implications for the client in the therapy process toward recognizing that "all God's children" have racial and cultural identities—even if those children grow up to be therapists.

Therefore, in this book, we examine the impact of both the therapist's and the client's racial and cultural perspectives throughout the therapy process. We do not offer prescriptive techniques for counseling individuals from specific ethnic groups; rather we apply more of an interpersonal model with race and culture as aspects of the therapeutic relationship to be processed in therapy.

For assisting us in this endeavor, we would like to thank Tina Q. Richardson, Lehigh University; Sylvia R. Balderrama, Vassar College; Nicholas Ladany, Lehigh University; and Maria Cecilia Zea, George Washington University for proofreading this book in its preliminary forms, and Lisa Paler Hargrove and Chalmer Thompson (Indiana University) for sharing their work and themselves with us. We also owe a great debt to our respective secretarial and administrative assistants (Eleanor Daino, Sherry Padgett, Denise Park, Toni Betton, Sarah Knox, Kathy Lynch, and Charity van Delft) for assisting us with various technical aspects of producing the manuscript. Also, the works of many of our present and former students are cited and integrated throughout the subsequent chapters. We thank them and appreciate them for being naive enough and brave enough to ask the hard questions. In part, this book was born because of them.

Janet E. Helms
Donelda A. Cook

CHAPTER

1 Introduction

We think that it is appropriate to share with you a few thoughts about the philosophy underlying our practice and study of counseling and psychotherapy. Our perspective emphasizes racial *and* cultural sensitivity, by which we mean listening to and integrating into the therapy process the racial and cultural themes that each person—client and therapist—brings to the counseling or psychotherapy session.

As we shall discuss in later chapters, cultural themes, as we use the concept, may evolve from one's racial history, ethnic socialization, social class experiences, religious orientation, gender identity, and sexual orientation, as well as a variety of other collective identity sources. However, we do not believe that cultural and racial dynamics are necessarily synonymous. Sometimes they may intersect, but they are not the same.

Obviously, it is impossible for an individual therapist to acquire a firm knowledge base or the specific competencies to deal effectively with each of the cultural and racial issues that accompany every client—particularly if one supposes that different skills and specific factual knowledge are required for each of the client's cultural groups. However, we do not believe that group-specific competencies are necessarily required to work with clients.

Instead our perspective is that practicing racially and culturally sensitive therapy requires that the therapist be open-minded enough to listen to the racial and cultural themes by which the client defines himself or herself. By being a good listener, the therapist can help the client to "see" the impact of race and culture on her or his everyday life. We think that by assisting the person to understand her or his behavior within the racial and cultural context in which it occurs, then we free him or her to reduce life stress by making more personally appropriate life choices.

As we will also discuss in subsequent chapters, we do not believe that all of a person's cultural-socialization groups are equally important and salient for all clients (or therapists) all of the time. For example, for some clients, race may be most germane to the problem for which they are seeking assistance, whereas for others, ethnicity (that is, ethnic culture) may be. Although our focus is primarily *sociorace* (i.e., societally defined racial categories), from time to time, we will also point out how we think other forms of cultural socialization (such as ethnicity and social class) might be used to work more effectively with clients.

Introducing Ourselves

Moreover, we should point out that we are both African American women. In our cases, this is a statement about our racial and cultural origins. Exercise 1.1 will introduce you to aspects of our cultural socialization. We believe that our racial and cultural socialization influence our perspectives as theorists, researchers, and practitioners.

Although we tried to be as racially and culturally inclusive of the other groups as possible, we feel that we were able to cover the African and White American therapist and client issues in greatest depth because those have influenced our own racial and cultural socialization most consistently. And to be fair, it is also the case that those two groups have received the most attention in traditional Western literature, albeit indirectly.

Finally, we do intend our perspective to encourage greater awareness of the racial and cultural issues of various groups. In other words, if you expose yourself only to socialization experiences common to your own socioracial or ethnic or social class group, then you will never know enough to be a racially and culturally sensitive therapist. In subsequent chapters, we intend to challenge the reader not only to know yourself better, but also to begin to ask better questions about the world around you. We like to think such curiosity has made us better therapists and that it will help you as well. Related to this goal, each chapter contains supplementary exercises or insights intended to stimulate your self-exploration. Most of these exercises should be beneficial to therapists or counselors at various professional levels, although each may benefit from them in different ways.

Overview of the Book

Our book is divided into three sections. The first section, Chapters 2 through 7, discusses the implications of conducting effective therapy when the client's and therapist's socioracial histories, ethnic culture, social class, and various other sociodemographics, which are often used as euphemisms or proxies for race, are recognized as viable aspects of the person. In Chapters 2 and 3, we attempt to illustrate the various ways in which such constructs have been used, and we provide our own conceptual definitions of relevant terms. Chapters 4 and 5 overview the histories of racial and cultural sociopolitical domination and subordination of the major racial groups as they are defined in the United States. Chapter 6 discusses implications of race for therapy, while Chapter 7 addresses therapeutic dynamics of culture.

The second section examines issues of therapy process. Here our focus is resolution of client and therapist racial and cultural issues within the therapy process. Chapter 8 begins this section with a discussion of the ways in which traditional theoretical schools of therapy might be modified to make them more responsive to issues of race and culture. In Chapter 9, we describe the process more pragmatically with a particular emphasis on reoccurring race- or culture-related themes and issues. Chapter 10 focuses on our manner of resolving controversial racial and cultural

Some Rules We Live By

One bright sunny day last summer, we generated the proverbs, sayings, and adages that follow from our collective socialization experiences as African-American women raised in the South and Middle West. We tried to record them in the vernacular in which we heard them, although they were generally said with a certain tonal quality that we can still hear, but cannot quite capture on paper. Sayings such as these represent the cultural values and beliefs that one has been taught.

In addition to reliving our youth with us, we thought you might like to compare your cultural socialization with ours. Therefore, we have provided a column for you to check *Yes*, if you heard the same or similar sayings when you were growing up, and a column for you to check *No* if the saying is unfamiliar to you.

Is Our Maxim

	Your Maxim?	
	Yes	*No*

Self-Concept

The blacker the berry the sweeter the juice
Beauty is only skin deep
Pretty as a picture

Morality

Don't turn away a stranger begging for food
Turn the other cheek
The Lord won't give you more that you can bear
Be careful what you ask for, you may get it

Respect for Authority

I brought you into this life, and I can take you out of it
Do what I say, not what I do

Social Rules

Smiling faces sometimes pretend to be your friends
I like my men like I like my coffee—hot and black
Don't judge a book by its cover

Achievement and Commerce

You're slower than molasses in January
The early bird gets the worm
See a penny and pick it up, all the day you'll have good luck
You're sharper than a rat's turd
If it was a dog, it would've bit you

Expression of Emotions

If looks could kill . . .
The empty wagon makes the most noise
There's a thin line between love and hate
Let the door knob hit you where the dog should have bit you

To determine how similar to us you are, count the number of checks in the *Yes* column. Notice that we subjectively clustered our sayings according to what underlying value or principle we thought they were intended to teach. So the more *Yes* checks you have in a category, perhaps the more similar our socialization was in these areas.

EXERCISE 1.1b

Now that you have seen what we're like and how much you have in common with us, you might want to try retrieving important sayings from your own childhood socialization. So, take about five minutes and list as many as you can.

_____

_____

_____

_____

_____

_____

Then go back and analyze them to determine what cultural principle or value you were intended to learn from each of them.

---

process dilemmas. Chapter 11 examines career theory and practice, while Chapter 12 examines racial and cultural aspects of group interventions. Chapter 13 concludes Part Two with an exploration of indigenous forms of healing.

Finally, the third section examines alternative ways of viewing the therapy process. These include examination of cultural and racial considerations in therapy supervision; that is, the process of teaching students to perform therapy (Chapter 14), research concerns (Chapter 15), and answers to questions we have been frequently asked by students, colleagues, and supervisees (Chapter 16).

PART ONE

Who Enters
the Process?

CHAPTER

2

Becoming a Race- and Culture-Sensitive Therapist

Becoming a therapist who can cope effectively with issues of race and culture in the therapy process begins with the recognition that race and culture are integral psychological aspects of every person as well as the social environments in which she or he functions, regardless of the person's (or one's own) physical appearance. It is also the case that race and culture are not synonyms. Consequently, they may serve separate as well as interactive functions in the person's life—even if the person is a therapist or a client. We are all survivors of our racial and cultural socialization.

For either participant—therapist or client—(socio)racial socialization (i.e., how others treat a person because of her or his perceived race) potentially shapes the person's feelings, thoughts, or behaviors toward himself or herself as well as others when racial dynamics are a consideration. In other words, the therapist's and client's reactions to each other are potentially influenced by the psychological qualities (e.g., attitudes, values, beliefs, and perceptual processes) that were acquired in response to racial socialization. Results of such socialization include the content of the in-group and out-group filters—learned from other members of pertinent societal racial groups—by which a person expresses racial attitudes, stereotypes, and differential expectations of racial "majority" and "minority" group members. On the other hand, cultural socialization (e.g., daily life rituals) determines how we structure our lives and what we construe as "normal" behavior.

Thus, the therapist's and client's manners of conceptualizing the mental health problems they intend to resolve result from culture-related life experiences (Betancourt & Lopez, 1993), whereas the power dynamics (i.e., their manner of interacting with each other when there are race-related aspects of the problem or the therapy process) reflect race-related life experiences (Helms, 1992; Peterson, 1991). To the extent that the therapists' and clients' socialization histories in either the racial or cultural domains of life have been incongruent, then one should expect differences in the ways in which the therapists and clients conceptualize the problem for which help is sought, as well as in what they consider to be appropriate "treatment" for the problem.

Each person—therapist or client—has been socialized to view herself or himself in a particular manner where race is concerned. Moreover, each has been socialized to perceive "the other(s)" in particular ways. These socialized racial perceptions may arise full blown during the therapy interaction or they may be camouflaged by professional techniques (in the case of the therapist), and/or by various forms of resistance (in the case of clients), or by racial stereotyping in the case of both participants (Block, 1981; Cook, 1994; Jones & Seagull, 1977).

Various personality theorists contend that best psychological adjustment is defined by the presence of an integrated sense of Self (Cross, 1990; Erikson, 1968; Taylor & Dube, 1986). This integrated Self consists of physiological (e.g., genotype) and psychological attributes (e.g., intelligence) that are specific to the person, as well as psychological attributes that evolve in response to societal socialization practices (e.g., Baptiste, 1990), particularly those practices that are centered around memberships in demographic categories (e.g., age cohort, gender, race, ethnic group, occupation, social class, sexual orientation, religion).

When various societal institutions (e.g., families, schools, governments) consistently promote practices, policies, and procedures with demographic category membership as their underlying theme, then members of the categories learn to think of themselves as being a part of a group and this "groupness" becomes an aspect of the Self to be integrated. If some measure of voluntary or involuntary physical segregation or separation accompanies membership in the demographic category, then members of shared categories inevitably shape one another's values, beliefs, and attitudes, but not necessarily deliberately. In other words, members of demographic groups often share a common culture because of sociological and political forces that place them in the same environment (Yee, Fairchild, Wizmann, & Wyatt, 1993).

We believe that when a demographic category has salience in society, focused socialization practices, and psychological meaning to the person, then it is a "demographic identity." Demographic identities have implications for behavior. In fact, it seems reasonable to assert that what changes a demographic category from merely a nominal variable to a demographic identity with implications for behavior is either a related culture or socialization practices that presume such a culture. Our primary focus is the psychological aspects of race as a demographic identity, and the cultures that have come to be associated with the existing racial categories. Race and culture have been virtually ignored as potentially distinguishable psychological constructs in counseling and psychotherapy theory, practice, and research. However, we intend to argue that each critically influences every aspect of the helping process.

Consequently, to ignore the racial or cultural dynamics of therapists and clients within the therapy relationship is to provide inadequate therapy. Regardless of the racial composition of the therapy dyad; that is, even when therapists and clients are of the same racial or ethnic cultural group, both are operating under certain assumptions and expectations regarding themselves and the other as racial (and perhaps) cultural beings. Consequently, it is unwise for therapists to assume that the client's perceptions are identical to their own. Therefore, gathering data regarding the client's racial history and examination of one's own racial attitudes toward members of the client's racial group should be a major part of the therapist's ongoing assessment process.

The notion of conceptualizing race and culture as vital aspects of the therapy process does not seem so foreign if one considers that clients are routinely asked to specify their racial and (sometimes) ethnic classifications as part of the intake process in most mental health agencies, although this information is rarely incorporated into the process in meaningful ways. Furthermore, if race influences the manner in which therapists interact with clients throughout the process—from intake to outcome (Jones & Seagull, 1977; Sue & Sue, 1990)—as many theorists contend, then therapists typically must form at least some tentative (perhaps unspoken) hypotheses about clients based on the client's racial classification. Otherwise, it seems unlikely that racial classification would be considered relevant identifying data so uniformly across mental health settings (Johnson, 1987; Pedersen, 1991; Smith, 1991).

Moreover, although clinicians are frequently advised to take a "multicultural" or "diversity" perspective (e.g., Axelson, 1993; Ridley, Mendoza, & Kanitz, 1994; Sue & Sue, 1990), it is rarely the case that such advisements refer to anything more than the client's or the therapist's racial categories. A missing link in programs for training therapists is the deliberate exploration of the ways in which therapists actually do or do not attend to racial and cultural dynamics and, for that matter, clients raise such issues.

Hills and Strozier's (1992) survey of Counseling Psychology training programs approved by the American Psychological Association (APA) revealed that race and ethnicity were rarely a primary focus in the curricula of Counseling Psychology programs, although several programs had at least one course with a "multicultural" emphasis. Bernal (1980) and Bernal and Padilla (1982) made similar observations about the training of clinical psychologists. Regan (1989) found that clinicians in training generally relied on one another rather than on their primary therapy supervisors for information about the impact of race on their therapy interactions and support in exploring such matters.

Furthermore, it can be argued that racial and cultural dynamics may be important aspects of therapeutic modalities in addition to individual therapy and programs for training therapists. Other relevant modalities include group and family therapy (Gushue, 1993; Tsui & Schultz, 1988), consultation and outreach services (Garcia, Wright, & Corey, 1991; Sue, 1991), therapy supervision and training, including supervisee-supervisor and supervisee-client interactions (cf. Cook & Helms, 1988; Cook & Paler Hargrove, 1997; Hunt, 1987), as well as the psychological theories and research that form the basis of such approaches (Ponterotto & Casas, 1991). Although we intend to apply our approach for using race and culture to these other modalities, the bulk of our attention will be on the individual therapist-client dyad.

Race and Culture as Themes in Therapy

The therapist's and client's internalized experiences related to their racial and cultural socialization can become important forces in the therapy process. We use the term *psychological* (abbreviated by the prefix *psycho*) to mean intrapsychic or *subjective* processes with the person as their center. That is, *psychoracial* refers to those person-level psychological attributes that a person develops in response to racial socialization, whereas "psychocultural" refers to characteristics that he or she develops in response to cultural socialization.

We use *sociological* (abbreviated by the prefix *socio*) to mean *external* or systemic processes, which include interpersonal interactions, with the person as their focus.

Thus, *socioracial* or *sociocultural* refers to societal practices, policies, and so forth that have the person's respective racial group or culture(s) as their focus. We call implicit or internalized racial or cultural messages *psychological* (e.g., psychoracial or psychocultural). Our usage implies, for example, that identifying with or committing to one's societally defined racial group is a psychological (i.e., "psycho") reaction to race, whereas one's racial classification per se is a sociological (i.e., "socio") category.

Sue and Zane (1987) use *proximal* and *distal* to refer to approximately equivalent constructs. As do Sue and Zane, we think that therapists' and clients' psychological (proximal) characteristics have more immediate, fluid, and remediative implications for

TABLE 2.1   Some Examples of Psychoracial and Psychocultural Factors in the Therapy Process

Indicator	Definition	Therapy Example
Psychorace		
Racial Identity (Helms, 1996)	Perceptions of oneself and others as members of a societally ascribed racial group	Client and therapist may not be able to relate to each other because of racial preconceptions.
Cultural (racial) Mistrust (Terrell & Terrell, 1984)	Expectations that one will experience racial discrimination from Whites	ALANA clients may have difficulty relating to White therapists because of histories of institutional racism.
Race-related Stress (Utsey & Ponterotto, 1996)	Quantity of stressful racial life experiences	Clients or therapists may experience high levels of stress due to ongoing acts of racism in their everyday lives.
Psychoculture		
Commitment to Ethnic Culture (Whittler et al., 1991)	Involvement in activities thought to characterize one's ethnic group	The therapist or client may engage in activities or practice group customs that are special for their in-group.
Cultural Knowledge (Doyle & Chng, 1994)	Conscious information about the traditions, customs, and rituals of one's ethnic group.	Confusion may occur when the therapist assumes the therapist and client share identical information about one another's cultural socialization.
Acculturation (Cuellar, Harris, & Jasso, 1980)	The process of learning or acquiring the rules of a cultural group	Stress may occur as the client or therapist attempt to interpret implicit rules of a culture in which he or she is expected to function.

Note: We use *ALANA* to refer to African Americans or Blacks, Asian Americans and Pacific Islanders, Latino/Latina Americans, and Native Americans, collectively.

the therapy process as such than do sociological ascriptions. Yet sociologic (distal) characteristics provide indirect information about how the therapist and client came to be the people they are and to be exposed to the messages that they have internalized.

Table 2.1 provides some examples of psychoracial and psychocultural characteristics related to the therapy process. Although a person potentially develops distinguishable psychological cultural characteristics related to his or her various demographic identities, our focus will be on normative subjective cultures within socioracial groups. Table 2.2 provides examples of socioracial and sociocultural therapist and client characteristics; that is, practices that might occur in the environments in which the person is expected to function.

The major socioracial groups in the United States; that is, the groups that are the focus of societal interventions or manipulations, are as follows: African Americans or Blacks, Asian Americans and Pacific Islanders, and White or European Americans. Latinos/Latinas or Hispanics, and Native or Indigenous Americans are commonly treated as distinct racial groups (Takaki, 1993). However, in terms of genotype, they are acknowledged combinations of the other three groups. We will discuss Latinos/Latinas and Native Americans as though they are distinct "racial" or socioracial groups since that is customary in the United States (Helms & Talleyrand, 1997).

For the socioraces Black and White, the respective cultural labels of *African* and *European* are used to acknowledge the alleged original cultures that typically are presumed to define these groups. In deferring to such usage, however, we are not

TABLE 2.2   Some Examples of Sociocultural, Socioracial, and Class Factors in the Therapy Process

Indicator	Description	Relevance to Therapy
Sociocultural		
Familial Childrearing Practices	Families define the rules for appropriate expression of emotions and mental health.	Psychotherapy theories assume a particular style of childrearing, which may not fit therapists' or clients' life experiences.
Socioracial		
Objective Racial Climate	Discriminatory societal practices based on people's perceived race influence how group members interrelate within and across groups.	Therapist and client may relate to one another based on societal racial stereotypes.
Socioeconomic Class		
Parents' Education	Education is one of the primary sources of exposure to the dominant culture.	When therapists' and clients' educational life histories differ markedly, so might their understanding of dominant culture.

intending to imply that Africa and Europe are the only continents from which so-called Black and White people may trace their ancestry. Furthermore, our usage does not imply that any of the socioracial groups is homogenous with respect to ethnicity. We *know* that many people in the United States in each of the socioracial groups are also potentially of one or more known ethnic group sources. However, this book primarily addresses socioracial and correlated cultural issues rather than ethnic-group cultures *per se*.

Summary

In this chapter, we presented several terms that we think are useful for examining client and therapist intrapsychic and interpersonal styles of functioning, as well as impasses in the therapy process as broadly defined. Chances are that you will not remember all of them at first reading. So, we will be repeating them as necessary in subsequent chapters, but, for now, try Exercises 2.1 and 2.2 to discover what meaning some of the terms already have for you.

EXERCISE 2.1

Who Are You?

List at least 10 characteristics that describe you.

Characteristic	Label	Ranking	Difference
1. White			
2. Intelligent			
3. Athletic			
4. Social			
5.			
6.			
7.			
8.			
9.			
10.			

Next, using our definitions, go back and label these characteristics according to whether they are either psychoracial or socioracial (*R*), psychocultural or sociocultural (*C*), or something else (*O*). The order and number of traits you list within each subgroup will give you an idea of which dimensions are most salient to your identity.

Now, rank order your characteristics from *1* (most important) to *10* (least important) to indicate how others identify you. If your rank ordering differs from the order in which you listed characteristics, consider what this reveals about your daily interactions with other people. You might want to meet with a small group and discuss your findings with them, especially as they might pertain to your interactions with clients.

EXERCISE **2.2**

The Meaning of Your Sociorace

In response to the following questions, list as many ideas as come to mind.

What does being a member of your racial group(s) mean to you?

_____

_____

_____

What does your racial group membership mean about you to other members of your racial group (in-group)?

_____

_____

_____

What does your racial group membership mean about you to nonmembers of your racial group (out-group)?

_____

As you review your answers, what consistencies or inconsistencies do you notice? How do you resolve the race-related inconsistencies in your day-to-day living, if there are any? If there are no inconsistencies, what sense do you make of that?

REFERENCES

Axelson, J. A. (1993). *Counseling and development in a multicultural society* (2nd ed.). Pacific Grove, CA: Brooks/Cole.

Baptiste, D. A., Jr. (1990). The treatment of adolescents and their families in cultural transition: Issues and recommendations. *Contemporary Family Therapy, 12*(1), 3–22.

Bernal, M. E. (1980). Hispanic issues in psychology: Curricula and training. *Hispanic Journal of Behavioral Sciences, 2*(2), 129–146.

Bernal, M. E., & Padilla, A. M. (1982). Status of minority curricula and training in clinical psychology. *American Psychology, 37*, 783–787.

Betancourt, H., & Lopez, S. R. (1993). The study of culture, ethnicity, and race in American psychology. *American Psychology, 48*, 629–637.

Block, L. B. (1981). Black Americans and the cross-cultural counseling and psychotherapy experience. In A. J. Marsella & P. B. Pedersen (Eds.), *Cross cultural counseling and psychotherapy* (pp. 177–194). New York: Pergamon Press.

Cook, D. A. (1994). Racial identity in supervision. *Counselor Education and Supervision, 34*, 132–141.

Cook, D. A., & Helms, J. E. (1988). Visible racial/ethnic group supervisees' satisfaction with cross-cultural supervision as predicted by relationship characteristics. *Journal of Counseling Psychology, 35*, 268–273.

Cook, D. A., & Paler Hargrove, L. (1997). The supervisory experience. In C. E. Thompson & R. T. Carter (Eds.), *Racial identity theory* (pp. 83–95). Mahwah, NJ: Lawrence Erlbaum Associates.

Cross, W. E., Jr. (1990). *Shades of Black*. Philadelphia, PA: Temple University Press.

Cuellar, I., Harris, L. C., & Jasso, R. (1980). An acculturation scale for Mexican American normal and clinical populations. *Hispanic Journal of Behavioral Sciences, 2*, 199–217.

Doyle, E. I., & Chng, C. L. (1994). Design and validation of a Mexican American Attitude and Knowledge Scale. *Health Values, 18*(2), 40–49.

Erikson, E. (1968). *Identity, youth, and crisis*. New York: Norton.

Garcia, M. H., Wright, J. W., & Corey, G. (1991). A multicultural perspective in an undergraduate human services program. *Journal of Counseling & Development, 70*(1), 86–90.

Gushue, G. V. (1993). Cultural identity development and family assessment: An interaction model. *Counseling Psychologist, 21,* 487–513.

Helms, J. E. (1992). Why don't psychologists study cultural equivalence in cognitive ability tests? *American Psychologist, 48, 629–637.*

Helms, J. E. (1996). Toward a methodology for measuring and assessing "racial" as distinguished from "ethnic" identity. In G. R. Sodowsky & J. C. Impara (Eds.), *Multicultural assessment in counseling and clinical psychology* (143–192). Lincoln, NE: Buros Institute of Mental Measurements

Helms, J. E., & Talleyrand, R. M. (1997). Race is not ethnicity. *American Psychologist, 52*(11), 1246–1247.

Hills, H. I., & Strozier, A. L. (1992). Multicultural training in APA-approved counseling psychology programs: A survey. *Professional Psychology: Research and Practice, 23,* 43–51.

Hunt, P. (1987). Black clients: Implications for supervision of trainees. *Psychotherapy, 24,* 114–119.

Johnson, S. D. (1987). "Knowing that" vs. "knowing how": Toward achieving expertise in multicultural training for counseling. *The Counseling Psychologist, 15*(2), 320–331.

Jones, A., & Seagull, A. A. (1977). Dimensions of the relationship between the Black client and the White therapist: A theoretical overview. *American Psychologist, 32*(10), 850–855.

Pedersen, P. B. (1991). Multiculturalism as a generic approach to counseling. *Journal of Counseling & Development, 70,* 6–12.

Peterson, F. K. (1991). Issues of race and ethnicity in supervision: Emphasizing who you are, not what you know. *The Clinical Supervisor, 9,* 15–31.

Ponterotto, J. G., & Casas, J. M. (1991). *Handbook of racial/ethnic minority counseling research.* Springfield, IL: Charles Thomas.

Regan, A. (1989). Discussion of race in the supervision process. Personal communication.

Ridley, C. R., Mendoza, D. W., & Kanitz, B. E. (1994). Multicultural training: Reexamination, operationalization, and integration. *The Counseling Psychologist, 22,* 227–237.

Smith, E. J. (1991). Ethnic identity development: Toward the development of a theory within the context of majority/minority status. *Journal of Counseling & Development, 70*(1), 181–188.

Sue, D. W. (1977). Barriers to effective cross-cultural counseling. *Journal of Counseling Psychology, 24,* 420–429.

Sue, D. W. (1991). A model for cultural diversity training. *Journal of Counseling & Development, 70*(1), 99–105.

Sue, D. W., & Sue, D. (1990). *Counseling the culturally different: Theory and practice* (2nd ed.). New York: John Wiley.

Sue, S., & Zane, N. (1987). The role of culture and cultural techniques in psychotherapy: A critique and reformulation. *American Psychologist, 42,* 37–45.

Takaki, R. (1993). *A different mirror: A history of multicultural America.* Boston: Little, Brown and Company.

Taylor, D. M. & Dube, L. (1986). Two faces of identity: The "I" and the "We." *Journal of Social Issues, 42,* 81–98.

Terrell, F., & Terrell, S. (1984). Race of counselor, client sex, cultural mistrust level, and premature termination from counseling among Black clients. *Journal of Counseling Psychology, 31,* 371–375.

Tsui, P., & Schultz, G. L. (1988). Ethnic factors in group process: Cultural dynamics in multi-ethnic therapy groups. *American Journal of Orthopsychiatry, 58,* 136–142.

Utsey, S. O., & Ponterotto, J. G. (1996). Development and validation of the index of the Race-Related Stress (IRRS). *Journal of Counseling Psychology, 43,* 490–501.

Whittler, T. E., Calantone, R. J., & Young, M. R. (1991). Strength of ethnic affiliation: Examining Black identification with Black culture. *Journal of Social Psychology, 131,* 461–467.

Yee, A. H., Fairchild, H. H., Wizmann, F., & Wyatt, G. E. (1993). Addressing psychology's problems with race. *American Psychologist, 48,* 1132–1140.

3 Applications of Racial and Cultural Terminology to Therapy

It might be obvious that our use of race and culture is rather atypical. Thus, before continuing our discussion of the influence of race and culture on the therapy process, it is important to compare our definitions of the terms *race, ethnicity* or *ethnic group,* and various derivations of *culture* to standard usages. Our usage implies that such terms are primarily social constructions that have psychological consequences for the person, whereas common usage treats them as objective, physiologically determined characteristics of the person (Helms, 1994a). These differences in perspective have implications for how race and culture have been considered in the counseling and psychotherapy literature heretofore, as well as how we think they should be considered.

Race As Social Construction

Race has no consensual biological or physiological definition. Allen and Adams (1992) argue that true racial differentiation requires satisfaction of the following criteria: (a) delineation of the criteria (biological or genetic) used to distinguish one race from another; (b) evidence of conformance to those criteria *within* racial groups; and (c) an a priori method for accounting for any observed overlap between races on the designated criteria. As we discuss in Chapters 4 and 5, it would be difficult for racial groups in the United States to conform to these criteria because of the country's long-standing history of miscegenation.

Whether one attributes people's genetic similarity to common ancient African origins or recent genetic mixing via sexual exploitation, accommodation, and intermarriage or interracial procreation, it is commonly accepted that any physical characteristic that one assumes can be used to differentiate one "racial" group from another can generally be found in other racial groups as well. In fact, it has been argued that the range of within-group variability among members of supposedly discrete racial categories with respect to various physiological traits (e.g., blood types, skin colors) exceeds that of between-group variability regarding the same traits (Allen & Adams, 1992; King, 1981; Zuckerman, 1990).

Yet people commonly *know* what is meant by the term *race*. Most persons can accurately tell you which racial group(s) they are a member of, although they may be unable to discuss coherently the sociopolitical or cultural implications resulting from such group membership. P. Katz (1982) has reported that by the age of three or four, children are able to differentiate among racial groups. In fact, children who cannot accurately classify themselves with respect to racial group membership are often the target of major remediative efforts (e.g., Hopson & Hopson, 1990). For example, Black children's racial misclassification of themselves was the primary psychological evidence presented in support of the Supreme Court's *Brown v. Topeka* decision (cf., Cross, 1990), which intended to prohibit racial segregation in the nation's elementary schools (see Table 4.2).

Why is there so much certainty about the meaning of such an ambiguous construct as "race"? Why do people persist in labeling persons as "belonging" to one racial group rather than another when it is quite possible that the persons being differentially classified share common genetic makeup? The reason is because race is a social construction intended to maintain certain societal norms—in the case of race, the norm of between-group disparity. A social construct has meaning in the minds and discourse of people who use it, but not in objective criteria. It defines who should have access to societal and ingroup resources as well as the rules by which such resources will be dispensed. As such, social consequences result from correct and incorrect racial classifications (Dobbins & Skillings, 1991; Johnson, 1990).

Race has been used as a nominal category in most psychological theory and research (Helms, 1994a, 1994b). Nominal conceptualizations involve the assignment of people to supposedly mutually exclusive racial groups by means of unspecified or inadequate quasi-biological criteria (Helms, 1992, 1996) such as phenotype or physical appearance. According to this usage, a person's racial label or category is assumed to imply stable, correlated biological and psychological characteristics beyond phenotype.

Thus, for instance, when one infers level of intelligence from skin color or clients' preferences for race of counselor from their racial classification, one is probably using a quasi-biological as well as a nominal definition of race. Such definitions are "quasi" because they are based on inferences. That is, generally no genetic assessment or biologically linked theoretical construct is offered to substantiate the proposed linkage between appearance and behavior.

For a group's modal phenotype (i.e., physical appearance) to become a racial category, it has only to satisfy the following criteria: The modal group-defining physical attributes must be easily seen, frequently occurring, difficult to change, and perceived as different in type and frequency of occurrence from the analogous modal physical attributes of the dominant or group-defining sociopolitical group.

When a person is perceived as being a member of a racial group, then the person's "racial" demographic identity typically obliterates his or her membership in other demographic categories or social affiliations. That is, one's access to society's rewards and punishments is more often based on one's alleged racial characteristics than on any other real or fictive human characteristics. Other potential demographic identities effectively do not exist independently of racial classification, and racial classification often obscures other aspects of a person.

Thus, for example, if a person's ancestry is English, Jewish, or German and the person's perceived race is White, then the United States society's rules, privileges, and sanctions for White people usually pertain to the individual. However, if one's ancestry is English, Jewish, or German and one is also perceived to be Black, then the person's Blackness rather than ethnicity more strongly determines the social conditions to which the person will be exposed.

Historical and Cultural Conceptions of Race

According to Gotanda (1991), in society, nominal conceptualizations of race have come in three versions formal, historical, and cultural. Historical and cultural conceptions of race are also environmental conceptualizations (Helms, 1994a). That is, they attribute psychological characteristics, at least in part, to influences outside of the person such as socioracial history (e.g., racism, oppression) or sociocultural socialization (norms, customs).

Formal.   When a formal definition is used, race refers to skin color and nothing else. Thus, formal conceptions assume that race has no more social significance than other observable, politically meaningless characteristics such as eye or hair color. Often universalistic theoretical perspectives on counseling and psychotherapy use formal conceptualizations of race.

Historical.   Historical conceptions focus on the sociopolitical implications of race, particularly the diverse racial-group histories of domination and subordination. Thus, historical definitions recognize the existence of long-term consequences attributable to one's racial group's experiences in the society. Race-related affirmative action graduate admissions criteria are based on historical definitions of race.

Cultural.   Cultural conceptions of race propose between-group diversity with respect to cultural values, attitudes, customs, products, and other factors assumed to comprise the concept of "subjective culture." More often than not, cultural definitions locate the origins of racial-cultural differences in classic civilizations such as those of Greece, Africa, and so forth. Thus, for example, in psychology, Afrocentric theories reflect cultural conceptualizations of race.

Implications of Race for Therapy

Perhaps it is worth noting that quasi-biological definitions are virtually useless to psychotherapists because there is nothing a therapist can do to modify the assumedly racial criteria. On the other hand, environmental definitions, whether cultural or historical in nature, provide a site at which the therapist can intervene to promote change. Pedersen (1994), for example, stresses the importance of discovering what the person has been taught by her or his "cultural" teachers. In other words, a goal of the therapist should be to make explicit implicit socioracial and sociocultural messages.

It is important for the racially competent therapist to recognize when and how the different types of racial and cultural conceptions are used by clients as well as by the therapist herself or himself. Often conflicts happen in clients' environments (including therapy sessions) because the participants are using different definitions of race without necessarily recognizing or acknowledging that they are. Moreover, "the problem" may be conceptualized differently by all parties depending upon what definition they are using.

For example, listen to the following newspaper columnist's analysis of why he is the last remaining proponent of racial integration.

"Was I the only person left in America who believed that the actual mingling of the races was a good thing, that it would erase cultural barriers and leave us all a lovely shade of tan? Should I have objected when anyone insulted a black [sic] by calling him [sic] an 'oreo,' which is to say black on the outside but despicably white on the inside? This statement had the same moral standing as one white [sic] person complimenting another by saying 'That was white of you.' But I didn't say anything. Hypocrisy? Cowardice?" (Allen, 1994, p. C4).

Were you able to recognize a variety of conceptualizations of "race" in his discourse? You might want to compare your analysis of his comments with ours in Exercise 3.1. Notice that one's solution to the "race problem" probably changes

---

EXERCISE 3.1

Recognizing the Different Meanings of *Race*

Here's our analysis of the dialogue presented earlier in this chapter (see above). You might want to compare our analysis with your own to get a better understanding of the ways that "racial" terminology is used.

Comment: Was I the only person left in America?
Analysis: The White cultural value of individualism is apparent in the person's conceptualization of race relations in terms of himself ("I") as the central figure in the situation.
Comment: Who believed that the actual mingling of the races was a good thing, that it would erase <u>cultural barriers</u> (underline added) and leave us all a lovely shade of tan?
Analysis: Here, he is using "races" to connote biologically distinct groups and seems to be oblivious to the fact that the races are already mingled and have been for some time. Also, he uses racial categories as though they necessarily are equated with distinct cultures.

Comment: Should I have objected when anyone insulted a black [sic] by calling him [sic] an 'oreo,' which is to say black on the outside but despicably white on the inside?
Analysis: Name calling here is a historical response to a between-group history in which Blacks (of various skin colors) who identified primarily with White racial values became confederates of these Whites and betrayed the Black group.
Comment: This statement had the same moral standing as one white [sic] person complimenting another by saying 'That was white of you.' But I didn't say anything. Hypocrisy? Cowardice? (Allen, p. 4).
Analysis: The power of Blacks and Whites to exercise power over others has never been equivalent. This "compliment" means that a White person has been caught using his or her power in an unmannerly way, which is not quite the same as being accused of betraying one's whole racial group.

depending on how the problem is conceptualized. In our experience, this is true in everyday life; it is also true in the therapy process.

Euphemisms for Race

how do u identify yourself
what background

Not only is race an ambiguous concept, but it is so emotionally laden that people try to find "nicer" terms to substitute for it. Some commonly used terms are (a) *ethnicity* or *ethnic group*, (b) *culture*, (c) *social class*, and (d) *religion*. Some less common terms used primarily by psychologists and other social scientists are derivatives of culture such as *multicultural* and *culturally diverse*. The use of so many terms to mean race makes specification of differential characteristics of these other potential demographic identities difficult. It also increases the confusion associated with race.

Ethnicity or Ethnic Culture

Presumably, the use of the terms *ethnicity* and *ethnic group* is based on societal perceptions that shared cultural characteristics often exist among people of the same socioracial groups. Members of a socioracial group typically have shared similar political and economic histories, which may or may not have been related to their ethnic origins. Under certain conditions (e.g., segregation), members of a socioracial group may also develop or maintain a shared cultural legacy, which typically is an amalgamation of ethnic cultures.

Consequently, it is not usually clear when "cultural group" is being used to discuss one thing (e.g., socioracial life conditions) rather than another (e.g., an ethnic group's sociocultural practices). The racially and culturally competent therapist needs to recognize the imprecision in the usages of the various terms and be able to explore their different implications for the client.

From our perspective, *ethnicity* refers to the national, regional, or tribal origins of *one's oldest remembered ancestors* and the customs, traditions, and rituals (i.e., subjective culture) handed down by these ancestors, which among the ethnic group members, are assumed to be their culture. Ethnic groups may exist within societal racial groups, but the two are not necessarily the same. Cultural and racial variability exists among members of the same racial or ethnic groups (Dobbins & Skillings, 1991; Pederson, 1991). For example, some Black people speak Spanish and others speak English; some Latinos/Latinas classify themselves as Whites, whereas others self-classify as Black or Native American.

The culture associated with one's ethnicity may be transformed to conform to American culture more generally, but to members of the ethnic group (and sometimes nonmembers) the resulting transformations still define their ethnic group. In the United States, a persons' loyalty to and identification with an ethnic group seems to vary according to (a) his or her familial history of immigration; (b) history of ethnic group segregation, separation or assimilation; and (c) visibility, cohesiveness, and density of the group in localized regions of this country.

Familial History.   Ordinarily, recent immigration of a person or the person's ancestors is associated with greater identification with an ethnic group rather than a racial group. Moreover, if members of the ethnic group continue to immigrate to this country in sizeable numbers, then ethnicity is likely to remain an important component of the group members' self-identifications through successive generations. In the case of long-term residents or native-born ethnic groups, the salience of group members' ethnicity may depend, in part, on the quality of the family's or tribe's valuing of that aspect of themselves. When the person's group (especially family) values its ethnicity, it is difficult for the person to abandon it without becoming a marginal member of the ethnic community.

Various practitioners (e.g., Baptiste, 1990; Facundo, 1990; Ho, 1990; Laureano & Poliandro, 1991) have pointed out the importance of assessing and attending to clients' immigration histories as well as those of their kinspeople. Both the therapist's and client's ethnic cultural adaptations may influence virtually every aspect of the therapy process, including symptom expression and diagnosis, relationship building, as well as transference and countertransference, i.e., distortions of the relationship (Cheatham, 1990; Tobin, 1986).

Separation.   The collective experience of forced racial or ethnic segregation as well as voluntary separation also tends to assist a person in maintaining ethnic group ties. Thus, many ethnic enclaves are the result of housing discrimination and other forms of political oppression that made it necessary for the ethnic group members to depend on one another for their survival. Moreover, within communities populated by single socioracial groups, one often finds blocks or enclaves comprised of different ethnic groups. So, among the White socioracial group, one can often find Polish, Irish, and Italian communities, for example. The ethnic tensions and rivalries and regional loyalties that characterized ancestral ethnic intergroup relations may still characterize the relationships of modern-day descendants to some extent.

Today the histories of subordination by separation of various ethnic groups are encoded in the dominant group's language. Thus, terms such as *ghetto, Chinatown, shanty Irish,* and *just off the boat* have in common their reference to subordination of groups due to socioracial or ethnic group membership. Unfortunately, it is possible to use such terms to blame the victims of oppression for their life circumstances and to ignore the contributions of the dominant society to their deprived circumstances.

For members of groups who have been negatively labeled, even if the person is not personally aware of experiencing discrimination himself or herself, personal use of group-disparaging labels may reflect internalized racism or ethnocentrism. Therefore, it behooves the therapist to explore her or his own history of oppression as well as that of the client, particularly when the therapist or client is prone to use such language to describe herself or himself or members of her or his racial or ethnic group. Ideally, therapist self-exploration of such issues will occur before the client arouses them.

Although cultural differences exist among recent immigrants and native-born ethnics, some adjustment themes seem fairly common. Where clients are concerned, these include: (a) conflicts and tensions associated with familial inter-generational differences in acculturation or the learning of U.S. culture; (b) assimilative stresses, that is, tensions or conflicts that arise as one strives to be accepted by members of the dominant racial and cultural groups, respectively; (c) intrapsychic cultural incongruence, defined as mismatches between one's own primary culture and the dominant culture. In Chapter 7, some of the models that have been proposed for assessing the cultural dynamics of clients who are recent immigrants are summarized.

Moreover, therapists also may distort the therapy process because of their own internalized history of immigration, even if they are native born. Of primary concern here are the therapist's unresolved issues of longevity and ownership, interethnic and interracial tensions, and social class. With respect to each of these dimensions, therapists who perceive themselves or their families as original inhabitants, long-term residents, or native born may resent "newcomers" who remind them of familial or their own histories of immigration.

If a recent immigrant client is not the same skin color or social class as most White Americans, or she or he belongs to a disfavored ethnic group in the client's or therapist's country of origin, then the client may arouse therapist distortions (i.e., *countertransference*). Also, it might be difficult for the therapist and client to have more than a superficial relationship with one another. Therapists who are members of recent immigrant groups may also experience countertransference reactions when interacting with clients who remind the therapist of his or her original ethnic group and the group's socialization experiences in the United States. In both types of interactions therapists or clients may exhibit anger and confusion and perceive one another as symbols of some sort. Therapists may mistrust their own level of competence under such cross-cultural conditions. Therefore, in addition to exploring the client's past and present immigration history, it is important that the therapist be aware of the immigration history and associated cultural values that he or she brings to the therapy process.

Culture

In general, *culture*, as psychologically defined (i.e., psychoculture), refers to the values, beliefs, language, rituals, traditions, and other behaviors that are passed from one generation to another within any social group, although our focus is socioracial groups and related cultures (Helms, 1994a). Hofstede (1980) identified several dimensions by which cultures can be differentiated. For our purposes, the most important dimension is "individualism-collectivism."

An *individualistic* culture favors self-definition based on gratification of the individual's personal needs and desires. Consequently, in such cultures, a person's behavior is more likely to be motivated by the quest for personal fulfillment and self-interests rather than group survival. *Collectivistic* cultures value survival and maintenance of the group over enhancement or fulfillment of the individual. Therefore, one's own behavior is governed by what is best for the group rather than what is best for oneself, although the definition of group may vary among cultures.

According to J. Katz (1985) as well as others (e.g., Helms, 1992b; Stewart, 1972), American and Western culture is individualistic, and this individualistic orientation is reflected in the principles of psychotherapy as it is typically taught and practiced. Thus, therapists trained in Western systems may be perplexed by clients who conceptualize their concerns from collectivistic perspectives. Also, therapists in training who are from collectivistic cultures may be confused by their training as well as by clients and colleagues who are of individualistic cultural origins. However, we do not believe that therapists or clients are collectivistic because of where they were born (e.g., Western countries), but rather because of what they learned about survival from their primary cultural socialization group(s).

Criteria of Culture.   Both *psychoculture* (one's manifestation of culture) and *socioculture* (societal socialization practices) are so ingrained and ever present in people's lifestyles that they often are invisible to members of the relevant groups (i.e., ingroups) as well as nonmembers. Culture so intertwines people with their racial and cultural environments that all human behavior is probably shaped by some aspect of one culture or another (cf. Pedersen, 1991).

Brislin (1990) has specified seven cultural criteria that might be useful for making cultures visible. Thus, a culture can be recognized when one can specify (a) aspects of a way of life made by a group of people; (b) ideas transmitted from generation to generation; (c) group-related childhood experiences resulting in internalized values; (d) group practices for socializing children into adulthood; (e) consistent group-related patterns of behaviors or ways of conceptualizing events; (f) cultural patterns that are maintained despite mistakes and oversights in the system that generates them; and (g) a feeling of helplessness and bewilderment among group members that results when cultural patterns are changed.

Sometimes when the client or therapist is experiencing a great deal of bewilderment or feelings of incompetence, examination of the relevance of Brislin's criteria for analyzing one's current situation might be helpful. Also, Brislin's criteria can be useful for assessing the pervasiveness of culture(s) in a client's or therapist's life. Presumably, the more criteria one can specify, the more salient is the person's culture.

Implications

The dominant ethnic culture in the United States is White American culture (Alba, 1990). White American culture is an amalgamation of the ethnic cultures of the smaller (especially) White Northern and Western European ethnic groups who originally settled in this country (see Chapter 4).

It has been our experience that White culture generally is more individualistic than is that of other socioracial groups. Thus, we think that people who have been socialized to be members of the White socioracial group tend, on average, to perceive and evaluate members of other groups from an individualistic perspective, but become increasingly collectivistic with respect to the White group as contact and perceived threat from members of other socioracial groups increase.

Most African, Latino/Latina, Asian and Pacific Islander, and Native American (ALANA) cultures, in their original forms, are assumed to have been more collectivistic than individualistic (cf. LaFromboise, 1988; Myers, 1988; Stewart, 1972).

Again, our experiences suggest that present members of these groups tend to be more collectivistic than individualistic unless they have strongly acculturated White culture. However, members of ALANA cultures are required to conform to White culture and are evaluated on the basis of how well they do so in a variety of domains (e.g., English language competence, social skills).

Consequently, clients from these groups often are confused by the change in cultural perspective that they must adapt when interacting with members of the White culture. For their part, adherents to White culture often have difficulty comprehending the dynamics of collectivistic cultures, and/or recognizing when they themselves are functioning according to the rules of collectivism.

When members of collectivistic socioracial and/or ethnic-cultural groups interact with other collectivistic groups, confusion or intergroup tensions sometimes arise because the two kinds of collectivistic groups either express collectivism differently or believe that they do. For example, it has been argued that their extended family is the primary reference group for Asian and Latino/Latina Americans whereas the socioracial group is the primary reference group for African Americans, although the criteria for racial group membership may be quite elastic.

Thus, a therapist competent in racial and cultural therapy must be capable of recognizing the common characteristics shared by members of the same socioracial and sociocultural groups, yet allow for individual differences. Also, therapists must be willing to examine the extent to which their clients' psychoracial and psychocultural characteristics are congruent with respect to the sociocultural and socioracial demands and expectations of the environments in which they must function.

Social Class

Interestingly enough, although social class is often used to explain between-group differences, it has no consensual meaning in psychology. Levels of education or income, which often are not under a person's control, are frequently used to "assess" social class, and psychological inferences are made from the person's class assignment. Yet Helms (1992b) points out that different criteria for judging social standing may be used by groups for whom access to society's rewards has been limited. In African American communities, for example, stability of one's employment may reveal more about the person's self-perceived and community-ascribed status in the community than the nature of the occupation per se. For example, a postal clerk in an African American community might be accorded the same class status as a teacher in White culture and, historically speaking, might have been equivalently educated.

For the most part, social scientists' efforts to analyze the effects of social class status on personal adjustment have focused on what Lewis (1966) called the "culture of poverty," by which he meant the behavioral patterns of especially Black Americans. The basic premise of this model is that poor people develop pathological strategies for surviving with limited economic resources. These "deviant" values, customs, and traditions (i.e., culture) supposedly are passed down to successive generations in a never ending cycle (Wilson, 1996). This deviant culture of poverty allegedly prevents individuals from achieving economic success because they do not acquire the internalized value system that would permit them to take education and work seriously.

Numerous labels for signaling an individual's lower social class status (e.g., *underclass*, *Welfare Queen*, *culturally deprived*) exist in everyday language, and each of the socially undesirable labels ordinarily implies individuals of a particular race— Blacks in most instances. Furthermore, in most of the psychotherapy research in which race or ethnicity allegedly was the focus of inquiry, only visible racial/ethnic group (VREG) clients of lower socioeconomic status were studied (e.g., Lorion & Felner, 1986).

Class labels often become attached to individual members of socioracial groups regardless of their actual socioeconomic status as individual members of the relevant group. With the possible exception of Native Americans residing on reservations, the majority of the members of every socioracial group are middle class or above accord- ing to 1990 census data (U.S. Department of Commerce, 1992; also, see Landry, 1987). Therefore, when a therapist uses a client's racial classification or skin color to assume the client is "disadvantaged" or "advantaged" economically, then he or she risks building class barriers in the therapy relationship. Such barriers may be mistaken for racial or cultural barriers, which serves to perpetuate between-group myths.

Sue and Sue (1990) may have been the first theorists to attempt to redefine social class as a psychological construct that might have implications for the psy- chotherapy process and interpersonal processes more generally. They hypothesized that the generic characteristics of (White) middle-class culture are inherent to tradi- tional psychotherapy and essentially do not match the generic characteristics of lower- class ALANA groups.

Table 3.1 is loosely based on their dimensions, but reflects our orientation in that we attempted to speculate about shared middle-class status of ALANAs and lower-class status of Whites. We think that when ALANA groups belong to the same social class, they manifest similar class-related cultural characteristics, although the means by which the separate groups acquired such characteristics may differ somewhat. For example, Sue and Sue (1990) attribute the "nonstandard English usage" of lower-class Asian, Native, and Latino Americans to bilingual backgrounds. We think multilingual language traditions may also explain nonstandard usage when it occurs within (espe- cially indigenous) African American and poor White ethnic groups, although their original languages often have been lost due to their historical experiences of cultural racism or ethnocentrism (Alba, 1990; Jones, 1972; see Chapters 4 and 5).

Comparison of Tables 3.1 and 2.1 might also suggest some dimensions along which social class can be distinguished from race and culture at the person level. Chances are if behavioral and social scientists were to investigate the patterns of lan- guage usage of various social-class groups within racial and ethnic categories, for example, they would find some within-group and between-class similarities and dif- ferences in communication styles (Helms, 1992a). Such variations might be misinter- preted if one attempts to ignore either the communicators' racial and ethnic or social class groups of origin.

Another implication of our observations about social class is that therapists need to acquire skills for assessing socioeconomic class and psychosocial class as distinct

TABLE 3.1 Summary of Potential Social Class Psychological (Proximal) Characteristics

Socioracial Group	
White (Anglo)	**ALANAs**
Middle Class	
Standard White American English	Traditional cultural-group adaptations of English
Formal universal verbal communication	Social-role status conscious verbal communication
Valuing of external structure (e.g., 50-minute sessions)	Valuing of social structure (e.g., a session ends when it ends)
White person of highest class determines rules for interaction	Status or social roles of participants defines style of interaction
Status relative to other in-group class and race members defines well being	Class-based cultural rules are used as the standard for well being
Lower Class	
Independent	Interdependent
Suspicious of persons of higher class	Formal toward persons of higher class
Class and race stereotypes shape cross-class interactions	Shared conditions of deprivation serve as in-group credentials
Direct, pragmatic, and solution-oriented	Indirect, pragmatic, and solution-oriented

Note: We used Helms (1992a), Lorion and Felner (1986), McLemore (1983), Sue and Sue (1990), and Triandis (1994) as catalysts for the ideas in this table.

(but not uncorrelated with) race and ethnic culture. One such set of skills is the capacity to listen for the underlying meaning of the client's communications even if he or she comes from a different social class than the therapist.

For example, a White male first-generation Polish American client of mine (JH) who was a doctoral candidate in chemistry thought of himself as "not doing real work" when he was engaged in conducting experiments. For "Jim" (and his family members), "real work" was defined as laboring in a factory for twelve hours a day for minimal wages as his deceased first-generation father had done to support a primary and extended family of eight. Thus, when confronted with an experiment to be done, Jim found himself wasting his psychological energy in planning more experiments than could possibly be done in the time available to him, or in self-disparagement ("They're going to find out that you don't know what you're doing." or "You're not working hard enough. Plan more experiments. You're never going to graduate.") rather than completing the task at hand. Helping Jim to conceptualize himself as a "first generation" white-collar worker also helped him to reconceptualize his definitions of work and of himself as a productive worker.

Some other ways that we have observed that "first-generation middle-classdom" appears is in the form of "survivor guilt." *Survivor guilt* and *affluent guilt* (i.e., the types of guilt sometimes associated with being a member of a relatively affluent social class) have similar psychological consequences for the therapist. One continually struggles with the question of how much to give back. If your client barely has enough food to survive, and you have more than enough, shouldn't you feed him or her? If you live in a house all by yourself, and your client is homeless, shouldn't you invite her or him to move in with you?

If you are a therapist who is prone to social-class survivor or affluent guilt, there are some things you can do to minimize its effects on the therapy process. First, we have found that it helps to invest some time or money in an organization or activity that symbolizes your unresolved social-class issues. Give enough so that you miss it, but not enough that it depletes your own resources. In that way, when confronted with a client who is consciously or unconsciously pulling on your social-class strings, you can assuage your guilt pangs by reminding yourself of what you are already doing to help people in circumstances similar to your client's situation.

Second, be realistic about the amount of disposable resources you actually have to spare. We have a theory that whatever your unresolved issue is, it will suddenly appear in your therapy chair in increasingly extreme forms until you take steps to deal with it. So, if the therapist resolves social-class guilt by taking care of clients' financial needs directly, sooner or later most therapists will encounter a client whose needs exceed the therapist's resources. If the therapist resolves such issues symbolically by, for example, overpatronizing or infantilizing the client, then the therapy process is ruined.

Nevertheless, use of our therapist guilt-reducing strategies does not absolve the therapist of the responsibility for helping the client find ways to improve the client's circumstances. If the therapist, who presumably knows the social-class system better than the client, teaches the client how to negotiate the system for the purpose of self- or group-improvement, then the client acquires skills that he or she can use after the therapy relationship no longer exists.

In this regard, we encourage therapists to be creative as well as action oriented. For instance, a therapist we know helped a client resolve his homelessness problem by advising the client to enroll in at least a credit hour of college coursework per semester in a local residential college. By doing so, the client had access to space in the college dormitory in addition to financial aid for his education. Whereas one can argue that attending college was not a perfect solution for the client, at least it provided him with self-empowering options.

We should also note that in our experience, many therapists have grappled with the feelings (e.g., jealousy, anxiety, anger, inadequacy) aroused when the client is much more well to do than the therapist. Often these feelings appear in the form of defenses such as minimizing the seriousness of the client's problem (e.g., "Why is she crying to me about losing her boyfriend, why doesn't she just buy another one?") or stereotyping the client (e.g., "She's just your typical 'JAP.'" "She's your typical YUPPIE." or "She's 'bourgie.'").

In such instances, we generally recommend that the therapist acknowledge (to oneself or to another therapist) the underlying feelings the client elicits, and try to understand its source so that the client does not become the target for the therapist's displaced social class aggression. It also helps to actively look for the client's pain (it must be there or the client wouldn't be seeking therapy) and redefine it in a way that helps the therapist feel some kinship with the client. Then, of course, there's always fantasy. If you do a very good job with this client, maybe he or she will refer all of her or his wealthy friends, and you can raise your fees—a lot.

Socioreligious Ethnics

Socioreligious ethnics might be defined as cultural groups whose actual or perceived religious practices and customs (e.g., dress, places of worship) define them as distinct social groups or enclaves within the dominant societal culture. In a predominantly Christian, Protestant country, these groups generally are a numerical minority relative to the larger society because of their religious origins or practices. However, to qualify for minority status the groups must exist in sufficient enough numbers in localized geographical areas for people who are not members of the groups to be aware of their existence. Sometimes these groups are described by one racial category (e.g., Amish); sometimes they cross the boundaries of racial categories, but are stereotyped by society (and sometimes in-group members) as belonging to only one racial category or another (e.g., Jews, Muslims). When people treat religion as though it is genetically transmitted, then they are probably using it as a euphemism for race. However, religious practices are learned, and consequently, are a potential aspect of a person's acculturation.

Therefore, therapists should inquire about clients' religious socialization because such information can reveal the types of cultural messages that motivate the client (Pedersen, 1994). In addition, it might be particularly important to explore a client's religious history if one anticipates using a therapy intervention with a spiritual or religious component. For example, self-help programs such as Alcoholics Anonymous often require clients to give up personal power to a "higher power." The nature of one's religious socialization may influence how easily one can accomplish such surrender.

The Sociopolitical Implications of Racial and Cultural Labels

The terminology that is used to describe people's racial-group membership and cultural socialization has implications for how society perceives them as individuals or members of groups. It also affects individual group member's self-perceptions.

Racial Terminology

The terms *ethnic minorities, subcultures, culturally diverse,* and *minorities* have been used in America to refer to ALANAs (i.e., African Americans, Asian Americans, Latinas/Latinos, and Indigenous Americans) collectively as well as separately. Terms such as *mainstream, majority,* and *dominant* have been used to refer to European (and other White) Americans. Moreover, Whites historically have assigned racial labels (e.g, *negro, Indians, Orientals*) to themselves as well as each of the ALANA groups. The fact that usually goes unacknowledged is that "Whites" are "white" because they so define themselves rather than because they are innately different from the other socio-racial groups in biological or genetic makeup.

When discussing the shared experiences of the ALANA groups, we prefer the terms *ALANA* or *visible racial/ethnic groups* (VREGs; Cook & Helms, 1988) to the more customary labels for them. The term *minorities* locates the subordinate economic, political, legal, and social positions of the aforementioned groups in this country in the persons within groups rather than the environments in which the conditions of disadvantage are practiced. Therefore, for ALANA in-group members, *minorities* becomes an inescapable psychological reminder of the disempowered status of individuals who are not White. Moreover, the term *minority* follows members of the ALANA groups and is used to describe them whether or not they are in fact the minority in any given setting. Similarly, the term *majority* is used to describe Whites regardless of the reality of their numerical circumstances.

Thus, use of the terms *minority-majority* serve to codify the existing racial power differences in this country. Therefore, if the White "majority" group continues to oppress (or benefit from the oppression of) racial and/or ethnic groups described as minorities, then use of the labels makes it too easy to decide who should feel the brunt of racial discrimination or ethnocentrism and who should be prevented from enjoying many of the privileges of society. Furthermore, VREGs who identify with their "minority" status may internalize the oppressive conditions by voluntarily segregating themselves or forsaking their share of the benefits of the "mainstream" society.

For their part, use of supposedly race-neutral terminology such as *majority* and *dominant* to describe themselves allows Whites to engage in discriminatory behavior by right, and consequently, to avoid responsibility for doing so. Such usage also permits them to be oblivious of the extent to which such behavior is socioracially related. That is, it permits them to deny racial bias. It is obviously dehumanizing and disempowering to "minority" persons to be victimized by racism or ethnocentrism, but it also robs the White person of his or her humanity when he or she automatically employs such strategies with a VREG person regardless of her or his actual status. Whether in the workplace, the classroom, the loan office, or the therapist's office, the individual so-labeled cannot help but feel separate from and less than the dominant-group person with whom she or he is interacting. Conversely, the White person using such labels cannot help but feel better than the VREG person with whom he or she is interacting.

Culture Variants

Two variants of culture, *cultural diversity* and *multiculturalism*, have been used as substitutes for "race". These usages of variants of culture also serve a disempowering function for ALANA persons in the United States. Both terms typically are used as umbrellas for one or more of the many demographic categories (e.g., gender, sexual orientation) by which individuals might be described. However, cultural diversity and multiculturalism refer to so many demographic characteristics that they have become virtually useless for explaining the ways in which the therapy process is influenced by racial or cultural factors (Helms, 1994b).

As members of various demographic identity groups in addition to ALANAs have fought for inclusion in mainstream America, the concepts of cultural diversity and multiculturalism have been adopted by mental health professionals and educators as a means of acknowledging the presence in U.S. society of many demographic groups with unresolved sociopolitical concerns. Also, use of ambiguous terminology makes it easier to encourage acceptance of the cultural heterogeneity present in society in various forms without actually acknowledging it. We will refer to this philosophy of treating virtually all aspects of human diversity as equivalent as the *principle of multiculturalism*.

The principle of multiculturalism has been proposed as an alternative to the "melting pot" or assimilationist principle. Proponents of these earlier philosophies considered it desirable to blend cultures such that the dominant cultural standards became the norm for all (cf. Hutnik, 1991; Sue & Sue, 1990). Theoretically, implementation of philosophies based on promoting cultural diversity and multiculturalism could represent a move toward equating racial groups with respect to status within the society.

However, practically speaking, such terms are often used to permit visible racial/ethnic groups to call attention to their unequal status within a particular social institution or system without threatening Whites (or one another) too much. Typically, when such terms are used, it is to sensitize White Americans to the cultural and sociopolitical differences that exist between themselves and members of other socioracial and underrepresented demographic groups so that they can learn to tolerate these differences. Yet a consequence of treating all demographic categories as equivalent to race and culture is that everyone can become an "oppressed minority" when it is convenient. As long as one is unaware of one's undeserved advantaged status, one feels little responsibility for rectifying the situation.

Use of all-inclusive cultural terminology also means that the small share of the societal pie that may have been reserved for the under-represented socioracial populations must be shared by all of the ALANA groups (as well as White women and religious minorities, for example). Consequently, White Americans still end up with the largest portion of the pie, and the visible racial/ethnic groups each end up with a sliver to share among in-group members. Therefore, the ingredients are necessarily in place for encouraging conflict amongst the disempowered groups, particularly if they are not aware of the societal structures that exist to promote such conflict.

Implications and Conclusions

Various authors (Allen & Adams, 1992; Johnson, 1990) have recommended that the ambiguity in racial terminology be resolved by substituting *ethnicity* for *race* (Phinney, 1996). We think this solution ignores the fact that race has specific meaning(s) in society as well as to the person being so labeled. It also trivializes ethnicity, making it no more than a euphemism for racial classification (Helms & Talleyrand, 1997).

There are at least two problems with the practice of using the concepts of cultural diversity and multiculturalism as they are typically used in the mental health fields. First, it encourages treating all of the ALANAs or VREG cultures as a single culture or (occasionally) as separate cultural groups with common socioracial socialization, contrasted against a standard White or mainstream American culture. Such comparisons perpetuate the orientation that White culture is normative, and only ALANA cultures must be explained. Consequently, by indirectly labeling VREG socioracial cultures as deviant or unusual, the society's sociopolitical power remains in the hands of White Americans who can continue to believe that they deserve the biggest piece of the societal pie because they are "better" adjusted to American culture than the visible racial/ethnic groups.

In the hands of therapists working with ALANA or White clients, treating White culture as universal may contribute to maintaining the societal status quo with respect to power differences. In addition, such a stance might make it very difficult to assist clients for whom the status quo is inappropriate or ineffective and unhealthy, regardless of their racial classification.

Nevertheless, we believe that having a language in common for discussing the emotion-laden constructs of race and culture will make it easier to manage them in the therapy process as well as in life more generally. Exercise 3.2 will help you judge how much of our terminology you have already acquired.

In this book, we use the terms *sociorace* and *race* interchangeably because we want to encourage consideration of the differential environmental significance of the various racial classifications as communicated through powerful societal socialization messages. We also intend to discourage continued misuse of race as a biological construct in psychotherapy literature because there is no evidence that it has such meaning in United States American society (Yee et al., 1993). By alternating sociorace and race, we recognize and intend to frequently remind the reader that race (as it has been used in psychotherapy literature) is virtually unexamined as a psychological construct.

Culture is used in this book to discuss particular cultural patterns of subgroups who are defined by shared cultural socialization regardless of ethnic origins or ethnicity. For us, *ethnic groups* refer to people who potentially share cultures defined by specific geographic regions of the world. *Ethnicity* is used to discuss particular cultural patterns of these peoples under the assumption that similarity in expressed culture results from similar cultural socialization. Such socialization might or might not have occurred in response to racial segregation.

Our usages depart from custom in that we do not consider *race*, *culture*, and *ethnicity* to be synonymous terms; nor do we consider them to be useful proxies for one another. Nevertheless, whether one uses our terminology or some other, we feel that the central point to keep in mind is that racial and cultural constructs are always present in the psychotherapy relationship in some form.

The psychotherapy experience as it pertains to the socioracial groups of the United States (rather than other countries) is discussed in this book because the historical, sociopolitical, and acculturative and assimilative circumstances that have occurred between the races and ethnic groups in the United States probably are unique to this country in many ways. In line with Helms's (1991) argument that

EXERCISE **3.2**

Terminology Quiz

Now, let's see whether we're speaking the same language. Respond to the following true (T) or false (F) statements by marking the response that you think is correct.

1.	In the U.S., race is a socially defined concept.	T	F
2.	In the U.S., racial groups are biologically distinct.	T	F
3.	A well-trained therapist can know a client's race by looking at her or him.	T	F
4.	*Race* and *ethnicity* are synonymous.	T	F
5.	Culture is passed from one generation to another within social groups.	T	F
6.	*Dominant culture* refers to the imposing of one group's behavioral ideals and values on other groups.	T	F
7.	In the U.S., "dominant culture" refers to White American culture.	T	F
8.	In collectivistic cultures, one's own behavior is governed by what is best for the group rather than what is best for oneself.	T	F
9.	If a therapist knows a client's racial background, then he or she also knows what the client's values are.	T	F
10.	When labels such as *minority* and *majority* are used to describe racial groups, these labels reinforce the power differences between racial groups in the United States.	T	F

Answers: 1. T; 2. F; 3. F; 4. F; 5. T; 6. T; 7. T; 8. T; 9. F; 10. T

---

groups empower themselves by naming themselves, we attempt to use racial, ethnic, and cultural labels proposed by members of the groups themselves. Yet we are aware that even group-selected labels either explicitly or implicitly use Whites as a standard or comparison group. Such in-group/out-group comparisons may be inevitable as long as Whites are the numerically and psychologically dominant group. Be that as it may, appellations are ever changing as groups struggle to define and empower themselves and, consequently, in some cases, we may be behind the times. If such is the case, we apologize in advance.

REFERENCES

Alba, R. D. (1990). *Ethnic identity: The transformation of White America*. New Haven: Yale University Press.

Allen, B. P., & Adams, J. Q. (1992). The concept "Race": Let's go back to the beginning. *Journal of Social Behavior and Personality, 7,* 163–168.

Allen, H. (May 29,1994). Black unlike me: Confessions of a White man confused by racial etiquette. *The Washington Post Section* C:Editorials/Columnists, C1 & C4.

Baptiste, D. A., Jr. (1990). The treatment of adolescents and their families in cultural transition: Issues and recommendations. *Contemporary Family Therapy, 12*(1), 3–22.

Brislin, R. W. (1990). *Applied cross-cultural psychology.* Newbury Park, CA: Sage.

U.S. Department of Commerce (1992) *1990 Census of population: General population characteristics, United States.* Washington, DC: Bureau of the Census.

Cheatham, H. E. (1990). Africentricity and career development of African Americans. *Career Development Quarterly, 38*(4), 334–346.

Cook, D. A., & Helms, J. E. (1988). Visible racial/ethnic group supervisees' satisfaction with cross-cultural supervision as predicted by relationship characteristics. *Journal of Counseling Psychology, 35,* 268–273.

Cross, W. E., Jr. (1990). *Shades of Black.* Philadelphia, PA: Temple University Press.

Dobbins, J. E., & Skillings, J. H. (1991). The utility of race labeling in understanding cultural identity: A conceptual tool for the social science practitioner. *Journal of Counseling & Development, 70,* 37–44.

Facundo, A. (1990). Social class issues in family therapy: A case-study of a Puerto Rican migrant family. Special Issue: Working with the urban poor. *Journal of Strategic and Systemic Therapies, 9*(3), 14–34.

Gotanda, N. (1991). A critique of "Our Constitution is Color-Blind." *Stanford Law Review, 44*(1), 1–68.

Helms, J. E. (1991). What's in a name change? *Focus, 4*(2), 1–2.

Helms, J. E. (1992a). Why don't psychologists study cultural equivalence in cognitive ability tests? *American Psychologist, 48,* 629–637.

Helms, J. E. (1992b). *A race is a nice thing to have: A guide to being a White person or understanding the White persons in your life.* Topeka, KS: Content Communications.

Helms, J. E. (1994a). The conceptualization of racial identity and other "racial" concepts. In E. Trickett, R. Watts, & D. Birman (Eds.), *Human diversity: Perspectives on people in context* (pp. 285–311). San Francisco: Jossey-Bass.

Helms, J. E. (1994b). How multiculturalism obscures racial factors in the therapy process: Comment on Ridley et al. (1994), Sodowsky et al. (1994), Ottavi et al. (1994), and Thompson et al. (1994). *Journal of Counseling Psychology, 41,* 162–165.

Helms, J. E. (1996). Toward a methodology for measuring and assessing "racial" as distinguished from "ethnic" identity. In G. R. Sodowsky & J. C. Impara (Eds.), *Multicultural assessment in counseling and clinical psychology,* (143–192). Lincoln, NE: Buros Institute of Mental Measurements.

Helms, J. E., & Talleyrand, R. M. (1997). Race is not ethnicity. *American Psychologist, 52*(11), 1246–1247.

Hills, H. I., & Strozier, A. L. (1992). Multicultural training in APA-approved counseling psychology programs: A survey. *Professional Psychology Research and Practice, 23,* 43–51.

Ho, C. K. (1990). An analysis of domestic violence in Asian American communities: A multicultural approach to counseling. Special Issue: Diversity and complexity in feminist therapy. *Women and Therapy, 9*(1–2), 129–150.

Hofstede, G. (1980). *Culture's consequences: International differences in work-related values.* Beverly Hills, CA: Sage.

Hopson, D. P., & Hopson, D. S. (1990). Different and wonderful: Raising Black children in a race-conscious society. New York: Prentice Hall.

Hutnik, N. (1991). *Ethnic minority identity: A social psychological perspective.* Oxford: Clarendon Press.

Johnson, S. D. (1990). Toward clarifying culture, race, and ethnicity in the context of multicultural counseling. *Journal of Multicultural Counseling & Development, 18,* 41–50.

Jones, J. (1972). *Prejudice and racism.* Reading, MA: Addison-Wesley.

Katz, J. (1985). The sociopolitical nature of counseling. *The Counseling Psychologist, 13,* 615–624.

Katz, P. A. (1982). Development of children's racial awareness and intergroup attitudes. In L. G. Katz (Ed.), *Current topics in early childhood education,* (pp 17–54).

King, J. C. (1981). *The biology of race.* Berkeley: University of California Press.

LaFromboise, T. D. (1988). American Indian mental health policy. *American Psychologist, 43*, 388–397.

Landry, B. (1987). (Ed.) *The new Black middle-class.* Berkeley: University of California Press.

Laureano, M., & Poliandro, E. (1991). Understanding cultural values of Latino male alcoholics and their families: A culture sensitive model. Special Issue: Chemical dependency: Theoretical approaches and strategies working with individuals and families. *Journal of Chemical Dependency Treatment, 4*(1), 137–155.

Lewis, O. (1966). *The culture of poverty.* San Francisco: W. H. Freeman.

Lorion, R. P., & Felner, R. D. (1986). Research on mental health interventions with the disadvantaged. In S. L. Garfield & A. E. Bergin (Eds.), *Handbook of psychotherapy and behavior change* (pp. 739–775). New York: John Wiley & Sons.

McLemore, S. D. (1983). *Racial and ethnic relations in America* (2nd ed.). Newton, MA: Allyn and Bacon, Inc.

Myers, L. J. (1988). *Understanding an Afrocentric world view: Introduction to an optimal psychology.* Dubuque, IA: Kendall/Hunt.

Pedersen, P. (1994). A culture-centered approach to counseling. In W. J. Lonner & R. Malpass (Eds.), *Psychology and culture* (pp. 291–295). Boston: Allyn & Bacon.

Pedersen, P. B. (1991). Multiculturalism as a generic approach to counseling. *Journal of Counseling & Development, 70*, 6–12.

Phinney, J. (1996). When we talk about American ethnic groups, what do we mean? *American Psychologist, 51*(9), 918–927.

Stewart, E. C. (1972). *American cultural patterns: A cross-cultural perspective.* LaGrange Park, IL: Intercultural Network.

Sue, D. W., & Sue, D. (1990). *Counseling the culturally different: Theory and practice* (2nd ed.). New York: John Wiley.

Tobin, J. J. (1986). (Counter)transference and failure in intercultural therapy. *Ethos, 14*(2), 120–143.

Triandis, H. C. (1994). *Culture and social behavior.* New York: McGraw-Hill.

Wilson, W. J. (1996). *When work disappears.* New York: Knopf.

Yee, A. H., Fairchild, H. H., Wizmann, F., & Wyatt, G. E. (1993). Addressing psychology's problems with race. *American Psychologists, 48*, 1132–1140.

Zuckerman, M. (1990). Some dubious premises in research and theory on racial differences: Scientific, social, and ethical issues. *American Psychologist, 45*, 1297–1303.

4 The Sociopolitical Histories of the Original Socioracial Groups

The socioracial and sociocultural histories of the five socioracial groups may influence the quality of therapy interactions. However, therapists are often trained to pretend obliviousness to socioracial cues (i.e., to treat everyone the same) and to ignore people's psychoracial responses (e.g., internalized racism) to the differential socialization messages these cues elicit. Therapy educators and supervisors commonly do not recognize that race is often intrapsychic and has emotional consequences on the person and group levels. Yet this type of universalistic racial perspective does not generally typify the experiences of people in the real world—the world from which clients (and therapists) come. Clients and therapists of color frequently come from environments in which knowledge of the racial mores of their environments is central to their survival in those environments.

As a result, more often than not, when faced with obvious racial tensions either within the counseling process per se or in the client's life more generally, therapists typically are afraid to tackle the racial aspects of the problem or do not have the knowledge and skills to do so. Clients are often more willing to attempt to resolve internalized racial traumas than the therapists who are supposed to assist them in resolving their life problems, but need informed guidance to do so.

Overview of Chapter

In this chapter, we examine the sociopolitical histories of three of the five major socioracial groups (as defined in Chapters 2 and 3)—White, Native, and African Americans. We address the other two groups, Latinas/Latinos and Asian Americans and Pacific Islanders, in Chapter 5. In this chapter and the next, we discuss the five socioracial groups in the order according to which they became racial groups. With the exception of Native Americans, the groups are also discussed in descending order of their numerical size in the United States, from largest to smallest. The size of socioracial groups generally influences, if not determines, the extent to which members of any particular group will appear in either the client or professional role in therapy settings. For example, the majority of mental health professionals and clients are members of the White racial group. In general, members of small groups are much more likely to find themselves in the client role rather than the mental health professional role, although Asian Indians may be an exception to this observation (Bernal, 1990; Fujita, 1990).

The first three groups we discuss are those whose beginnings as distinct socioracial groups can be traced back to the exploitative conditions that characterized the origination of this country. In particular, we attempt to identify group historical themes that might appear symbolically in the therapy process. Also, we discuss implications of these histories for therapy involving clients and therapists either of different socioracial groups or who manifest different types of psychoracial reactions to similar conditions of racial socialization.

As mentioned in the previous chapters, the prefix *socio* refers not only to the groups' race and culture-related experiences of domination, oppression, and coexistence, but also to their experiences of advantaged status based on the groups' designated racial or cultural characteristics. Sometimes *sociopolitical* is used as an umbrella term for these conditions of deprived or advantaged life status. Although socioracial and sociocultural socialization need not be mutually exclusive, one can often discern differential impacts of them on the person's way of being.

In considering the enduring impacts of the racial and cultural histories of the socioracial groups, it is important to recognize and accept the fact that the various socioracial groups typically have had vastly different experiences of acculturation and assimilation, as well as domination and oppression, in this country. Therefore, psychoracial and psychocultural (i.e., internalized) remnants of these experiences may influence the manner in which therapists and clients interact with one another even when they are not consciously aware of their own identification with the culture or sociopolitical experiences of their racial or cultural groups as ascribed by society.

Furthermore, it is important that the therapist be somewhat cognizant of the unresolved historical issues of each of the major socioracial groups because often the therapist may have to assist the client in realizing the extent to which the client's therapy issues are influenced by his or her racial and cultural socialization histories—alone or in combination. Moreover, the therapy process frequently is influenced by the socioracial and sociocultural experiences of the client's (and therapist's) primary socializing group(s). Thus, the therapist needs to be able to query the client about relevant historical dynamics in order to understand the course of the process.

Of course, the histories of the various socioracial groups have been quite different, both with respect to how newcomer members of the socioracial groups have been assimilated into their own socioracial group as well as into the other existing societal socioracial out-groups. Consequently, therapists and clients can be expected to reflect those accommodations made by members of their group even if such accommodations occurred before the particular group member was born.

Nevertheless, the sociopolitical historical experiences of all five of the socioracial groups generally have not been pleasant for any of them, which may explain why relevant issues are rarely discussed. We did not enjoy writing about them. Chances are they will not make pleasant reading, but we think Chapters 4 and 5 cover the bare minimum of the kinds of racial history necessary, but not sufficient, for delivering racially sensitive service. Perhaps Exercise 4.1 will help you understand why we believe that it is extremely important to be aware of the subtle ways in which remnants of the groups' racial histories still are present in everyday life.

EXERCISE 4.1

Sometimes oppressive socioracial socialization is so subtle that one often cannot recognize it. The following exercise is intended to help you become aware of the many ways in which racism exists in everyday life. This exercise works best if you have someone read it to you so that you can be free to let your mind wander where it will.

A New Racial World Order

Janet E. Helms
University of Maryland

Imagine a new world order. Imagine a new racial world order. Visualize how it would appear in the United States.

Think about growing up in a country where the majority of the "real Americans" are Asian or Black or Hispanic or Indigenous Americans—People of Color—and the minority or the second-class citizens are, of course, Whites. Imagine that it will always be that way. Enjoy the sense of power and accomplishment one feels as a member of the colorful groups— the mainstream, the majority, the superior cultures. Then recall that one can only belong to this group if one has color; that is, if one is Black or Asian or Hispanic or Native American.

Experience the hopelessness and lack of power one feels as one recognizes that one is "a minority," "culturally deprived," culturally disadvantaged," "a suburb dweller," "unqualified"— and White. And that these things will always be true for you no matter what you personally accomplish in life—for as long as you are White.

In this new world order, because of their selfish tendencies, almost all Whites are segregated by law or social customs in places called "suburbs." And when a couple of them accidentally move into neighborhoods of color, the decent people say, "there goes the neighborhood"— meaning that Whites will try to take over other people's property and shape it to fit their own needs, a process called "gentrification."

In school, you learn to revere liberators of the people such as Chief Joseph, Cesar Chavez, Marcus Garvey, Rosa Parks, and to celebrate days of national liberation of Peoples of Color— Juneteenth day, Cinco de Mayo, the Battle of the Little Big Horn, and so on. You learn that Columbus should be remembered as the White man who brought transcontinental slavery to the Americas and he is often used to portray the bad things that can happen if you allow Whites to move into your neighborhoods.

Imagine textbooks that portray Whites only as oppressors, slaveholders, thieves, bootleggers, and rapists. Imagine textbooks with no White heroes. Then consider that the local football team is called the "rednecks" and their sheet-dressed fans typically celebrate touchdowns by bashing cars or throwing food at each other—all in good fun, of course!

Visualize a media industry controlled by Black people, and they control who reports the news, what stories are reported, who stars in movies and on TV. Consider an educational system controlled by Hispanic people, the advocates of bilingual education. Or a banking system controlled by Asians who used their talent for kinship banking to rescue the national banks following the Whites' savings and loans scandal of the '90s. Rejoice for the original Americans who were finally able to prove through the court system that the country really belongs to them, and now rent it out as they choose.

Think about a socioeconomic system in which all of the major industries and corporations are controlled by People of Color who, of course, hire only people who look like them. When Whites ask for opportunities, they are politely reminded that "quotas" are unfair to hardworking People of Color, and besides, it's hard to find a qualified White anyway.

Now, recall that your civil rights are protected by a President and Vice President, who are People of Color, and have been since the last White President was impeached for race-baiting. Of course, the Supreme Court has one White Justice, appointed after a public hearing during which he promised to forget that he was White. In the Senate, two of 102 Senators are White. But they don't create much of a problem because few people even know that they are there.

Finally, recognize that whether you hate my fantasy or love it, it could become a reality during the next century if we don't change how we deal with race in this country.

That's the end of my fantasy—for now.

Processing the Fantasy

Take a few minutes to respond briefly to the following questions. You may share your responses in discussion groups.

1. What did you feel?
2. What part of the fantasy disturbed you most?
3. What part of the fantasy did you find most positive?
4. At what point during the fantasy (if any) did you try to escape the experience?
5. What strategies did you use to escape or cope with the fantasy?
6. What did you learn about how you manage race-relations in the real world?
7. What did you identify as racial problem areas for you as a therapist?

White Americans

The second-longest surviving and largest group in this country (but not the world) is Whites as self-defined. According to the 1990 census, approximately 87% (199,686,078) of Americans classified themselves as Whites. This figure includes Asians, Latinas/Latinos, and Indigenous Peoples who self-classify as White. Moreover, protestations to the contrary, Whites are likely to remain the largest *single* socioracial group for some time, and members of immigrant groups are likely to aspire to membership in the White group as long as it is the most powerful of the socioracial groups. Thus, concern in the predominantly White lay media and among demographers about the displacement of the White population by People of Color generally stems from the erroneous practice of combining all of the ALANA groups, regardless of how they classify themselves racially. The classification is then used to treat them all as though they have the same intragroup and interracial sociopolitical and cultural concerns and problems, regardless of the reality of the respective group's life conditions.

Almost from the beginning of this country, those Whites who are not viewed as members of the ALANA groups, have set the standards by which other groups are defined, acculturated, and assimilated both with respect to the White group and the relevant groups of color to a large extent. We use *acculturation* to mean the process by which a person learns available culture(s) generally, but especially the dominant White culture. We use *assimilation* to mean the process by which the person is accepted and/or incorporated into a group.

Whites as the Dominating Socioracial Group

The dominant racial theme in White American history to which its members must find some resolution is Whites' history of political and economic domination and subjugation and efforts to annihilate peoples of color and their cultures. Jones (1972) calls laws, policies, and customs designed to establish and maintain the superior political and economic status of a racial group "institutional racism"; he calls the devaluation and abolishment of the culture of one socioracial group by another "cultural racism"; and acts of racism committed by a person "personal or individual racism."

In this country, Whites' history of institutional and cultural racism or political oppression of other groups began with the invasion of the Americas' shores by White explorers of various ethnicities including Spanish, British, French, Dutch, and Portuguese. However, the groups who gained the strongest toehold in what became the United States were the English or Anglo-Saxons. According to Feagin (1984, p. 53), the American Historical Association's percentage estimates of the ethnic origins of the White population in the United States in 1790 were as follows:

English	60.1
Scotch, Scotch-Irish	14.0
German	8.6
Irish (Free State)	3.6
Dutch	3.1
French, Swedish	3.0
Other	7.6

In 1990, Alba, using census data, reported the following estimated percentages of White ethnic groups:

English	26.7
Scotch	5.3
German	26.5
Irish	22.0
Dutch	3.4
French/French Canadian	7.3
Italian	6.5
Polish	4.2
Native American	2.8

Consequently, it has been primarily English Americans and other northern Europeans who have created the structures that underlie institutional racism and define "American culture." All of the various White ethnic groups who were here prior to the 1900s formed the core of the aristocracy and are sometimes called "old immigrants." They eventually came to call themselves "Americans" rather than their original ethnic appellations to denote their superior status relative to the other "hyphenated" groups who entered the country or were already present.

According to sociologists and historians, most of the original White settlers who came to this country with the intent of making it their permanent home apparently were deviants or misfits in their countries of origin. That is, many were religious dissidents, economically oppressed, derelicts, criminals, or n'er-do-wells who had no reason for going back to their country of origin. Many were urban dwellers who had no skills for surviving in an agricultural environment, but viewed residence in this country as an opportunity to improve their life circumstances. Some were merchants and their employees who were drawn to the country by the opportunity to benefit economically from its natural resources (Feagin, 1984; McLemore, 1983; Weatherford, 1991; Zinn, 1980).

Thus, the "American dream" was born in the sociopolitical and historical experiences of this original group. The dream included a heavy emphasis on individualism, religious freedom (for Christian Protestants), and materialism. Each successive generation was encouraged to buy a share of this dream by abandoning its traditional cultural mores in order to be assimilated into the larger White and more politically powerful group.

It is virtually impossible to explore the sociopolitical racial and cultural dynamics of the White group without addressing the manner in which the group persecuted other socioracial groups, particularly Native and African Americans. The roots of Native and African Americans' negative expectations and perceptions of Whites began with these groups' unique and prolonged experiences of domination and subjugation by White people. Moreover, White people's discomfort with these groups probably also has its roots in their own ancestoral history of institutional and cultural racism.

Three consequences of the White group's capacity to dominate other groups were that they were able to (1) impose White Anglo-Saxon culture on the country as the standard of normality; (2) maintain the structure of racism so that it worked to the advantage of White peoples; and (3) define the criteria by which one could enter the White group. Feagin (1984), quoting Michael Novak, noted the following: "In the country clubs, as city executives, established families, industrialists, owners, lawyers, masters of etiquette, college presidents, dominators of the military, fundraisers, members of blue ribbon committees, realtors, brokers, deans, sheriffs—it is the cumulative power and distinctive styles of WASPs [White Anglo-Saxon Protestants] that the rest of us have had to learn in order to survive. WASPs never had to celebrate Columbus Day or march down Fifth Avenue wearing green. Every day had been their day in America" (Feagin, 1984, p. 69).

Much of the tension and conflict that occurs in interracial and intraracial as well as intercultural interactions can be traced back to the legacies of racism and the imposition of White Anglo-Saxon socioracial and sociocultural standards on ALANA socioracial groups. However, most members of the ALANA groups would never be able to achieve full membership in the White group because selected physical characteristics (e.g., skin color) made it difficult for them to blend into the White group. Thus, inferior sociopolitical status was preordained by these groups' appearances rather than by their accomplishments.

Domination and Assimilation
of White American Ethnic Groups

At a general societal level, the groups for whom ethnic group discrimination per se is most relevant are Whites, Asians, and Latinas/Latinos. Generally, Native and African Americans were treated with similar levels of inhumanity regardless of ethnicity, although for a short period, because of their efforts to acculturate to White culture, the so-called "civilized" (i.e., Cherokee, Creek, Chickasaw, Choctaw, Seminole) Native American communities did enjoy privileged status relative to their African and other Native American counterparts.

Furthermore, to escape the form of discrimination expressed toward their racial or ethnic groups, sociracial norms emphasizing acculturation to White culture have existed in many ethnic groups. Often these norms involved physical changes intended to make one "look" White enough to be assimilated into White American society. If one's physical appearance naturally approached the White norm in some aspects, then both within and outside of their sociracial groups, such individuals were likely to enjoy advantaged status relative to their in-group counterparts. The supposed White ancestry responsible for such appearance was seen as evidence of a person's superior quality relative to the person's in-group counterparts.

The closer in appearance to the White physical ideal, the easier the self-transformation was—at least externally. Thus, successive generations of White seekers of the American dream frequently gave up their cultural identity in exchange for entry into the White sociracial group. Many visible racial/ethnic group (VREG) seekers of the dream may have lost or abandoned their cultural identities as well, but access to the dream was not guaranteed in exchange for their sacrifice.

White Ethnics.   According to Franklin (1991), in the United States in the late 1800s, (racial) social Darwinism became the primary "scientific" rationale for sociracial segregation. The basic tenet of racial social Darwinism was maintenance of the purity of the White race in order to assure its survival, superiority, and dominance in the world. Fernandez (1992) asserts that Europeans and Americans of European ancestry readily adopted and internalized the theory of their racial superiority, "perhaps noting how conveniently it displaced onto 'nature' human responsibility for discriminatory laws and practices . . ." (p. 138).

To protect their sociopolitical position, the original White Americans used a racial hierarchy to differentiate themselves from Whites of "mixed" and, therefore, inferior ancestry. Thus, Anglo-Saxons and Nordics anchored the superior end of the White racial continuum and Mediterraneans anchored the lower end of the continuum (see Feagin, 1984, and Spikard, 1992). As recently as 1916, Hutnik (1991, pp. 26–27) cites Madison Grant as having written that, ". . . the new immigration, while it still included many strong elements from the north of Europe, contained a large and increasing number of the weak, the broken and the mentally crippled of all races drawn from the lowest stratum of the Mediterranean basin and the Balkans, together with hordes of the wretched, submerged populations of the Polish ghettos."

In response to their limited access to the benefits of the White sociopolitical systems, White ethnics on the lower levels of the hierarchy learned to hide those aspects of themselves that would reveal that they were not truly White. Because this camouflage has worked so well, many White people have no collective memory of when circumstances were otherwise. Still others may remember the sacrifices, but consider the rewards that ensued worth the losses. Consequently, members of the affected groups often have difficulty recognizing how their collective experiences differ from those of visible racial/ethnic groups, and/or why such groups might not easily relinquish their cultures or forget their socioracial histories.

The term *White ethnics* is typically used to refer to those White people who themselves or whose ancestors were not successfully assimilated into White American culture, and for whom cultural markers signaled the group's lowly racial or cultural status relative to other White Americans. Thus, it was not unusual for members of White ethnic groups to give up parts of themselves by changing their names and manner of dress, abandoning or camouflaging their religion if they were not Protestant, discarding languages other than American English, or changing their physical characteristics, all as a means of fitting into the dominant group.

Still other excluded Whites attempted to "become" White by allowing the characteristics that marked them as distinct to be used as the target of "good-natured" ribbing. During the 1988 Presidential election, for instance, candidate Michael Dukakis (of Greek ancestry) sometimes began his speeches by poking fun at his own nose size. Media commentators generally interpreted such actions as a show of good humor rather than as a self-deprecating attempt to conform to White standards of beauty.

Thus, within the general White American socioracial group, people may differ in the extent to which their ethnic group has had to change itself as the price for assimilation. However, in virtually all cases, their self-diminishment allowed individual members of the ethnic groups to compete for access to the resources controlled by the White American group. Sometimes self-transformation required several generations, but as soon as the White ethnic person could blend into the White group with respect to appearance, language, and culture, the person was assimilated or accepted into the dominant White group.

In discussing the self-transformation that Arab-Americans undergo in order to fit into the White world, James Abourezk, a former Senator of Arab-American heritage notes: " 'We've found in ADC [American Arab Anti-Discrimination Committee] that some Arab-Americans have changed their names to make them sound more Anglo, because they just don't want to get in trouble,' he adds. For example, F. Murray Abraham—the American-born, Oscar winning actor (*Amadeus*)—uses an initial because, as he told one reporter, his Syrian name Fahrid, 'would typecast me as a sour Arab out to kill everyone' " (cited Kasem, 1994, pp. 4–5).

Very little empirical information is available concerning whether the effort to acculturate exacted any psychological toll from White people. Some evidence does exist to suggest that many of the smaller in number and more recently immigrated White ethnics are able to maintain at least superficial aspects of their original cultures. For example, Alba (1990) reported that more than 85% of American Whites could name the countries or parts of the world of their ancestoral origins. In addition, as members of formerly distinct White ethnic groups seek to reclaim their particular relinquished cultural identity or realize that it cannot be reclaimed, they also may begin to acknowledge how much they have lost.

"Certainly it [my 'affinity for Black people and their culture'] must go back to the times I grew up in, my peculiar family, the fact that they were Jewish—or, better, the way we suppressed that reality. This produced a vacuum in my inner self that demanded filling, the need for a tube, some sense of identity, a set of loyalites outside the immediate family" (Blauner, 1993, p. 2).

Now, it is true that certain members of the White ethnic groups continued to practice aspects of their culture within the privacy of their homes, but many did not. Presumably, those individuals, who assert that they have no culture other than American, are people whose ancestors abandoned their cultural heritage in exchange for a piece of the American dream or whose culture defines the American dream.

The primary difference between the so-called White ethnics and the groups of color is that the former did and do eventually come to be recognized as Americans and are accorded the prima facie rights intended by that appellation. That is, "whiteness" is a criterion for full citizenship. Most of the groups of color have yet to achieve that status regardless of their numbers of generations in this country, their material or economic success, or their intellectual accomplishments. Consequently, when Whites use themselves or their ancestors as a symbol of what can be accomplished if one "merely pulls up one's bootstraps," they are setting themselves up for a conflictual interaction unless (perhaps) they are interacting with a White ethnic person who has "made it" and has been assimilated into the White American group.

Implications

Although not much literature exists concerning therapist/client relationships when ethnic power differences exist among members of the same socioracial group, it is reasonable to assume that tensions may occur. Diverse histories of acculturation and assimilation mean that Whites may enter the therapy process with unresolved issues related to their own group's racial socialization. For example, the White therapist whose appearance conforms to a Northern or Western European standard may not recognize the ways in which he or she generalizes his or her own White socialization experiences to other White ethnic groups. Moreover, if either the therapist or client believes that he or she has successfully acculturated and been assimilated into White culture, then that party might have difficulty working with a White therapist or client who has refused to make such accommodations.

Clients whose socioracial or ethnic group members have experienced domination by White people may react to the particular White therapist as though the therapist has personally oppressed the client's people, even though the client may have no conscious knowledge of having been personally oppressed. That is, for the client, the therapist may become a symbolic representation of White people. Moreover, the White therapist may be perceived and perceive himself or herself as being guilty of oppression even when the therapist has no conscious awareness of having personally committed any acts of oppression.

In working with VREG clients, White therapists may experience feelings of frustration, anger, or resentment toward People of Color based on a lack of recognition of differences between their own ethnic experiences in the United States and the experiences of People of Color. Others may have unresolved feelings of guilt and/or shame. "White guilt" may be elicited by the awareness that one is a member of the racial group that continues to wield power over the ALANA socioracial groups. Shame or "survivor guilt" may be aroused as the White ethnic person begins to realize how much of value has been relinquished in order to earn membership in the White group.

White clients who find themselves working with VREG therapists may enter the process with questions about the therapist's competence. These questions typically are fueled by a (sometimes) unconscious internalization of White historical socialization in which they were taught that People of Color are never innately the equals of White people, although the precise reasons for the alleged inequality may be group-specific. Alternatively, White clients with liberal racial attitudes or who belong to White ethnic groups may idealize a VREG therapist simply for having achieved professional status in a racially discriminatory society. This positive bias may facilitate the development of a therapeutic alliance, but it could inhibit the client's therapeutic expressions of anger toward the therapist during the working stages of the therapy process.

In either the case of negative or positive bias, the VREG therapist must be attuned to the possibility of relevant dynamics. If the VREG or White ethnic therapist finds herself or himself "proving" her or his objective qualifications, then chances are White racial sociopolitical socialization (i.e., racial superiority) is an unspoken issue. If the therapist finds herself or himself succumbing to flattery and believing that he or she is the perfect therapist, then chances are unresolved racial issues are the source of considerable idealization of the therapist. In either case, the therapist might do well to bring the racial issues directly into the therapy relationship.

Native Americans

In the beginning in the Americas, there were "the people," and the people knew themselves by many names. Some of these names might have been Apache, Dakotas, Pawnees, Pima, Navajos ("Dine"), Innuit, Hohokam, Chumesh, and so forth. (However, these may also only be names that the peoples were given and chose to keep to facilitate communication with the White invaders.) To the White invaders, the people were known as "Indios," "Indien," "Indianer," or "Indian," or "heathens" or "redskins" depending on what language the White people spoke and during what period of conquest they spoke it (Brown, 1981; Weatherford, 1991; Zinn, 1980).

It is not clear how many peoples existed in what became the continental United States when the Pilgrims landed at Plymouth in 1620. President Bill Clinton met with 547 "tribes" (many Indigenous People prefer the appellation "nations," "societies," or "communities" to tribes) in 1994. However, Voyles (1994) noted that an additional 500 peoples were not invited, including 300 who are recognized by the governments of the states in which they reside, but not by the federal government, and another 200 who are recognized by neither state nor federal governments. Moreover, an unknown number of groups were annihilated during the "westward expansion" as it is euphemistically called.

Estimates vary as to how many Native Americans populated North and South America when Christopher Columbus's crews landed wherever they landed in 1492. In analyzing the various available statistical estimates, Feagin (1984) concluded that there were between one and ten million Native American persons in North America in the 1600s, and that the population was reduced to about 200,000 by 1850, where it stabilized until about 1930.

It is clear that successive White explorers virtually annihilated the original Native American population via warfare, disease, slavery, and exportation. McNeill (1976) and a U.S. congressional report (*Indian Health Care*, 1986) estimate that over 90% of the indigenous population was killed by epidemics, wars, and other scourges within a century after Columbus arrived. Thus, the first holocaust in the Americas involved Whites' virtual destruction of the indigenous populations.

Perhaps the reader should be reminded that much of the recorded history of that era describes Native peoples who were initially welcoming and hospitable toward the invading White hoardes. Feagin (1984) notes that contrary to media depictions of them as dangerous and treacherous "redmen," the Native inhabitants actually assisted White settlers in their westward expansion by voluntarily providing food and shelter, and acting as guides. Whites probably would not have survived in this country if the Indigenous Peoples had not been willing to share their resources with them. However, it is also the case that Native Americans' generosity of spirit was repeatedly repaid with lies, deception, and needless aggression at every level of the governmental structure (i.e., federal, state, regional) as well as by White individuals who were supposedly friends.

So that the reader can acquire a sense of the level of betrayal to which Native Americans were exposed, we have summarized some critical historical events in Table 4.1. Some critics argue that the Native peoples were not entirely peaceful prior to the White European invasion. Indeed, there does seem to be evidence of intergroup skirmishes prior to the arrival of White people (Weatherford, 1991). However, there is no evidence (to our knowledge) that Native Americans attempted to annihilate their enemies during these battles. War was waged for pragmatic purposes (e.g., personal revenge, capture of horses) rather than for the destruction of a people per se. Furthermore, Native American weaponry was better suited for limited destruction (e.g., game hunting) than for massacres. Nabokov (1991) notes that in contrast to European powers, indigenous nations never kept standing armies.

Of course, it could be argued that Whites went to battle for pragmatic purposes also—to acquire for themselves the land that was occupied by Indigenous Peoples. Yet such battles were not limited to the destruction of other combatants who held the desired territory, but rather frequently included elderly people, women, children, and warriors under flags of truce or running away from the battle. Most of the massacres (e.g., the Seminole War of 1818, Sand Creek massacre, Wounded Knee Creek massacre) described in history are "honored" because of the Anglo combatants' total disregard for the welfare and humanity of noncombatants who occupied desired territory or assets that White people wanted (Feagin, 1984; Zinn, 1980).

Furthermore, in the long run, the weaponry of Native peoples was no match for the arsenals of the White people who sought to destroy them for personal profit. According to Nabokov (1991), during the 17th and 18th centuries, the indigenous people held their own against the European aggressors with bows and arrows against muzzle-loader rifles. But in the latter half of the 19th century, they were overwhelmed by the Europeans' repeating rifles, never-ending troop replacements, and the contributions of Indian scouts to the Europeans' cause. In support of these observations, Feagin (1984) noted that between the years of 1840 and 1860, of the approximately 250,000 White settlers who traveled westward, far less than 1 percent were killed by indigenous peoples.

Historians do not typically report that war was waged against women and children in battles involving only Native American groups, but the same cannot be said of battles involving White protagonists. The slaughter of women and children by White warriors is evidence that the warriors intended to destroy their enemy, and this intention was obvious in many of the acts of White aggression (some of which are summarized in Table 4.1) toward the Native populations. Zinn (1980) attributes the Europeans' attempts to destroy the Native American population to their desire to acquire material wealth (e.g., land, minerals); that is, the pursuit of the American dream.

Nevertheless, although the numbers of Native Americans were severely decimated by the 1900s, the Native American population had achieved a remarkable comeback by the 1990 census year. Thus, according to the census, almost two million Americans were self-classified as Indians, Eskimos, and Aleuts (Paisano, 1993). Of these, the five largest groups (listed in descending order of size) were as follows: Cherokee (308,000), Navajo (219,000), Chippewa (104,000), Sioux (103,000), and Choctaw (82,000).

In part, the growth, most of which occurred between 1950 and 1990, can be attributed to the people of mixed-socioracial ancestry (White-Native American, African-Native American) or mixed nationhood (e.g., Cherokee-Pawnee) claiming their Native American socioracial ancestry. Wilson (1992) notes that whereas 56.5% of the 265,583 Native Americans counted in the 1910 census were "full bloods," 20 years later, only 46.3% were so classified. Within the Native American socioracial group, being of "mixed" ancestry can be problematic both in terms of assimilation to the group as well as personally.

With respect to within-group assimilation, people of mixed ancestry may be rejected by "full bloods," particularly if part of that mixture is White. If the person's mixture includes African American ancestry, then he or she may be "invisible" to other members of the relevant group as well as to other socioracial groups within the society because of the societal tradition of classifying anyone with any assumed African ancestry as Black (See Wilson, 1992; Weatherford, 1991).

With respect to personal adjustment, the person who has White ancestry must resolve conflicts encountered by being aware that the blood of the "oppressor" and the "victim" courses through her or his veins, and he or she may be accepted by neither group. Notice the personal conflict inherent in Insight 4.1.

TABLE 4.1   Some Moments in Native American and European American Intergroup History

Event	Year	Description of Consequences
		Land Acquisition
First deed of Native lands to English colonists	1625	To humor Plymouth Rock colonists, Samoset "signed over" 12,000 acres of Pemaquid communal land in a "land transferring ceremony." Waves of successive colonists, not understanding that people cannot own the Great Spirit's land, appropriated land as desired.
King Philip's (a.k.a. Metacom) War	1675	Provoked by arrogant actions of New Englanders, Metacom (son of the chief of the Wampanoags), led a confederacy of Native tribes in a war intended to save them from extinction. Of the 52 English settlements that were attacked, 12 were destroyed. Superior English weaponry eventually resulted in the virtual extermination of the Wampanoags and Naragansetts and the death of Metacom. His head was displayed at Plymouth for 20 years and his wife, son, and other captured women and children were sold into slavery in the West Indies.
Andrew Jackson ("Sharp Knife") took office as President	1829	In his first message to Congress, President Jackson recommended that all of the southern Indigenous people be moved west beyond the Mississippi. Although this recommendation violated many treaties between the Indigenous peoples and the U.S. government, it became law on May 28, 1830.
Congress passed act to regulate trade and preserve peace with the Indigenous peoples on the frontiers	1834	All of the U.S. west of the Mississippi excluding Missouri, Louisiana, and the Arkansas territory was designated as "Indian country." White persons were prohibited from settling in Indian country, or trading there without permission, and the U.S. military was charged with apprehending any White person who violated the act. Before the law went into effect, new waves of White settlers had already claimed chunks of Native lands and were never required to return it.
"Trail of Tears"	1838	In response to the discovery of gold on Cherokee homelands, General Winfield Scott forced the Cherokees into concentration camps and then westward to "Indian Territory." During the long winter trek, 25% of the Cherokees died from the weather conditions, starvation, or disease. Other southern peoples were also forced to abandon their southern homelands and "immigrate" to the homelands of the free Plains people.
		Assimilation Pressures
Dawes Act	1887	By government decree reservations were divided into parcels that were allotted to tribal members; "surplus" land could be sold to the United States, which held the proceeds in trust to promote activities to hasten the tribes' movement toward Anglo assimilation. The end result of the act was to transfer considerable portions of Native lands to White people, generally through fraud and deceit.

TABLE 4.1 Continued

Event	Year	Description of Consequences
		Land Acquisition
Boarding Schools Started	1879	Richard H. Pratt, an army officer at Hampton Institute in Virginia, conceived the idea of educating Indians at boarding schools away from the reservation the previous year. The famous Carlisle boarding school in Pennsylvania was established to teach the Native Americans the skills and attitudes of the Anglo society.
"Civilization Funds"	1819	Grants of money were given to Christian missionary societies to convert the Native peoples and "encourage" them to give up their indigenous beliefs.

Unless otherwise noted, the events summarized in this table were also summarized in McLemore (1983), Nabokov (1991), and/or Zinn (1980).

INSIGHT 4.1

A Personal Account of Being Caught between Two Races

"Within myself I feel rejected or feel the threat of rejection. My mother married a White man. Her family wanted her to marry an Indian. My aunt excludes my father from the address on her letters. As the offspring of such a[n Indian-White] marriage, I am in a precocious [sic] position. I feel like an outsider . . . When I was growing up I feared being rejected for my dark skin. . . . My White relatives talked about 'Dagoes' in reference to Latin Americans and Italians. They are dark and so again I felt defensive about my skin color. As a halfbreed, I was not fully accepted by either set of relatives" (Anonymous, cited in Nabokov, 1991, pp. 412–413.

When working with Native American clients, it is important for the therapist to be attuned to the manner in which the client self-identifies. Also, it is important not to avoid dealing with the historical issues of this group because of personal feelings and conditions of shame, guilt, or ignorance. In our experience, we have seen therapists attempt to identify with Native American clients by romanticizing the clients' circumstances. Thus, it is not unusual to hear therapists make comments such as, "I think having a little Native American blood would be exotic," without realizing the past and present socioracial-group(s) trauma that may be salient for the client.

In addition, therapists should be aware that regional differences may influence how Native American clients interact with members of other VREG groups. For example, one frequently hears of the strong alliances among Native Americans and African Americans in the eastern and southeastern United States, but rarely hears of

Native Americans' bitterness toward African Americans in the West because of the deeds of the Buffalo soldiers. Therefore, a VREG therapist cannot assume that he or she will automatically be accepted by Native American clients simply because he or she is not White.

African Americans

The second holocaust in this country involved the abduction and enslavement of African peoples. According to Turner and Singleton (1978), the era of enslavement of Africans in this country (approximately 1650 to 1865) had several phases, and various rationales were offered to justify it. During its first phase, White captors took potential slaves by the millions from various nations on the continent of Africa. The rationales offered by Whites for the abductions and enslavement successively were as follows: (a) God considered "blackness" to be evil and therefore "black" people needed to be protected from their base instincts; (b) Blacks needed to be controlled because of their subhuman natures; (c) Blacks were incapable of surviving freedom; and (d) slavery helped the nation and benefitted "uncivilized" Black people.

There is some disagreement about the probable origins of the first Africans or Black people who were enslaved in the United States. Because the United States entered the slave trade so late in the history of the global enterprise, it is estimated that the people who were enslaved came from West Africa, from Senegal inland as far as the countries that are now called Mozambique and Angola. "[The enslaved peoples] came from a variety of ethnic [or kinship groups] including Igbo, Tiv, Kongo, Fante, Asante, Ibibio, Fon, [and so forth]" (Shuffelton, 1993, p. 270).

According to Shuffelton, unlike their Native or European counterparts, "[African "immigrants"] were simply 'blacks,' unlike European immigrants and their descendants who continue to point to their origins as Scots, Welsh, Germans, or Dutch" (Shuffelton, 1993, p. 270). Throughout their history in the States, African peoples have been treated as an homogeneous group virtually without regard to ethnic group, social class, or personal accomplishments. Thus, when one attempts to find statistics describing the various African ethnic groups in the United States similar to those reported by Alba (1990) for White ethnic groups, it is virtually impossible to do so. The primary social criterion for inclusion in the African American group has been skin color or inferred skin color.

Millions of the potential slaves died in route to the Americas in what has been called "the Middle Passage." Conditions on slave ships were inhuman and resulted in incalculable numbers of deaths. Others committed suicide prior to boarding the slave ships rather than submit to slavery. Still others were killed trying to resist.

Charles Johnson (1991), a novelist, gives this fictionalized account of conditions on a slave ship in 1830: "Once the Allmuseri [African villagers] saw the great ship and the squalid pit that would house them sardined belly-to-buttocks in the orlop, with its dead air and razor-teethed bilge rats, each slave forced to lie spoon-fashion on his [sic] left side to relieve the pressure against his [sic] heart—after seeing *this*, the Africans panicked. . . . They saw us [slavers] as savages. In their mythology Europeans had once been members of their tribe . . . but fell into what was for these people the blackest [sic] of sins. The failure to experience the unity of Being everywhere was the Allmuseri vision of Hell . . ." (Johnson, 1991, p. 65). Some historians estimate that as many as 30 million Africans died in route to the Americas, and for many African Americans, America's lack of acknowledgement of their holocaust is a source of unresolved bitterness.

Throughout much of the duration of slavery, White slave owners replenished their slave "stock" through selective in-group breeding and by raping and sexually exploiting African and, occasionally, European women. In fact, according to Giddings (1984), between 1661 and 1669, Virginia passed legislation that successively exempted African-descended women from the limited protections of the law granted European women, and violated English law by according children the status (free or bond servant) of their mothers regardless of the race and status of their fathers. Intermarriage between Whites and Negroes, mulattos, and Indians was discouraged by banishment in Virginia. In Maryland, a law that enslaved free-born English women for the lifetime of their husbands if they married a Black slave, had to be lifted because so many White women were purchased by White men for the explicit purpose of marrying them to enslaved Black men.

Consequently, many people who are considered White today can find some African ancestry and many African Americans can find some White ancestry in themselves if they follow the limbs of their family tree back far enough. Also, because many people who were attempting to escape from slavery were given refuge in Native American communities, or shared the condition of slavery with Native Americans, and/or were enslaved by some of these groups as well, a large percentage of the African American population also has Native American ancestry.

Regardless of how slavery was rationalized, at its core was Whites' psychological and physical domination of their African captives with the sanction of law, and the support of much of the White population. Africans were property and, consequently, could be treated as less than animals.

In order to justify the mistreatment of peoples who had first entered the country as explorers and bond servants as had their White counterparts, slaveholders developed a mythology of White superiority and Black inferiority. Africans (and Indigenous Americans) were slaves because their alleged inferior intellectual, moral, and cultural conditions dictated that slavery should be their status.

According to Zinn (1980), only a relatively small number of wealthy Whites were slaveholders. Thus, he states that "[in] the South, beneath the apparent unity of the white Confederacy, there was also conflict. Most whites [sic]—two thirds of them—did not own slaves. A few thousand families made up the plantation elite" (p. 231). Takaki (1993) estimates approximately 6% of the Southern White population were slaveholders. However, probably neither Zinn's nor Takaki's figures account for the small "business" owners, because records for slaveholders with fewer than 20 slaves often were inadequate (Shuffleton, 1993; Zinn, 1980). Moreover, Weatherford (1991) contends that slave breeding became a more profitable enterprise in some states (especially in South Carolina and Georgia) than cotton production. Accordingly, he contends that "[t]he number of slaves in the United States grew from less than a million at the time of American independence from Britain to 4 million at the time of the Civil War, less than a century later. The Southern states probably had more money invested in slaves than in all their land combined" (Weatherford, 1991, p. 125).

Be that as it may, it is also the case that hundreds of thousands and perhaps millions more were willing to condone the institution of slavery in exchange for a share of the myth that their White skin made them superior to others, and still others actively practiced their own versions of institutional racism. So seduced were they by the myth of White superiority that Whites were enticed to fight each other in a Civil War so that one group (Confederates) could maintain an economic base that could not survive without the free labor that the slaves provided.

Also, the foundations and principles of personal, cultural, and institutional racism were developed during this era and are still present in perhaps more subtle form in contemporary society. In the North, where slavery was legally abolished after the Revolutionary War, laws, policies, and practices were put in place that successfully excluded free-born and freed Blacks from fair participation in the societal political and economic structures (Takaki, 1993). Thus, it is likely that if the various forms of racism had been eradicated when the institution of slavery was legally abolished, then White-Black intergroup tensions would have disappeared as well. However, as shown in Table 4.2, the history of Blacks in this country has been one of repetitious battles over their desire for a share of the American dream.

The themes of the intergroup struggles can be categorized approximately as follows: (a) access to education—during the slavery era a Black person caught reading could be punished by death; afterward access to the same level of educational opportunities available to their White and other VREG cohorts became an ongoing goal; (b) reparations and political enfranchisement—efforts to achieve the reparations promised former slaves following the Civil War and restitution for the more than 100 years of institutional racism; (c) economic and employment inequities—concerns about the lack of access to well-paying (traditionally White male) occupations, pay inequities, and racial discrimination in the workplace; (d) equal access to public accommodations, thoroughfares, and institutions; and (e) victimization by and reactions to violence as epitomized by Whites' use of riots, massacres, and uprisings to control Black people, and Blacks' use of civil disturbances and uprisings as a form of rebellion against governmental systems perceived to be engaged in institutional racism.

Nevertheless, in spite of the fact that no rights were granted them without significant bloodshed on the part of themselves and their advocates, the history of African Americans in this country is a remarkable story of survival at every phase of the country's development. The reader might like to test her or his own knowledge of some of that history in Exercise 4.2.

Few therapists or clients, regardless of sociorace, are taught much about African and White American history. In fact, slavery and racism are virtually taboo subjects in Western psychology and psychotherapy. African Americans as a group are often blamed and clients in particular are "pathologized" if they do succomb to the conditions of oppression under which they find themselves (see Thomas & Sillen, 1972). Consequently, African American clients who need to focus on reactions to

TABLE 4.2 **Some Moments in African American and European American Intergroup History**

Year	Event
	Reparations and Equal Opportunity
1865	Union Army General William T. Sherman issued "Special Field Order No. 15" at the request of 20 Black ministers and church officials (some of whom were formerly enslaved). The order designated the entire southern coast of Georgia inland for 30 miles for the exclusive use of freed people. In August of the same year, President Andrew Johnson ordered 40,000 African freed people off the land, some at gun point, and returned it to Confederate owners.
1865	The Thirteenth Amendment to the Constitution outlawed slavery and "involuntary servitude."
1868	The Fourteenth Amendment defined citizens as "all persons [regardless of race] born or naturalized in the U.S."
1870	The Fifteenth Amendment guaranteed the right to vote to all citizens of the U.S.
1964	The Civil Rights Act originally prohibited employment discrimination on the basis of race, but was modified to include gender, nationality, and religion.
1991	The Civil Rights Act allegedly extended civil rights protections for disenfranchised groups, but prohibited the use of race-based norms in employment testing.
	Educational Opportunity
1873	With the advocacy of newly elected Black officials, free public schools were created for the first time in South Carolina. Numbers of Black and White students attending school increased from 0 to 70,000 and from 20,000 to 50,000, respectively.
1954	In Brown v. Board of Education, the Supreme Court reversed the separate-but-equal doctrine that it had supported in Plessy v. Ferguson and ruled that in public education "the doctrine of 'separate but equal' has no place."
1957	Nine Black teenagers, handpicked by the National Association for the Advancement of Colored People (NAACP), attempted to integrate all-White Central High School in Little Rock, Arkansas. Each day for a period of three weeks, the armed National Guard, operating under the governor's orders, prevented their entry. President Dwight D. Eisenhower sent federal troops to ensure their entry and to maintain the peace in the school for the remainder of the year.
1974	In Milliken v. Bradley, the Supreme Court ruled that suburban (predominantly White) schools could not be used to desegregate urban city schools.
1978	In Bakke v. Regents of the University of California, the Supreme Court ruled that set-aside affirmative action plans (for the benefit of increasing the numbers of People of Color) in higher education institutions were illegal unless the imparting institution could show clearly how its specific plan remedied past discrimination.

(continued)

TABLE 4.2   Continued

Year	Event

Educational Opportunity

1992	In <u>Freeman v. Pitts,</u> the Supreme Court reversed the 11th Circuit Court of Appeals, which had tried to keep <u>Brown v. Board of Education</u> alive by insisting that 'demographic changes' could not let the school board off the hook. "It must continue to work toward eliminating all *vestiges* of the dual [racial] system." The Supreme Court ruled unanimously that, "if public schools remain racially unbalanced because of where the races live, school districts are 'under no duty to remedy imbalance that is caused by demographic patterns.' " (Hentoff, 1994, p. 28).
1995	The Supreme Court heard a case to decide whether institutions of higher education could continue to offer "race-based" scholarships to underrepresented socioracial groups.

Employment Legislation and Policies

1948	President Harry S. Truman issued an executive order charging the armed forces to desegregate as soon as possible (a process that historians, who believe it has happened, contend took over 10 years).

Public Accommodations

1875	Civil Rights Act outlawed discrimination against Blacks in public accommodations including hotels, theaters, railroads, and so forth.
1883	The 1875 Civil Rights Act was nullified by the Supreme Court.
1896	In <u>Plessy v. Ferguson,</u> the Supreme Court ruled that a railroad could segregate Blacks and Whites as long as the separate facilities were equal. Thus began a long history of legal "separate, but equal" public institutions and accommodations throughout the country.

Riots, Uprisings, and Rebellions

1923	In the "Rosewood Massacre," a week-long rampage, a mob of 200 to 300 Whites murdered at least six Black people and torched the predominantly Black town of Rosewood, Florida when a White woman claimed that she had been raped by a Black man. Eleven elderly survivors and their descendants sought retribution from the Florida Legislature for the government's failure to protect them, and in 1994, were awarded $150,000 per survivor (Booth, 1994; "Florida to Pay 1923 Riot Victims," 1994).

Note. Unless otherwise indicated, the events described were adapted from Feagin (1984), McLemore (1983), and Zinn (1980).

racial oppression in a therapeutic environment can generally expect little comfort and understanding from therapists whose training has been limited to traditional programs.

With regard to this point, Comer (1991) asserts that the practice in the mental health professions in the United States of projecting the negative sexual and aggressive impulses of Whites onto Blacks (and other groups of color) also began

EXERCISE 4.2
African American History Quiz

Because the exposure to African American history that is taught in schools often occurs during only one month of the year and typically is limited to the Civil Rights Movement of the 1960s, many people's knowledge of African American history lacks breadth. The purpose of this quiz is to help you think about what you know about African American history.

In the *Names* rows are listed some famous African Americans who made significant contributions to American history (Reasons & Patrick, 1971). The *Deeds* rows describe their specific contributions. Your task is to match each name with the appropriate deed. The correct answers are shown below.

Names:
1. Louis Latimor
2. Marian Anderson
3. Catherine Ferguson
4. Charles Drew
5. Althea Gibson
6. Benjamin Banneker

Deeds

A. In 1793, this person established the first Sunday school in New York to care for poor children of any race.

B. Using self-taught knowledge of mathematics acquired at the age of 50, this person helped plan the District of Columbia and authored an almanac.

C. The child of a sharecropper, this formidable "street fighter" won the Wimbledon tennis championship and the U.S. Nationals at the age of 30.

D. Born and educated in Washington, D.C., this doctor established the American Red Cross Blood Bank and organized the world's first mass blood bank project, Blood for Britain.

E. This inventor invented and patented a carbon filament for the Maxim electric incandescent lamp and helped prepare the patents for a variety of electric and telephone inventions.

F. This critically acclaimed vocalist was the first African American to sing with the Metropolitan Opera Company; discrimination against the nationally and internationally acclaimed singer led Eleanor Roosevelt to resign from the Daughters of the American Revolution.

Answers: 1. E, 2. F, 3. A, 4. D, 5. C, 6. B.

---

during the slavery era. Thus, according to Comer: "Psychoanalysts have repeatedly found among their patients a psychic association of blackness with darkness, fear, evil, danger, sexuality, and aggression" (p. 595).

Much speculation and many proposals exist for describing how best to work with Black clients who generally are assumed to require yeoman interventions just to achieve a minimal level of human functioning. More has been written about African Americans as clients than any other VREG. We discuss some of this literature in subsequent chapters. However, it is very difficult to find anything hopeful or encouraging about them in this literature. We suspect this is because many theorists and therapists, regardless of race, have never been required to face the unresolved racial issues aroused by African American clients.

REFERENCES

Alba, R. D. (1990). *Ethnic identity: The transformation of White America*. New Haven: Yale University Press.

Bernal, M. (1990). Ethnic minority mental health training: Trends and issues. In F. C. Serafica, A. I. Schwebel, R. K. Russell, P. D. Isaac, & L. B. Myers (Eds.), *Mental health of ethnic minorities* (pp. 249–278). New York: Praeger.

Blauner, B. (1993). "But things are much worse for the Negro people": Race and radicalism in my life and work. In J. H. Stanfield, II (Ed.), *A history of race relations research: First-generation recollections* (pp. 1–36). Newbury Park, CA: Sage Publications.

Brown, D. (1981). *Bury my heart at wounded knee*. New York: Washington Square Press.

Comer, J. P. (1991). White racism: Its root, form, and function. In R. L. Jones (Ed.), *Black Psychology* (pp. 591–596). Berkeley, CA: Cobb & Henry.

Feagin, J. R. (1984). *Racial and ethnic relations* (2nd ed.). Englewood Cliffs, NJ: Prentice-Hall, Inc.

Fernandez, C. A. (1992). La raza and the melting pot: A comparative look at multiethnicity. M. P. P. Root (Ed.), *Racially mixed people in America* (pp. 126–143). Newbury Park, CA: Sage Publications.

Franklin, V. P. (1991). Black social scientists and the mental testing movement, 1920–1940. In R. L. Jones (Ed.), *Black Psychology* (pp. 207–224). Berkeley, CA: Cobb & Henry.

Fujita, S. (1990). Asian/Pacific-American mental health: Some needed research in epidemiology and service utilization. In F. C. Serafica, A. I. Schwebel, R. K. Russell, P. D. Isaac, and L. B. Myers (Eds.), *Mental health of ethnic minorities* (pp. 249–278). New York: Praeger.

General population characteristics: 1990 census of population, United States (1992). U.S. Department of Commerce, Bureau of the Census.

Giddings, P. (1984). *When and where I enter: The impact of Black women on race and sex in America*. New York: Bantam Books.

Hutnik, N. (1991). *Ethnic minority identity: A social psychological perspective*. Oxford: Oxford University Press.

Johnson, C. (1991). *Middle passage*. New York: Penguin Group.

Jones, J. (1972). *Prejudice and racism*. Reading, MA: Addison-Wesley.

Kasem, C. (1994, January 16). I wanted my son to be proud. *The Washington Post*, 4–6.

McLemore, S. D. (1983). *Racial and ethnic relations in America* (2nd ed.). Boston: Allyn and Bacon, Inc.

McNeill, W. H. (1976). *Plagues and peoples*. Garden City, NY: Anchor Books.

Nabokov, P. (1991). *Native American testimony: A chronicle of Indian-White relations from prophecy to the present*. New York: Penquin Books.

Paisano, E. L. (1993). *We, the first Americans*. Census Bureau, Washington, DC: United States Printing Office.

Shuffleton, F. (1993). *A mixed race: Ethnicity in early America*. New York: Oxford University Press.

Spickard, P. R. (1992). The illogic of American racial categories. In M. P. P. Root (Ed.), *Racially mixed people in America* (pp. 12–23). Newbury Park: Sage Publications.

Takaki, R. (1993). *A different mirror*. Boston: Little, Brown and Company.

Thomas, A., & Sillen, S. (1972). *Racism and psychiatry*. New York: Brunner/Mazel, Inc.

Turner, J. H., & Singleton, R., Jr. (1978). A theory of ethnic oppression: Toward a reintegration of cultural and structural concepts in ethnic relations theory. *Social Forces, 56*, 1001–1018.

Voyles, L. C. (1994, May 19). Letter to the editor on Indian heritage. The *Washington Post, Section A*, p. 20.

Weatherford, J. (1991). *Native roots: How the Indians enriched America*. New York: Fawcett Columbine.

Wilson, T. P. (1992). Blood quantum: Native American mixed bloods. In M. P. P. Root (Ed.), *Racially mixed people in America* (pp. 108–125). Newbury Park, CA: Sage Publications.

Zinn, H. (1980). *A people's history of the United States*. New York: Harper & Row Publishers.

5 The Sociopolitical Histories of the Culture-Based Socioracial Groups

Latina/Latino and Asian/Pacific Islander Americans' socioracial categorization is based on supposed differences in cultural practices (e.g., language, religion) as compared to the American Anglo-Saxon Protestant norm. Perhaps because the criteria for classifying these groups are subtle, the acculturation process often involves their learning that resources in the United States are given to or withheld from socioracial groups rather than ethnic groups.

Latinas/Latinos

Of the various VREG socioraces we have discussed, Latinas/Latinos have perhaps the most perplexing sociopolitical history for non-Latino/Latina therapists to comprehend. This confusion stems in part from the fact that Latinos/Latinas in the United States are descendants of various ethnic and socioracial groups, each of which collectively carries the socialization of the oppressor as well as the oppressed. Furthermore, although this polarity of oppression occurs within and among the Latino/Latina groups, it was and presumably continues to be enhanced by the early history of domination of Latino/Latina peoples contiguous to the continental United States by the federal government.

Spanish Oppression

What defines the various Spanish ethnic groups as a socioracial group is supposedly Spanish (or Latin) ancestry and culture. Moreover, many members of the socioracial group itself have chosen the label *Latinas/Latinos* to replace the more familiar *Hispanics* because the former includes all of the versions of Spanish culture that exist in Central America, Latin America, and the Caribbean as well as presumably the ethnic groups of Portuguese and other European ancestries and cultures in these regions. The term *Hispanic* is derived from the island of Hispaniola (now the Republic of Haiti and the

Dominican Republic) and presumably connotes a narrower range of ethnic groups. Nevertheless, because most of the sociopolitical history of these groups is based on the interactions between the U.S. government and the Spanish and/or Spanish ethnic groups in the Western Hemisphere, it is perhaps useful to examine some of the themes that pertain to these groups in particular.

When Axelson (1993) placed nationality or ethnic groups into socioracial categories, Spaniards were classified as "White" whereas Mexicans were classified as "Hispanics." However, people of Spanish descent were not always perceived and, consequently treated as Whites in the United States or in the world more generally. Spain was conquered and occupied by the Moors, an African people. According to Weyr (1988), this occupation resulted in Spain's becoming an appendage rather than an integral part of Europe. Moreover, because the Moors were not "white," other Europeans (and Anglo Americans) did not consider Spaniards to be "pure" white (McLemore, 1983; Takaki, 1993).

Yet compared to the Native American inhabitants of the lands on which Columbus's crews landed and the enslaved Africans who later populated the Spanish and Portuguese territories, the original Spaniards were of lighter skin color on average. Consequently, in their roles as conquerors and slaveholders, they could define themselves as White and superior, and enforce that self-definition because they also controlled the military, economic, and political power in those regions that they invaded and occupied. Thus, the ingredients for promulgating institutional racism were in place—a self-defined White group with sociopolitical power and military might.

In their initial colonization efforts in this part of the world, Spain took control from Indigenous Peoples in much of what is now Latin America, including South America, Central America, many of the surrounding islands in the Caribbean (e.g., Puerto Rico), and various regions of present day United States (e.g., California, Texas, Florida). This control was gained by annihilating or virtually annihilating Indigenous peoples in many cases and raping and sexually exploiting Indigenous women in many other cases (Weatherford, 1991). Furthermore, in certain regions (e.g., Mexico), the Spanish adopted a policy of "civilizing" the native population by indoctrinating them into the Catholic religion, requiring that Spanish replace their indigenous languages, and by miscegenation.

In those instances wherein Indigenous populations were annihilated at too fast a rate to satisfy Spanish and Portuguese rulers' agricultural and mining goals, enslaved Africans were imported to replace them. They, too, were subjected to rape and legal and exploitative conjugal alliances with their Spanish conquerors. Consequently, the group known as Latinos/Latinas or Hispanics consists of numerous mixtures of peoples, who on the basis of physical appearance categorize themselves socioracially as European Spanish, native-born Whites ("Criollas"), Blacks ("Negros"), or Native Americans ("Indios") and various Indigenous-Spanish ("Mestizo") and African-Spanish ("Mulatto") mixtures. In addition, Latinos/Latinas today tend to classify themselves according to skin color with the lighter skin colors being perceived as more socially desirable and for the most part, contributing to greater access to sociopolitical and economic resources.

According to Rich (1987), the Latino population in the United States is predominantly Mexican (63%; 11,762,000), Puerto Rican (12%; 2,284,000), and Cuban

(5%; 1,017,000). Of these three ethnic groups, Cubans have fared best in terms of education, employment, and economic status. Although their differential achievement is frequently attributed to their middle-class and professional status before they fled Fidel Castro's Communist regime in the 1950s, what goes unnoticed is the fact that the majority of Cubans who immigrated and have been assimilated into the society also on average were of lighter skin color than either their Puerto Rican or Mexican counterparts or much of the population that remained in Cuba. Thus, it also is possible that immigration to a system in the United States that favors "white" peoples may account for some part of their (as well as other "white" Latino/Latinas') success.

Although the 1990 census does not provide a breakdown of Latino/Latina ethnic groups by socioracial classifications (U.S. Department of Commerce, 1992), it does offer the following racial classification figures for Americans of "Hispanic origins": 52% White (11,557,774), 7% Black (769,767), .7% American Indian, Eskimo, Aleut (165,461), 1.4% Asian/Pacific Islander (305,303), and 43% "other race" (9,555,754). The largest percentages are self-classified Whites and other race. Canabal's (1995) research suggests that this other-race category includes people whose ancestors claim more than one category of racial ancestry, people who use ethnic or national groups in place of racial classification, as well as people who use the *Hispanic* or *Latina/Latino* label for their racial self-designation. In addition, within these groups, various ethnic groups may differentially prefer labels such as *Chicano, Mexican American, Cubano,* and so forth rather than Hispanic or Latino/Latina.

It appears to us that Latino/Latinas have not recognized and/or acknowledged the sociopolitical implications of race in their (or their ancestors') countries of origin. In part, the denial of the existence of institutional racism can probably be explained by the fact that conscious integration of aspects of the *cultures* of the various peoples in the regions did occur to some extent. Also, because Africans or Native Americans did outnumber the Spanish in many areas, and often Spanish invaders arrived with no women of their own nationality group with whom to mate, many people in the various regions are of mixed ancestry.

For example, Takaki (1993) reports that the original Mexican settlers of Los Angeles were primarily of Native American and African ancestry with only a trace of Spanish. Among Anglo Americans in the States, Spanish ancestry in itself was considered a potential stain on what Ben Franklin called the "lovely white [sic] race." However, visible mixed heritage was considered a defect that made the Spanish-Mexicans inferior in every way to Anglo Americans. On the other hand, the Mexicans considered themselves more civilized than and superior to Anglo Americans because they could trace their ancestry to ancient Native American civilizations such as the Aztecs, Incas, Mayans, and so forth.

Among Latino/Latinas, the prevalence of "mixed-race" people theoretically also is acknowledged. Often Latino/Latinas will naively use phrases such as, "De que color es detra su orejas?" ("What color is behind your ears?"), to remind one another of their non-White ancestry. However, when one considers that dirt is usually what one finds behind one's ears, then it becomes clearer that such adages really imply that melanic skin is dirty and unclean.

In his autobiography, Richard Rodriquez (1982, p. 116), a Mexican American, discusses the specific ways in which his family of origin taught him that his dark skin color was bad. "It was the woman's spoken concern: the fear of having a dark-skinned son or daughter. Remedies were exchanged. One aunt prescribed to her sisters the elixir of large doses of castor oil during the last weeks of pregnancy. (The remedy risked an abortion.) Children born dark grew up to have their faces treated regularly with a mixture of egg white and lemon juice concentrate. . . . One Mexican-American friend of my mother's, who regarded it a special blessing that she had a measure of English blood, spoke disparagingly of her husband, a construction worker, for being so dark. . . . Nothing I heard outside the house, regarding my skin, was so impressive to me."

Also, it seems to be the case that even those Latino/Latinas who are at the bottom of the sociopolitical hierarchies in their countries of origin do not notice the relationship between skin color and status. Instead one frequently hears Latinas/Latinos attributing differential social statuses to social class differences or cultural disadvantage rather than to skin color differences or implicit racism, similar in kind to its manifestation among their Anglo and African American counterparts.

Consequently, when Latino/Latinas immigrate to the United States, they often are unprepared for the facts that a narrower range of skin colors defines the White socioracial group, that people of color automatically are assigned to lower levels of the sociopolitical hierarchy, and that skin color (i.e., socioracial classification) supercedes social class in importance. Therefore, people who may have enjoyed real or imagined superior socioracial status in their country of origin are frequently flabbergasted to discover that upon entering the United States, they not only no longer enjoy such status, but they are relegated to one hypothetically homogeneous "Hispanic" socioracial group, a group of color.

Furthermore, treatment of the members of the group is largely controlled by governmental laws and policies that were initially developed during eras of U.S. colonialization of primarily Mexican and Mexican American peoples. The resulting form of institutional racism was later generalized to incoming and colonialized Latino/Latina groups of color. In addition, the societal stereotypes and expectations for this group typically are modifications of those that were used to justify Anglo Americans' acquisition of Spanish-controlled territories.

Latino Domination within the United States

As shown in Table 5.1, the lust after Spanish and/or Mexican-controlled land by Anglo Americans has a long history. For example, almost as soon as Mexico gained its independence from Spain, national leaders in the States began to call for the appropriation of and confiscation of Spanish lands, and private citizens immediately began to oblige them, often using the myth of Anglo American superiority as the justification for their avarice.

On the level of the national government, as has been true with respect to Native Americans, treaties between the United States and Mexican governments were made and often unilaterally violated by the United States (see Feagin, 1984; McLemore, 1983). Friendly overtures by Mexican governments toward Anglo American citizens

TABLE 5.1   Moments in Spanish/Mexican and Anglo History

Year	Description of Events
	Anglo Land Acquisition
1769	The Spanish colonization of California territory began when Father Junipero Serra founded the mission of San Diego de Alcas. Most of the settlers and workers were of Native and African ancestry with a trace of Spanish, although *criollas* (ostensibly "pure" Spanish) tended to be the landed gentry.
1803	Louisiana Purchase, a treaty with France, ceded the Louisiana territory to the U.S., but did not clearly specify the boundaries of the territory. Unclear boundaries became the pretext for ongoing conflict between the U.S. and Spain and Mexico over ownership of Texas and the lands west to the Pacific.
1819	Spain and the U.S. completed a treaty by which the U.S. was given Florida in exchange for relinquishing its claims to Texas. The Sabine River was designated as the boundary between Louisiana and Texas.
1820	Thomas Jefferson advocated acquiring the Spanish colony of Texas because of its wealth of resources.
1821	Mexico achieved independence from Spain and all of Spain's territories in the Western Hemisphere.
1830	Mexican government outlawed slavery and prohibited the further immigration of Anglo Americans into Texas.
1846	Provoked by Texas joining the Union and various other treaty violations by the U.S., the U.S.-Mexican war began. In California, armed civilians initiated a separate war to capture California. Massacres, murders, rape, and pillaging of Mexican civilians typified both engagements.
1848	The Treaty of Guadalupe Hidalgo ceded to the U.S. over half the territory of Mexico (most of present day southwestern U.S.) and demarcated the Rio Grande as the boundary of Texas. Mexicans living north of the new boundary were required to formally retain their Mexican citizenship and move south or become U.S. citizens by fiat. Subordination of peoples of Spanish ancestry became legal for the first time.
1898	Spanish-American War began and resulted in the U.S. acquisition from Spain of the Philippines, Puerto Rico, and the liberation of Cuba from Spain.
	Anglo Domination of Latino/Latina Peoples
1904	In the first year that the number of legal Mexican immigrants exceeded 1,000, the border patrol became active and attempted to control Mexican immigration.
1943	Zoot-Suit Race Riots—violence was perpetrated against Chicanos dressed in zoot-suits (a style of male dress with ballooning trouser legs) by off-duty police and U.S. servicemen in Los Angeles. The clothing was used as an excuse for seriously wounding thousands of Chicanos and for arresting Chicano victims rather than the mobsters.
1926	Employers began pushing efforts to "repatriate" Mexican Americans; 60% of those who were forced to leave the U.S. were American citizens. It was one of many cycles of using Mexican workers when they were needed, and sending them back to Mexico under pressures from White workers when they were not.

Notes: Dates in the table are approximate since many events lasted over extended periods of time. Unless otherwise noted, the events are summarized from McLemore (1983) and Takaki (1993).

were generally repaid with violence and duplicity. Private citizens took what lands they wanted, often with the support of the U.S. government and its military (Takaki, 1993).

Spanish and later Mexican efforts to salvage their lands were repulsed by the superior numbers and weaponry of the United States as well as by its greater experience in drafting and implementing oppressive legislation. Consequently, more than half of former Mexican territory became the property of the United States (see Table 5.1), chunk by chunk. Various skirmishes and wars in which the United States was victorious permitted the government to dictate national boundaries in the Southwest. Nevertheless, many Mexicans and Mexican Americans consider the Southwestern United States to be their ancestral homeland, and consequently, resent American efforts to prohibit the free entry of Mexican nationals into the United States.

Moreover, some authors contend that Mexican Americans in the United States were and continue to be treated as second-class citizens or foreigners. Thus, as was true of African Americans, Mexican Americans were victimized by White-initiated riots and massacres. When business leaders perceived the numbers of Mexican Americans were so large that they threatened (White) Americans' economic security, laws and policies were passed to permit the "repatriation" of Mexican American citizens and the deportation of Mexican nationals, most of whom had been enticed to the United States to perform the menial labor that White workers considered too lowly for White people to perform (See McLemore, 1983; Takaki, 1993).

Furthermore, access to educational institutions and other public accommodations used by Whites was forbidden to Mexican Americans. It was a common view that they should be trained only for lowly work. To the extent that work was available, it was grimey, back-breaking work such as cotton picking and beet harvesting for very low wages. U.S. boundaries historically have been permeable such that Latino/Latinas (especially Mexicans) have been lured to the country when there is much low-skill menial labor to be done, but discarded when such work is not available. Also, as previously mentioned, U.S. citizenship generally has not afforded the socioracial group as a group any particularly beneficial status in this country; its individual members are often devalued and stereotyped according to their physical appearance and English language competence. Negative psychological attributes are inferred from failures to meet the White American ideals with respect to such characteristics.

Domination of Asian Americans and Pacific Islanders

The smallest in number and most recent socioracial group to enter the United States is the collection of ethnic groups classified as Asian Americans and Pacific Islanders. As is true of all of the groups discussed so far, the Asian American label subsumes a variety of Asian ethnic groups. Fujita (1990) estimates that there are at least 29 different Asian cultural groups presently in the United States. According to the 1990 census, the largest of these groups in descending order of size presently are as follows: Chinese (1,079,000), Pilipinos (1,052,000), Japanese (766,000), Vietnamese (634,000), Koreans (542,000), and Asian Indians (526,000).

Most of the larger groups were enticed to the continental United States to fulfill menial labor needs of White business interests here. Because they came "voluntarily," the Asian group is possibly the only group of color that genuinely can be considered to be "immigrants." The first of these groups to enter the United States in sizable numbers were the Chinese, followed by the Asian Indians and Japanese, and then the Pilipinos (Takaki, 1993).

In general, White domination of this socioracial group occurred by means of discriminatory laws and immigration policies (that is, institutional racism). The exception to this observation is the Pilipinos whose homeland was ceded to the United States following the Spanish-American War (see Table 5.2) and the indigenous Hawaiians. In order to subjugate the Pilipino people, many of whom did not want to "belong" to either Spain or the United States, this country engaged in a brutal and bloody war, which Zinn (1980, p. 308), quoting the Philadelphia *Ledger*, describes as follows: "The present war is no bloodless, opera bouffle engagement; our men have been relentless, have killed to exterminate men, women, children, prisoners and captives, active insurgents and suspected people from lads of ten up, the idea prevailing that the Filipino [sic] as such was little better than a dog. . . . Our soldiers have pumped salt water into men to make them talk, and have taken prisoners people who held up their hands and peacefully surrendered, and an hour later, without an atom of evidence to show that they were even *insurrectos*, stood them on a bridge and shot them down one by one, to drop into the water below and float down, as examples to those who found their bullet-loaded corpses."

Thus, the United States' conquest of the Philippines was reminiscent of its bloody acquisition of the Native American territories. However, in spite of firepower that was much inferior to that of the United States, the Pilipinos resisted colonialization from 1899 to 1902. Nevertheless, the islanders subsequently became United States "nationals," but not citizens. This status gave them greater freedom to immigrate to the United States than other Asian ethnic groups, but not greater acceptance. Moreover, with this history of brutality toward a people in the Pacific who theoretically were under U.S. protection, it was perhaps easier for the U.S. government to callously uproot Japanese Americans during World War II (see Table 5.2).

Nor were United States immigration policies for other Asian groups benign. Beginning with the first group to immigrate—the Chinese— the general immigration policy was to solicit workers to perform work considered to be too menial for White workers, use the services and skills of the incoming group until the task for which they were recruited was completed or obsolete, while paying substandard wages. For each of the groups, once White workers began to perceive the group as economic or sexual competitors, group-specific restrictive immigration policies were implemented to limit or prohibit the immigration of the group, and local laws were created to ensure segregation of the group from Whites.

What makes Asians (of color) and Pacific Islanders a socioracial group is that although most laws and policies were initially created to get rid of a specific Asian ethnic group, eventually most were generalized to all Asian/Pacific Island ethnic groups of color and their descendants, regardless of their country of origin or their manner of immigration. Moreover, their differential treatment occurred because they were not "white."

As evidence of the correlation between skin color and access to economic and political power, Takaki (1993) notes that once Armenians were reclassified from "Asiatics" to ("white") "Caucasian," their economic status far exceeded that of their Japanese counterparts who were not Caucasians. In other words, commonalities in physical appearance were used to differentiate Asian/Pacific Islanders from other "racial" groups, and to infer psychological characteristics.

In addition, the experiences of the original Asian Indian immigrants indicate that "white appearance" per se rather than Caucasian classification was the criterion used to determine citizenship status. Asian Indians by law were classified as Caucasians, but not "white." By way of justifying the denial of citizenship and the imposition of other racist national policies for this group, the Supreme Court made it clear that (perceived) "whiteness" was the criterion that determines one's access to citizenship and the power such status affords.

In a series of Supreme Court decisions in response to Asian Indian immigrants' attempts to become naturalized citizens (see Table 5.2), the Court ruled "that the definition of race had to be based on the 'understanding of the common man [sic],' . . . [and that] the term 'white person' meant an immigrant from northern or western Europe . . . [and although] the blond Scandinavian and the brown Hindu [Asian Indian may] have a common ancestor in the dim reaches of antiquity, . . . the average man knows perfectly well that there are unmistakable and profound differences between them today. . . . The law does not employ the word 'Caucasian' but the [common speech] words 'white persons' . . . (cited in Takaki, 1989, p. 299). Therefore, the obvious conclusion was that whereas Asian Indians were "Caucasians," they were not "white," and therefore (unlike the Armenians) were not entitled to the protection of "White men's" laws.

As far as racial classification is concerned more generally, at least initially, most of the Asian/Pacific Island ethnic groups were classified as fictive or "as if" "blacks" or "Indians." For example, in discussing the 1852 California Supreme Court decision of People v. Hall, Takaki (1993, p. 206) reports that the conviction of a (presumably White) man convicted of murdering a (presumably) Chinese person on the testimony of three Chinese witnesses was overturned because in California law, "the words 'Indian, Negro, Black, and White' were 'generic terms, designating races,' and that therefore 'Chinese and other people not white' could not testify against whites."

Consequently, the stereotypes that were used to characterize these other socioracial groups were also used to define Asian/Pacific Islanders, and to justify their particular experiences of discrimination and institutional racism (Takaki, 1989; 1993). And they, in turn, often came to apply the existing stereotypes to other socioracial and Asian ethnic groups (other than their own). It seems to be the case that the issues of internalized racism for this group often involve the theme of being accepted as "Americans" (that is, assimilation) because it was the combination of being perceived as non-White foreign competitors that brought down the full force of racial oppression in its various manifestations upon the shoulders of this group.

In addition, because the various Asian ethnic groups were often recruited because they could be forced to work under deplorable conditions for very low wages, they were frequently used as strike breakers and/or to force earlier Asian ethnics and

TABLE 5.2   Moments in Asian/Pacific Islander and White American History

Year	Description of Event
	Immigration and Citizenship
1848	Plans were set in motion to recruit Chinese immigrant laborers to the U.S. to build the transcontinental railroad and mine and cultivate the lands of the newly acquired California.
1853	As a result of intimidating Japan by sailing warships into Tokyo Bay, Commodore Matthew Perry won a treaty granting the U.S. trading rights with Japan.
1860	The first sizable wave of Chinese immigrants began a 30-year migration.
1870	Chinese immigrant laborers were brought to Massachusetts to break a strike by Irish immigrants.
1882	*Chinese Exclusion Act*—prohibited Chinese immigration into the U.S., and was in the forefront of laws and court decisions that segregated Chinese with other "colored" citizens.
1893	In Yue Ting v. The United States, the Supreme Court ruled that Congress could deport immigrants of a racial group who did not or could not take steps to become citizens under the existing naturalization laws.
1898	The Supreme Court ruled in <u>The United States v. Wong Kim Ark</u> that a person born in the U.S. of Chinese parents is an American. This ruling became the basis for most Chinese Americans' claims to citizenship (Kingston, 1980). Also, Hawaii became a U.S. territory, giving Whites control of the islands. Japanese laborers were recruited to work the lands seized from the indigenous Hawaiians.
1908	In the <u>Gentleman's Agreement</u>, negotiated by President Theodore Roosevelt and the Japanese government to assuage Whites' anti-Japanese racism, the Japanese government agreed not to give passports to any workers except those already in the U.S. and their close relatives.
1922	In <u>Ozawa v. The United States</u>, the Supreme Court ruled that only immigrants of "free white" or African origins could become citizens of the U.S., which effectively excluded Japanese as well as most other Asian immigrants.
1924	An Immigration Act implied that citizenship status was intended for "Nordic[s]" but not Asians who were "aliens" ineligible for citizenship. Under the law, any (white) American who married a Chinese person lost his or her citizenship.
1965	Immigration and Nationality Act removed *explicit* anti-Asian immigration restrictions.
1968	Amendments to the Immigration Act directed that the allocation of immigrants to the U.S. be based on hemispheres (i.e., Eastern versus Western) rather than race or nationality. In the first act to limit Western immigration, an annual quota of 120,000 from the West and 170,000 from the East (but no more than 20,000 from any one Eastern country) was acceptable.

(continued)

TABLE 5.2 Continued

Year	Description of Event

"Racination" and Racial Classification

Year	Description of Event
1854	In the District Court of San Francisco, Chinese immigrant Chan Young was denied citizenship because he was not "white."
1870	The Nationality Act specified that only "free whites" and "African aliens" were eligible for naturalization in a country, which was intended for those of "Nordic fiber."
1880	Anti-miscegenation law in California forbade Whites to marry "Negroes [sic], mulattoes, or Mongolians" (Takaki, 1993, p. 330). The law was modified in 1933 to include Pilipinos ("Malays") "to protect the nation, as well as [the states] against the peaceful penetration of another colored race" (Takaki, 1993, p. 329).
1882	*Chinese Exclusion Act*—prohibited Chinese immigration into the U.S., and was the forerunner of laws and court decisions that segregated Chinese with other "colored" citizens.
1909	Armenian immigrants were classified as "Asiatics" by immigration authorities, making them ineligible for citizenship. In the *Halladjian* decision, the U.S. Circuit Court reclassified them as (white) "Caucasian" because of their appearance. Their present-day assimilation into the White group reveals the advantage of having "white" characteristics.
1923	In <u>The United States v Bhagat Singh Thind,</u> the Supreme Court ruled that Asian Indians were Caucasians, but were not "white," and therefore were ineligible for naturalized citizenship.
1930	A Monterey Superior Court judge ruled that White immigrant women married to Pilipinos were not entitled to naturalized citizenship. The ruling was used to deprive (White) Americans who married Pilipinos of their U.S. citizenship.

Discriminatory Social Policies

Year	Description of Event
1852	In response to the governor of California's call for some action to stem the "tide of Asiatic immigration," mobs of Whites slaughtered hundreds of Chinese.
1869	The transcontinental railroad was completed and thousands of primarily Chinese workers were unemployed. As competitors for "white jobs," they became the focus of anti-Asian violence and discriminatory regulations.
1906	With the backing of the local White community, the San Francisco mayor, newspapers, and local leaders sought to establish a separate school for Asian students. A rapid increase in anti-Asian violence followed.
1942	The California legislature passed a bill to limit the number of people of Japanese ancestry in state government. President Franklin Roosevelt issued and Congress validated Executive Order 9066. The Order gave the military authority over the civilian population. It was the basis of the relocation of Japanese Americans (two-thirds of whom were native-born citizens) to concentration camps during World War II. Italian and German "aliens" were not "relocated."

Note: Information summarized in this table was obtained from Kingston (1980), Takaki (1993), and Zinn (1980).

African and Mexican American workers to accept lower wages and poor employment conditions as well (Takaki, 1989). Thus, in many instances, in addition to the ongoing conflict between Whites and Asian/Pacific Islanders, intergroup tensions developed among Asian ethnic groups, as well as between Asian/Pacific Islanders and other groups of color. Many of these tensions probably still exist in subtle forms today.

Furthermore, members of subgroups within the Asian/Pacific Islander community have tended to continue to think of themselves as distinct ethnic groups, and to locate their groups along a status hierarchy without recognizing or acknowledging the extent to which all of the groups have been treated as a socioracial entity in and by the United States The hierarchy seems to have its origins in intergroup tensions that occurred among the various national groups (e.g., Japanese-Korean conflicts) and European-Asian colonialism (e.g., British conquest of India, Spanish conquest of the Philippines) that occurred prior to the groups' encountering the United States, as well as in the particular forms of institutional racism designed for them once they entered the United States.

Also, our discussions with Asian American students of various ethnic groups suggest to us that the status hierarchy also is based on ethnocentricism, racism, and internalized racism. With regard to ethnocentricism, at least among early generations, apparently longevity and "purity" of one's traditional Asian culture locates one at a better position along the hierarchy than otherwise; "mixed racial" ancestry places one at a lower level than "racial purity"; and, in the case of Asian ethnic groups within the United States, whose country of origin was colonialized by Europeans and/or European Americans, "white" appearance (though not necessarily White people) often is valued.

Thus, Asian parents often encourage their offspring to select marital partners with light skin without recognizing the internalized racism inherent in this dictate. Moreover, Asian youth tend to associate dark skin color within their group with undesirable social characteristics such as poverty, recent immigrant status (as in the phrase "just off the boat"), and lack of class or refinement (Paler Hargrove, 1993).

Consequently, the therapist who intends to work with Asian American clients may be perceived as inadequate by Asian clients if he or she forces the client to fit a homogeneous Asian stereotype. Moreover, if the therapist is not at least receptive to the client's definition of her or his "Asianness," then it is unlikely that the therapy process will be of much benefit to the client.

Implications and Conclusions

Therapists are often oblivious to the fact that cultural cues of VREGs are sometimes used as surrogates for race. In the case of the two culture-based socioracial groups, this oversight may be particularly damaging because sometimes their families attempt to protect them from the ravages of racism by not telling them about it. Consequently, clients from these groups often do not develop the necessary cognitive framework for differentiating stress due to systemic barriers from personal weaknesses.

EXERCISE 5.1
Learning about American People

We have found that gaining insight into the cultural and racial life experiences of clients from different cultural backgrounds or socioracial groups makes it easier for us to use appropriate counseling interventions with them. In addition to the references that we cited in this chapter, we have found the "nonscientific" resources listed below to be useful for helping us to enter clients' frames of reference.

Films

The Great Indian Wars, 1840–1890. Plymouth, MN: Simitar Entertainment.

Eyes on the prize: America's civil rights movement (1991). Boston, MA: Blackside, Inc.

Who killed Vincent Chen? (1989). New York: Filmmakers Library.

The stories of Maxine Hong Kingston, parts 1 and 2. New York: WNET.

Books

Beal, M. D. (1963). *I will fight no more forever: Chief Joseph and the Nez Perce War.* New York: Ballantine Books.

Helms, J. E. (1992). *A race is a nice thing to have: A guide to being a White person or understanding the White persons in your life.* Topeka, KS: Content Communications.

McLauren, M. A. (1987). *Separate pasts: Growing up White in the segregated south.* Athens, GA: University of Georgia Press.

Rodriquez, R. (1982). *Hunger of memory: The education of Richard Rodriguez.* New York: Bantam Books.

Tan, A. (1989). *The Joy Luck Club.* New York: Putnam. (also available on videocassette)

Tatum, B. D. (1987). *Assimilation blues: Black families in White communities.* New York: Greenwood.

X, Malcolm. (1993). *The autobiography of Malcolm X.* New York: Ballantine Books.

The foregoing list is just a sampling of the wide array of cultural and racial vicarious-participation immersion experiences that are available. Now that we have encouraged you to think about it, you may have recalled favorites that you found educational and worthy of recommending to a friend. If so, list them below, and try to describe in a few words what you learned from them.

_____

_____

_____

As a consequence, such clients may possess the same perspectives on matters of race as therapists of color who have learned to survive in "humanistic" training programs by denying sociorace as a significant part of who they are. They may also appear to be satisfactorily acculturated to White therapists who have not informed themselves about how race functions as an impediment for these clients. The majority of therapy interactions will be intraracial (i.e., White therapist/White client). However, most interracial interactions will also involve a White person. Therefore, a conclusion to be drawn from this chapter and Chapter 4 is that therapists must prepare themselves to cope with racial matters even if they strongly believe that they will never need such preparation. Exercises 5.1 and 5.2 might help therapists begin their preparation.

EXERCISE 5.2

Do You Suffer from "Racial Oppression Syndrome"?

Dr. Andrew Baines, a retired psychiatry professor from Howard University, uses the concept of "Post-slavery Syndrome" or "slave mentality" to explain the sense of internalized servitude that prevents many African Americans from developing the self-confidence necessary to function effectively in society. As did Malcolm X, Dr. Baines views the lack of self-confidence as a lingering residue of the enslavement of African people in the United States. We think that members of all of the VREG socioracial groups whose ancestors experienced racial oppression might still feel the residues of that ancestral experience. So, we have taken the liberty of generalizing some of Dr. Baines's questions to pertain to the common experiences of domination of African, Latina/Latino, Asian/Pacific Islander, and Native Americans (i.e., ALANAs).

Below, we have selected 10 items from a 30-item quiz that the *News Dimension* developed to assess slave mentality. The quiz is not a standardized measure, but should be regarded as a paper-and-pencil interview that will help you explore possible issues of internalized servitude. Even if you are not an ALANA, you might want to try this quiz for what it can reveal about your own racial socialization. Place a mark next to the item beneath the column that best represents your viewpoint.

1. Do you believe that schools run Yes No by people of your race are incapable of providing a quality education?

2. If you worked for a large White company and later went to work for a small ALANA company in the same capacity, would you feel that you are better than the other ALANA workers in the new company?

3. If a White waiter or waitress at a White-owned restaurant accidently spills some sauce on you, are you quick to excuse the person?

4. Are you finding that you are usu- Yes No ally critical of your neighbors of your own race?

5. When shopping for a car, do you feel you can get a better deal from a White salesperson than from an ALANA salesperson?

6. If you buy tennis shoes for yourself or your children, is it important to buy expensive shoes?

7. When you're leaving a store, do you automatically look for the detection device near the door and hope it doesn't go off while you are passing by?

8. Do you ever use "special" racial terms (e.g.,the N-word, negrita) when referring to others of your racial group, whether you're angry or not?

9. If a White police officer stops your car, do you believe that the officer did so because of your race?

10. Within the past month, have you looked at yourself in a mirror and had thoughts about what it would be like to be White?

Count the number of yes responses, and use the prorated scoring key below to assess your level of "Racial Oppression Syndrome."

If you answered yes to a maximum of two questions, consider yourself relatively free of Racial Oppression Syndrome. If you answered yes to more than two but less than five of the items, you may have periodic attacks of internalized servitude. If you have more than five yes responses, consider the possibility that you consistently have race-related feelings of low self-esteem and a negative self-concept.

Note: This Exercise was adapted from Are You Still A Slave? (1994, May 27), In B. A. Murray (Ed.), *News dimensions: The nation's most progressive Black newspaper,* (pp. 2 & 25). 1221 Massachusetts Avenue, N.W., Suite 522, Washington, DC 20005.

REFERENCES

Axelson, J. A. (1993). *Counseling and development in a multicultural society* (2nd ed.). Pacific Grove, CA: Brooks/Cole Publishing Company.

Canabal, I. (1995). Latino group identities and collective and personal self-esteem. Unpublished doctoral dissertation, University of Maryland, College Park, MD.

Fairchild, H. P. (1926). *The melting pot mistake.* Boston: Little, Brown and Company.

Fujita, S. (1990). Asian/Pacific-American mental health: Some needed research in epidemiology and service utilization. In F. C. Serafica, A. I. Schwebel, R. K. Russell, P. D. Isaac, & L. B. Myers (Eds.), *Mental health of ethnic minorities* (pp. 249–278). New York: Praeger.

Grant, M. (1916). *The passing of the great race.* New York: Charles Scribner's Sons.

Kingston, M. H. (1980). *China men.* New York: Ballantine Books.

McLemore, S. D. (1983). *Racial and ethnic relations in America* (2nd ed.). Boston: Allyn and Bacon, Inc.

Paler Hargrove, L. (1993). *Skin color.* Unpublished videotape. University of Maryland, College Park, MD.

Reasons, G., & Patrick, S. (1971). *They had a dream.* New York: New American Library.

Rich, S. (1987, September 11). United States Hispanic population up sharply. *The Washington Post,* p. A9.

Rodriguez, R. (1982). *Hunger of memory: The education of Richard Rodriguez.* New York: Bantam Books.

Takaki, R. (1993). *A different mirror.* Boston: Little, Brown and Company.

Takaki, R. (1989). *Strangers from a different shore.* New York: Penguin Books.

U.S. Department of Commerce. (1992). *General population characteristics: 1990 census of population, United States.* U.S. Department of Commerce, Bureau of the Census.

Weatherford, J. (1991). *Native roots: How the Indians enriched America.* New York: Fawcett Columbine.

Weyr, T. (1988). *Hispanic United States of America: Breaking the melting pot.* New York: Harper & Row.

6 Models of Racial Oppression and Sociorace

It is impossible for us to provide a thorough review of the socioracial group issues of each of the five major groups. Nevertheless, in previous chapters, we sought to provide enough of a flavor of the tensions so that therapists can have a basis for thinking about possible socioracial tensions that might impact the therapy process with themselves as the symbolic catalyst. Social scientists of various theoretical persuasions and orientations have attempted to provide explanations of racism's impact on individuals and/or intergroup relations, but rarely (with the possible exception of psychoanalytic theorists) have they considered the impact of racial factors on the therapy process per se.

Most contemporary theories of race and culture have tended to focus on the societal structural dynamics and implications of race and (occasionally) culture, but have rarely examined their intrapsychic and interpersonal consequences at the level of the individual. Yet therapists ought to be concerned about the interplay between the person's objective reality or circumstances (e.g., conditions of oppression) and her or his subjective well-being (e.g., manner in which experiences are interpreted).

Moreover, it is important to realize that although both race and culture involve person-environment socialization, for each individual client, psychorace and psychoculture may be differentially salient to the client in any given situation (see Table 2.1). For some people, racial socialization will be a more important aspect of their personality development, and for others, cultural socialization will be more important. In this chapter, we examine models of racial oppression and sociorace for their usefulness in assessing client dynamics.

Socioracial Racial Theory

In order to maintain control over a group, it is necessary for the group in power to psychologically debilitate the target group's members. Not only must the members of the VREGs (in this case) be convinced that the inferior status of their group is pre-ordained or deserved, but the benefactors, beneficiaries, and perpetrators of the psychological and systemic oppression must also convince members of their own group that their superior status is justly deserved and that they bear no personal responsibility for the inferior status of the other socioracial out-groups.

Of course, as we mentioned in Chapters 3 and 4, one set of strategies that White Americans collectively have used to achieve and maintain functional control over visible racial and ethnic groups (VREGs) is differential dispensation and allotment of social, political, and economic power according to White-defined racial criteria. The efficient use of such strategies requires that mutually exclusive racial categories be created, regardless of whether these categories have any biogenetic basis in fact.

Moreover, members of the oppressed group(s) must be "de-cultured," by which we mean exposed to pervasive, systematic, ongoing indoctrination to the effect that their traditional culture as well as the members of that cultural group are inferior and worthless. The resulting cultural vacuum is then filled with the dominant group's stereotypical depictions of the various socioracial groups.

Also, members of the deculturated groups must be taught to which "racial" group they belong, and what observable socially undesirable characteristics define their group membership. That is, they must be "racinated" (see Cross, Parham, & Helms, 1991). This sequence of events makes it possible for the dominating group to maintain control over those groups considered to be threats to the status quo. In this society, groups of color (ALANAs) have been the primary focus of societies' demoralizing deculturation and racination tactics.

Whites, the preservers of the racial status quo and definers of the dominative group, must also be taught the fabricated observable criteria for innately belonging to or earning membership in the privileged group. As mentioned in the previous chapter, the racination process for them involves learning the sociopolitical rules of the dominant group (a process that presumably begins at birth); it also requires replacement of traditional European and Asian cultures with amalgamated (White) American culture. In addition, they must create and/or learn the rationale for why VREGs do not have or deserve equivalent status in this country.

For both Whites and VREGs, a discernible manifestation of the deculturation-racination process is the internalization of racial stereotypes. The mental health professions as well as politicians have contributed mightily to the content of existing racial stereotypes. Thus, in their analysis of racism in the mental health literature, Thomas and Sillen (1972) outlined the following racial stereotypic assumptions: (a) Blacks are endowed with "less gray matter" and smaller brains and consequently, are more prone (than Whites) to "insanity"; (b) social protest by People of Color is an infallible symptom of mental derangement; (c) less evolved or "lower races" (on the racial hierarchy) have not evolved sufficiently beyond their "simian past" to practice appropriately the conventions of civilized society (e.g., monogamous marriage); (d) VREGs cannot control their emotions and demonstrate a lack of morality, particularly with respect to sexuality; (e) VREGs are inappropriate candidates for psychoanalysis because of their "simplistic minds," but make excellent research specimens; and (f) living in close proximity to Blacks and other "lower races" (especially Asians and Native Americans) contaminates Whites, and so forth.

Perhaps not surprisingly, these stereotypes do not differ markedly from the racial stereotypes that prevail in contemporary society more widely. However, perhaps more surprising is the fact that the themes underlying the stereotypes are still a strong aspect of the conceptualization of racial dynamics in mental health and psychotherapy literature.

Interestingly, as Axelson (1993) noted, there is no consensual derogatory stereotype of Whites as a *racial* group. Their superiority is assumed. White stereotypes, such as they are, pertain to particular "deviant" ethnic groups (e.g., Polish jokes) or White subgroups who otherwise are assumed (without evidence) to differ in major ways from most White people (e.g., "rednecks").

For both the oppressors and oppressed, internalized racial stereotypes about oneself as well as others are a major component of what is meant by the term *internalized racism*, or psychological reactions to racial oppression. Among mental health practitioners, personalized psychological reactions are assumed to have major therapeutic implications, although they typically only discuss these implications as they pertain to Blacks and other VREGs.

For example, Landrum and Batts (1985) proposed a variety of related symptoms including poor self-concept, misdirected anger, in-group discord, drug addiction, and so forth as the potential focus of race-related interventions. When internalized racism is expressed overtly, it can have implications for the quality of a person's interactions with others. In the case of therapists and clients, in particular, the quality of the therapy process may be detrimentally influenced by the nature of the psychological reactions to race that each party has internalized.

Models of Racial Oppression

Feagin (1984) divides the existing explanatory models of racism and ethnocentricism into two categories—*order* and *power-conflict*. The focus of these models tends to differ depending on whether they were intended to explain the life circumstances of the dominative group (Whites) or one or more of the dominated groups. In the former case, one typically sees a greater emphasis on describing White people's negative reactions to "non-White" or "non-American" others; in the latter, one sees most emphasis on explaining adaptations of African, Latina/Latino, Asian, and Native Americans (ALANAs) to societal racism and ethnocentricism.

According to Feagin (1984), order theories generally emphasize the outcomes of assimilation and/or racism, that is, the manner by which nondominant groups adapt to or become like the dominant group. Power-conflict theories focus on the social control and conflict associated with subordinating other groups, in this case, White strategies for controlling other groups.

Nevertheless, virtually none of the models discussed by Feagin is of much use in analyzing the psychological implications of race in the psychotherapy process because they tend to treat race as group or structural dynamic rather than individual-difference dimensions. Structural dynamics pertain to societal conditions of racial classification (such as racial integration in housing and schools), and differential access to power (such as voting patterns and numbers of elected officials), whereas individual difference dimensions pertain to subjective reactions to one's conditions of racism (such as depression, exhilaration, and so forth). Using our terminology, structural models identify distal or sociological characteristics, whereas psychological models describe psychological (subjective) or proximal reactions to race.

In this chapter, some models that pertain specifically to issues of structural conditions of racism and ethnocentricism, that is, power-conflict and order models, are briefly summarized. We think these models are most useful for forming hypotheses about the societal racial conditions under which individual members of the various socioracial groups may exist. We also present models of racial identity development (Helms, 1990a) as one manner of conceptualizing clients' psychological adaptations to racism that we have found useful for explaining client and therapist racial dynamics in individual and group psychotherapy.

White Power-Conflict Models

The central question driving the quest for White models of racial oppression has concerned the group's propensity to seek and maintain dominative relationships with people who are assumed to be of a different race (see Chapters 4 and 5). At least up until 1964, when the first Civil Rights Act was signed, the relationship of Whites to groups of color was unapologetic domination, segregation, and oppression. Again the details of the domination differed depending on which group one considers.

However, the common thread running through race relations involving Whites as the protagonists is that Whites considered themselves to be superior to *all* non-White groups, and therefore entitled by birthright to "life, liberty, and the pursuit of happiness." Naturally, all groups of color were considered subservient and inferior and were expected to earn any of the rights to life, liberty, or justice that White society was willing to accord them.

Even the White people who are often portrayed as being sympathetic to the causes of people of color often were practitioners of racism. Abraham Lincoln, the "Great Emancipator," reveals his level of personal and institutional racism in the following quote: "I will say, then that I am not, nor ever have been, in favor of bringing about in any way the social and political equality of the white [sic] and black [sic] races (applause); that I am not, nor ever have been, in favor of making voters or jurors of negroes [sic], nor of qualifying them to hold office, nor to intermarry with white [sic] people . . .

And inasmuch as they cannot so live, while they do remain together there must be the position of superior and inferior, and I as much as any other man am in favor of having the superior position assigned to the white [sic] race" (cited in Zinn, 1980, p. 184).

Most social scientists have been unable to explain why Whites have adhered to the principles of White supremacy, privilege, and domination for so long and so consistently with so many socioracial groups. Several theoretical explanations have been offered and we briefly summarize them here, not necessarily because we subscribe to them, but because therapists should be aware of the theories that may underlie their clients' expectations of them.

Theoretical explanations of Whites' dominative status can be categorized approximately as follows: (a) racial superiority; (b) racial inferiority; and (c) circumstantial. We intend only to describe these perspectives briefly, and consequently, in the case of those perspectives that are purported to be theories of "development" or "evolution," we may have done the perspectives a disservice. Therefore, the reader is referred to the original sources for a fuller elaboration of the perspectives.

White Racial Superiority

The general premise of White superiority explanations is that Whites deserve their dominant sociopolitical status because they are genetically, intellectually, and/or culturally superior to those whom they have dominated. Consequently, the characteristics of the White group are the standards by which members of other groups are evaluated.

In psychology more specifically, White superiority explanations have existed in both implicit and explicit versions. To the extent that they are based on the experiences of White people and their culture, universalistic perspectives are implicit White superiority perspectives (see Wrenn, 1962). Explicit models typically are founded on principles of sociobiology and directly base their premises on racial classifications, but not necessarily measurable physiological "racial" characteristics.

Universalistic Perspectives

In a sense most of the traditional theories of counseling and psychotherapy are based on universalistic principles. According to Ridley, Mendoza, and Kanitz (1994), universalistic perspectives are of two types—*generic* and *etic* or *true universalistic*. Proponents of generic perspectives argue that there are principles, aspects, or processes of human existence that transcend (socio)racial and cultural boundaries and, therefore, are applicable to all human beings. Proponents of etic universalistic frameworks contend that aspects of traditional theories are universally applicable to all people or that new culturally inclusive models can be created that will be applicable to everyone regardless of socioracial and/or cultural boundaries.

Generic models, theories, and principles are implicitly White racial and/or cultural superiority perspectives because they typically are explanations of human adaptations using the socialization experiences of White westerners and Europeans as the basis of such interpretations (see Chapter 8). Such perspectives rarely consider the possibility that different life circumstances might contribute to alternate adaptations, which might be equally "healthy" for members of those groups to whom they pertain.

Consequently, the behavior of Whites is considered to be normative for other groups, and deviations from such norms are considered to be deficits. Explanations for these alleged deficits are then presumed to lie in the group's genetic makeup (in reality, racial classifications) or environmental deprivation. Hypothetical "group deficiencies" then become the justification for a wide range of dominative behaviors on the part of Whites.

With regard to the history of intergroup racial and cultural relations in general, group deficiencies of various sorts were used to justify the domination of all of the visible racial and ethnic groups. According to Hacker (1992), "From the premise of genetic inferiority, there follows the corollary that members of a lesser race should be content to perform tasks unsuited to other strains. This was the rationale for slavery, and it has by no means disappeared. (There are even hints of this in the plea to create more blue-collar jobs for black [sic] men.)" (p. 28). In the mental health professions more specifically, alleged ALANA inferiority has been used consistently to explain why ALANAs' behaviors supposedly do not conform to White-based standards in most aspects of the helping process.

Sociobiology

The basic premise of race-related sociobiological theory is that the racial-classification groups can be aligned along a superiority/inferiority hierarchy based on their presumed ancestry regardless of national or continental boundaries. Franklin (1991) contends that the underlying "scientific" basis of this perspective is Social Darwinism, and suggests that it was the philosophy underlying much of the "founding fathers'" and their descendants' mistreatment of VREGs in this country (see Helms, 1994).

According to Hutnik (1991) and Spikard (1992), some of the earliest spokespersons in U.S. society for this perspective were Madison Grant (1916), Henry Pratt Fairchild (1926), Howard C. Hill (1919), and Ellwood P. Cubberly (1929). In psychology, some spokespersons have been G. Stanley Hall (1904), J. Phillip Rushton (1990, 1995), and Arthur Jensen (1969). Originally, as previously noted, advocates of the racial sociobiological perspective argued that the northern and western European "races" were superior to all other racial groups, including southern and eastern Europeans. Although the order of the alignment of the racial categories shifted slightly over the ensuing decades, with Asians occasionally replacing Whites at the top of the hierarchy (see, for example, Rushton, 1995), according to Spikard (1992, p. 14), the typical order devised by the dominant European group was as follows: ". . . Caucasians at the top, Asians next, then Native Americans, and Africans at the bottom—in terms of both physical abilities and moral qualities [such as dishonesty, poverty, uncleanliness]."

The notion that psychological characteristics (e.g., physical abilities, personality characteristics) were inherited provided the justification for White Americans' domination and exploitation of other groups. Each racial group was assumed to be defined by a distinctive combination of psychological characteristics, and consequently, to occupy a different rung on the Darwinian evolutionary ladder. Since they were presumably the most evolved, Anglo-Saxon Americans had the right to force other groups to conform to their standards and/or to take from misfits that which was necessary (e.g., land, life, personhood, culture) to ensure the dominance and unity of the White American group.

White Racial Inferiority Models

White inferiority models attribute Whites' history of other-group domination to inherent aspects of the condition of being White, such as physiological or environmental deficits relative to other socioracial groups. Both psychoanalytic and cultural explanations of the "White personality" have been offered, according to which the sociopolitical characteristics of the White group are attributed to physiological or evolutionary deficiencies, and consequent psychological impairment resulting therefrom

As is true of the other perspectives, our rationale for presenting these perspectives is not necessarily because we endorse them wholeheartedly, but rather because many clients will have internalized them as a form of folk psychology, a way of ameliorating the pain of institutional and cultural racism. The therapist who first hears about these views of White people from the mouths of her or his client is likely to be caught unawares.

Psychoanalytic.   Although psychoanalytic theory often has been used to account for White racism (Comer, 1991; P. Katz, 1976), psychiatrist Frances Cress Welsing (1974) is probably the first person to use this theoretical orientation to account for Whites' propensity to dominate other sociocracial groups. Psychoanalytic theory originated with Sigmund Freud. In general, psychoanalytic theorists locate the motivation for human behavior in (usually) unconscious drives and instincts as Freud did. In many versions of psychoanalytic theory, these motivations have themes of sexuality and/or aggression.

For Welsing, the conscious or unconscious force that motivates Whites' domination of others is the drive to compensate for their whiteness; that is, their "color inadequacy" or "albinism." Thus, the basic premises of Cress's "Color-Confrontation Theory" are as follows: (a) When white people encounter any part of the massive numbers of peoples of color of the world, they become painfully aware of their minority status with respect to their own relative lack of color and number; and (b) in response to the wounded sense of identity that is based on an unchangeable part of themselves—their external appearance—they develop a number of defensive reactions and mechanisms to protect themselves from their own feelings of inadequacy.

Among the reactions are uncontrollable hostility and aggression, and defensive feelings that continuously have had peoples of color as their target throughout history. Among the defense mechanisms are repression of feelings and awareness of their genetic color inferiority; reaction formation in which the valued and desired skin color is psychologically imbued with opposite characteristics such as dirtiness, evil, and so forth; and "compensatory logic" (also a form of reaction formation) in which the lack of color or genetic deficiency is transformed into White supremacy. Thus, according to Welsing, White supremacy then becomes Whites' justification for their participation in the varieties of institutional and cultural racism that prevail in the society.

Environmental.   Michael Bradley (1978), an anthropologist, proposed the theory of the "ice-man inheritance." According to his theory, White people are the descendants of Africans of color who migrated into the Northern Hemisphere, where their efforts to survive during the Ice Age (from 100,000 to 10,000 years Before the Present, B.P., which he defines as beginning in 1950) resulted in the evolution of definitive physiological and psychological characteristics, vestiges of which were transmitted to successive generations.

Thus, Bradley (1978, p. 26) contends that "glacial evolution demanded certain special adaptations of Neanderthal man [sic] and that present-day Caucasoids still show vestiges of these adaptations. *These special adaptations had incidental side effects which resulted in an exceptionally aggressive psychology, an extreme expression of the cronos complex, and a higher level of psychosexual conflict compared to all other races of men [sic]."*

In Bradley's thesis, "Caucasoid" refers to "White peoples." By *cronos complex*, he means territorial behaviors designed to protect one's identity and status across time (past, present, and future). In other words, people compete with their ancestral past (i.e., one must achieve more than one's ancestors), the present (i.e., one should accomplish more than the living including one's own offspring), and the future (i.e., one attempts to leave a legacy that others cannot surpass). Whereas Bradley contends that the cronos complex is a theme in all human societies, he argues that it is stronger in White groups because they were the only group to have evolved in a glacial environment, and consequently, they alone developed the exceptionally high level of aggression used to impose their identity on others. Unlike other racial groups, evolution in such austere circumstances allegedly narrowed the range of physical (e.g., sexual enjoyment) and psychological (e.g., empathy) options available to Whites for sublimating their self-protective aggressiveness.

Circumstantial

These explanations generally attribute Whites' exploitation of other groups to the circumstance of Whites' being the political majority in the country. Most such perspectives tend to begin the search for descriptions of the White condition post Civil War. More often than not, some simplistic form of racism or other manner of out-group prejudice is seen as the cause of Whites' self-aggrandizement. Richardson (1989) pointed out that these theories of racism generally treat VREG people as stressors to White people rather than conversely. Nevertheless, based on their reviews of racism literature, various authors (e.g., Allport, 1958; Katz, 1976; Richardson, 1989; Singer, 1962) have classified existing power-conflict racism-prejudice theories as follows:

Historical.   The root causes of contemporary interracial-group conflict are located in the histories of the visible racial and ethnic groups (VREGs) that are participants in the conflict. Recall that the opportunity to convert and save the souls of African and Native Americans was frequently used as a rationale for slavery (see Chapter 4), an option that presumably is no longer available. Therefore, if ALANAs are discriminated against, it is because the options to civilize them are no longer readily available, and/or they no longer take maximal advantage of existing remedies. In other words, to understand Whites' anti-Black or anti-Native sentiments, then one needs to examine the histories of enslavement of these groups. Typically such perspectives do not explicate the reasons why or the manner in which the historical experiences of VREGs are responsible for shaping White people's feelings, attitudes, or behaviors.

Sociocultural.   Societal and cultural (actually racial) trends cause people's individual racism. So, for example, urbanization (the tendency of large groups of especially People of Color to move into cities) has been hypothesized to account for Whites' antipathy toward Blacks because it promotes racial isolation and segregation, and because the incoming group does not share the same cultural values as the host group. Yet as Richardson (1989) notes, such explanations disregard the fact that even people who are not involved in the societal trend (e.g., urbanization) may express or experience the same types and levels of racism as those who are involved.

Earned Reputation. Alleged offensive characteristics of VREGs (e.g., bad odor, diminishment of property values, intellectual deficits) may provoke White people's abhorrence and aggression. Then these racial stereotypes may be used to justify Whites' negative attitudes toward other socioracial groups. This perspective is implicit in much of the psychotherapy literature pertaining to racial factors.

White Order Models

Although race- and culture-focused theorists have tended to be oblivious to the impact of White racism and Anglo-Saxon ethnocentrism on White people, if we stretch our imaginations some, we can adapt a couple of the existing frameworks to discuss Whites' potential adaptations to racism at the individual level.

Frustration-Aggression Hypothesis. Originally proposed by Dollard (1957; Dollard, Doob, Miller, Mowrer, & Sears, 1939), this explanation of the causes of racism and ethnocentricism continues to exist in the psychotherapy literature in sometimes modified forms. The basic premise here is that people respond to frustration, hostility, or unpleasant feelings of day-to-day arousal by taking them out on (displacing) convenient substitutes (scapegoats) for the more powerful aggressors or uncontrollable events. In this case, people of other perceived races or cultures become the scapegoats or targets for the frustration-reducing expressions of racism-ethnocentricism.

According to McLemore (1983), any guilt aroused by recognition that one is displacing aggression is assuaged by using racial stereotypes to rationalize former behaviors as well as new feelings of adverse arousal to daily frustrations, resulting in a cycle of out-group aggression. Since Whites are in the numerical majority and hold the institutional power, it is more likely that their frustration-aggression cycle will be overtly expressed, whereas VREGs are assumed to use covert forms of expression such as passive aggression or urban riots (Simpson & Yinger, 1972).

Although the frustration-aggression hypothesis was proposed as a universally applicable explanation of the manner by which people acquire personal racism, we think it may be more useful for understanding some, but not all, White people's racial reactions. In our experience, some White clients use a race-specific lay version of the frustration-aggression hypothesis to explain their antipathy toward other groups. "Some (fill in the socioracial group) person was mean (fill in a specific act) to me and ever since then, I have hated (or other appropriate affective verb) all (fill in the blank) people."

Obviously, a certain amount of personal racism and inadequate skills for managing one's emotions underlie such assertions. The therapist can use the frustration-aggression hypothesis to aid her or him in identifying the client's specific manner of resolving daily frustrations, and to assist the client in learning more competent strategies for coping explicitly with life in general, and incidentally, other racial groups.

VREG Models

Interestingly, theories of VREGs' adaptation to their group's particular conditions of exploitation and domination have generally focused on describing the circumstances of African Americans. This singular focus on African Americans when addressing matters of race, and the other groups (i.e., Asian, Latino/Latina, and Native Americans) when examining issues concerning cultural adaptation, probably has occurred for two reasons.

First, as noted in Chapters 3 and 4, throughout mental health history until the mid-1970s, all of the groups of color were generally considered to be no different than Blacks for all practical purposes (Thomas & Sillen, 1972). Consequently, theoretical formulations that pertained to one group were considered to be applicable to members of the other socioracial groups as well.

As it became expedient for economic and political reasons to expand the varieties of socioracial groups to accommodate differential prejudices and discrimination against immigrants of color and/or from undesirable parts of Europe and Asia, mental health theorists, practitioners, and researchers joined the rest of society in focusing on cultural differences as the justification for their alleged psychopathology rather than the maladaptive racial climate. Moreover, because Native Americans were generally considered to have a distinct culture whereas African Americans were not (Shuffleton, 1993; see Chapter 4), the effect of racism on Native people's well being has been as absent as the study of cultural incompatibility has been for people of African descent in the United States.

Thus, with respect to theoretical perspectives, one finds some allegedly racial psychological models with Black Americans as their focus, and some cultural models with Native, Latino/Latina, and Asian Americans as their focus. One rarely sees cultural factors addressed with respect to African Americans or racial factors addressed vis-à-vis the other groups of color. Consequently, in our experience, we have found that many of our colleagues and students have difficulty realizing that both cultural and racial factors might be of concern to VREG clients, regardless of their particular socioracial membership group.

In this chapter, we discuss racial sociological and psychological models. In the next chapter, we focus more explicitly on group-relevant cultures.

Sociological Perspectives

Most of these theories are intended to explain the psychological consequences of and/or the psychological motivations (i.e., internal mechanisms) for what is considered to be group-specific antisocial or deviant behavior. Most locate the stimuli for these consequences in the conditions of institutional racism and personality deficits of African Americans.

Geschwender (1968; cited in McLemore, 1983) proffered three theoretical models based on the proposition that civil disturbance is a reaction to people's increased dissatisfaction as they compare their real circumstances to their ideal circumstances. They are as follows: (a) Rising-expectation hypothesis—in response to improving group-related conditions, people begin to hope and believe that significant change is possible. Discontent occurs when the hoped-for ideal and one's reality are too discrepant, and consequently, collective action may occur; (b) Relative-deprivation hypothesis—People of Color compare their lives to those of Whites, and if the gap between one's group's real status and the status of Whites is not perceived to be narrowing, then discontent may occur. Such discontent would not be based entirely on one's group's objective circumstances, but rather one's circumstances relative to the more advantaged group(s); (c) Rise-and-drop hypothesis—if an era of improvement for one's group is perceived as being followed by a period of stagnation or decline, then frustration and anger may result from unfulfilled expectations, even if individual members of the group are better off than before.

Note that each of these models infers individual psychological reactions (e.g., frustration, discontent, anger) from one's ascribed socioracial membership group.

Psychological Models

Some theorists have presented the perspective that all Black people are irrevocably scarred by their circumstances of being the victims of the societal conditions of racism (see Helms, 1990b, for an overview). Contemporary versions of this perspective conceivably can find their antecedents in the work of Kardiner and Ovesey (1951). Therefore, we believe that it might be useful to examine their formulation in some detail.

Mark of Oppression.   Kardiner and Ovesey contend that the "central problem" of personality adaptation for "Negro" people is racial discrimination. Racial discrimination creates chronically low self-esteem among members of this population because they are constantly receiving negative images of themselves from other people's behavior toward them. Because the pain of racial discrimination is unremitting and constant, the person adopts "restitutive maneuvers" (defense mechanisms) to maintain internal equilibrium. Some of these defenses protect the person's intrapsychic status by preventing her or him from being overwhelmed by the pain of discrimination; some enable the person to present an acceptable social facade so that he or she can interact with the relevant social environments, albeit in a maladaptive manner. All of this self-management requires a constant expenditure of psychic energy that deprives the person of the psychological resources necessary to build a more healthy personality structure.

Figure 6.1 illustrates the personality structure of Black people as conceptualized by Kardiner and Ovesey. In the model, (racial) discrimination fuels development of the Black personality constellation of low self-esteem (the self-focused consequence of discrimination) and aggression (the other focused reaction to discrimination).

The figure portrays the primacy of low self-esteem and aggression in the Black personality, but was intended to be only a skeletal outline of the ways in which these

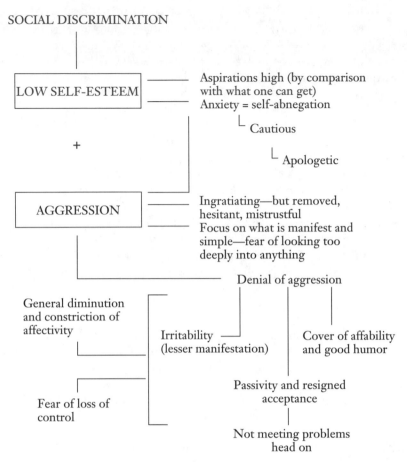

SOCIAL DISCRIMINATION

LOW SELF-ESTEEM — Aspirations high (by comparison with what one can get)
Anxiety = self-abnegation
      Cautious
      Apologetic

+

AGGRESSION — Ingratiating—but removed, hesitant, mistrustful
Focus on what is manifest and simple—fear of looking too deeply into anything

General diminution and constriction of affectivity

Denial of aggression

Irritability (lesser manifestation)

Cover of affability and good humor

Fear of loss of control

Passivity and resigned acceptance

Not meeting problems head on

FIGURE 6.1   Kardiner and Ovesey's (1951) Model of the Black Personality.

From THE MARK OF OPPRESSION: A Psychosocial Study of the American Negro by Abram Kardiner and Lionel Ovesey. Copyright 1951. Reprinted by permission of W. W. Norton & Company, Inc.

dynamics manifest themselves. Thus, not only is low self-esteem evident in Black people's allegedly high levels of anxiety and tendencies to have higher aspirations than society will permit them to realize, but also in their self-contempt, idealization of Whites, and "frantic efforts to be white [sic]," hostility, apathy, hedonism, "living for the moment," "criminality," and hatred of oneself and other members of one's racial group.

Similarly, not only are anxiety, ingratiation, simplistic thinking, and denial of aggression symptoms of Black people's underlying aggression, but so too are the following: (a) rage and fear, which eventually become interchangeable because of the societal prohibitions against expressing the former if one is Black; (b) submission or compliance, which become increasingly more abject with greater levels of rage and hatred; (c) laughter, gaiety, or flippancy, which, of course, are evidence of denied rage; and (d) masochism, depression, migraine headaches, and hypertension resulting from repressed rageful feelings toward a loved object.

It is fairly easy to find the psychological themes proposed by Kardiner and Ovesey reverberating throughout the mental health literature in which visible racial and ethnic groups are depicted. For example, Smith (1980) noted the overwhelming focus on the alleged psychopathology of Black people rather than of society in the career development literature (see Chapter 11).

Moreover, even the cursory overview of Kardiner and Ovesey's perspective that we have presented reveals that their (and similar) perspectives make "healthy personality" and (especially) Black people oxymorons. In addition, although we will not present the rest of their perspective here, suffice it to say that the contemporary themes of restricted emotionality, family pathology, absentee fathers, emotionally ungratifying mothers, lack of positive Black "role models," and so forth may not necessarily have begun with Kardiner and Ovesey, but were certainly embellished by them.

In addition, Kardiner and Ovesey believed that their depictions pertained to Black people regardless of social class or any other life conditions. According to them, ". . . the Negro [sic] has <u>no possible basis for a healthy self-esteem and every incentive for self-hatred.</u> The basic fact is that in the Negro [sic] aspiration level, good conscience and even good performance are irrelevant in face of the glaring fact that the Negro [sic] gets a poor reflection of himself [or herself] in the behavior of whites [sic], no matter what he [or she] does or what his [or her] merits are" (Kardiner & Ovesey, 1951, p. 197, underlines added).

Racial identity theorists were the first to offer the perspectives that healthy personality development is possible for People of Color, White people are not necessarily the main objects of identification and reinforcement for People of Color, and that racism in its various forms has implications for the personality development of White people.

Racial Identity Models

In actuality, racial (in fact "socioracial") identity models are psychological models because they intend to explain individuals' intrapsychic and interpersonal reactions to societal racism in its various manifestations. That is, they are descriptions of hypothetical intrapsychic pathways for overcoming internalized racism and achieving a healthy socioracial self-conception under varying conditions of racial oppression. We find these models useful for assessing the influence of racial factors on the client's concerns as well as the reactions of the client and therapist to one another.

Table 6.1 summarizes some of the models that have been proposed to describe the socioracial adaptations of specific socioracial groups. Most of these models are "typologies" that propose static character types, which develop in response to being deprived by or benefitting from racism in its various forms. A few are stage theories that propose a sequential process by which an individual's growth toward healthy adjustment occurs.

Many of the models purport to be descriptions of "ethnic" or "cultural" development or adaptation. However, if to us, the particulars of the models seemed to pertain more to socioracial dynamics as we have defined them than to culture, then they were included in Table 6.1. In some instances, we modified the original theorists'

TABLE 6.1   Selected Summary of Visible Racial or "Ethnic" Group (VREG)

Author	Kind	Group	Description of Types/Stages
Banks (1981)	Stage	African American	**Ethnic Psychological Captivity**—Person internalizes society's negative view of his/her socioracial group. **Ethnic Encapsulation**—Person participates primarily with own socioracial group, which is idealized. **Ethnic Identity Clarification**—Person learns self-acceptance. **Biethnicity**—Person possesses healthy sense of socioracial identity and can function in own group and in White culture. **Multiethnicity**—Person is self-actualized and can function beyond superficial levels in many cultures.
Cross (1971)	Stage	African American	**Preencounter**—Person identifies with White people and culture, and rejects or denies kinship with Black people and culture. **Encounter**—Person repudiates previous identification with Whites, seeks identification with Blacks. **Immersion-Emersion**—Person completely identifies with Blacks and abhors Whites. **Internalization**—Person incorporates a positive Black identity and transcends psychological effects of racism. **Internalization-Commitment**—Person maintains Black identity while resisting the various forms of societal oppression.
Dizard (1970)	Typology	African Americans	**Assimilated**—Person moves as comfortably and easily in White environments as White prejudice will permit. **Pathological**—Person exhibits some form of psychopathology as the primary response to life's hardships. **Traditional**—Person attempts to preserve one's own-group identity, integrity and dignity.
Gay (1984)	Stage	African American	**Preencounter**—Person's socioracial identity is subconscious or subliminal or dominated by Euro-American conceptions of one's group. **Encounter**—Person's perceptions of her/his socioracial group are shattered by an event, which initiates search for new group conceptions. **Post-Encounter**—Person experiences and exudes inner security, self-confidence, and pride in one's socioracial group.

TABLE 6.1   Continued

Author	Kind	Group	Description of Types/Stages
Carney & Kahn (1984)	Stage	White American	**Stage 1**—Person's perceptions of VREG people are based on societal stereotypes.
			Stage 2—Person recognizes own-group embeddedness, but deals with other groups in a detached scholarly manner.
			Stage 3—Person either denies the importance of race or expresses anger toward one's own group.
			Stage 4—Person attempts to blend aspects of White culture with aspects of VREG cultures.
			Stage 5—Person has commitment to promoting social equality and cultural pluralism.
Hardiman (1982)		White Americans	**Acceptance**—Person shows active or passive endorsement of White superiority.
			Resistance—Person has initial conscious awareness of racial identity.
			Redefinition—Person attempts to redefine Whiteness from a nonracist perspective.
			Internalization—Person internalizes nonracist White identity.
Terry (1977)		White Americans	**Color blind**—Person equates acknowledgment of color with racism, feels one can exonerate oneself from being White by asserting one's "human-ness."
			White Blacks—Person abandons Whiteness by overidentifying with Blacks and rejecting one's Whiteness.
			New Blacks—Person recognizes that racism is a White problem and ascribes to a pluralistic racial world view.

Note: More extensive versions of this table appear in Helms (1990a, 1990b).

language to reflect our interpretation. Therefore, we include them here as exemplars of racial rather than cultural psychological models.

The majority of the models summarized have single socioracial groups as their focus (either African American or White American). Although some models attempt to describe the adaptations of a variety of groups exposed to similar conditions of oppression (e.g., Atkinson, Morten, & Sue, 1989; Myers et al., 1991), these latter theories presumably are examples of what Ridley et al. (1994) mean by etic-universal perspectives.

Still other theories not summarized in Table 6.1 are either efforts to integrate existing theories with similar themes and constructs (e.g., Sabnani, Ponterotto, & Borodovsky, 1991) or derivatives or restatements of those theories (e.g., Rowe, Bennett, & Atkinson, 1994). Despite the many versions of racial identity theory from which one might choose, we will use Helms's (1984; 1990a; 1994) version of racial identity theory because that is the perspective that we have found most useful in our own work with therapists, clients, and ourselves.

Helms's Racial Identity Theory

Helms (1984; 1990a) originally proposed White and Black racial identity models and used them to describe the psychotherapy process involving these two groups. Subsequently, she expanded the Black model to pertain to other VREGs in recognition of the commonalities of experience with respect to racial (but not necessarily cultural) societal forces.

Thus, as is our central premise, the models are based on the assumption that racial classifications are sociopolitical constructions whose existence signals socioracial groups' differential rankings or access to resources in the political and economic societal hierarchy. Predictable psychological consequences (e.g., internalized racism) are assumed to result from being socialized as a member of one group rather than another; that is, either a dominant or nondominant collective.

The racial identity models are intended to describe the process of development by which individual members of the various socioracial groups overcome the version of internalized racism that typifies their group in order to achieve a self-affirming and realistic racial-group or collective identity. The need for such development exists because society differentially rewards or punishes members of societally ascribed racial groups according to their racial classifications.

Common Themes

The two racial identity models (as well as her gender identity model) share some common themes, which are summarized in Table 6.2. However, to discuss these, it is necessary to take note of another alteration in Helms's Black/White model, which is the replacement of the construct of "stages" with "ego statuses" (Helms, 1996). Statuses are cognitive-affective-conative intrapsychic principles for responding to racial stimuli in one's internal and external environments. Helms (1996) contends that the change was necessary to encourage mental health workers who use racial identity models to conceive of the process of development as involving dynamic evolution rather than static personality structures or types. Therapists presumably cannot modify types whereas they may be able to alter processes.

For both models, the developmental process involves successive differentiations of increasingly more sophisticated racial identity ego statuses whose objective or measurable manifestations are schema or information-processing strategies. The maturation or evolution of the more sophisticated statuses makes it possible for the person to perceive and respond to racial information in one's internal and external environments in increasingly more complex ways. Thus, Helms makes a distinction between racial identity *development* and racial identity *expression*. Development or maturation refers to the sequence by which racial identity statuses potentially become available

TABLE 6.2   Summary of Common Ego Status Themes in Helms's Racial Identity Models

Themes

Persons must overcome societal definitions of one's socioracial group by redefining oneself in personally meaningful terms.

Self redefinition involves a sequential differentiation or maturation of ego statuses.

Simplest or least complex statuses develop first.

The seeds of more complex statuses are inherent in earlier statuses.

Statuses that are most consistently reinforced in the environment become strongest and potentially dominant.

A status is dominant when it occupies the largest percentage of the ego and is used most frequently for interpreting racial material.

Statuses that are not reinforced recede in importance and become recessive.

Recessive statuses are infrequently used to govern responses to racial stimuli.

Ego statuses are hypothetical constructs that cannot be measured.

The strength of ego statuses is inferred from their behavioral expressions—schemata.

Schemata typically reflect the themes that are present in the person's socioracial environment(s).

Environments can be internal (psychological) or external (environmental).

for self-expression, and schema or expression is the manner(s) in which a person's available statuses actually are manifested.

Although the general process of developing a racial identity (that is, self-referential commitment to a societally ascribed racial group) is considered to share some similarities, the content of the developmental process within the two models differs markedly because of group differences in access to social, economic, political, and numerical resources. Thus, although the underlying thematic content of the models as described is susceptible to change as the racial dynamics of the global society change, it seems to require major societal cataclysms for societal racial dynamics to be transformed—at least in positive directions.

People of Color (POC) Racial Identity

In the POC model, a basic assumption is that, in the United States, the symptoms or consequences of racism directed toward one's racial group are a negative conception of one's racial group and oneself as a member of that group. In this model, *POC* refers to Asian, African, Latino/Latina, and Native Americans of color living in the United States regardless of the original continental origins of their ancestry. Even our cursory overview of the history of race (rather than ethnic) relations in the United States (e.g., Takaki, 1993; Zinn, 1990) reveals that peoples of the so-designated groups have been subjected to similar (but not necessarily identical) deplorable political and economic conditions because they were not perceived to be "pure" white.

Moreover, as Alba (1990) notes, the conditions of oppression that "undesirable" White ethnic immigrants to this country originally faced virtually had disappeared by their third generation in this country. Yet racism continues to follow members of the visible racial groups well beyond the third generation in this country, and has become a "tradition" that they must learn to survive.

Thus, a primary collective identity developmental task for them all is to overcome or abandon socialized negative racial-group conceptions (that is, internalized racism) as previously discussed in order to develop a realistic self-affirming collective identity. Therefore, abandonment of internalized racism involves similar processes for each of the groups of color, regardless of the specific group to which they have been relegated.

Helms's model to explain the process by which this adaptation potentially occurs is a derivative and integration of aspects of Cross's (1971) Negro-to-Black conversion model, Atkinson et al.'s (1989) Minority Identity Development model, and Erikson's collective identity model, with some influence from Kohut's (1971) self psychology. Table 6.3 summarizes the sequence by which the ego statuses as well as the correlated schema become differentiated for VREGs. The labels for the ego statuses in parentheses are the names appropriated from Cross (1971), and Helms tends to use them when only African American people are the population being assessed.

Conformity.   Accordingly, *Conformity*, the original or least sophisticated status and schema, involves the person's adaptation and internalization of White society's definitions of one's group(s), either by conforming to the existing stereotypes of one's own group(s) or attempting to become White and assimilated into White culture. Thus, this status tends to foster information processing in which White people and their culture are idealized and anything other than White is denigrated. When the person is using the Conformity schema or information processing strategy (IPS), he or she is oblivious to the racial dynamics in her or his environment, and if they are forced into the person's awareness, he or she may respond with selective perception in which information is nonconsciously distorted and minimized to favor the White group.

The Conformity speaker in Table 6.3 illustrates the manner in which those aspects of oneself that are perceived to be White (heritage, culture) are elevated and those that are not are devalued or ignored. However, she also demonstrates a basic principle of racial identity development—the seeds of latter statuses are present in the original status. Thus, that part of herself that is proud of her White heritage will still be present if she develops the status of Integrative Awareness, but she will be able to demonstrate equal pride in her African American heritage.

Dissonance.   *Dissonance*, the ego status characterized by disorientation, confusion, and unpredictable responses to racial events, begins to evolve as the person begins to acknowledge her or his lack of fit in the White world. Notice that the speaker in Table 6.3 seems to be caught between two cultures, Black and White, in this instance. A common theme underlying the Dissonance schema is the ambivalence and anxiety caused by the lack of familiarity with the nature of one's own group's cultural and sociopolitical battles and accomplishments and the lack of positive material about one's own group with which to replace one's waning idealization of the White group.

TABLE 6.3   Summary of ALANA Racial Identity Ego Statuses, Examples, and Information Processing Strategies (IPS)

Status and Example

Conformity (Pre-encounter)—External self-definition that implies devaluing of own group and allegiance to White standards of merit. Person probably is oblivious to sociracial groups' sociopolitical histories. IPS: Selective perception, distortion, minimization, and obliviousness to sociracial concerns.

Example: "If you are a mixed race [Black-White] person, don't deny your European heritage just because Black people [in the U.S.] try to force you to choose. We are special because of our White heritage! We can be mediators of peace between these two warring peoples."

Dissonance (Encounter)—Ambivalence and confusion concerning own sociracial-group commitment and ambivalent sociracial self-definition. Person may be ambivalent about life decisions. IPS: Repression of anxiety-evoking racial information, ambivalence, anxiety, and disorientation.

Example: "I talked 'white,' moved 'white,' most of my friends were white. . . . But I never really felt accepted by or truly identified with the white kids. At some point, I stopped laughing when they would imitate black people dancing. I distanced myself from the white kids, but I hadn't made an active effort to make black friends because I was never comfortable enough in my 'blackness' to associate with them. That left me in sort of a gray area. . . ." (Wenger, 1993, p. 4).

Immersion—Idealization of one's sociracial group and denigration of that which is perceived as White. Use of own-group external standards to self-define and own-group commitment and loyalty is valued. May make life decisions for the benefit of the group. IPS: Hypervigilence and hypersensitivity toward racial stimuli and dichotomous thinking.

Example: "So there I was, strutting around with my semi-Afro, studiously garbling the English language because I thought that 'real' Black people didn't speak standard English, . . . contemplating changing my name to Malika, or something authentically black . . ." (Nelson, 1993, p. 18).

Emersion—A euphoric sense of well-being and solidarity that accompanies being surrounded by people of one's own sociracial group. IPS: Uncritical of one's own group, peacefulness, joyousness.

Example: "A jubilant [Black] scream went up . . . we had a feeling, and above all we had power . . . So many whites [sic] unconsciously had never considered that blacks [sic] could do much of anything, least of all get a black [sic] candidate this close to being mayor of Chicago" (McClain, 1983, cited in Helms, 1990, p. 25).

Internalization—Positive commitment to and acceptance of one's own sociracial group, internally defined racial attributes, and capacity to objectively assess and respond to members of the dominant group. Can make life decisions by assessing and integrating sociracial group requirements and self-assessment. IPS: Intellectualization and abstraction.

Example: "By claiming myself as African American and Black, I also inherit a right to ask questions about what this identity means. And chances are this identity will never be static, which is fine with me" (L. Jones, 1994, p. 78).

Integrative Awareness—Capacity to value one's own collective identities as well as empathize and collaborate with members of other oppressed groups. Life decisions may be motivated by globally humanistic self-expression. IPS: Flexible and complex.

(continued)

TABLE 6.3   Continued

Status and Example

Example: "[I think of difference not] as something feared or exotic, but difference as one of the rich facts of one's life, a truism that gives you more data, more power and more flavor . . . [You need a variety of peoples in your life.] . . . so you won't lapse into thinking you're God's gift to all knowledge as North American Negro" (L. Jones, 1994, p. 80).

Note: Descriptions of racial identity statuses are adapted from Helms (1994). Statuses are described in the order they are hypothesized to evolve.

Immersion.   The *Immersion* status evolves in response to the person's need to replace the group-specific negativity that resides in her or his identity constellation with positive group information, and thereby alleviate the anxiety triggered by awareness of the lack of a viable racial self-definition in a society that so values racial classifications. When a person is using the Immersion status, he or she idealizes everything considered to be of his or her group and denigrates everything considered to be of the "White world." When this schema is operative, the person maintains stability and predictability by indulging in simplistic thinking in which race or racism is virtually always a central theme, and one's own group members are always right as long as they conform to externally defined standards of group-appropriate behaviors. In Table 6.3, Nelson demonstrates the seemingly mindless conformity to stereotypic ideals of Blackness, whether or not those ideals are personally meaningful.

Emersion.   Thematically, community, communalism, and commitment to one's own group are the driving forces of the *Emersion* status. The appearance of this status is the recognition of the person's need for positive group definition. When the person is using this status, he or she feels grounded when surrounded by members of her or his own group. As is the case for the Dissonance status, Emersion is primarily an affective status (e.g., joyousness and euphoria in response to the presence or accomplishments of one's own group).

The example in Table 6.3 demonstrates the joyousness that may be experienced when a member of one's groups accomplishes something of note. The solidarity is often evident in people's clustering with people of their own group, particularly in predominantly White environments.

Internalization.   A positive commitment to one's group, internally defined racial attributes and perspectives, as well as the capacity to objectively assess and respond differentially to members of one's own as well as the dominant racial group characterize the *Internalization* status. When using this status, the person uses abstract reasoning or intellectualization and is capable of weighing and integrating complex racial information.

The speaker using the Internalization schema in Table 6.3 illustrates the person's ability to be self-analytic, self-exploratory, and flexible with respect to her identity. She also illustrates the principle that one's manner of resolving racial dilemmas becomes more complex as one gains access to increasingly more sophisticated ego statuses.

Integrated Awareness. The most sophisticated status and schema (i.e., *Integrative Awareness*) involve the capacity to express a positive racial self and to recognize and resist the multiplicity of practices that exist in one's environment to discourage positive racial self-conceptions and group expression. In addition, when this status is accessible, the person is able to accept, redefine, and integrate in self-enhancing ways those aspects of herself and himself that may be deemed to be characteristic of other socioracial and cultural groups. Furthermore, her or his conceptualization of other people and environmental events can be as complex as needed to ensure healthy intrapsychic and interpersonal functioning. When speaking from this status, L. Jones demonstrates the thirst for diversity that often characterizes this status.

Summary. To summarize, the evolution of ego statuses for People of Color begins with the most primitive status whereby the person primarily interprets and responds to racial information in a manner that suggests negative own-group identification, endorsement of societal prejudices toward one's group, and uncritical esteem for the White group. The last status to evolve permits the person to resist many types of oppression of one's own and others' collective identity groups without abandoning one's primary commitment to one's own group(s). The end goal of the maturational process is to acquire the latter status and be able to use it most of the time in coping with a racially complex world in which one's integrated and positive sense of self is frequently at risk.

White Racial Identity

In the White model, it is assumed that being a member of the acquisitive socioracial group contributes to a false sense of racial-group superiority and privilege. Thus, the process of overcoming internalized racism for Whites is assumed to require the individual to replace societally ordained racial group entitlement and privilege with a non-racist and realistic self-affirming collective (racial) identity. Helms and Piper (1994) define *White people* as follows: "those Americans who self-identify or are commonly identified as belonging exclusively to the White racial group regardless of the continental source (e.g., Europe, Asia) of that racial ancestry" (p. 126).

As a consequence of growing up and being socialized in an environment in which members of their group (if not themselves personally) are privileged relative to other groups, Whites learn to perceive themselves (and their group) as being entitled to similar privileges. In order to protect such privilege, individual group members and, therefore, the group more generally, learn to protect their privileged status by denying and distorting race-related reality, and aggressing against perceived threats to the racial status quo. Consequently, healthy identity development for a White person involves the capacity to recognize and abandon the normative strategies of White people for coping with race.

Helms's (1984, 1990a, 1994) theory proposes a process by which White people develop racial identity. As shown in Table 6.4, for White people, the maturation

TABLE 6.4   Summary of White Racial Identity Ego Statuses, Examples, and Information Processing Strategies (IPS)

Status and Example

Contact—Satisfaction with racial status quo, obliviousness to racism and one's participation in it. If racial factors influence life decisions, they do so in a simplistic fashion. IPS: Obliviousness, denial, superficiality, and avoidance.

Example: ". . . The Balls have prided themselves on the ancestral image of compassion, emphasizing that masters tried as best they could not to separate slave families in sale; that no Ball masters perpetrated violence or engaged in master-slave sex. Ed Ball's research is viewed by some family members, especially the elderly ones, as a threat to long-held beliefs. Some would prefer not to know too many details about their ancestors' slave practices, one relative says" (Duke, 1994, p. 12).

Disintegration—Disorientation and anxiety provoked by unresolvable racial moral dilemmas that force one to choose between own-group loyalty and humanism. May be stymied by life situations that arouse racial dilemmas. IPS: Suppression, ambivalence, and controlling.

Example: "I was upset. I couldn't do anything for a couple of weeks . . . Was I causing more pain than healing? Was this somebody else's history, not mine? Was I an expropriator, as Stefani Zinerman [a Black woman newspaper editor] accuses me of being? Should I just stop [investigating my family's history of slave ownership] and let black [sic] people do their own history?" (Duke, 1994).

Reintegration—Idealization of one's socioracial group; denigration and intolerance for other groups. Racial factors may strongly influence life decisions. IPS: Selective perception and negative outgroup distortion.

Example: "When someone asks him, 'Don't you feel bad because your ancestors owned slaves?' his response is 'No, I don't feel bad because my ancestors owned slaves. I mean, get over it. If Ed wants to go around and apologize, Ed's free to go around and apologize. But quite frankly, Ed didn't own any slaves. He isn't responsible for slavery or anybody's misfortunes . . . ' " (Duke, 1994, p. 24).

Pseudo-Independence—Intellectualized commitment to one's own socioracial group and subtle superiority and tolerance of other socioracial groups as long as they can be helped to conform to White standards of merit. IPS: Selective perception, cognitive restructuring, and conditional regard.

Example: "He has also said to them [the descendants of his family's slaves]: I am sorry . . . his mother, brother and a few other relatives believe the apology had a healing effect . . . " (Duke, 1994, p. 12).

Immersion—The searching for an understanding of the personal meaning of Whiteness and racism and the ways by which one benefits from them as well as a redefinition of Whiteness. IPS: Hypervigilance, judgmental, and cognitive-affective restructuring.

Example: "I'm interested to look at whiteness [sic] as carefully as white [sic] people look at blackness [sic]. As a white [sic] person, I'm interested to understand how my ethnicity [sic] has produced me as an individual . . . and how whiteness [sic] produces the majority experience of Americans. My plantation research might be a way for me to do this intellectually as a writer" (Duke, 1994, p. 12).

Emersion—A sense of discovery, security, sanity, and group solidarity and pride that accompanies being with other White people who are embarked on the mission of rediscovering Whiteness. IPS: Sociable, pride, seeking positive group-attributes.

TABLE 6.4 Continued

Status and Example

Example. "But Ed's apology [for his family's ownership of slaves] produced positive reactions as well. Janet and Ted Ball, Ed's mother and brother, both were moved by [his apology]: 'I was crying too,' says Janet Ball . . . Ted Ball . . . says he whispered a private 'thank you' to his little brother. . . . He feels grateful to Ed 'for doing the hard work it took to get to the apology.'" (Duke, 1994, p. 24).

Autonomy—Informed positive socioracial-group commitment, use of internal standards for self-definition, capacity to relinquish the privileges of racism. Person tries to avoid life options that require participation in racial oppression. IPS: Flexible and complex.
Example: ". . . It's [the exploration of his familial history of slave ownership] about me personally trying to find some way as a white [sic] person, quite apart from my family's history, to acknowledge what's happened in this country. I mean during the time that English-speaking people have been in this country, for more years were black [sic] people enslaved than not enslaved" (Duke, 1994, p. 25).

Note: Descriptions of racial identity statuses are adapted from Helms (1994). Racial identity ego statuses are listed in the order that they are hypothesized to evolve.

process of recognition and abandonment of White privilege begins with the ego's avoidance or denial of the sociopolitical implications of one's own and others' racial-group membership (Contact status) and concludes with its capacity to strive for non-racist own-group membership and humanistic racial self-definition and social interactions (Autonomy status).

Contact

The racial identity evolutionary process for Whites begins with *Contact*, a primitive status, primarily characterized by simplistic reactions of denial and obliviousness to the ways in which one benefits from membership in the entitled group and only superficial acknowledgement of one's membership in the White group. Thus, when this status is dominant, the person reacts to racial stimuli with denial, obliviousness, or avoidance of anxiety-evoking racial information, especially when such information implies something derogatory about the White group or the person as a member of that group.

Notice that in the example, the historian's family rejects him when he attempts to move from the family's pie-in-the-sky romanticization of its ancestors' slave ownership. Their obliviousness serves a protective function in that those family members who can avoid facing their ancestors' history of ownership of Black people can also avoid present-day responsibility for doing something to make amends.

Disintegration. *Disintegration* begins to evolve when one can no longer escape the moral dilemmas of race in this country and one's participation in them. Sometimes it is initiated by People of Color's reactions to one's naivete or superficiality, but usually it evolves and becomes stronger as one is continuously exposed to circumstances where one cannot afford to ignore one's Whiteness and the socialization rules that characterize the group because of the risk of ostracism by the White group.

The basic nature of the moral dilemmas is that one is continuously forced to disassociate with respect to race and racism while acting toward People of Color in inhumane ways in order to be loved, accepted, and valued by significant members of the White group. When this status is in charge of the person, it is expressed as disorientation, confusion, general (sometimes debilitating) distress, and nonreceptivity to anxiety-evoking information.

In the example in Table 6.4, the speaker illustrates the type of disintegration that frequently follows the White person's rebuffed attempts to "do good" for People of Color. Whereas the speaker thinks his turmoil is attributable to a Black person's animosity, a more likely explanation is that family members' antipathy is causing him to question whether the costs of being beneficent outweigh the benefits.

Reintegration.   The *Reintegration* status evolves as a system for mitigating the anxiety that occurs when one's Disintegration status is dominant. The person reduces pain and avoids personal anxiety by adopting the version of racism that exists in her or his socialization environments, which then relieves her or him of the responsibility for doing anything about it. The general theme of this status and correlated schema is idealization of one's own socioracial group, denigration and intolerance toward other groups, and protection and enhancement of the White group and thereby the maintenance of the racism status quo. Thus, selective perception and distortion of information in an own-group enhancing and out-group debasing manner describe this status and correlated schema.

The need to avoid personal responsibility for racism is evident in the Reintegration example. By minimizing the significance of his family's role in perpetuating slavery, and consequently, his personal advancement because of it, he eliminates his own and his entire family's responsibility to do anything about it.

Pseudo-Independence.   The *Pseudo-Independence* status is characterized by an intellectualized commitment to one's racial group in which one identifies with the "good" nonracist Whites and rejects the "bad" racists. Identification and commitment are made possible by acknowledgement of superficial group (rather than personal) culpability for Whites' racial wrongdoing, and by not necessarily conscious efforts to resolve "the race problem" by assisting People of Color to become more like Whites. Schematic expression or information-processing strategies involve reshaping racial stimuli to fit one's own "liberal" societal framework, avoidance of negative information about oneself, and selective perception.

Immersion.   The *Immersion* status involves the search for a new, humanistic, nonracist definition of Whiteness. When this status is operative, the person attempts to recover from prior distorted racial socialization and seeks accurate information about race and racism and their pertinence to oneself. The information-processing strategies operative here are searching for internally defined racial standards or reeducating oneself, hypervigilence, and activism.

In Table 6.4, the Immersion schema is expressed by the person's frenetic search for the meaning of Whiteness to himself or herself as well as to other White people in society. Although he or she is not certain where his or her inquiry will end, it is fueled by the inexplicable belief that such self- and other exploration is virtually ordained. This sensation of being on a mission of recovery characterizes the Immersion status and its schematic expression.

Emersion. The *Emersion* status is the appreciation of and withdrawal into the community of reeducated White people for the purposes of rejuvenating oneself and solidifying one's goals of seeking new self-knowledge. This is primarily an affective status and so one finds a variety of emotional themes including the joyous tears and prayerful gratitude toward kindred sojourners described in Table 6.4.

Autonomy. The last and most advanced status to evolve permits complex humanistic reactions to internal and environmental racial information based on a realistic, nonracist self-affirming conception of one's racial collective identity. When a person is operating from the *Autonomy* status, he or she no longer has to impose arbitrary racial definitions on others nor must succumb to others' arbitrary racial criteria. The Autonomy schema permits flexible analytic self-expression and responses to racial material.

Racial Identity Expression

As previously discussed, the model describes the development or process by which the statuses come into being. Consequently, the highlights or distinguishable aspects of the statuses and related schemata are described. However, most individuals develop more than one status, and if multiple statuses exist, then they can operate in concert. That is, they may each influence a person's reactions to racial stimuli.

Thus, in Tables 6.3 and 6.4, although we have categorized the examples according to what appears to be the strongest status-schema theme, it seems to us that aspects of other status-schema are present in virtually every instance. For example, in Table 6.4, the Reintegration segment is classified as *primarily* Reintegration because of the person's subtle dehumanizing and unwillingness to acknowledge even his ancestors' role in perpetuating slavery and racism. However, the minimization and intellectualization of racial tensions that characterize the Contact and Pseudo-Independence statuses also waft through this example. Similar blends of statuses can be found in the other examples as well, and presumably blends describe people's reactions more often than do "pure" statuses.

Also apparent in the examples in Tables 6.3 is the fact that racial identity themes may be blended in the individual's reactions to racial catalysts regardless of their socioracial classification. As we just observed with respect to White identity development, most people probably do not express their racial identity in pure forms. Thus, the second example in Table 6.3 illustrates expression of both the Conformity and Dissonance statuses in that the VREG speaker acknowledges his White cultural socialization and consequent greater familiarity with White people on one level (Conformity), but also is able to describe his lack of fit with either the Black or White socioracial group (Dissonance).

Nevertheless, each of the examples has a racial identity theme that seems to be stronger than the others, and to determine which is a person's strongest status, one would need to analyze the themes inherent in several samples of a person's race-related behavior. Themes that frequently occur presumably signal stronger underlying statuses, and conversely, stronger statuses conceivably contribute to more consistent thematic race-related expressions. Insight 6.1 should give the reader an opportunity to try her or his hand at this type of qualitative analysis of racial identity.

However, more often than not, researchers have attempted to develop quantitative paper-and-pencil inventories for assessing racial identity. Burlew and Smith (1991) and Ponterotto and Casas (1991) critically reviewed some of them. Of these measures, the ones used most frequently are the Black and White racial identity research scales developed by Helms and her associates (Helms & Parham, 1996; Helms & Carter, 1990; Carter, 1996; Corbett, Helms, & Reagan, 1992). From these measures, Helms (1996) proposed racial identity assessment inventories, which she suggests might be useful in mapping the person's racial identity expression.

Using the scoring procedures Helms proposed for the assessment of Whites' racial identity expression (WRIAS Social Attitudes Inventory), we generated a racial identity profile for the White female group leader whose race-related group behavior is presented in Chapter 12 (see Figure 6.2). The profile suggests that this person's racial identity resting-state expression is characterized by equally strong Contact, Pseudo-Independent, and Autonomy schemata. Thus, she does not have a clearly dominant schemata, although Disintegration and Reintegration appear to be recessive for her. In response to race-related stimuli other than the paper-and-pencil inventory, one would expect her to be rather naive about such matters, but to express her naivete in a liberal and intellectualized manner with traces of personal independence and non-conformity to derogatory group norms. The reader might want to skip to Table 12.1 to see whether you think her profile accurately predicted her race-related behavior in a group discussion of race.

INSIGHT 6.1

A Proud American

Whoopi Goldberg doesn't hesitate when filling out nationality questions on census forms.

"I wouldn't put 'African-American.' I just put down 'American,' because that's what I am," she says.

"Yes, I've been criticized by the black [sic] community, and loudly. But I'm fifth- or sixth-generation American, and I also have Chinese and white [sic] in me.

"I'm not culturally from Africa. I've been in Africa—I know better. I'm real proud that I helped build America, so I'm not going to let anybody call me anything except American.

Note: This excerpt is reprinted from "A proud American," *The Kansas City Star,* August 30, 1994, p. E-6.

Ego Status Expression

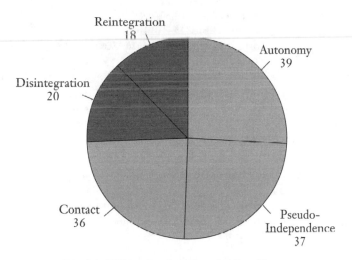

FIGURE 6.2 Linda's White Racial Identity Profile

Linda's profile suggests that her strongest expressed statuses are a combination of Contact, Autonomy, and Pseudo-Independence. Her weakest statuses are Disintegration and Reintegration. Subscales followed by asterisk(s) are higher (single) or very much higher (double) than the subsequent subscale. The ordering of Linda's scores is similar whether one examines subscale scores relative to her immediately adjacent clockwise raw score (see pie), or her scores as compared to Carter's (1996) percentile norms (% tile column). Pie slices of the same shade do not differ significantly. Contact (i.e., lack of sophistication about the significance of race) appears to be a strong influence in her interpretation and reaction to racial information. For more information about interpreting racial identity profiles, see Helms (1996).

Mode of Expression	Raw Score	% tile	Comment
Contact	36*	81	Contact is stronger than Disintegration
Disintegration	20	19	Disintegration does not differ significantly from Reintegration
Reintegration	18**	11	Reintegration is much weaker than Pseudo-Independence
Pseudo-Independence	37	70	Pseudo-Independence does not differ significantly from Autonomy
Autonomy	39	70	Autonomy does not differ significantly from Contact
Total	150		Profile appears to be valid

Conclusions and Implications for Therapy

It is possible to add some depth to our discussion of socioracial and psychoracial characteristics that we initiated in Chapters 2 and 3 (e.g., Table 2.1). As symbolized in
Figure 6.3, the first question one needs to ask is whether issues of commitment to a
socioracial group are germane to the problem for which the client is seeking assistance. The possibilities are: (a) yes, either implicitly or explicitly the client's problem
involves race, racism, or racial identity; (b) maybe, the possibility exists that such factors are relevant, but if so, their manner of influence is not unambiguously evident;
(c) no, the person is experiencing a "universal" life problem for which racial tensions
and/or dynamics in particular do not seem to be relevant.

In the case of the first two options, the general sociological models of oppression *might* provide some insight into the racial life conditions experienced by clients
and/or therapists. However, inferring that any particular circumstances or characteristics of a group necessarily pertain to individual members of the group is ill-advised.
Rather one might use such perspectives to form hypotheses about the relevant dynam-

Excerpt: "We're special because of our European ancestry."
Therapist considerations: ARE SOCIORACIAL DYNAMICS RELEVANT?

YES	MAYBE	NO
Relevant Sociological Factors		
Psychological Reactions		
Interventions		

Relevant Sociological Factors	Psychological Reactions	Interventions
Apparent racial classification	Anger	Empathy
Skin color	Defensiveness Conformity status	Factual race-related information
Parents' differential experiences of sociorace	Naivete	Communication skills

FIGURE 6.3   Some Socioracial Dimensions of Clients and Therapists

ies in the person's life, but these should be confirmed or disconfirmed in one's actual interactions.

Moreover, the content of one's own or one's client's racial stereotypes might reveal the racial perspective on which they are based. It may be easier to countermand such stereotypes when one understands their origins. In any case, one dimension of our perspective concerns examining whether the client has *personally* experienced socioracial oppression or benevolence because of her or his racial classification, and, if so, in what form. Remember that cues to such experiences can be factors so subtle as differential treatment due to skin color differences within and between socioracial groups, or so overt as job promotions accorded on the basis of racial classification.

The psychological perspectives might be more useful in conceptualizing the race-related dynamics of clients with respect to any of the three options, although we think that the early historical perspectives that we summarized (e.g., frustration-aggression) might pertain to certain clients rather than all clients. For example, if one's client is clearly aggressing against someone of another socioracial group, then one should look initially toward daily life frustrations to identify provocations or socialization experiences.

However, if the client is the target of the aggression, then it is not certain that any of the power-conflict or most of the traditional psychological race-related models will be of benefit to her or him. Particularly, if the client is a VREG person, such models may be inapplicable because for the most part, they were created to assist White people in comprehending People of Color.

In our experience, client's reactions to socioracial dynamics tend to be complex on the cognitive, affective, and behavioral levels regardless of the person's socioracial group. Therefore, we tend to prefer the more complex psychological (i.e., racial identity) theories for making sense of these dynamics because they make it possible to conceptualize racial reactions as common human responses in the racial environment(s) of the United States rather than as inexplicable peculiarities of the visible racial and ethnic groups.

If one thinks that history of oppression-domination is relevant, then one needs to specify the kinds that are relevant for this particular client and perhaps her or his social system. Next, one attempts to move inside the client by choosing some psychological model (e.g., racial identity) for describing her or his reactions to these stimuli. Then one shapes one's interventions according to what seems appropriate for the client's conditions. Several authors, some of whom are summarized in Table 6.2, have proposed interventions matched to the client's levels of expressed racial identity (Carney & Kahn, 1984; Gay, 1984; Helms, 1990a; Sabnani et al., 1991). These may need to be modified somewhat to match the client's needs.

Figure 6.3 is an example of how one might perform such an analysis using the first example in Table 6.3. The comment suggests that the person is experiencing anxiety, anger, and perhaps confusion (psychological reactions) apparently in response to others' communications about her racial classification (sociological), and perhaps her own manner of communicating about her socioracial group allegiances.

Others might intuit from her statement that she devalues membership in the African American group, and that she is ignorant of the racial histories of both of her parents' socioracial groups. Moreover, she is attempting to resolve her Conformity status issues with respect to the two groups—Blacks and Whites—that have the longest continuous history of racial conflict in this country, perhaps without the conceptualization and communication skills necessary to do so.

Thus, in her case, a racially sensitive therapist would need to understand the multiple ways in which issues of racial oppression and dominance might be expressed within the client (e.g., Does she perceive that she acquires higher or lower status because of her parentage?) as well as her significant socialization environments (e.g., How does each parent cope with race?), and communicate this understanding to the client in an empathic manner. Moreover, since the client may be caught in a familial and societal war that is not of her making, the therapist will need to help her acquire information and teach her communication strategies to help her disentangle herself, as well as help her learn to explore and recognize the complex racial dynamics that seem to be playing themselves out in her environment.

The issues presented in the figure for discursive purposes are based on a rather small excerpt of this person's behavior and may not be accurate even for her. Therefore, they should not automatically be generalized to someone else who makes a similar comment. Rather the framework should be used to suggest the kind of investigation in which the therapist should engage in order to be appropriately responsive to racial dynamics.

Also, at the risk of being redundant, let us remind the reader that information about a person's racial identity does not reveal anything about her or his cultural socialization, except perhaps how much the person values her or his socioracial group's traditional culture. That is, a person may have developed a positive racial identity (e.g., have positive feelings about her or his socioracial group) without ever having been socialized in the relevant culture. Conversely, a person may have been socialized in a particular culture, and consequently, be capable of practicing its customs, traditions, and so forth without having any understanding of the sociopolitical racial dynamics that the groups consider to be central to their survival.

REFERENCES

Alba, R. D. (1990). *Ethnic identity: The transformation of White America*. New Haven: Yale University Press.

Allport, G. (1958). *The nature of prejudice* (abridged edition). New York: Doubleday Anchor Books.

Atkinson, D. R., Morten, G., & Sue, D. R. (1989). *Counseling American minorities: A cross-cultural perspective* (3rd ed.). Dubuque, IA: Wm. C. Brown.

Axelson, J. A. (1993). *Counseling and development in a multicultural society* (2nd ed.). Pacific Grove, CA: Brooks/Cole Publishing Company.

Banks, J. A. (1981). The stages of ethnicity: Implications for curriculum reform. In J. A. Banks (Ed.), *Multi-ethnic education: Theory and practice* (pp. 129–139). Boston: Allyn & Bacon.

Bradley, M. (1978). *The iceman inheritance: Prehistoric sources of Western man's racism, sexism, and aggression*. New York: Warner Books.

Burlew, A. K., & Smith, L. R. (1991). Measures of racial identity: An overview and a proposed framework. *Journal of Black Psychology, 17*(2), 53–71.

Carney, C. G., & Kahn, K. B. (1984). Building competencies for effective cross-cultural counseling: A developmental view. *The Counseling Psychologist, 12*(1), 111–119.

Carter, R. T. (1996). Exploring the complexity of racial identity attitude measures. In G. R. Sodowsky & J. Impara (Eds.), *Multicultural assessment* (pp. 193–223). Lincoln, NE: Buros Institute of Mental Measurement.

Comer, J. P. (1991). White racism: Its root, form, and function. In R. L. Jones (Ed.), *Black psychology* (pp. 591–596). Berkeley, CA: Cobb & Henry.

Corbett, M., Helms, J. E., & Regan, A. (1992). The development of a White racial identity immersion scale. Paper presented at the American Psychological Association Convention, Washington, D.C.

Cross, W. E., Jr. (1971). The Negro-to-Black conversion experience: Toward a psychology of Black liberation. *Black World, 20*(9), 13–27.

Cross, W. E., Jr., Parham, T. A., & Helms, J. E. (1991). The stages of Black identity development: Nigresence models. In R. L. Jones (Ed.), *Black Psychology* (pp. 319–338). Berkeley, CA: Cobb & Henry Publishers.

Cubberly, E. P. (1929). *Changing conceptions of education.* Boston: Houghton & Mifflin.

Dizard, J. E. (1970). Black identity, social class, and Black power. *Journal of Social Issues, 26*(1), 195–207.

Dollard, J. (1957). *Caste and class in a Southern town* (3rd ed.). Garden City, NY: Doubleday.

Dollard, J., Doob, L., Miller, N., Mowrer, O. H., & Sears, R. R. (1939) *Frustration and aggression.* New Haven: Yale University Press.

Duke, L. (1994, August 28). This harrowed ground. *The Washington Post Magazine*, pp. 8–13; 20–25.

Fairchild, H. P. (1926). *The melting pot mistake.* Boston: Little, Brown and Company.

Feagin, J. R. (1984). *Racial and ethnic relations.* Englewood Cliffs, NJ: Prentice-Hall, Inc.

Franklin, V. P. (1991). Black social scientists and the mental testing movement, 1920–1940. In R. L. Jones (Ed.), *Black Psychology* (pp. 207–224). Berkeley, CA: Cobb & Henry.

Gay, G. (1984). Implications of selected models of ethnic identity development for educators. *The Journal of Negro Education, 54*(1), 43–52.

Geschwender, J. A. (1968). Explorations in the theory of social movements and revolutions. *Social Forces, 47*, 127–135.

Grant, M. (1916). *The passing of the great race.* New York: Scribner.

Hacker, A. (1992). *Two nations: Black and White, separate, hostile, unequal.* New York: Charles Scribner's Sons.

Hall, G. S. (1904). *Adolescence.* New York: Appleton.

Hardiman, R. (1982). *White identity development: A process oriented model for describing the racial consciousness of White Americans.* Unpublished doctoral dissertation, University of Massachusetts, Amherst.

Helms, J. E. (1984). Toward a theoretical explanation of the effects of race on counseling. A Black and White model. *The Counseling Psychologist, 12*, 153–165.

Helms, J. E. (1990a). *Black and White racial identity: Theory, research, and practice.* Westport, CT: Greenwood Press.

Helms, J. E. (1990b). Three perspectives on counseling and psychotherapy with visible racial/ethnic group clients. In F. C. Serafica, A. I. Schwebel, R. K. Russell, P. D. Isaac, & L. B. Myers (Eds.), *Mental Health of Ethnic Minorities* (pp. 171–201). New York: Praeger.

Helms, J. E. (1994). Racial identity and other "racial" constructs. In E. J. Trickett, R. Watts, & D. Birman (Eds.), *Human Diversity* (pp. 285–311). San Francisco: Jossey Bass.

Helms, J. E. (1996). Toward a methodology for assessing "racial identity" as distinguished from "ethnic identity." In G. R. Sodowsky & J. Impara (Eds.), *Multicultural Assessment.* Lincoln, NE: Buros Institute of Mental Measurement.

Helms, J. E., & Carter, R. T. (1990). Development of the White racial identity attitude scale. In J. E. Helms (Ed.), *Black and White racial identity: Theory, research, and practice* (pp. 67–80). Westport, CT: Greenwood Press.

Helms, J. E., & Parham, T. A. (1996). The Racial Identity Attitude Scale. In R. L. Jones (Ed.), *Handbook of tests and measurements for Black populations* (Vol. 2), (pp. 167–174). Hampton, VA: Cobb & Henry Publishers.

Helms, J. E., & Piper, R. E. (1994). Implications of racial identity theory for vocational psychology. *Journal of Vocational Psychology, 44*, 124–138.

Hutnik, N. (1991). *Ethnic minority identity: A social psychological perspective.* Oxford: Oxford University Press.

Jensen, A. R. (1969). How much can we boost IQ and scholastic achievement? *Harvard Educational Review, 39,* 1–123, 126.

Jones, L. (1994, May). Mama's White. *Essence Magazine,* pp. 78, 80, 148.

Kardiner, A., & Ovesey, L. (1951). *The mark of oppression: Explorations in the personality of the American Negro.* Cleveland, OH: Meridian Books.

Katz, P. A. (1976). The acquisition of racial attitudes in children. In P. A. Katz (Ed.), *Toward the elimination of racism* (pp. 125–150). New York: Pergamon.

Kitano, H. H. (1982). Mental health in the Japanese American community. In E. E. Jones & S. J. Korchin (Eds.), *Minority Mental Health* (pp. 149–164). New York: Praeger.

Kohut, H. (1971). *Analysis of the self.* New York: International University Press.

Landrum, J., & Batts, V. A. (1985). *Internalized racial oppression.* Unpublished working paper. Cited in J. Landrum-Brown, Black mental health and racial oppression. In D. S. Ruiz (Ed.), *Handbook of mental health and mental disorder among Black Americans* (pp. 113–132). New York: Greenwood Press.

McClain, L. (1983, July 24). How Chicago taught me to hate Whites. *Washington Post, Section C,* 1, 4.

McLemore, S. D. (1983). *Racial and ethnic relations in America.* Boston, MA: Allyn and Bacon.

Myers, L. J., Speight, S. L., Highlen, P. S., Cox, C. I., Reynolds, A. L., Adams, E. M., & Hanley, C. P. (1991). Identity development and worldview: Toward an optimal conceptualization. *Journal of Counseling and Development, 70,* 54–63.

Ponterotto, J. G., & Casas, J. M. (1991). *Handbook of racial/ethnic minority counseling research.* Springfield, IL: Charles C. Thomas.

Richardson, T. Q. (1989). White racial consciousness and the counseling profession. Unpublished paper, LeHigh University, Bethlehem, PA.

Ridley, C. R., Mendoza, D. W., & Kanitz, B. E. (1994). Multicultural training: Reexamination, operationalization, and integration. *The Counseling Psychologist, 22,* 227–289.

Rowe, W., Bennett, S. K., & Atkinson, D. R. (1994). White racial identity models: A critique and alternative proposal. *The Counseling Psychologist, 22,* 129–146.

Rushton, J. P. (1990). Differential K theory: The sociobiology of individual and group differences. *Personality and Individual Differences, 6,* 441–452.

Rushton, J. P. (1995). *Race, evolution, and behavior: A life history perspective.* New Brunswick, NJ: Transaction Publishers.

Sabnani, H. B., Ponterotto, J. G., & Borodovsky, L. G. (1991). White racial identity development and cross-cultural counselor training: A stage model. *The Counseling Psychologist, 19* (1), 76–102.

Shuffleton, F. (1993). *A mixed race: Ethnicity in early America.* New York: Oxford University Press.

Simpson, G. E., & Yinger, J. M. (1972). *Racial and cultural minorities* (4th ed.). New York: Harper and Row.

Singer, L. (1962). Ethnogenesis and Negro Americans today. *Social Research, 29,* 419–432.

Smith, E. J. (1980). Profile of the Black individual in vocational literature. In R. L. Jones (Ed.), *Black Psychology* (pp. 324–357). New York: Harper & Row.

Spikard, P. R. (1992). The illogic of American racial categories. In M. P. P. Root (Ed.), *Racially mixed people in America* (pp. 12–23). Newbury Park, CA: Sage Publications.

Takaki, R. (1993). *A different mirror: A History of multicultural America.* Boston: Little, Brown.

Terry, R. W. (1977). *For Whites only.* Grand Rapids, MI: William B. Erdmans.

Thomas, A., & Sillen, S. (1972). *Racism and Psychiatry.* New York: Brunner/Mazel, Inc.

Welsing, F. C. (1974). The Cress theory of color-confrontation. *The Black Scholar, May,* 32–40.

Wenger, J. (1993). Just part of the mix. *Focus, 21*(9), 3, 4.

Wrenn, G. C. (1962). The culturally encapsulated counselor. *Harvard Educational Review, 32*(4), 444–449.

Zinn, H. (1980). *A history of the United States.* New York: Harper & Row.

CHAPTER

7 Aspects of Culture
in Personhood

In this chapter, we ponder culture models and consider how they might be used and/or modified to be of value to therapists. In doing so, we begin with a discussion of what might be called the "process of culture," that is, the social rules or principles by which people co-exist both within and between relevant cultural groups. Then we consider the content of the cultures of the primary socioracial groups; in other words, the dimensions, aspects, or traditional cultural patterns of these groups. Following our descriptions of cultures, we summarize some of the acculturation (psychological) and assimilation (sociological) models that have been proposed for assessing the manner in which the person fits herself or himself into cultures and/or is accepted into cultural groups. Finally, of course, we hypothesize some therapy implications of our observations.

The Process of Cultures

When groups segregate themselves from other socioracial groups (as has been true of the White group) or are segregated from other groups through law, custom, or social sanctions (as have been the groups of color), members of the group are able to hold onto and enhance elements of the cultures of their forebearers, which thereby permits the group to survive its collective life circumstances in this country.

According to Triandis (1994), a culture can be classified according to its objectively discernable products such as tools, languages, art forms, and so forth or its subjective principles, which include norms, rituals, values, information-processing strategies, and so forth. He calls those aspects of culture that pertain specifically to the psychological aspects of the person within a cultural context *subjective culture* and those concrete indicators from which culture may be inferred *objective culture*. The work of the culturally responsive therapist has subjective culture as its primary focus.

When we use the term *culture* in our discussions, we not only mean it in the sense that Triandis defines the term, but we also use it to mean those psychological dimensions that characterize the "at-home" culture rather than the "public" or "marketplace" culture since those two are not always the same. What is meant by *at-home* or *marketplace* can vary according to whether one is from an individualistic or collectivistic culture (see Chapter 2).

In general, in collectivistic cultures more people or social units participate in the cultural socialization of its members than is true of individualistic cultures. Thus, the at-home culture may be more complex; that is, require satisfactory performance of specific roles and fulfillment of more rules and social obligations than is the case for the public culture. Consequently, the mental health of persons from collectivistic cultures may be dependent upon more persons within the relevant group than is the case for persons from individualistic cultures.

Moreover, people from collectivistic rather than individualistic cultures may define "at-home" and "public" differently. For example, for collectivists the ideal at-home culture often includes the people with whom one works as well as the people with whom one lives, as long as such people are perceived as following the "correct" cultural mores; whereas for individualists, the at-home culture is likely to be more narrowly defined and transient. In-groups or at-home culture for individualists are people whose goals, expectations, and so forth are perceived to match and not threaten one's own fate for as long as such is the case. Moreover, individualists can become collectivists when it is necessary to resolve some threat to one's personal well-being, but can easily leave the collective once the problem is resolved.

In general, for individualistic people and cultures, satisfaction of personal needs, goals, and desires are primary. Thus, in such cultures, it is not considered unusual for a person to forsake significant others (e.g., family, friends) in one's life in order to achieve great things for oneself. In fact, in the United States, such people are considered heroic; in the Constitution and the corresponding legal system the protection of individualism is fundamentalism. Based on his analyses of average worker responses in 50 national cultures and three geographic regions, Hofstede (1983) ranked the United States first in individualism. Thus, the "American way" is to be independent, self-reliant, emotionally detached, and egocentric. Consequently, collectivistic people are considered to be rather odd because they often violate many of the societal expectations.

In psychology and the mental health disciplines, the individualistic orientation has been virtually sanctified. Thus, for example, a language of pathology (e.g., enmeshed, dependent, immature, field dependent) has evolved to describe people who do not separate from their families and go their own way once they reach adulthood, a process that is supposed to begin as soon as the person is born.

For their part, collectivists and collectivistic cultures tend to be other-focused; that is, concern about the needs, expectations, and evaluations of others is central to one's own sense of well being. Pannu (1994) argues that collectivistic people internalize aspects of their cultural groups so that significant sociocultural communicators in their lives become an inseparable part of themselves internally. Thus, whereas an individualist is more likely to speak in terms of what he or she (i.e., "I") wants or how he or she is affected by social events, the collectivist is more likely to speak in terms of what is expected of him or her and to interpret environmental cues as signaling certain expectations to which he or she should conform.

To make the cultural diagnostic picture even more complex, not all collectivistic cultures look the same. Hofstede's (1980, 1983) research suggests that in addition to collectivism-individualism, there are several dimensions on which global cultures and individuals can be described. These are as follows: (a) power-distance (also

EXERCISE 7.1

Thinking about Your Value Orientations

Kluckhohn and Strodbeck (1961) contended that there are five universal questions (see *Questions* below) to which humans, regardless of sociorace or ethnic background, must find answers. According to them, each question has three potential answers from which each person or cultural group necessarily selects. We have provided the answer-alternatives (see *Answers*) below, along with a sample of items adapted from the Intercultural Values Inventory (Carter & Helms, 1983), intended to demonstrate appropriate responses for each orientation. For each of the items, answer "*Y*" (yes) if the item reflects a value by which you live your life and/or would raise your children, and "*N*" (no) if it does not.

Questions and Potential Answers

What is the nature of human character?

Evil	*Mixed*	*Good*
People are basically evil. Y N	People are both good and bad. Y N	People are basically good. Y N

What is the relationship of people to nature?

Subjugation	*Harmony*	*Mastery*
People have little control over natural forces. Y N	People are one with nature. Y N	Nature is supposed to be controlled by humans. Y N

What is the proper time focus?

Past	*Present*	*Future*
Remember where you come from. Y N	Strike while the iron is hot. Y N	A person must plan for the future. Y N

What is the proper form of human activity?

Being	*Being in Becoming*	*Doing*
Show what you feel when you feel it. Y N	One's inner world should be nurtured. Y N	Those who can't, teach; those who can, do. Y N

What is the proper form of social relations?

Hierarchical	*Collateral*	*Individualistic*
Honor your father and your mother. Y N	The nail that sticks out gets hit. Y N	Each person is an island. Y N

Your *yes* responses are suggestive of your value-orientation tendencies. However, you cannot accurately assess your orientations from single responses. Nevertheless, you might use your responses to think about potential areas of therapist-client cultural conflict.

sometimes conceptualized as hierarchical-collateral relations or horizontal-vertical collectivism by other authors)—the amount of respect and deference accorded to persons of higher perceived social status by persons of less status; (b) uncertainty avoidance—reliance on stability and structure to avoid ambiguities in life; (c) femininity (expressiveness)—emphasis on promoting harmonious interpersonal relations and focus on the affective aspects of such relationships; and (d) masculinity (instrumentality)—emphasis on task management and mastery over one's environment, striving for personal achievement and material rewards (also see Kluckhohn and Strodtbeck, 1961; Triandis, 1994).

In addition to being predominantly collectivistically or individualistically oriented, a person can also vary along any of the dimensions that Hofstede (1980) or other culturalists have proposed. For example, it is not difficult to imagine a client whose life goals are defined by her or his personal desires (i.e., individualistically oriented), who believes power in relationships should be granted according to social status (power distance or hierarchical relations), and is committed to maintaining emotional, supportive interpersonal relationships (femininity). Exercise 7.1 is based on Kluckhohn and Strodtbeck's (1961) alternative cultural formulation, which is often used to describe Native American cultures in particular (Trimble, 1981).

In Table 7.1, we contrast the cognitions, emotions, and behaviors of individualists and collectivists. Although we present the two types of cultures as though they are mutually exclusive, in fact, it is possible for a person to be collectivistic or individualistic with respect to some of the dimensions and the opposite with respect to the others. In addition, it is possible that people feel internal discord when their cognitive, affective, and behavioral strategies reflect different types of cultural socialization.

The Self

As summarized in Table 7.1, the person's manner of construing or perceiving oneself can vary according to cultural socialization, and should be an immediate area of inquiry for the therapist since our work so often involves interventions designed to alter the person's self-conceptions. However, typically the therapist can discover this information merely by listening to the way in which the client discusses or describes herself or himself.

When clients use individualistic orientations, they tend to describe themselves in terms of internal personality traits such as abilities (e.g., "I'm an intelligent person."), affective states (e.g., "I'm depressed."), behavioral styles (e.g., "I am shy."), and so forth. "I" occurs as a central theme in the individualistic client's conceptualization of her or his problem. By listening for the stable personality characteristics that consistently are joined with the client's "I" statements, the therapist often can obtain a picture of how the client typically sees herself or himself. Moreover, individualistic persons tend to construe themselves as having the same traits across social contexts, and consequently, have difficulty describing themselves in terms of or conforming to the differential performance criteria and social obligations inherent in various social roles.

TABLE 7.1   A Comparison of Individualistic and Collectivistic Cultural Cognitions, Emotions, and Behaviors

Individualistic	Collectivistic
Cognitions about Self	
Self is separate and discrete.	Self depends on group relationships and obligations.
Environments should be changed to make the self comfortable.	One changes oneself to promulgate a harmonious environment.
One's achievements define oneself.	One's achievements define the group.
Cognitions about Others	
Others' needs, rights, and expectations are secondary to one's own.	One must fulfill one's obligations to one's group; the group's needs are central.
To depend on others is a major character flaw.	To be rejected by others is a major character flaw.
Behavioral Principles	
One's own social status defines how one should be treated and should treat others.	A person's social role defines how he/she should be treated and should treat others.
Members of one's own group are generally treated the same.	Members of one's own group of equal status are treated the same.
The same rules of deportment generally apply to everyone.	One's deportment for in-group and out-group members differs.
Rules for Expressing Emotions	
One expresses one's negative feelings whether one is alone or with others.	One expresses negative feelings when one is alone but hides them when with others.
Emotions are determined primarily by one's inner experience.	Emotions are determined primarily by the social context in which they occur.

When the client's predominant cultural orientation is collectivistic, then the person tends to conceptualize the self within an often complex conglomeration of social roles and contexts. Thus, such persons often describe themselves and/or their problems through the eyes of other people or situations in which they find themselves. For example, "My parents want me to be a doctor," "My mother says that I am lazy," and so forth. Collectivists can generally describe themselves in terms of a number and variety of social roles, but, unlike their individualistic counterparts, have trouble listing general self-descriptive personality traits. By listening to whose perceptions the client reports, one can obtain a sense of who or what constitutes the client's salient at-home or in-group cultural-group members.

Conceptions of Others

It logically follows that clients (and therapists) assume that others in their environments construe themselves in the same way as they do. Thus, collectivists expect others' behaviors to be rule- and context-defined, whereas individualists rely on internal personality attributions to explain others' behaviors. Such interpretations apply to the therapist as well as other people in the client's life.

In explaining other people's behaviors, the collectivist can make use of external explanations or attributions such as luck, other people's expectations, and other situational constraints. The individualist, however, uses the behavior of other people, including the therapist, to make inferences about the person's internal psychological status. Often such inferences are based on the assumption that, "What I would be (or am) feeling under these circumstances must also be what the other person is feeling."

Behavioral Patterns

As far as observable behavior is concerned, for collectivists, the therapist fits into a certain social role and the client will accord him or her the status due that role and interpret the therapist's behavior accordingly. Thus, if in the client's at-home culture the therapist is perceived as a healer and healers routinely actively intervene in people's everyday lives, then the client from such a culture might expect the therapist to behave in a similar manner. Although therapists in traditional Western training programs are taught to be rather passive recipients and interpreters of information that the client proffers, collectivistic clients often expect more direct, active, and structured interventions (e.g., advice-giving, information-seeking and providing) with obvious relevance to their everyday life.

On the other hand, individualistically oriented people are more likely to expect therapists to delve into their inner world and assist them in examining and manipulating it, because the inner-self is where their experiencing happens most consistently. Thus, passive therapy interventions such as reflection of feeling, paraphrasing, minimal encouragers, and so forth might feel more culturally congruent in such cases.

Emotional Expression

Matsumoto (1994) points out that certain categories of emotions (e.g., joy, fear, sadness, and disgust) are present in all cultural groups. However, he points out that the various types of emotions may serve different functions within the two types of cultural groups and different social principles may govern when, how, and with whom they are expressed.

In discussing differential function, Matsumoto (1994) distinguishes between socially disengaged and socially engaged emotions. *Socially disengaged emotions* help one sustain one's conception of oneself as an independent and separate entity. Thus, feelings of pride or superiority derived from one's own personal accomplishments as well as feelings of anger and depression based on the failure to satisfy personal needs are both types of emotions that serve to separate one from other people.

Socially engaging emotions, according to Matsumoto (1994), encourage communal relationships and interpersonal bonding. Such emotions can be "positive" emotions such as friendliness, love, and respect or "negative" emotions such as guilt and shame due to one's dysfunctional behavior within a social context. The positive emotions stimulate group engagement because they feel good, and the negative emotions stimulate group-related behavior because one needs to interact with the group in order to redress the wrong and restore harmonious relationships.

Neither collectivists nor individualists "own" one type of emotions rather than the other. People from either type of culture can and do express both types of emotions. However, collectivists and individualists may experience both socially engaging and disengaging emotions with different levels of intensity and pervasiveness depending on what underlying meanings such emotions have for them.

For individualists, emotions generally are catalysts for further self-fulfillment or self-alteration, and they occur within oneself. If one does not share them with others, then others do not know what the person's emotional status is or what specific emotions the person might be experiencing. Thus, when working with such persons, the therapist has to guess or intuit what emotions characterize the client's experiencing, and if the therapist does so accurately, then the therapist is said to be capable of expressing "accurate empathy."

However, the existence of socially engaging or disengaging emotions can portend ostracism from a meaningful social network for the collectivist because the "appropriate" emotion is often defined more by the social contexts in which it occurs than by the subjective experience per se. Also, more people are aware of the person's emotional state, if they play a role in defining it. Thus, if something happens that "should" be embarrassing or the person behaves in an embarrassing manner (e.g., the person "loses face" or is "dissed"), then he or she is assumed to be ashamed by those who witness the situation, if they know the rules of the at-home culture.

Moreover, citing Ekman et al. (1972) as his original source for this concept, Matsumoto (1994) notes that the "cultural display rules" governing emotional expression within and across cultures may be different, and he summarizes a variety of cross-national and cross-cultural studies to illustrate this point. His review revealed the following influences on emotional expressions within groups:

1. *Social Roles.* For example, when the emotional expressiveness of Americans (of unspecified sociorace or cultural dimensions) and Japanese were compared, both groups responded to disgusting films (e.g., portrayals of amputations, sinus surgery) with expressions of disgust, anger, and so forth when they thought that they were alone. However, when they viewed the films in the presence of a presumably high status experimenter (of unspecified characteristics), Americans continued to express such emotions whereas Japanese smiled so as not to offend the experimenter.

2. *Social Context.* When asked to rate the appropriateness of expressing a standard set of positive and negative emotions in various social situations, White Americans rated the expression of emotions in public and with children as being more appropriate than did Latinos/Latinas. They also indicated that emotional

expression was more appropriate with casual acquaintances than did African, Asian, or Latino/Latina Americans. Moreover, in general, Whites tended to report that expression of negative emotions such as disgust, fear, and contempt was more acceptable than did one or more of the other groups.

3. *Intensity of Emotion.* Citing his own research, Matsumoto (1993) reported that when African, Asian, Latino/Latina, and White Americans were asked to rate how intensely they perceived the "universal" facial expressions of emotions, there were significant between-group differences. They found that African Americans differed most consistently from Asian and/or White Americans in that they perceived anger and fear more intensely than did Asian Americans, and disgust more intensely than did both groups; Asian Americans also perceived fear less intensely than did Latino/Latina Americans.

4. *"Decoding Rules"* (Matsumoto, 1994, p. 126). Cultural socialization influences the rules or principles that a person uses to recognize emotions and interpret them. Thus, decoding rules are the principles that people learn and automatically use to help them comprehend other people's emotional expressions.

Although much of the literature pertaining to emotional expression focuses on cross-national comparisons, it is sufficient to suggest that the therapist should at least entertain the possibility that different rules may underlie the therapist's and the client's interpretation and expression of emotions. In addition, it may not be sufficient to be aware of the client's mode of processing emotional information if one is unaware of the rules that predominate in the environments in which the person has to function on a day-to-day basis.

The Content of Cultures

Theorists from each of the major visible racial/ethnic groups argue for the existence of subjective cultures for their people independent of or perhaps in addition to their socialization in response to conditions of oppression. Some authors (Helms, 1992; J. Katz, 1985; Stewart, 1971) also argue for the existence of a White or "American" culture whereas others (Ivey & Ivey, 1993) argue against such a proposition. Nevertheless, in addition to discussing the cultures of the visible racial and ethnic groups, we will also discuss White culture.

Here, it might be useful to repeat Helms's (1994a, 1994b) discussions of what culture is and is not from her psychological perspective. Starting with the last point first, she argues that culture is *not* the following: (a) a person's socioracial classification per se; (b) skin color, which is generally used as a synonym for race; (c) nationality or citizenship-status classification; (d) a synonym for racial identity; or (e) necessarily conscious. As we have argued throughout this book, each of the foregoing categories are sociological classifications that might reveal something about the nature of the systems and institutions in which the person has been socialized, but reveal nothing about the nature of the person's incorporation of that socialization. Racial identity is a form of psychological reaction to one's socioracial socialization that is only superficially revealed by how a person classifies herself or himself. Neither cultural nor racial reactions are necessarily apparent to the person experiencing them. In fact, one might argue that most of the time, our cultural and racial psychological adaptations are not conscious to us.

On the other hand, some aspects of culture defined from a psychological perspective are in-group-defined values, traditions, norms, behaviors, and rituals. These aspects are internalized or learned, passed down from generation to generation, and are ways that cultural in-groups control the behavior of or "civilize" their members. Since internalized culture does contribute to the products of culture about which Triandis (1994) spoke, sometimes one can "see" or at least infer the nature of a group's culture from the products that it produces.

For all of the socioracial groups, the cultural content that we summarize should be considered to represent central tendencies common to ethnic groups observed by theorists and/or practitioners familiar with the relevant cultural group. However, "central tendency" does not mean that everyone within the group expresses all (or perhaps any) of the requisite dimensions. Moreover, because culture is learned (i.e., acculturated) rather than inborn, it is possible for a person who "looks like" he or she should practice a certain culture to be unfamiliar with any aspects of it. One *learns* best the culture(s) in which one was socialized.

White Culture

Most culturalists (i.e., researchers and theorists who use principles of cultural socialization to analyze human behavior) traditionally have treated the concepts of "American culture" and "White culture" as synonymous, often without recognizing that they have done so. Moreover, White culture has been invisible to many White theorists, researchers, and practitioners because they are immersed in it and, as members of the numerically and politically dominant group, never have to venture into other cultures unless they choose to do so. Consequently, one rarely finds delineations of White culture per se in the psychotherapy literature.

Nevertheless, Katz (1985) proposed dimensions of White culture and discussed how they influence the counseling process, and Helms's (1992) adaptations of these dimensions are summarized in Table 7.2. Other authors have used similar dimensions to describe "American culture" (e.g., Stewart, 1972). Perhaps you will notice that the dimensions that Katz describes are virtually the same as those that define individualistically oriented cultures as we have previously described them. Therefore, maybe it is not necessary to reiterate the discussion of them here.

However, the point we would like to emphasize here is that White cultural dynamics are the central themes in counseling and psychotherapy theories, models, and measures. Therefore, it is important for theorists and practitioners to examine the tools they use to assure themselves that they are aware of the ways in which individualism (White culture) is implicit in their own perspectives and methodologies.

TABLE 7.2 Some of Katz's (1985) White Cultural Components and Dimensions of Therapy

Component	Description	Therapy Implication
Rugged individualism	Individuals are primary social units and are valued for being independent, autonomous, and masters of their environments.	A person's problems are intrapsychic and can be resolved by knowing oneself better and taking charge of one's circumstance.
Action orientation	A person must control one's life and environments.	Clients must be helped to replace passivity and inaction with control and mastery.
Status and power	External credentials, material possessions, and prestige determine one's social status and power.	A therapist must have the appropriate paper credentials to be an effective therapist.
Communication rules	A person must write and speak standard (White) English to be worthy of respect.	Clients are expected to discuss their problems in fluent English.
Time	Time is a valuable commodity that can be quantified.	Therapy appointments are scheduled for a fixed amount of time.
Aesthetics	The best people exhibit European physical credentials and cultural components.	Clients who do best in traditional therapy are young, attractive, verbal, intelligent, successful (YAVIS), and White.
History	Anything worth knowing or being has its basis in the experience of European immigrants in the U.S.	Clients are viewed as pathological if they do not define or redefine themselves to conform to individualistic frameworks.
Family structure	The male-dominant nuclear family is the ideal and normative socialization unit.	Clients who do not conform to gender-based familial roles or whose families do not are considered abnormal.
Emphasis on scientific method	Everything of importance can be quantified, and that which is rational or objective or those who use such strategies are best.	Traditional Western theories and measures are assumed to describe the client's reality better than the client can.

Native American Cultural Content

Coupled with their struggles against socioracial domination were the efforts of the Native peoples (with some exceptions) to resist acculturation to the White American culture and abandonment of their own cultures. Once the White Americans encountered the Natives, it became evident that not only were the cultures of the two socioracial groups incompatible, but also that the Whites intended to impose their culture on the Native peoples. Thus, it became impossible for Whites and Natives to peacefully co-exist.

In the words of Big Eagle, a Santee Sioux: "The whites [sic] were always trying to make the Indians give up their life and live with white [sic] men—go to farming, work hard and do as they did—and the Indians did not know how to do that, and did not want to anyway. . . . If the Indians had tried to make the whites [sic] live like them, the whites [sic] would have resisted, and it was the same way with Indians" (cited in Brown, 1981, p. 38). Insight 7.1 illustrates the impact of acculturation and assimilation pressures as expressed through the eyes of contemporary Native American youths.

Several authors have attempted to delineate the dimensions that define Native American cultures. In our terminology, these dimensions define the at-home "traditional" culture. It should be noted that such summaries were not intended to homogenize the various Native American cultures, but rather to emphasize the dimensions that many of the traditional groups (i.e., those that chose to resist conformance to White culture) are assumed to have in common.

INSIGHT 7.1

Native American Children Speak

See if you can find examples of personal, cultural, and institutional racism in the following discussion with Native American teenagers. Then, think about the implications of their experiences for the acculturation and assimilation into Anglo-American culture of a people.[1]

Minton: What do you want from other American teenagers?

Wenona Littlewolf: I want to them to know about us. At school, they showed *Roots* [about African Americans], and a series about Nazis and the Jews, about the Holocaust, but they don't focus as much on the Native American background. . . . Even if you have elders in the house, sometimes they've been through so much, in boarding schools, growing up, where they were made fun of for talking their own language or when they talked about their culture. . . .

Jamie Littlewolf: But a lot of our own families don't really know our background, because they weren't taught it.

Angela Charwood: I had this friend once, and I couldn't go over to her house because her mom doesn't like Indians, so she didn't want me there. She thought we were these no-good people.

Elizabeth Day: I want trust. A lot of people feel, "I've got to watch them closely. They might steal something from me." . . . And when my dad goes into a store, people give him dirty looks. Once he was sitting in a restaurant for a half hour, and he just couldn't get waited on. Finally, he just walked out.

Eugene Walters: Native Americans have been discriminated against a lot longer than African-American or any other race. From the minute Columbus set foot on this land, they were taking advantage of the Indians. Where I used to live, they'd say, "Oh, why don't you do a rain dance?". . . It's what they saw on TV. . . .

Brenda Lang: Independence Day and all that—it's good for them, but I think they should also try to appreciate the people we honor and respect, to appreciate us.

[1]This dialogue is an excerpt from Lynn Minton's (1994) conversation with six Chippewa students attending a college preparatory program at Bemidji State University.

Locust (1990) contends that the following descriptors pertain to the majority of Native Americans with a tribal affiliation:

1. A belief in a Supreme Creator, who has a name, a personage, and often a place of residence. Terms of reverence (e.g., *Grandfather*) are typically used in place of the Supreme Creator's name, which is rarely spoken because it is so sacred. According to Locust, the Creator is an omnipotent spiritual rather than physical presence that controls all aspects of existence.

2. Humans are a composite of spirit, mind, and body. Of the three components, the spirit (the "I AM") is most important because it defines the essence of the person. The physical body is the "house" prepared by the parents in which the spirit dwells, and the mind serves as the mediator between body and spirit in a manner somewhat analogous to the role of the ego with respect to the id and super-ego in psychoanalytic psychology.

3. "Plants and animals, like humans, are part of the spirit world. The spirit world exists side by side and intermingles with the physical world" (Locust, 1990, p. 223). Thus, many Native Americans believe that they share a spiritual kinship with all living things because all things originate with the Supreme Creator.

4. The spirit is immortal, and immortality is circular; that is, it has no beginning or ending. When the body dies or is "shed," the spirit is free to move (be born) into another body or life, and the spirit continues to repeat the birth-death process until it reaches perfection and can "return" to the Supreme Creator.

5. Illness is a disruption of the mind-body-spirit homeostasis. When a traditional person becomes ill or experiences problems in life including mental health concerns, then she or he must discover and take steps to correct whatever condition or circumstance is weakening the spirit and permitting the illness or physical injury or life-problem to occur.

6. Wellness is equilibrium or harmony of spirit-mind-body. "To be in harmony is to be at 'oneness' with life, eternity, the Supreme Creator, and oneself" (Locust, 1990, p. 225). Traditional Native Americans strive for harmony—a state of being that comes from within rather than from one's physical or interpersonal environments.

7. Unwellness or disharmony within the spirit-mind-body triad is caused by suppressed socially disengaging emotions (e.g., anger, heartache, fear) that serve as catalysts for physical and mental deterioration if spiritual energy is low. Therefore, disharmony is to be avoided.

8. Illness or unwellness can result from natural or unnatural causes. Natural illness occurs when one accidentally or intentionally violates a sacred tribal interdiction. Such violations can influence one's own health as well as that of one's family. So, eating prohibited foods, injuring an animal, marrying into one's own clan, and so forth might result in natural illnesses. Unnatural illness results from evil forces that are symbolized by tribe-specific incarnations such as the bear, owl, or reptiles. Evil-doers (approximately analogous to "evil witches or warlocks" or "root workers"), manipulators of evil (especially mental) energy, influence the person either directly if her or his spirit is weak or indirectly through

the person's interpersonal environment (e.g., family members). Accidents, depression, irrational thinking, unusual behavior, and so forth are examples of the kinds of conditions that can be caused by evil-doers.

9. Each person is responsible for her or his own health status. If a person allows disharmony in her or his life, then the person risks that her or his spiritual energy will ebb and her or his body will become diseased or ill. Thus, if one wishes to remain healthy, then one should strive to maintain spirit-mind-body harmony. However, a healer who recognizes the interconnectness of the human triad can often assist the person in recovering such harmony once it is lost. Even healers who are not skilled in remediating unwellness in all three components of the triad themselves can assist the person by collaborating with healers whose areas of expertise are the other domains. In either case, respect for the client's view of life is central.

The Nature of African American Culture

As previously mentioned, most traditional culturalists have not identified an African culture different from the culture that allegedly evolved in response to slavery and racial oppression or social class deprivation (see Chapters 4 and 5). Furthermore, those theorists who have attempted to describe an African American culture have focused on classic African cultures with a specific emphasis on Egypt (or Kemet) as the origin of that culture (see Jackson, 1993, for a summary of these models). For example, the following dimensions are Helms's (1992) adaptations of those that Boykin (1983) and Baldwin (1985, 1991) propose as characterizing African cultures in the Diaspora:

1. *Spirituality*—the belief that immaterial forces, especially a Supreme Being who can appear in many manifestations, have power in determining what happens in people's everyday life; includes a moral code that promotes altruism, fairness, and justice.
2. *Harmony*—the self and one's surroundings are interconnected and are intended to operate in synchrony.
3. *Movement*—personal conduct is organized through movement and motion.
4. *Affect-Mind-Body*—the person's mind, body, and emotions form an interconnected triad that is intended to function in equilibrium, whatever alters one component also influences the others.
5. *Communalism*—one's group is a significant definer of who one is; one's group is as important as one's self.
6. *Expressiveness*—the unique aspects of one's personality are expressed through one's behavioral style and creative flair.
7. *Orality*—knowledge is gained and transmitted orally and aurally, and one achieves credibility by being an effective oral communicator. Effective communication is rhythmic, symbolic, and occurs on cognitive-affective-behavioral levels.
8. *Time*—is measured by socially meaningful events and customs rather than quantity.

However, those Africans who survived the slavery era and subsequent institutional and cultural racism in the United States also developed a unique African American ethnic culture that is typically overlooked as a source of strength and pride. This culture is a blend of those elements of the various African peoples that have come to the Americas over the centuries, and became assimilated into the African American socioracial group. It combines those themes that are and were common across African tribal and ethnic groups, but does not necessarily obliterate all traces of other ethnicities. This blended African culture is probably strongest in the South where it was developed, but presumably exists in some form wherever groups of African Americans reside in significant numbers. This hypothesized blended culture is what we mean by "African American culture."

Landrine and Klonoff (1994), the only theorists to our knowledge who have attempted to define indigenous African American ethnic culture as we conceptualize it, hypothesize that this culture consists of the dimensions illustrated in Table 7.3. Compare African American culture as they operationally define it and racial identity (an adaptation to racism) as Helms (1996) operationally defines it in Table 7.4 to get another view of how psychological adaptations to cultural and racial socialization differ.

Latino/Latina Culture

The proximity of the Latino/Latina groups to the United States has made it easier for this socioracial group to maintain various derivatives of Spanish culture in the United States because newcomer immigrants bring it with them and citizens and permanent residents often can maintain contact and connections with bearers of the culture. Nevertheless, Latino/Latina cultural theories and models differ in the extent to which they emphasize particular aspects or domains of the cultures. Sometimes differences seem to be linked to the particular ethnic group under consideration, and sometimes they seem to be linked to the gender of the theorist. For example, Latinas seem to attend more to the differential psychological implications of gender roles and sexual orientation within the cultural group than do their male counterparts.

Even so, some dimensions appear rather consistently in discussions of Latino/Latina cultures (e.g., Chin, De La Cancela, & Jenkins, 1993; Comas-Diaz, 1992; Fouad, 1994; Marin, 1994). They are as follows:

1. *"Allocentrism"* (collectivism)—personal interdependence that is characterized by sensitivity to the social and physical environment, empathic understanding of others' feelings, willingness to sacrifice one's own self-interests to benefit one's cultural group, and reliance on in-group or at-home cultural members for sustenance (Marin & Marin, 1991; Marin, 1994).
2. *Simpatia*—a preference for smooth, conflict-free social relationships and affiliations that contributes to a behavioral style intended to protect the self-esteem and dignity of in-group members. It involves being responsive to others' feelings and avoiding conflicts that might contribute to confrontations, wounded feelings, or assaults to one's dignity.

TABLE 7.3   Landrine and Klonoff's (1994) Dimensions of Indigenous African American Culture

Scale Item	Response
Preferences for Own-Group Things	
1. Most of the music I listen to is by Black artists	Totally Agree
2. I read (or used to read) *Jet* magazine.	Totally Agree
Traditional Family Values and Practices	
1. One or more of my relatives knows how to do hair.	Totally Agree
2. When I was young, my cousin, aunt, grandmother, etc. lived with me and my family for awhile.	Totally Agree
Traditional Health Beliefs, Practices, and Folk Disorders	
1. I know what "falling out" means.	Totally Agree
2. Prayer can cure disease.	Totally Agree
Traditional Socialization	
1. I went to mostly Black elementary school(s).	Totally Agree
2. I used to sing in the church choir.	Totally Agree
Traditional Foods and Food Practices	
1. I usually add salt to my food to make it taste better.	Totally Agree
2. I know how to cook chit'lins.	Totally Agree
Religious Beliefs and Practices	
1. I believe in heaven and hell	Totally Agree
2. I like gospel music.	Totally Agree
Interracial Attitudes	
1. Whites don't understand Blacks.	Totally Agree
2. IQ tests were set up purposefully to discriminate against Black people	Totally Agree
Superstitions	
1. I avoid splitting a pole.	Totally Agree
2. I eat black-eyed peas on New Year's Eve.	Totally Agree

This table is based on Landrine and Klonoff's (1994) African American Acculturation Scale.

TABLE 7.4   Some Dimensions of Helms's (1996) People of Color (and Black) Racial Identity

Scale Item	Response
Conformity (Pre-encounter)	
1. I feel uncomfortable when I am around Black people.	Strongly Agree
2. I believe that being Black is a negative experience.	Strongly Agree
Dissonance (Encounter)	
1. I am determined to search for my Black identity.	Strongly Agree
2. I can't feel comfortable with either Black people of White people.	Strongly Agree
Immersion	
1. I limit myself to Black activities as much as I can.	Strongly Agree
2. White people can't be trusted.	Strongly Agree
Emersion	
1. I feel an overwhelming attachment to Black people.	Strongly Agree
2. I feel excitement and joy in Black surroundings.	Strongly Agree
Internalization	
1. People, regardless of their race, have strengths and limitations.	Strongly Agree
2. Being Black just feels natural to me.	Strongly Agree

Note: Racial identity dimensions are from Helms (1996). Names for dimensions in parentheses historically have been used to describe Black people.

3. *Familialism*—loyalty, strong identification with, attachment to, and interdependence on one's (blood-related) extended family, which includes parents, uncles, aunts, siblings, grandparents, cousins, and so forth. Each member of the family is expected to provide emotional and financial support to all members of the extended family who, in turn, are each expected to fulfill specific culturally defined social roles.

4. *Respeto* (respect)—deference or respect accorded to people because of their status due to gender, age, and family role or position.

Some cultural themes appear in various discussions but sometimes under different labels or definitions. Some examples of these are as follows:

1. *Espiritismo*—belief in traditional healing and health practices in which the material and spiritual worlds are assumed to interact.

2. *Marianismo*—a gender role in which the woman is expected to emulate the spirituality of the Virgin Mary and to endure all suffering inflicted upon her by the

men in her life. Also, she is expected to be submissive, passive, dependent, and defined by her home and family.
3. *Machismo*—the male gender role in which the man is expected to be the primary provider for the family and to be responsible for the family's welfare, honor, and protection. The gender role also permits him to be chivalrous toward women and sexually accessible to many of them.

Asian Americans

Theorists' and researchers' discussions of Asian American culture have generally pertained to specific Asian ethnic groups rather than the entire socioracial group, perhaps in part because Asians were initially enticed to this country as distinct cultural groups (see Chapter 5). Nevertheless, although it may not be immediately obvious to members of the various Asian ethnic groups, some common cultural themes do appear to occur across groups and to contribute to their acculturation and assimilation stresses.

Consider, for example, the following list of cultural themes derived from Lee's (1989) description of traditional Chinese American families and Yamamoto, Silva, Justice, Chang, and Leong's (1993) description of traditional Japanese civilization:

1. Familism-primacy of the family, group, or community.
2. Socialization occurs within the context of an extended family, and family practices promote development of a group or collectivistic consciousness.
3. Confucianism, Taoism, or Buddhism is the philosophy by which one's ethics, social relationships, and role within the community are defined.
4. Interdependence, such that the person is expected to function in harmony within her or his social context.
5. Hierarchical relationships—one's obligations and duties to the collective are defined by one's social role (for example, masters, experts, employers, and subordinates express loyalty; fathers and sons share intimacy).
6. Filial piety—the parent-child bond is more critical than virtually any other, and has implicit in it a reciprocal set of duties and obligations that maintain family harmony.
7. Emotions expressed through actions (e.g., taking care of one's parents' physical needs) rather than verbalizations.
8. Respect for authority.
9. Males are more valued than females.
10. The mind and body are indivisible, so that mental illness or problems may be expressed as somatic symptoms.

There is also evidence to suggest that these dimensions may characterize other Asian ethnic groups as well (Pannu, 1994). Nevertheless, the therapist does need to remind herself or himself that similar themes do not necessarily signify identical cultural content or expression. In the United States especially, one must be aware that the different histories of immigration of the various groups imply different group-level acculturation of the marketplace culture. Therefore, some groups, and consequently, some client members of those groups, may be more marketplace acculturated than others.

Acculturation and Assimilation Processes

The foregoing discussion suggests that many collectivist cultures exist within a society in which individualism predominates. Consequently, members of the nondominant groups are exposed to societal pressure to abandon their own culture in exchange for access to an opportunity to strive for a personal share of societal resources and inclusion in the dominant group. Whereas this exchange worked for White American ethnic groups because they did not have easily recognizable physical characteristics by which they could be excluded, it has never truly occurred for People of Color, in part because their physical characteristics make them easily classifiable.

Because the groups of color were segregated with other people who looked like them and shared some cultural dynamics, it was possible for them to hang onto their own particular versions of collectivism. Consequently, when individual members of these groups must function in unfamiliar cultural environments, they experience the acculturation stress associated with learning to function in a new culture. Moreover, since it is usually the case that People of Color are never fully accepted into the dominant cultural group, they usually must negotiate assimilation stresses as well.

Acculturation Stresses

Acculturation concerns the extent to which the person learns and expresses her or his own as well as the dominant cultures, although some theorists prefer the term *enculturation* for the own-group learning process. For each of the socioracial groups, theorists have proposed models of acculturation. Most of these hypothesize acculturation types or stages that vary from total internalization or identification with one's traditional culture to total identification with White culture. Some of these are summarized in Table 7.5. We could easily have included them with the racial identity perspectives summarized in Table 6.1 because many of the models do not necessarily elucidate cultural characteristics as such. However, many of the theorists did intend their models to be relevant to the cultural adaptation processes of particular Asian ethnic groups. So, in that narrow sense, they are cultural models.

Native Americans

The relationship of Native Americans to Whites in this country in many ways has been and continues to be quite complex, in part because Indigenous Peoples have not consistently been considered to comprise a distinct racial group (Wilson, 1992). Many historians assert that for most of Whites' history in this country, they considered Native Americans to be a "heathen" or "savage" variant of the White race rather than a different race as was the case for African Americans (Shuffleton, 1993).

TABLE 7.5 **Acculturation Models for Native, Asian, and Latino/Latina American Socioracial and Ethnic Groups**

Author	Dimension	Description of Dimensions
	Native Americans	
Chance (1965)	Traditional Indian	Rejects middle-class individualistic values; value orientations are present-time; harmony with nature, cooperation, conformity.
	Nontraditional Indian	Attempts to be assimilated into White culture; value orientations are future time; competitive, and individualistic.
Lowrey (1983)	Traditional People	The Native person practices the cultural language and customs, and shares the beliefs of her/his Native ancestors.
	Acculturated People	Person of Native ancestry attempts to accommodate to White culture by straddling the Anglo/Native cultural fence.
	Autonomous people	The Native person is able to choose the best values and beliefs from each group.
Kitano (1982)	Type 1 Marginal	Negative Japanese/negative White—the person of Japanese-American ancestry identifies with neither her/his own group or with the White group.
	Type 2 Mono-Anglo	Positive White/negative Japanese—the person identifies with White culture and rejects Japanese-American culture.
	Type 3 Mono-Japanese	Negative White/positive Japanese—the person rejects White culture, but identifies with Japanese-American culture.
	Type 4 Bicultural	Positive Japanese/positive White—the person identifies with Japanese and White American cultures.
	Asian Americans	
Lee (1989)	Traditional	Conforms strongly to traditional Chinese cultural emphasis on agricultural background and morals guided by traditional religious/philosophical values.
	Transitional	A Westernized person being socialized by parents and grandparents with traditional beliefs.
	Bicultural	People socialized to be bilingual and capable of functioning effectively in either culture.
	Americanized	Chinese people, born and raised in the U.S., for whom Chinese culture and identity are no longer salient.

(continued)

TABLE 7.5   Continued

Author	Dimension	Description of Dimensions
Asian Americans		
Sue & Sue (1971)	Asian-American	The person of Chinese American ancestry idealizes Chinese American culture while denigrating White culture.
	Traditional Chinese	The person identifies with traditional Chinese culture while essentially disregarding White culture.
	Marginal	The person identifies with neither group.
Latinos/Latinas		
Baptiste (1990)	Immigrants	People whose preadolescent cultural socialization occurred in a country other than the U.S.
	Reluctants	Immigrants who resist moving to and engaging in the "new" culture, usually by means of behavioral problems.
	Optimists	Immigrants, usually older children, who mirror their parents' adaptational strategies.
	Immigrant Americans	Persons who emigrated to the U.S. at such a young age that they are able to forget and replace the old culture with the new.
	Americans	People born in the U.S. of immigrant parents whose connection to the traditional culture is only as seen through their parents' eyes.
Szapocznik et al. (1978)	Type 1	Person identifies primarily with Anglo culture.
	Type 2	Person identifies primarily with Cuban culture.
	Type 3	Person identifies with both Cuban and Anglo culture.
	Type 4	The person does not identify with either culture.

Thus, Thomas Jefferson advocated intermarriage as a means of civilizing Native Americans whereas he proposed no such remedy for any of the other VREGs.

"More than once . . . he [Jefferson] told the Indians, 'Your blood will mix with ours; and will spread, with ours, over this great island. . . . [Our goal is] to let our settlements meet and blend together, to intermix, and become one people' " (a Native American, cited in Shuffleton, 1993, p. 273).

Nevertheless, White Americans considered the practice of Christianity to define who was civilized. However, the traditional Native peoples practiced indigenous religions other than Christianity, most of which were based on different conceptualizations of spirituality (Locust, 1990). Consequently, considerable military and sociopolitical pressure was used to force Native Americans to abandon their traditional religions (see Insight 7.2). One could argue that Christianity has often been used as a

INSIGHT 7.2
A Quest for Religious Freedom

In the late 1800s (around 1890), Wovoka, the "Painte Messiah," founded the religion of the Ghost Dance. The purpose of the Ghost Dance religion was to bring the warrior ancestors back from the dead. Although the Ghost Dancers' ritualistic expression of their religion differed from Christianity as expressed by Whites at the time, the tenets of Ghost Dancing were a combination of Christian and indigenous philosophies. Believers were obliged to: (a) refrain from harming others, (b) practice nonviolence and humanistic love, and (c) dance and sing to encourage the Messiah to bring back the ancestors. Symbols of their religion were Ghost shirts that many believed could not be penetrated by bullets.

Hundreds of Native Americans of many tribal origins and languages came to see the Christ returned to earth as a Native American, and to dance the dance of the Ghosts. Wovoka promised the faithful a new earth in which White men would be buried by new soil, and the land would be as it was before the coming of the White man. The Ghost Dancer faithful would join their ancestors on the new earth, where only Native peoples would live. The religion spread quickly among the indigenous peoples of the West.

U.S. Indian Bureau inspectors and army officers, from Dakota to Arizona, from Indian Territory to Nevada, were alarmed by the ghost dancing because they feared a resurgence of indigenous religious beliefs and practices. Leaders of the Ghost Dance were accused of being insurrectionists. Sitting Bull, the Chief of the Hunkpapa Sioux (apparently not a strong Ghost Dance believer himself), was arrested ostensibly for leading the religious insurrection on the Sioux reservation.

Under dubious circumstances, Chief Sitting Bull was killed during the arrest by two Indian police. In the military massacre that followed, Big Foot (a Ghost Dance leader) and 350 Minneconjon Sioux (mostly women and children) were slaughtered. It has been estimated that approximately 40% of the tribe was lost that day at Wounded Knee.

And so (for a time) ended the hopes of the Native Peoples for tribal independence and religious freedom.

This historical account was based on information provided by Brown (1981) and McLemore (1983).

tool to exterminate Native American traditional religions, and consequently, the people themselves.

Consequently, many of the socialization principles that were used to promote the civilization of supposedly depraved Whites were also applied indiscriminantly to Native Americans, only in more drastic form (see Table 4.1). Thus, slightly different versions of the Anglo-conformity or assimilation models that were invented for White ethnics also were generally used to prescribe the adaptation and adjustment process of Native Americans.

The Native American acculturation models summarized in Table 7.5 describe possible types or dimensions of individual Native American people's psychological reactions to attempts to extinguish their culture. Although the models differ in the number and labels attached to the various psychological adaptations, they all suggest that Native Americans' reactions to assimilation processes can be predicted and described.

African Americans

As previously mentioned, one rarely finds culture-based models for describing the psychological adaptations of African Americans, perhaps because it has been assumed that they do not have a legitimate culture (Shuffleton, 1993). Therefore, although a number of models have been proposed for describing their racial adaptations (see Chapter 6; Helms, 1990; Cross, Parham, & Helms, 1991), virtually none has been proposed for describing the cultural learning and adaptation processes that result when one's culture is invisible; that is, when it is automatically assumed that oneself and one's cultural group have been deculturated.

Nevertheless, it is possible that many of the acculturation models that have been proposed for the other visible racial and ethnic groups may also pertain to African Americans, if one replaces the other groups' cultural dynamics with African American cultural dynamics such as those described in Insight 7.3. Yet where African Americans are concerned, it is important to take note of the special assimilation pressures that appeared in the form of detrimental governmental research practices in the health and mental health fields because these have implications for the ways in which many African Americans view institutions that supposedly exist to "help them."

While it is not clear to us whether these detrimental practices occurred because of perceived cultural or racial differences of the African American victims, we include them here because the language that has been used to describe African Americans' long-standing reactions to societal systems often uses the language of culture.

INSIGHT 7.3
African Cultural Principles

Many African-based self-help and mental health outreach programs center their interventions around specific cultural themes. M. A. McKenzie's outreach program in Washington, D.C. was designed to assist African American women recover from histories of substance abuse and incarceration by inspiring them to become *Mudiwas* (Swahili for *queens*), and is based on collectivism and the *Kwanzaa* principles described below.

During *Kwanzaa*, a spiritual (rather than religious) period that occurs at the end of the year, many African Americans reflect on the previous year, give gifts, and celebrate their kinship with one another and the ancestors.

Collectivism—what one does to harm oneself (taking drugs, having multiple sex partners) also harms everyone in one's community in one way or another
Umojo—unity
Kujichagulia—self-determination
Ujima—collective work and responsibility
Ujamaa—cooperative economics
Nia—remember the ancestors and the struggles they endured to make the world a better place for their descendants
Kuumba—creativity
Imani—faith

Condensed from D.L. Brown (1994).

Examples of the types of events to which we allude are as follows: (a) the Federal government-sponsored research known as the "Tuskegee experiment," a study conducted over a 40-year period during which 600 Alabama African American men who thought they were being treated for syphilis actually were unwitting subjects in a study to investigate the damage the disease would do to the body, if it remained untreated (Sue & Sue, 1990). It should be noted that although information is now available about the fate of these men, no one even discusses the fates of their wives, mates, and children; (b) the Federally sponsored radiation cancer studies, which are just now coming to light, in which an unknown number of African American cancer patients who thought they were being treated for their disease, were actually injected with radiation in unrelated body sites so that scientists could study the effects of radiation on the body; and (c) ongoing sterilization and reproduction research involving African American women (Reid, 1978).

With respect to this latter point, Reid reported the following data on percentages of contraceptive sterilization (tubal ligations, hysterectomies, vasectomies, and combined procedures) conducted on Black and White women and men: Black women, 11.1%; White women, 4.9%; Black men, .6%; and White men, 5.5%. About these data she observes, "How many of these contraceptive operations constituted involuntary sterilizations is not clear. It is known, however, though not documented in any systematic way that: 'Involuntary, coercive sterilizations have been performed on black [sic] women for decades.' " (Reid, 1978, p. 208). Because mental health professions are less attuned to the societal abuse of African American women relative to other socioracial gender and socioracial groups, it is quite easy to misconstrue their mistrust of health systems.

Now, it could be argued that the events just described were not necessarily the misdeeds of mental health professionals (although we have elaborated on their misdeeds in earlier chapters). However, often mental health professionals colluded in these efforts, often by misusing psychological and psychiatric diagnostic procedures. Moreover, the therapist intending to be responsive to the racial and cultural dynamics of African American clients must realize that often clients do not make such fine discriminations among the "helping" fields, in part, because the mind and body are not separate entities in their traditional culture.

Therefore, an immediate acculturation implication of these observations is that therapists should be aware that some African American clients may enter or avoid entering mental health as well as medical institutions because of an historically based "cultural mistrust" (Terrell & Terrell, 1981; Nickerson, Helms, & Terrell, 1994) of such institutions. Moreover, if they do enter, a considerable amount of suspicion may accompany and remain with them for as long as the therapist is perceived as representing the goals of the institution rather than the needs of the African American community.

In addition, although many clients may not be able to recall specific historical events contributing to their feelings of wariness and suspicion, suffice it to say that many will express such feelings. Furthermore, many African American clients will have personally relevant contemporary stories of real and perceived mistreatment by health and mental health institutions within their own regions and neighborhoods.

Rather than automatically assuming that such beliefs are a form of delusion or "cultural paranoia," the effective therapist will have to work with the client to identify the sources of the client's feelings and negative expectations, and to alleviate them insofar as that is possible.

Latinos/Latinas

Latinos/Latinas have had considerable success in holding onto crucial elements of their cultures and resisting the assimilative forces of "Anglocization." In addition, they have been remarkably successful in forcing out-groups to acknowledge the social implications of their cultural inclusion in the society. Nevertheless, their visibility and identifiable cultural-group specific characteristics (e.g., Spanish language) often have made them catalysts for ethnocentric and racist policies and practices in the United States. For example, the English-only language movement in the United States is in direct response to xenophobic fears that English (and English culture) will be replaced by Spanish and Spanish culture as the language and culture of the marketplace (Booth, 1993).

Proposed Latino/Latina acculturation models are also shown in Table 7.5. Typically, these models describe the consequences of attempting to maintain a Spanish identity in an English language and culturally oriented environment.

White Acculturation

The Anglo-conformity perspective is the dominant theme inherent in White acculturation pressures. According to this perspective, White immigrants do and should shed their traditional cultures in favor of the histories and experiences and cultural dimensions of the (predominantly White-defined) host culture. It has been contended by prominent theorists across time that by internalizing the host culture (which supposedly includes only selected trace elements of other cultures), incoming groups could be absorbed into the "melting pot" of the dominant culture (Gordon, 1964; Park, 1950). It is from this perspective that mental health professionals have adopted the notion that enhancement of acculturation and assimilation are necessarily desirable therapy (and socialization) goals for people regardless of their cultural origin.

In fact, Alba (1990) does present evidence to suggest that Anglo-conformity accurately portrays the acculturation process by which White people become "Americans," that is, are assimilated into the dominative sociopolitical and economic group. He asserts that, "Ethnic distinctions based on European ancestry, once quite prominent in the social landscape, are fading into the background; other ethnic distinctions appear more highlighted as a result. In a sense, a new [White] ethnic group is forming—one based on ancestry from *anywhere* on the European continent" (Alba, 1990, p. 3).

With respect to the matter of learning Anglo-American culture, his research indicates that about 26% of his native-born "European American ethnic group" did not report having any cultural experiences that they associated with their ancestral ethnic groups, and approximately 77% reported fewer than six of the ethnic cultural activities shown in Exercise 7.2.

In his tripartite model for African Americans, Boykin (1986) also contends that to the extent that the marketplace culture is strikingly different from one's home culture and proficiency in the marketplace culture is imposed as a condition of worth, then one's psychological adjustment is at risk. Thus, according to his perspective, Whites as a group are at less mental-health risk due to cultural factors because their at-home and marketplace cultures typically are identical and, at most, vary only along a few dimensions.

In addition, since Whites are members of the numerically and politically dominant group, each one has a role in choosing the extent to which aspects of his or her

---

EXERCISE 7.2

What Remains of Your Ethnic Culture?

What is your ethnic background? _____

_____

With this answer in mind, respond to the following questions. During the past five years, how many times on average did you do or experience each of the following (put a number on the line)?

1. Eat special foods or dishes of your ethnic background _____
2. Practice customs or traditions of your ethnic background _____
3. Teach your children about your ethnic background _____
4. Attend or participate in ethnic festivals or celebrations _____
5. Visit an ancestral homeland _____
6. Use words or phrases from an ancestral language _____
7. Feel strongly about an issue because of your ethnic background _____
8. Discrimination against you because of your ethnic background _____
9. See or hear about discrimination against others who have your ethnic background

   _____
10. Come into contact with stereotypes or fixed ideas about people with your ethnic background _____

11. Feel curious about the ethnic background of someone else _____
12. Someone asking questions about your ethnic background _____
13. Feel a special sense of relationship to someone else because that person has your ethnic background _____
14. Discuss your ethnic background with someone else
15. Feel special interest in the career of a public figure or celebrity because that person has your ethnic background _____
16. Get special help in your business or profession from someone with your ethnic background _____

To obtain an idea of how you compare to Alba's (1990) White American native-born sample ($N = 460$), sum your responses to the 16 items. Alba reported that 25.9% had no experiences, 12.8% had one experience, 13% had two experiences, 12.2% had three experiences, 12.6% had four or five experiences, and 23.5% had six or more experiences. Item 1 (eating special foods) was the most frequently reported experience (47%), and item 16 (business help) was the least reported (2.2%). Ethnic discrimination (item 8) was reported by only 4.3% of the sample.

This exercise was adapted from Alba (1990, p. 79).

own ethnic cultures become a part of the marketplace culture as well as which aspects remain private. If one "looks" White, then one is assumed to be practicing the marketplace culture at home unless one chooses to reveal otherwise. Consequently, presumptions about the White person's at-home culture are not used by others to handicap him or her unless some other major "defect" (e.g., lower socioeconomic status) is made evident. Moreover, because the central tendencies of White culture are primarily individualistic, White people typically are not directly socialized by very many people and therefore, each one is responsible for or obligated to fewer people than are traditional members of the visible racial and ethnic groups.

Assimilation Pressures

Assimilation generally pertains to a group's level of acceptance by and inclusion in the dominant society on a structural level. However, the term does have some potential implications for people on an individual level as well; one shares the status of one's ascribed socioracial and cultural groups. Thus, from our perspective, the term *assimilation* pertains to the sociologically defined status of groups within the country, but it also pertains to the potential societal status of the individual client who is a member of these groups; that is, the extent to which he or she is accepted in personally relevant social environments.

Therefore, assimilation pressures as we conceptualize them can contribute to acculturation, but the two are not the same things. A culturally and racially responsive therapist not only should be aware of the global societal ethnocentrism and racism that often underlie assimilation pressures, but also the racism and cultural bias as they appear in the client's immediate environment. An awareness of macro- and micro-level racial and cultural dynamics is important for the therapist intending to assist the client to assess options and interpret reality more effectively.

On the macro-level, Gordon's (1964) model of assimilation is often used to assess the degree of dominant-group acceptance of particular racial or cultural groups in the society or the group's level of merging into the dominant group. Gordon identified three forms of assimilation: (1) cultural assimilation—the disappearing of a group due to replacement of the traditional group's culture with the dominant group's culture; (2) structural assimilation—equal-status interactions among group members at various levels of societal discourse; and (3) marital assimilation—selection of marital partners among ostensible groups without regard to their cultural or socioracial classifications.

McLemore (1983) further subdivides structural assimilation into "secondary" and "primary" structural assimilation. *Secondary structural assimilation* pertains to dominant and subordinate group relations in impersonal (marketplace) settings that are of equal status or are nondiscriminatory. Examples of relevant settings from an individualistic perspective are occupations, schools, and neighborhoods. *Primary structural assimilation* refers to status differentials in close, intimate, and personal settings involving dominant-group and subordinate-group members. Examples of relevant definers of this construct are families, fraternities or sororities, churches, and so forth.

In line with Gordon's original formulation, McLemore contends that cultural assimilation precedes secondary assimilation, which, in turn, should precede primary assimilation, and all three should precede marital assimilation. However, he departs from earlier theorists in that he contends that groups may be culturally assimilated without necessarily ever attaining the other kinds of assimilation. The levels of assimilation vary in the amount of access to intimacy with dominant-group members that is permitted.

The usefulness of this assimilation perspective for therapists is that it suggests that tolerance and acceptance of members of oppressed groups may occur at multiple societal levels and at different rates. If progression through the levels is inevitable as Anglo-conformity theorists contended, then by examining the levels of remaining disparity, the group's status within the society becomes more evident. At the level of the individual client, cross-group disparities in status may predict or explain the particular areas in which a person is likely to encounter cross-group as well as within-group conflict.

Further Implications for Therapy

Be that as it may, the client's cultural style may be quite complex. Therefore, the therapist should avoid adopting simplistic descriptions of the client's cultural dynamics because simplistic portrayals are not necessarily the most functional. Of course, the therapist should also avoid assuming that a person's appearance reveals anything about that person's cultural socialization. Rather, the therapist needs to perform a cultural appraisal of some sort, which might include assessment of the person's own cultural style, typical reactions to acculturation pressures, and relevance of the person's group-specific assimilation history to the problem he or she is attempting to resolve.

As one performs a cultural assessment, it is important to remember that just as it is possible for people to shift with respect to individualism-collectivism when necessary, they may also shift with respect to any of the other cultural dimensions discussed in this chapter under the appropriate circumstances. In fact, it is sometimes mandatory for one's psychological survival to be able to shift with respect to the various cultural dimensions as the situation requires. In this country, if a person is visibly different from the White group, the group that defines the marketplace culture, then the person also is assumed to be from a "different" subjective culture, and different typically means "deficient." Therefore, the capacity to shift cultures may become a compensatory strategy for surviving in potentially hostile environments.

Be that as it may, it is just generally the case that a person feels more comfortable and functional in the cultural mode(s) in which he or she was socialized because it is easier to comprehend one's own culture's unspoken rules. Nevertheless, as we mentioned in Chapter 3, in our experience, collectivistic orientations of some sort seem to be modal for clients socialized in VREG cultures whereas individualistic orientations seem to be modal for clients socialized in White culture, regardless of their actual socioracial classification. In our experience, the other cultural contents and dimensions are much less predictable.

By and large, being from collectivistic cultures and facing daily pressures aimed at discounting and eliminating those cultures, works against the psychological well-being of People of Color, regardless of whether they were socialized in the attacked culture themselves, because such pressures demonstrate that deviance is punished. Thus, for members of such groups, the at-home and marketplace cultures may be and remain quite different from one another because the significant aspects of the at-home culture are not viewed as worthy of emulation.

Also, members of collectivistic cultures who are not equivalently adept in the dominant individualistic culture may have difficulty performing up to their potential in "foreign" environments. Not only do they typically have little control over what aspects of their own culture will become public property, but they also have little control over which parts of the marketplace culture they will be required to internalize and perform if they wish to be evaluated positively. Although they do not control the contents of the marketplace culture, they are evaluated by its standards, particularly after the first generation. Therefore, sometimes it may be necessary to teach the client the rules for functioning in the alternate culture, that is, whichever culture is unfamiliar to the client. To accomplish the relevant educational process, it may be necessary to assist the client in recognizing the rules in her or his own culture, and then use that understanding to illustrate the other culture.

Finally, it should be noted that real and perceived socialization for collectivistic groups may involve large groups (sometimes, as in the case of African Americans, virtually an entire racial classification group or in the case of Asian Americans, ancestors who are no longer living as well as those yet to be born). Consequently, members of a collectivistic socioracial or cultural group may be obligated to many people, some of whom they may not even have met, some of whom may not be born yet, some of whom may be deceased, and some of whom may be fictive or "as-if" kinspeople.

REFERENCES

Alba, R. D. (1990). *Ethnic identity: The transformation of White America.* New Haven: Yale University Press.

Baldwin, J. A. (1985). Psychological aspects of European cosmology in American society. *The Western Journal of Black Studies, 9*(4), 216–223.

Baldwin, J. A. (1991). African psychology and Black personality testing. In A. G. Hilliard (Ed.), *Testing African-American students* (pp. 56–80). Morriston, NJ: Aaron Press.

Baptiste, D. A. (1990). The treatment of adolescents and their families in cultural transition: Issues and recommendations. *Contemporary Family Therapy, 12*(1), 3–22.

Booth, W. (1993, May 19). Dade county repeals ordinance declaring English official language. *The Washington Post,* p. A3.

Boykin, A. W. (1983). The academic performance of Afro-American children. In J. T. Spence (Ed.), *Achievement and achievement motives* (pp. 322–371). San Francisco: Freeman.

Boykin, A. W. (1986). The triple quandary and the schooling of Afro-American children. In U. Neisser (Ed.), *The school achievement of minority children* (pp. 57–88). Hillsdale, NJ: Erlbaum Press.

Brown, D. (1981). *Bury my heart at wounded knee.* New York: Washington Square Press.

Brown, D. L. (1994, September 14). African principles turn troubled women into "Queens." *The Washington Post*, pp. B1, B3.

Carter, R. T., & Helms, J. E. (1983). The Intercultural Values Inventory (ICV). *Test & Microfiche Collection*. Princeton, NJ: Educational Testing Service.

Chance, N. (1965). Acculturation, self-identification, and adjustment. *American Anthropologist, 67,* 372–393.

Chin, J. L., De La Cancela, V., & Jenkins, Y. M. (1993). *Diversity in psychotherapy: The politics of race, ethnicity, and gender.* Westport, CT: Praeger.

Comas-Diaz, L. (1992). Counseling Hispanics. In D. R. Atkinson, G. Morten, & D. W. Sue (Eds.), *Counseling American minorities: A cross-cultural perspective* (4th ed.). Dubuque, IA: Wm. C. Brown.

Cross, W. E., Jr., Parham, T. A., & Helms, J. E. (1991). The stages of Black identity development: Nigrescence models. In R. L. Jones (Ed.), *Black Psychology* (pp. 319–338). Berkeley, CA: Cobb & Henry Publishers.

Ekman, P., Friesen, W. V., & Ellsworth, P. (1972). *Emotion in the human face.* New York: Pergamon.

Fouad, N. A. (1994). Career assessment with Latinos/Hispanics. *Journal of Career Assessment, 2,* 226–239.

Gordon, M. M. (1964). *Assimilation in American life.* New York: Oxford University Press.

Helms, J. E. (Ed.) (1990). *Black and White racial identity: Theory, research, and practice.* Westport, CT: Greenwood Press.

Helms, J. E. (1992). Why is there no study of cultural equivalence in standardized cognitive ability testing? *American Psychologist, 47,* 1083–1101.

Helms, J. E. (1994a). How multiculturalism obscures racial factors in the therapy process: Comment on Ridley et al. (1994), Sodowsky et al. (1994), Ottavi et al. (1994), & Thompson et al. (1994). *Journal of Counseling Psychology, 41,* 162–165.

Helms, J. E. (1994b, October 21). Mentoring African American youth to preserve their culture and history in potentially hostile environments. Paper presented at the United Negro College Fund/Andrew W. Mellon Conference on Mentoring, Memphis, TN.

Helms, J. E. (1996). Toward a methodology for measuring and assessing "racial" as distinguished from "ethnic" identity. In G. R. Sodowsky & J. C. Impara (Eds.), *Multicultural assessment in counseling and clinical psychology* (143–192). Lincoln, NE: Buros Institute of Mental Measurements.

Hofstede, G. (1980). *Culture's consequences: International differences in work-related values.* Beverly Hills, CA: Sage Publications.

Hofstede, G. (1983). Dimensions of national cultures in fifty countries and three regions. In J. Deregowski, S. Dzuirawiec, & R. Annis (Eds.), *Explications in Cross-Cultural Psychology* (pp. 335–355). Lisse, Netherlands: Swets and Zeitlinger.

Ivey, A. E., & Ivey, M. B. (1993). *Counseling and psychotherapy: A multicultural perspective.* Boston: Allyn and Bacon.

Jackson, S. L. (1993). *An exploration of the relationships between African self-consciousness, Africentric belief systems, and racial identity attitudes in a college sample.* Unpublished paper, University of Maryland, College Park, MD.

Katz, J. (1985). The sociopolitical nature of counseling. *The Counseling Psychologist, 13,* 615–624.

Kitano, H. H. (1982). Mental health in the Japanese American community. In E. E. Jones & S. J. Korchin (Eds.), *Minority Mental Health* (pp. 149–164). NY: Praeger Publications.

Kluckhohn, F. R., & Strodtbeck, F. L. (1961). *Variations in value-orientations.* Evanston, IL: Row, Peterson.

Landrine, H., & Klonoff, E. A. (1994). The African American Acculturation Scale. *The Journal of Black Psychology, 20,* 104–127.

Landrum, J., & Batts, V. A. (1985). *Internalized racial oppression.* Unpublished working paper. Cited in J. Landrum-Brown, Black mental health and racial oppression. In D. S. Ruiz (Ed.), *Handbook of mental health and mental disorder among Black Americans* (pp. 113–132). New York: Greenwood Press.

Lee, E. (1989). Assessment and treatment of Chinese American immigrant families. *Journal of Psychotherapy and the Family, 6*(1–2), 99–122.

Locust, C. (1990). Wounding the spirit: Discrimination and traditional American Indian belief systems. In G. E. Thomas (Ed.), *U. S. Race Relations* (pp. 219–232). New York: Hemisphere Publishing.

Lowery, L. (1983). Bridging a culture in counseling. *Journal of Rehabilitation Counseling, 14,* 69–73.

Marin, G. (1994). The experience of being a Hispanic in the United States. In W. J. Lonner & R. Malpass (Eds.), *Psychology and Culture* (pp. 23–27). Boston: Allyn and Bacon.

Marin, G., & Marin, B. V. (1991). Research with Hispanic populations. *Applied Social Research Methods Series.* Newbury Park, CA: Sage Publications.

Matsumoto, D. (1993). Ethnic differences in affect intensity, emotion judgments, display rule attitudes, and self-reported emotional expression in an American sample. *Motivation and Emotion, 17,* 107–123.

Matsumoto, D. (1994). *People: Psychology from a cultural perspective.* Monterey, CA: Brooks/Cole.

McClain, L. (1983, July 24). How Chicago taught me to hate whites. *Washington Post, Section C,* 1,2.

McLemore, S. D. (1983). *Racial and ethnic relations in America.* Boston: Allyn and Bacon.

Minton, L. (1994, July 3). Fresh voices: 'I don't feel like I'm a part of America.' *Parade Magazine,* p. 12.

Nelson, J. (1993). *Volunteer slavery: My authentic Negro experience.* Chicago: Noble Press.

Nickerson, K. J., Helms, J. E., & Terrell, F. (1994). Cultural mistrust, opinions about mental illness, and Black students' attitudes toward seeking psychological help from White counselors. *Journal of Counseling Psychology, 41,* 378–385.

Pannu, R. (1994). Being true to the self: A cultural perspective on Kohut's theory of self psychology. Unpublished paper. Available from the Psychology Department, University of Maryland, College Park, MD.

Park, R. E. (1950). *Race and culture.* New York: Free Press.

Reid, I. S. (1978). Health issues facing Black women. In *Women's Research Program Educational Equity Group: Volume 2 Research Papers* (pp. 203–224). Washington, DC: U. S. Department of Health, Education and Welfare.

Shuffleton, F. (1993). *A mixed race: Ethnicity in early America.* New York: Oxford University Press.

Smith, P. B., & Bond, M. H. (1993). *Social psychology across cultures: Analysis and perspectives.* Boston: Allyn and Bacon.

Stewart, E. C. (1972). *American cultural patterns: A cross cultural perspective.* Chicago: Intercultural Press.

Sue, D. W., & Sue, S. (1990). *Counseling the culturally different.* New York: John Wiley and Sons.

Sue, S., & Sue, D. W. (1971). Chinese-American personality and mental health. *Amerasia Journal, 1,* 36–49.

Szapocznik, J., Scopetta, M. A., Kurtines, W., & Aranalde, M. D. (1978). Theory and measurement of acculturation. *Inter-American Journal of Psychology, 12,* 113–130.

Terrell, F., & Terrell, S. L. (1981). An inventory to measure cultural mistrust among Blacks. *Western Journal of Black Studies, 3,* 180–185.

Triandis, H. C. (1994). *Culture and Social Behavior.* New York: McGraw Hill.

Trimble, J. E. (1981). Value differentials and their importance in counseling American Indians. In P. B. Pedersen, J. G. Draguns, W. J. Lonner, & J. E. Trimble (Eds.), *Counseling Across Cultures* (pp. 203–226). Honolulu, HI: East-West Center.

Wilson, T. P. (1992). Blood quantum: Native American mixed bloods. In M. P. P. Root (Ed.), *Racially mixed people in America* (pp. 108–125). Newbury Park, CA: Sage Publications.

Yamamoto, J., Silva, J. A., Justice, L. R., Chang, C. Y., & Leong, G. B. (1993). In A. C. Gaw (Ed.), *Culture, ethnicity, and mental illness* (pp. 101–124). Washington, DC: American Psychiatric Press.

PART TWO

The Process

CHAPTER

8

The Therapy Process: Theoretical Orientations

Just as therapists are socialized by their life experiences to adopt certain cultural and racial perspectives, they are also socialized to adopt certain theoretical orientations by their therapist training experiences. Furthermore, just as the therapist's racial and cultural perspectives shape her or his perceptions and conceptualizations of her or his clients' dynamics, a therapist's theoretical orientation shapes her or his conceptualization of the dynamics of the therapy process, from beginning to end. In other words, the therapist's conceptualizations of (a) desirable therapeutic goals or outcomes, (b) assessment procedures, and (c) therapy principles or interventions are governed by a particular theoretical perspective, usually the one(s) that dominated in her or his professional training environments.

Some therapists contend that specific theoretical perspectives are more or less appropriate for ALANA clients or clients from collectivistic cultures than for White clients. For example, psychoanalytic therapy traditionally has been considered an inappropriate therapy modality for Black clients and lower socioeconomic status clients (of unspecified race), allegedly because they are incapable of the insight required by psychoanalytic approaches (see Lerner, 1972, for another view). Client-centered therapy has been advocated for traditional Japanese clients because of the indirectness of its interventions (Hayashi, Kuno, Osawa, & Shimizu, 1992), but opposed for Latino/Latina clients for the same reason (Valdes, 1983). Cognitive and behavioral approaches have been recommended for Black American clients because of the approaches' emphasis on structure, and for all clients without regard to racial, cultural, or socioeconomic conditions (see Casas, 1988, for a critique).

For the most part, prior recommendations and admonitions concerning which interventions are appropriate for clients of which culture or socioracial group have been speculative rather than empirically based. Sue, Zane, and Young (1994) note that empirical investigations specifically focused on examining the nature of the therapy process involving cultural or socioracial groups are extremely rare. A consequence of the lack of race- and culture-specific analyses of the therapy process is that therapists who intend to use race and cultural dynamics in their work usually must rely on clinical experience and intuition as the basis of their interventions without very much guidance as to how to do so effectively.

In this chapter, we discuss some ways in which three traditional Western theoretical perspectives— psychodynamic, client or person-centered, and cognitive-behavioral—

can be modified to be more sensitive to racial and cultural dynamics in the therapy process than they typically are. We contend that it is possible to use most of the contemporary theoretical perspectives to work with clients of various racial and cultural origins. However, the therapist must remember to compensate for the theories' lack of attention to cultural or racial dynamics as potential aspects of the therapy process at every phase, including her or his conceptualization of therapy goals, assessment, and selection of therapy interventions.

Psychodynamic Therapy

Psychodynamic is the name for a variety of theoretical perspectives in which clients' change or growth is conceptualized as occurring from the inside to the outside. That is, the client is hypothesized to change by means of overcoming those internal, unconscious personality characteristics (needs, instincts, drives, motivations, etc.) that impede effective functioning in her or his everyday life. Thus, psychodynamic therapy is an individualistically focused orientation. Psychoanalysis, as originated by Sigmund Freud, was the first version of psychodynamic therapy, and, in our opinion, continues to be the most influential of the genre. Therefore, our cultural critique of psychodynamic therapy focuses primarily on Freud's version of psychodynamic therapy, but should have implications for those developed by other psychodynamic theorists as well.

Goals of Therapy

Overview.   The primary goal of psychodynamic psychotherapy is to promote major character or personality changes in the client. Personality reconstruction is accomplished by helping the client to become aware of unconscious needs and motives derived from early childhood. The therapist helps the client to uncover unconscious thoughts, feelings, and behaviors, and to relive early childhood memories and experiences. Thus, the client's current presenting problems become the context in which her or his uncovered experiences are discussed, interpreted, and analyzed.

In focusing on past experiences, the therapist's primary function is to assist the client in examining the connections between traumatic situations and his or her unresolved past and present feelings about these situations. To encourage the requisite self-examination, the therapist initially explores the client's relationship with his or her parents. Emphasis is given to the client's view of the parent of the same gender as a source of identification for the client, and the parent of the opposite gender as a source for the client's view of current relationships with significant others of the opposite gender.

In addition, a major focus of therapy includes the client's reactions toward and expectations of the therapist because such reactions are thought to symbolize unresolved material from earlier phases in the client's life, particularly early childhood. The therapist examines ways in which the client's reactions to the therapist are similar to the client's reactions to the client's parent of the same gender. These metaphorical or displaced reactions are assumed to symbolize the client's initial interpersonal conflicts, and is referred to as "transference." Through the evolution of the transferential relationship, it is possible for the therapist to recognize patterns that connect the client's childhood behavior and current struggles, and assist the client in becoming aware of them. That is, the therapist assists in bringing repetitive patterns into the client's awareness or conscious. Through this ongoing process of revealing and analyzing unconscious material, the therapist gradually aids the client in achieving self-understanding, integrating the various parts of the client's self, and developing an independent, unconflicted identity.

Racial and Cultural Considerations.   From our brief overview of the goals of psychodynamic therapy, it might be obvious that there are several aspects of goal formulation in which the therapist needs to be open to the possibility that the realities of the clients' racial and/or cultural socialization may require alternate interpretations of her or his unconscious or recalled experiences. As they interpret the client's past, therapists who consider the past an important source of information must be careful to avoid superimposing their own cultural, racial, and socioeconomic biases on their interpretations of the client's experiences. Insight 8.1 provides an example of such misinterpretations.

Especially where early childhood experiences are concerned, it is important for the therapist to remember that experiences that may sound like aberrations to the

---

INSIGHT 8.1

Tashi Enters Psychotherapy

Negro women, said the doctor, are considered the most difficult of all people to be effectively analyzed. Do you know why?

Since I was not a Negro woman I hesitated before hazarding an answer. I felt negated by the realization that even my psychiatrist could not see I was African. That to him all black people were Negroes.

I had been coming to see him now for several months. Some days I talked; some days I did not. There was a primary school across the street from his office. I would listen to the faint sound of the children playing and often forget where I was, forget why I was there.

He'd been taken aback by the fact that I had only one child. He thought this was unusual for a colored woman, married or unmarried. Your people like lots of kids, he allowed.

But how could I talk to this arranger of my lost children? And of how they were lost? One was left speechless by all such a person couldn't know.

Negro women, the doctor says into my silence, can never be analyzed effectively because they can never bring themselves to blame their mothers.

Blame them for what? I asked.

Blame them for anything, said he.

It is quite a new thought. And, surprisingly, sets off a kind of explosion in the soft, dense cotton wool of my mind.

But I do not say anything.

An excerpt from Walker (1992).

therapist may be normal for the client in the racial or cultural environment in which he or she was socialized. Clients who were raised in environments in which they were subjected to environmental oppression because they were members of particular groups, as well as clients who were raised in dominating environments, may recall experiences of intimidation that might sound fictional at best on first hearing. Still others may recall as factual experiences events that are, in actuality, misinterpretations of cultural or racial or socioeconomic dynamics that were occurring at the time of the person's early childhood. Moreover, the therapist must recognize that it is quite plausible that external factors related to racism, ethnocentrism, sexism, and classism may contribute to clients' current presenting problems as well as to their previous development.

The therapist's conceptualization of trauma is another area in which the therapist might expect racial or cultural variations. Some aspects of a client's life that might be considered traumatic in traditional Anglo culture may not be considered as such in some immigrant cultures or collectivistic cultures within the United States. Conversely, some experiences that might not be considered to be indicative of trauma in individualistic culture in the United States might be so considered in other types of cultures. For example, in the former category might be included some childrearing practices, traditional cures, and rites of passage (e.g., physical punishment, coining, and female genital mutilation). Examples of individualistic practices that collectivistic cultures might find peculiar are early childhood weaning and toilet training, separate beds for parents and children, separate rooms for household members, and burying one's dead underground.

As the therapist attempts to identify the nature of the client's particular trauma, he or she must continuously ask himself or herself whether a particular experience is perceived as traumatic in the environment from which the client comes. Moreover, the therapist must be aware that it is not necessarily the objective event that is or is not traumatic, but rather the client's and her or his environment's reaction to the event.

Psychodynamic theory ordinarily assigns considerable responsibility to the parents (especially the mother) for the client's maladaptive personality development. In such formulations, the family is generally conceptualized as a nuclear family in which the father is the head and breadwinner and the wife is subordinate and the caregiver. Deviations from this structure are assumed to be a major cause of the client's problems.

However, as we mentioned in earlier chapters, family and parenting may be defined differently in collectivistic cultures. It is not unusual, for example, for the parent-child bond to supercede the spousal bond in importance. Thus, parents may lavish attention on their (usually male) children because they are expected eventually to assume the responsibility for the family's material and economic well-being. Moreover, in cultures in which extended families are normative, the parenting roles may be dispersed across several adults (e.g., aunts, uncles, grandparents, god parents, fictive or "play" relatives), whose role within the family defines their responsibility.

Therefore, in general it is important for the therapist to acquire knowledge of the various types of families that exist in this society. Moreover, by understanding (or at least being able to ask appropriate questions about) the racial and cultural dynamics inherent in the familial roles of parents and other relatives, relationships between children and parents, and the family system and the larger society, the therapist can avoid unduly pathologizing the client.

It is important for the therapist to be able to assist clients from collectivistic cultures to develop an understanding of themselves within the context of their own social communities as well as the larger society. However, the therapist should not expect the client to know automatically that her or his problems may be due to incongruence of some sort between the dominant culture and her or his own culture. Therefore, the culturally and racially sensitive therapist may find herself or himself educating the client about racial or cultural dynamics that the client "should" already have known about. Nevertheless, as we mentioned in previous chapters, immigrants to this country often must learn the rules of racism and ethnocentrism and how such rules pertain to them; whereas native-born ALANA clients may have long histories of attempting to be assimilated into the dominant group, and consequently, may have become oblivious to the impact of such rules on their group and on themselves as members of their group.

Also, if clients from racially subjugated groups are also from collectivistic cultures, then the therapist should entertain the possibility that they were raised to conceptualize themselves as irretrievably connected to others in their (especially racial) group, even if their objective circumstances appear to distinguish them from the average member of their group. In such instances, comments intended to be laudatory (e.g., "I think your success shows that racism can't stop a person if he or she works hard," "You're a credit to your race, if more of your people were like you.". . .) can in fact be quite insulting to the client. Therefore, the therapist should develop the habit of exploring the costs and benefits of racial integration to the client rather than assuming that he or she already knows its impact.

Furthermore, if the client is collectivistic with respect to cultural dynamics and expresses herself or himself in that manner, the therapist should be able to interpret the relevant contrasting dimensions of the individualistic culture for the client. When the therapist serves as an interpreter, it is important to consider where the client's and the dominant culture's values and beliefs might be in conflict. For example, how does one live in harmony or cooperatively with one's environment if most other people in the environment in which the client is expected to function advocate mastery and competition?

With respect to the goal of assisting the client in developing an integrated autonomous identity, the therapist must make sure that the client considers that an appropriate goal as well. It is important for the therapist not to assume that a strongly individualistic personality is necessarily best for everyone. Rather the matter of who the client should be at the end of therapy must be mutually decided by taking into consideration the conditions of the racial and cultural environment(s) in which he or she intends to function.

In addition to avoiding the imposition of her or his racial or cultural biases on the client, the therapist must always be aware of herself or himself as a potential transferential symbol for the client. After all, based on the therapist's appearance, the client will decide to which racial group the therapist belongs. More than likely, the client will also make assumptions about other characteristics of the therapist (including socioeconomic status, racial attitudes, cultural traditions) based on the therapist's "racial" appearance.

Therefore, the therapist should not ignore the client's perceptions of the therapist's race and culture as aspects of the transferential relationship. It may be difficult for the client to develop transference related to parents (however "parents" are defined) if racial transference develops as an overriding concern. Under such circumstances, the therapist may come to symbolize whatever past traumatic experiences or socialization—personal or vicarious—that the client or the client's salient identity groups have had with members of the therapist's racial or cultural group(s). Sometimes it is necessary to work through this racial-cultural transference before the more mundane issue of parental transference can even be expected to occur.

Assessment

In the psychodynamic perspective, the primary data for the assessment process are the client's defensive system and her or his manner of resolving developmental conflict across selected portions of the lifespan. Thus, adequate assessment involves mapping the client's particular dimensions with respect to these domains.

Defense Mechanisms

During the initial course of therapy, the therapist identifies and diagnoses the client's problems and major defense mechanisms. According to Corey (1985), Freud identified several ego defenses that individuals use to protect themselves from anxiety-provoking experiences. These are described in Table 8.1. Because not all clients use the same set of defenses, the therapist's task is to assess the particular defenses typically used by the client to deal with anxiety. The therapist accomplishes this task by eliciting subject matter from the client that he or she typically avoids.

The therapist helps the client to understand his or her defenses by interpreting the purpose that the defenses served during the client's childhood. The therapist and client will also explore ways in which the defenses may be disruptive in the client's current life.

The various schools of psychodynamic therapy each propose some usually stage-wise developmental sequence, the successful resolution of which is required for healthy personality development. The characterizations of these developmental entities provide a basis for assessing normal and abnormal personal and social functioning, the satisfaction or frustration of critical needs, the source of faulty personality development and adjustment problems, and healthy and unhealthy uses of defenses (Corey, 1985).

Racial and Cultural Considerations

When assessing defenses as used by clients of various socioracial and cultural groups, it is important for the therapist to recognize that defenses may serve different

TABLE 8.1   Description and Racial and Cultural Examples of Freud's Defense Mechanisms

Description of Defense Mechanism

Repression—the automatic or not-conscious pushing from awareness impulses that could have problematic consequences if they were revealed.
Example: A VREG person who hates White people might be totally unaware of such feelings.

Denial—the person's refusal to perceive that an unpleasant external event is real.
Example: White people's refusal to believe that racism still exists.

Reaction Formation—converting an undesirable impulse into its opposite.
Example: A VREG person who hates her or his racist employer, but treats her or him with exaggerated politeness and kindness.

Projection—a person attributes his or her own undesirable characteristics to others.
Example: A person who hates members of another racial group insists that they hate him or her instead.

Displacement—the use of a "safe" outlet to express one's threatening impulses rather than the person or object who originally triggered the impulses.
Example: Expressing one's anger at one's employer for being fired by lynching or otherwise hurting someone of another racial group.

Rationalization—the justification of one's behavior through use of plausible but inaccurate explanations.
Example: A White pre-med applicant with good grades and average test scores concludes that he or she was not admitted because of affirmative action.

Sublimation—an acceptable impulse or form of behavior is substituted for an unacceptable impulse.
Example: A VREG person expresses his or her anger at society by becoming a youth worker rather than a gang member.

Regression—reemergence of immature or earlier forms of coping with life stress.
Example: Using racial epithets (name-calling) to express one's anger.

Identification—alleviating anxiety by taking on the characteristics of someone of importance in one's life.
Example: Father-absent boys sometimes act like the prominent men or older boys in their communities, regardless of their occupations or social status.

Compensation—engaging in actions intended to make up for real or imagined defects.
Example: Suntanning to acquire skin color; wearing makeup that is much lighter than one's own skin color.

Undoing—performing some compensatory action to make up for a previous undesirable behavior or impulse.
Example: Attending church or paying homage to a deity to make up for a previous action.

purposes for such individuals, depending on their personal or group status in the society as well as the quality of their life experiences. Sometimes defenses that might be maladaptive for a White middle-to-upper class client may be necessary for the psychological and physical survival of a Person of Color. For example, several authors use the (unfortunately named) construct of "cultural paranoia" to describe the suspiciousness of White people that many African American people developed as an adaptive response to White racism. When African American clients exhibit this form of adaptive reticence in their interactions with White therapists, it is often mistakenly interpreted as general passivity and inhibition (Ridley, 1984).

Also, it is possible that clients' normal behavioral styles may be misread and misinterpreted by therapists from other cultural groups. For example, Tafoya (1989) warns that the traditional Native American cultural expression of anger and frustration is often mistaken for passivity and resistance. However, if the therapist is aware that such emotions are not overtly expressed in traditional Native cultures for fear of harming someone else's spirit (see Chapter 7), then he or she might interpret and treat the client's ostensibly "passive" behavior differently.

Therefore, the therapist must use the client's (especially racial) historical and cultural socialization experiences as a basis for the evaluation of the client's defense mechanisms. Moreover, the client's group's migratory or immigration experiences might be relevant influences on the composition or expression of the client's defensive system, particularly if these experiences were not positive and/or voluntary.

However, it may be difficult to differentiate the client's typical defense mechanisms from her or his idiosyncratic reactions to the therapist and the therapy process. Especially if the therapist and client are of different socioracial groups, and the groups have a history of intergroup conflict or tension, then the client may be reluctant to reveal intimate aspects of herself or himself to the therapist. Sometimes this reluctance is fueled by the client's belief that the therapist is not worthy enough to merit such personal information, but sometimes it is also fueled by a fear of how the therapist will use such a "weapon" against the client. Several therapists have noted that clients frequently withhold racial and cultural information about themselves because they are afraid that the therapist will merely use it to affirm preexisting stereotypes about them and/or their groups (Lau, 1984; Boyd-Franklin, 1989).

Therefore, the therapist must be willing to elicit the client's own cultural interpretations of her or his behavior. That is, the therapist may make the client aware of certain observable patterns or defenses and their interpretation from the therapist's racial and cultural perspective. However, then the therapist must be sensitive to the client's cues ("Yes, but . . . ," "Am I doing this right?," "Man, you just don't understand.") that he or she is not accepting the therapist's interpretations. Sometimes clients use passive resistance to communicate to the therapist that he or she does not understand the racial necessity or the cultural meaning of the client's defenses.

In fact, since the term *defense mechanisms* is generally used to imply internal strategies used to protect oneself from essentially self-induced anxiety, it may not be appropriate to think of client's racial and cultural behavioral styles as defense mechanisms per se. Rather if the style is common to many members of the person's group, it is probably best to think of it as a cultural or racial norm that may have served some adaptive function for the group, although it may or may not be presently serving the same function for the client.

Developmental Sequences

Freud originally hypothesized that an individual's personality is shaped by successful progression through "psychosexual" stages, by which he means movement of "libido" or life energy from one area of the body (erotogenic zone) to another. The manner in which the person's needs are (or are not) fulfilled by her or his parents at each stage of the progression determines the content of her or his personality structure and characteristics.

Thus, Freud proposed the following sequence (and approximate age of onset) of psychosexual stages: (a) *oral* (birth)—the infant obtains pleasure and gratification from feeding and sucking the mother's breast; (b) *anal* (age two)—the child obtains pleasure and gratification from expulsion and retention of feces and from her or his parents' pride in the child's mastery of her or his bowels; (c) *phallic* (age three years)—the child finds pleasure and gratification of her or his needs in her or his genitals, and develops appropriate sex-role characteristics if he or she is able to resolve successfully the consequential sexual fears, anger, rivalries, and anxieties the child feels toward her or his parents; (d) *latency* (age six years)—the child's overt expression of sexuality enters a period of dormancy and trauma and/or material associated with previous stages is repressed, although it will exert influence on the individual's behavior and personality; and (e) *genital* (puberty)—the child's sexuality reawakens and is probably directed toward a member of the opposite sex.

Although it may not be evident from our brief synopsis, Freud's perspective does acknowledge nominal interactions between the person and her or his environment as being critical aspects of the person's developmental maturation. However, most of the person's personality development is actually driven by forces within the person rather than from her or his interpersonal environment.

Erikson (1959) attempted to integrate the person's social context more fully into her or his lifespan developmental process. Thus, he proposed a stagewise developmental cycle. During the cycle, the individual's personality is thought to develop in concert with his or her progressively developing readiness to interact with society. Society, in turn, defines the person's identity for her or him by its manner of reacting to the person.

Thus, Erikson's "psychosocial" stages of development (briefly defined) are as follows: (a) *basic trust vs. mistrust* (infancy)—if successfully resolved, the person learns to trust her or his primary provider(s) (usually parents) and to view the social world as safe and predictable; (b) *autonomy vs. shame and doubt* (early childhood)—capacity to function independently, make one's own choices, and to practice self-control; (c) *initiative vs. guilt* (pre-school age)—being able to perform a task from beginning to end for the pleasure of doing so (i.e., develop a "doing" value orientation); (d) *industry vs. inferiority* (school age)—learning to become an effective worker and contributor to society; (e) *identity vs. role confusion* (adolescence)—development of a consistent and predictable self-concept and self-presentational style; (f) *intimacy vs. isolation* (young adulthood)—development of the capacity to engage in committed, responsible, and moral relationships with others; (g) *generativity vs. stagnation* (middle adulthood)—capacity to reflect on one's life and pass on life's lessons to the next generation; (h) *ego integrity vs. despair* (maturity)—the integration of prior stages to form a self that is confident and comfortable with one's own way of being.

Although we have described only the positive resolutions of the bipolar life crises that Erikson contended must be resolved during a person's lifetime, it is fairly clear that his perspective intends to specify the social roles and functions (i.e., outcomes) that characterize completion of a successful maturation process. Also, as we have shown in parentheses, typically Erikson's stages are associated with particular ages or phases of the lifespan. Thus, not only should a person mature by means of the proposed process, but he or she should do so within a prescribed time frame.

More contemporary psychodynamic theories such as self psychology (e.g., Kohut, 1971) and object-relations theory also propose predictable developmental stages or life experiences that are said to characterize the person's sequential differentiation of themselves from others (Corey, 1985). Pannu (1994) has discussed the limitations of such perspectives with respect to cultural dynamics where members of collectivistic cultures are concerned.

Regardless of their specific orientation, psychodynamic therapists attempt to assess some aspect of the client's psychosexual or psychosocial development. His or her particular theoretical framework defines for the psychodynamic therapist which criteria (e.g., developmental tasks) are to be used for assessing the client. From this ongoing assessment, the therapist infers the client's unresolved childhood issues, which then become material for modification through therapy.

Racial and Cultural Considerations

The sequential conceptualizations of personality development that characterize psychodynamic theories are lacking in cultural and racial responsivity in at least three ways. First, they define the content of stages in a manner that may have meaning within traditional individualistic culture, but may not be very meaningful within the context of collectivistic cultures. Second, they propose an invariant age-appropriate sequence of development. Finally, given the presumed importance of familial (or at least parental) socialization or childrearing practices on the person's development, very little is said explicitly in psychodynamic theory about the characteristics of the family. It is almost as though the family is assumed to be defined in the same manner for everyone.

With respect to the first two points, some evidence exists to the effect that many cultures within and outside the United States do not necessarily traverse the lifespan in the same manner as the normative White American. For example, Triandis (1994) reports that in some African cultures children are weaned from their mothers' breasts at age 36 months as compared to six months in Anglo-American culture. Some of our traditional Chinese and West Indian graduate students have informed us that toilet training is not the major source of distress in their cultures as it is in White culture—children will learn to master their bodily functions when they are ready. On the other hand, some of our African American colleagues with children express amazement at how long it takes White children to develop bowel mastery relative to their own children.

We admit that much of our ethnographic observation is based on hearsay and our observers might have been biased in one way or another. However, even if only a small portion of our second-hand information is accurate, then it suggests that the content of a person's character might be defined differently across cultures. It also suggests that what is considered to be fulfillment of age-appropriate developmental tasks or roles may occur at different ages in some cultures or might never occur in other cultures if it serves no pragmatic purpose.

Concerning cultural and racial variations in familial roles and childrearing practices, Lau (1984) points out that the (White) British or Western family structure is often used as the prototype for families from other cultural or racial groups. In the "standard" families, parents (i.e., a mother and father) are the authority figures who role-model the appropriate behavior for their offspring; the generations are differentiated from one another, and typically grandparents do not reside in the same household; and siblings' rank relative to one another is equivalent.

The family structure that Lau describes seems to be implicit in psychodynamic formulations of the family, to the extent that it is described at all. Vital aspects of the individual's personality (including sex-role identification, capacity to form intimate relationships, particular personality traits) depend on the quality of interplay between a traditional mother and father.

However, various authors contend that different family structures exist within the United States and are quite effective in promoting the development of mentally healthy people as long as the cultural integrity of the concerned group is not violated. According to Tafoya (1989), traditional Native American grandparents parent their grandchildren while the children's parents are involved in the age-appropriate tasks of breadwinning and building a home. Both Tafoya with respect to Native American culture and Boyd-Franklin (1989) with respect to African American culture describe multigenerational family structures, and also suggest that it is not unusual for children to move in with a relative other than their parents to maintain family harmony or for economic reasons.

Also, Boyd-Franklin notes that children sometimes serve a parenting role to their siblings in African American families, and apparently learn independence and responsibility from doing so. Lau and Boyd-Franklin each contend that single-parent (typically female) headed households in African American and West Indian families are not atypical or dysfunctional when they occur within the context of the extended family structure that is typical of these ethnic groups. Furthermore, traditional Asian/Pacific Islander and Latina/Latino Americans apparently are not expected to differentiate from or leave their families, and may consider their parents a lifetime responsibility (Baptiste, 1990; Lau, 1984). Exercise 8.1 illustrates one family value said to typify traditional Asian American families.

In short, a variety of family structures exist among the various cultural groups within the United States. Therefore, perhaps it is sufficient to say that the therapist who assumes that theoretical formulations based on the traditional Anglo-American

EXERCISE **8.1**

Understanding Cultural Dynamics

Consider the following tabloid: [A] hungry, toothless old mother [is] lying prone and weak on the ground, a crying baby [is lying beside her], and a young nursing mother, breasts dripping with milk [kneels between them]" (Lau, 1984, p. 93).

Before reading on, answer the following questions from *your* cultural perspective:

1. Assuming that she can only feed one of the two, which person should the young mother feed?
2. What rule did you use to make your decision?

Answer: If you answered "old mother," then you were probably socialized in an hierarchical culture of some sort. If your reason for responding as you did is some version of "responsibility to one's parents transcends responsibilities towards spouse and children" (Lau, 1984, p. 93), then you understand the cultural principle of "filial piety."

If you chose the baby, then take this opportunity to think about other ways in which your cultural socialization may have differed from that of someone raised in a collectivistic culture.

---

family structure necessarily do (or do not) pertain to all clients, risks damaging those clients for whom the model is inappropriate.

Therapy Interventions

When using a psychodynamic perspective to treat clients, the therapist maintains a relatively nonstructured approach to therapy, relying heavily on the client to initiate the process of verbally recounting present-day concerns and historical events. Initially, the therapist deals with the client's resistance to the process of therapy. The client may be ambivalent about becoming aware of his or her unconscious motives or needs, for fear that they will again not be fulfilled. Thus, even though the client may have entered therapy voluntarily, the therapist's interventions are based on the assumption that the client will not easily surrender his or her defenses as he or she interacts with the therapist.

A basic technique for surmounting the client's defenses is to interpret the client's avoidance patterns so that the client can work through the barriers or resistances that are impeding the therapy process. Thus, the therapist helps the client to gain insight, self-explore, and work through his or her resistances. Initially, the therapist deals with the client's resistance by providing interpretations of relevant issues that are the least threatening to the client.

Throughout the process, the therapist intentionally fosters the development of a transference reaction by maintaining as much mystery about his or her personal life as possible. This "blank-screen" demeanor ensures that the client's reactions within the process are based on past relationships rather than a real relationship with the therapist. As the process progresses, the client gradually grows frustrated with the therapist for not giving enough (that is, gratifying the client's needs) in the relationship. The client may become irritated because the therapist does not share information about her or his personal life with the client. Furthermore, the therapist intentionally does not reassure the client because the therapist is trying to encourage the client's expression of transference.

As the therapist becomes a significant symbolic figure in the client's life, eliciting both positive and negative feelings, the therapist begins to explore the client's reactions to the therapist. Together, the therapist and client examine the ways in which the client's reactions to the therapist are analogous in significant ways to the client's relationship with the parent of the same sex as the therapist.

A deliberate effort is made to assist the client in exploring her or his relationship with the client's same-sex parent. The focus of this exploration is the client's childhood and present feelings toward that parent. During the therapy process, the therapist and client explore parallels between the client's past and present ways of dealing with the parental relationship, and consequently, other people (such as the therapist) who arouse feelings associated with that relationship.

The therapist helps the client to work through the patterns that he or she experienced with significant others in his or her past as these feelings are expressed toward the therapist. By repeated interpretations of the client's behaviors and feelings, and by assisting the client in overcoming his or her resistance, the therapist helps the client to resolve old problematic relationship patterns. Through the facilitation and recollection of past events and insight, the therapist helps the client to see patterns from the past and the continuity of these patterns in the client's current life. When the client realizes how the past is still operating, personality change is possible, and the client is open to new options in his or her life.

Racial and Cultural Considerations

The possibility of racial and cultural impasses exists in slightly different forms in virtually every aspect of the therapy process as described by psychodynamic theorists. However, the general theme that runs through most of our subsequent comments is that we think that psychodynamic theorists' disregard of the racial and cultural contexts of potential clients is unwise.

Therapist's Stance.   When the therapist uses a passive, relatively unstructured stance or approach to helping the client, there are several places where a client's cooperative and respectful participation in the process as he or she understands it might be misconstrued as avoidance or resistance. Proceeding via an unstructured style assumes that from the beginning, the client knows that he or she is expected to begin telling his or her story, and that the telling of the story in and of itself will somehow help the client to solve his or her problems.

However, as we mentioned in Chapter 7 with regard to members of collectivistic cultures, a passive, nonresponsive therapist might be unwittingly forcing the collectivistic client to violate several cultural norms. Some that come to our mind are as follows: (a) cooperativeness and/or harmony with one's environment—the person of lower social status (in this case the client) is expected to listen patiently to what the higher status person (the therapist) has to impart in recognition of the fact that the therapist will communicate the relevant healing information when the client is ready to receive it. And readiness is revealed by the client's nonverbal communication that he or she is patiently listening; (b) hierarchical social roles—often it is considered impolite for the person with lesser status to hog the conversational floor or to call attention to herself or himself especially when in the presence of a higher status person such as the therapist (e.g., "Children should be seen and not heard." "The nail that sticks out gets hit."); and (c) the healer's role—the collectivistic client may come with a strongly held expectation that the therapist will take an active role in the client's "cure," and thus, may be confused by the therapist's lack of involvement.

In psychodynamic therapy, the term *resistance* has a connotation that clients are fighting the process of therapy, when in fact they may not be responding according to the therapists' expectations because the therapist and client have different expectations for the process of therapy. What may be interpreted as "defenses" may in actuality be cultural patterns of communicating, such as respect for authority (e.g., "Speak when spoken to." "An empty wagon makes the most noise.").

Also, clients may interpret the therapist's blank screen demeanor differently than the psychodynamic therapist intends. Some clients infer that the therapist is restraining strong negative feelings (such as anger and frustration) about the client, and the client may assume that the therapist is modeling how one is supposed to manage such feelings. For other clients, the therapist's restraint might imply the therapist's lack of involvement or interest in the process and/or the therapist's disrepect or devaluing of the client. In either case, the collectivistic client may seek guidance as to how he or she is expected to behave by observing the therapist's behavior, and by reacting in a complementary fashion according to the rules of the client's culture.

Furthermore, if the therapist and client are of different racial classifications, then their respective internalized histories of domination or subjugation may come to the forefront when the therapist's behavior is perceived as ambiguous. If the histories of the groups from which the client and therapist come have been contentious, then it is reasonable to assume that the client will begin to interpret the therapist's impassivity by means of whatever stereotypes about the therapist's group the client has internalized, and the client will react accordingly. In a like manner, the therapist may use his or her psychodynamic stance to misinterpret the client according to whatever between-group stereotypes the therapist has internalized.

Thus, in interpreting clients' avoidance patterns, it is important to do so in the context of the client's cultural values and sociopolitical defenses. Interpretations should not be directed solely at intrapsychic issues, but the therapist should invite clients to discuss their cultural values regarding talking to others about personal and family problems, and their expectations about how communication should flow when it involves them and an authority figure of the clients' gender. Especially if the interaction is cross-racial, then the therapist should also explore with the client the ways in which the client and people of the client's socioracial group have learned to protect themselves from people of the therapist's socioracial group. Furthermore, the therapist should be prepared to discuss her or his own racial biases. People of Color may be aware of the stereotypes that people in other socioracial groups hold regarding their groups; White people tend to be less aware of stereotypes that members of other groups hold about them. Consequently, clients of any socioracial group may be attempting to protect their socioracial group by not revealing anything about themselves or their families that would reinforce societal stereotyped images.

Therapeutic Alliance.   If a bond is formed in cross-racial therapy, however, the client may have exaggeratedly positive reactions to the therapist because a cross racial therapy bond may be the first significant nurturing experience that the client has had with a member of the therapist's race. As a way of rationalizing the incongruence between the client's stereotypic images of members of the therapist's race and his or her positive perceptions of the therapist, the client may perceive the therapist as a "special" member of that racial group.

Parental Dynamics.   As previously mentioned, when a client exhibits frustrated feelings in response to a therapist's withholding style, it is commonly assumed to signify something about the client's parental dynamics. However, such feelings may have nothing to do with the client's transferential feelings toward his or her parents. Rather they may result from inconsistencies between the client's cultural ways of relating to significant people in his or her life and the "cultural" norms of the psychodynamic therapist. The therapist's distance may be perceived as contrived and the client may terminate prematurely because of the artificiality of the relationship.

Particularly when White therapists are interacting with VREG clients, or White clients are working with VREG therapists, or VREG clients and VREG therapists are receiving therapy from someone from a group other than their own, clients may need to receive enough information and gratification from therapists to warrant their trusting them. Given the various histories of oppressive relationships between Whites and People of Color, many visible racial and ethnic groups have feelings of antipathy toward Whites. However, what is less often acknowledged is the fact that the ongoing between-VREG fights for a share of the small piece of the proverbial societal pie of opportunity allotted to them, may contribute to hostility in cross-racial therapy dyads among People of Color.

It is often the case that once the therapist becomes a special person in a collectivistic client's life, the therapist in effect becomes a member of the client's extended family. If such cultural transference occurs, therapists may not elicit the type of negative feelings that they anticipate because the client may come from a value system in which one's parents or authority figures are revered no matter how they treat the person of lesser status.

Thus, clients from collectivistic cultures may have difficulty expressing any negative emotions or attitudes toward their parents due to cultural values regarding the reverence of parental figures, and also for fear of reinforcing any stereotypical beliefs that the client thinks the therapist might hold toward members of the client's cultural group. In addition to perhaps having their needs unfulfilled by parents, many People of Color have ongoing pain associated with White society's vicarious and direct mistreatment of them. Native Americans and African Americans may be particularly offended by the perceived efforts to infantilize them because their "childlike" status often has been used as justification for the societal discriminatory practices that resulted in severe societal neglect and indifference to their needs.

Person-Centered Therapy

The client- or (more recently) person-centered approach to counseling and psychotherapy was originated by Carl Rogers. It too is a perspective with an individual intrapsychic emphasis. However, much of what the person internalizes results from the quality of her or his interactions with influential (originally familial) figures in her or his life.

Goals of Therapy

The primary goal of person-centered therapy is to assist the client in achieving self-actualization, where *self-actualization* is defined as becoming all that one was intended to be at birth. The therapist facilitates the search for self by providing a safe, accepting, and trusting atmosphere in which the client can explore his or her problems, come to know his or her true self, and as a consequence, enjoy all aspects of her or his life more fully and completely.

Assessment

Person-centered therapy does not involve formal assessment practices. Through listening to what the client says and implies, the therapist attempts to understand how the client experiences herself or himself and to discover any incongruence in who the client is (real self) and who the client would like to become (ideal self).

Therapeutic Procedures

To encourage the client's self-exploration, the therapist assumes a nondirective, attentive listening style as the client leads the in-session discussions. As the client presents his or her problem, the therapist exhibits an attitude of congruence, realness, or genuineness; and unconditional positive regard or acceptance, while communicating accurate empathic understanding of the client. These aspects of the therapist's attitude often collectively are considered to be the *necessary conditions* for therapeutic change (Rogers, 1980).

The therapist exhibits *genuineness* by expressing to the client the feelings and attitudes that the therapist is experiencing with respect to the client. Similarly, *unconditional positive regard* involves the therapist's allowing the client to be and express whatever feelings he or she is experiencing, while the therapist demonstrates total acceptance of the client and the client's worldview. *Empathic understanding* occurs when the therapist listens to the client's spoken and unspoken feelings and the personal meanings the client accords her or his feelings, and accurately reflects back to the client what has been said. Accurate reflection includes not only the client's verbal content and overt expression of feelings, but also the client's essence or manner of being.

In Rogers's (1986) later work, he described another therapist characteristic—transcendence or spirituality. *Transcendence* occurs when the therapist is strongly in touch with his or her inner and intuitive self such that his or her inner spirit seems to connect with the client's inner spirit, which produces a profound growthful and healing energy in the client.

In the *Psychotherapist's Casebook*, Rogers (1986) described this phenomena in his work with one client as follows: "This sensitive empathy is so deep that my intuition takes over at one point and, in a way that seems mysterious, is in touch with a very important part of her with which she has lost contact. At this point we are perhaps in a mutual and reciprocal altered state of consciousness" (207). However, Rogers explains that while simultaneously experiencing such a oneness with a client, the separateness of the client and the therapist is still clearly maintained.

As a result of the client's experiencing of the therapist's expression of the necessary conditions, the client then explores his or her feelings and attitudes at a deeper level and moves forward and takes actions toward living a more self-fulfilling life. In the midst of the safe, accepting, and trusting relationship that the therapist provides, the client is assumed to be capable of identifying and solving his or her own problems. The client will eventually get in touch with his or her true self and become the independent and integrated person that he or she is capable of becoming.

Racial and Cultural Considerations

A primary source of the difficulty involved in using person-centered therapy in a culturally and racially responsive manner is that the theory relies so heavily on mutual therapist-client understanding of the spoken word for its success. Over-reliance on verbal interactions to assess the client's dynamics may pose a problem for clients who are reluctant to discuss their feelings for any of the race- or culture-related reasons that we have previously discussed. Also, in cross-racial pairings, verbal communication may be distorted by clients' initial mistrust of their therapists. Some clients may need a more directive approach in the early stages of therapy as they become familiar with the therapy process and learn to recognize the therapist's manner of dealing with people of their racial group.

Therefore, not only must therapists be aware of their own racial and cultural biases and prejudices, but they must also work through such feelings so as not to communicate these attitudes to the client. Furthermore, by being able to discuss issues of race and culture with clients, therapists can engage in more authentic relationships. Also, given the society's history of complex racial relations, therapists must be prepared to accept the rage that clients of different racial backgrounds may hold toward therapists as symbols of the country's racial dynamics.

Furthermore, as we have noted in this chapter as well as earlier chapters, many clients from visible racial and ethnic groups or collectivistic cultures may express their stronger feelings nonverbally. Thus therapists must monitor clients' nonverbal communications, and use their knowledge of different cultural communication patterns to reflect clients' experiences back to them accurately.

Nevertheless, Rogers's most recent version of person-centered therapy with its attention to spiritual connectedness makes it possible to communicate with the client at a deeper level than seems permissable with the psychodynamic and cognitive behavior approaches. The therapist-client spiritual connection that Rogers describes is consistent with the spiritual dimension inherent in many collectivistic cultures, and the use of spirituality per se is often an important therapeutic ingredient in traditional healing practices (see Chapter 13).

Finally, it should be noted that the ultimate goal of person-centered therapy—the quest for self-actualization—should not be undertaken without considering the societal barriers that might impede the complete fulfillment of ALANA clients' dreams. The development of the true self for ALANA clients may be complicated by the necessity of their being bicultural in order to be accepted by the dominant culture as well as by their own racial and/or ethnic cultural group. It is often the case that the identity one must adopt to survive in the marketplace culture is at odds with the identity one must use to remain a member of the at-home culture. The therapist's responsibility is to help the client to discover where the interfaces and conflicts in her or his multiple identities lie.

Cognitive-Behavioral Therapy

The *cognitive-behavioral approach* to therapy is actually a meshing of two approaches—behavioral and cognitive. Both emphasize modifying maladaptive behavior as broadly defined. However, strictly speaking, behavioral approaches focus on external behaviors as the locus of change, whereas cognitive approaches focus on internal or intrapsychic behaviors (e.g., irrational thoughts). Because the approach is a blending of approaches, no one therapist is generally considered to define the perspective. However, Albert Ellis and Aaron Beck are often associated with various cognitive approaches.

Goals of Therapy

The therapist helps the client to identify and reframe the cognitions that are assessed as contributing to the client's self-defeating behavior. Cognitive-behavioral theory holds that an individual's behaviors and feelings are determined by the manner in which the person thinks about the world. Thus, the therapist helps the client to monitor and articulate his or her cognitions (e.g., thoughts, beliefs, fantasies, images, etc.) and modify maladaptive cognitions, which presumably lead to changes in the client's feelings and behaviors (Sacco & Beck, 1985).

Assessment

Prior to beginning treatment, the therapist thoroughly assesses the client to rule out severe thought disorders or suicidal behaviors that are considered to be inappropriate

INSIGHT **8.2**

Use of Person-Centered Therapy with an Asian Woman Client

The subsequent excerpt is abstracted from Hill (1989) to illustrate cultural impasses that can occur when the therapist does not integrate the client's unconscious cultural themes into the process. However, we refer the reader to the original source for a fuller presentation of the case because we think that it is an excellent illustration of how the client, therapist, and researcher each misread or do not understand the client's version of collectivistic culture.

According to Hill, the client in this case, "Marie," is "a 44-year-old, Chinese [first-generation American] woman" (p. 125); the therapist, "Dr. M," is "a 37-year-old, Black [African American], female [sic] psychologist" (p. 125). In column 1, we reproduce the actual therapist and client dialogue; in column 2, we present our speculations about the possible cultural themes and hypotheses that may have been relevant in the interaction. This excerpt is taken from the end of Marie's third session of therapy. Marie is responding to Dr. M's question about why she sought therapy.

Dialogue	Cultural Issue
Marie: The opportunity, you know, (Dr. M: the opportunity . . .) was there and I always felt I needed help. (Dr. M: MmHmm) You know, I said, "I bet you my life would be different if I could only get the direction to do things right or get some advice on how to go about straightening things that are so disorganized or whatever it is that's causing me to be like I am (Dr. M: MmHmm) or s-, whatever obstacles in the way. Maybe someone can tell me what it is so I can try to get around it." I've always felt that I had to have some kind of direction, (Dr. M: MmHmm) but it was just the expense of it (Dr. M: MmHmm) that, you know, made, made it just say well it would be nice to have, (Dr. M: MmHmm) to talk with, and, and straighten you out. But there are other things that are, come first (Dr. M: MmHmm) you know, before I, you know can even consider it.	The client seems to be externally focused; an intrapsychic therapy focus may not work. The client expects her therapist to be active and structured. Dr. M needs to explore Marie's value orientations. Who does she consider more important than herself?
Dr. M: So you're saying, what you're saying is that you have hope of finding some ways to make this better, this kind of heaviness and the problems that now feel very weighty, of dealing with them better.	This externalized conceptualization of Marie's problem could work if Dr. M uses it consistently.
Marie: MmHmm. I hope to get some directions (Dr. M: MmHmm) and some advice you know on what to do for all things that I, you know, have been bothering me and stood in the way (Dr. M: MmHmm) and, you know, the problems that I have, I hope that someone can tell me, "This is why it is and this is what you have to do to overcome it."	The client restates her preference for a structured, educational approach.

(continued)

INSIGHT 8.2   Continued

Dialogue	Cultural Issue

Dr. M: You know, as, as we have talked, we've just really begun. We've had our initial sessions. And then we had the break and did not meet. But as we've talked, you know, the first impression is that s-, several things, first of all it seems that you've got some ideas of where the hurts are. And you're not sure what kinds of things to do differently to handle things better. And that's part of what I hope will come out of our working together and getting some direction. But the other part of that that I want to say is that I think that, I know that that direction will come out of our talking, but more important that out of you, out of your getting confidence and deciding which step you want to take, which things feel like the next thing to do. And step by step, things will get lighter. But you'll find that some of those things, if not all of them will come from your beginning to feel better about making the next step. Does that make sense?

Dr. M attempts to shift Marie to an intrapsychic focus, to teach her to accept responsibility for her own change. A more effective strategy for this client might have been for Dr. M to assume responsibility for Marie's change, at least initially (e.g., "I will teach you how to feel better" . . .).

Marie: Well, I never had any confidence in myself. So I'm not sure if I'm going to come up with all this. You know, (Dr. M: MmHmm) I don't really have any confidence that's coming, going to come out of, from me, (Dr. M: MmHmm) because if it would, it would have happened already. (Marie laughs)

In several more speaking turns, Marie continues to request that Dr. M serve as an advice-giver, and Dr. M continues to urge Marie to look inward for such advice.

---

for treatment by means of cognitive-behavioral therapy. Standardized assessment tools such as the Beck Depression Inventory (Beck, 1967) may be used to determine the client's level of psychological disturbances or psychopathology. In a collaborative manner, the therapist helps the client to identify and monitor automatic dysfunctional thoughts, that is, specific self-statements that occur in a habitual manner without conscious effort.

By involving the client in the assessment process, the client learns to evaluate his or her thinking more objectively, and to disrupt the cognition-affective reaction-behavioral cycle that typically follows such thinking. Assessment of automatic dysfunctional thoughts may involve the therapist asking the client directly about her or his cognitive reactions to events that evoke intense emotional responses. The therapist may indirectly assess the client's thoughts by asking the client to imagine the sequence of events occurring prior to a specific negative reaction, and then focusing the client on identifying the specific thoughts that he or she was thinking at the time.

Therapeutic Procedures

The therapist uses a variety of cognitive and behavioral techniques to reframe the client's negative thoughts. However, cognitive-behavioral therapy stresses that the therapy process should involve collaboration between the therapist and client. The collaboration empowers the client by permitting her or him to be actively engaged in setting goals and doing self-assessments. Yet it is still quite important that the collaboration occur within the confines of a strong therapeutic relationship—a relationship based on trust, concern, and acceptance of the client—and accurate empathy.

Prior to each session, the client and therapist develop a list of prioritized issues to be dealt with during the session. While monitoring and directing the sessions to ensure that the highest priority issues are addressed during the session, the therapist uses both a nondirective and directive style.

Beck (1967; Sacco & Beck, 1985) developed a model of cognitive behavioral therapy that includes the following therapeutic procedures: (a) identifying and monitoring the client's dysfunctional automatic thoughts; (b) recognizing the connection between thoughts, emotion, and behavior; (c) evaluating the reasonableness of the automatic thoughts; (d) substituting more reasonable thoughts for the dysfunctional automatic thoughts; and (e) identifying and altering the client's dysfunctional silent assumptions.

Typically, as the therapist assists clients in identifying and monitoring dysfunctional automatic thoughts, he or she also must assist the client in identifying unreasonable cognitions and in recognizing the distortions of reality underlying the cognitions (Sacco & Beck, 1985). Rather than attempting to use words to persuade the client that his or her thoughts are unreasonable, the therapist uses a variety of data-gathering techniques as well as reinforcement of the client's involvement in the process.

In addition, the therapist uses didactic instruction to teach clients the basic concepts of cognitive-behavioral therapy, describing automatic thoughts and providing relevant reading material to facilitate the client's understanding of cognitive-behavioral therapy. Specific techniques such as role-playing or weekly homework assignments such as recording thoughts between therapy sessions may be used to facilitate recall of events and cognitions and to enhance the client's degree of involvement in the process.

In the beginning of therapy, therapists inform clients that homework will be an integral part of their therapy. Initially, cognitive-behavioral therapists are rather directive in assigning homework. They might instruct clients to keep a weekly diary of their dysfunctional thoughts. In their diary, clients are instructed to describe objective situations, the accompanying emotions, and the nature and frequency of the automatic thoughts that may have contributed to the emotions.

In helping clients to recognize the connection between thoughts, emotion, and behavior, therapists ask clients to articulate how they were feeling and behaving when they had specific thoughts. Therapists normalize the process by explaining to clients that feelings, behaviors, and thoughts are interconnected for everyone. As the therapy process continues, the therapist encourages clients to develop their own homework assignments to be completed between therapy sessions.

Also, the therapist teaches the client techniques to use to evaluate the reasonableness of his or her automatic thoughts. The techniques include teaching the client to ask himself or herself for evidence to support the thoughts, to proffer alternative interpretations of events, and to consider sources of blame other than oneself for negative events.

In addition, clients can be assisted in developing techniques to gather data from external sources as a means of testing the soundness of their thinking about specific situations. Finally, clients are asked to consider the possibility that their negative thoughts are in fact true, and if so, to consider what about the particular situation is so terrible. This latter technique helps clients to confront the most severe possiblities in their lives and to gain more realistic perspectives about their abilities to cope with them.

Clients are encouraged to develop their own positive self-statements to substitute for the dysfunctional automatic thoughts. In the beginning stages, clients are asked to write down their dysfunctional thoughts and to develop rational counter-thoughts that they truly believe. As the process becomes more natural for clients, they are not required to write them down. Therapists are expected to be particularly attentive to clients' unstated reservations regarding the rational thoughts that they have developed, and help clients to examine the underlying automatic thoughts that are impeding their acceptance of the rational thoughts. This process continues until clients truly believe the rational cognitions.

Behavioral techniques are also used to identify and modify dysfunctional cognitions. In these instances, the reward structure that maintains dysfunctional cognitions is identified, and a reinforcement schedule is designed to reward rational cognitions.

Clients' silent assumptions can be identified and altered by examining the recurring themes that arise from clients' specific automatic cognitions. Silent assumptions are the basic underlying beliefs that predispose clients to maintain particular dysfunctional thoughts. Theoretically, silent assumptions are more related to the client's world view than are automatic thoughts because they are ingrained common beliefs that tend to be rigid and pervasive. An example of such global beliefs is "To be happy, I must be accepted by all people at all times" (Sacco & Beck, 1985). The same procedures used for identifying and altering automatic dysfunctional thoughts are used for eliminating dysfunctional silent assumptions.

Racial and Cultural Considerations

The clear separation of mind (cognitions) and body (emotions) required for successful cognitive-behavioral therapy may contribute to very confusing therapy dynamics for clients whose cultures consider mind, body, and spirit inseparable. Also, since ALANA clients are often victims of severe racism in various aspects of their lives, if the therapist does not consider the impact of societal racial dynamics on client's (and therapist's) thinking processes, then he or she risks over-simplifying the client's cognitive processes.

Because of the constant bombardment of racial provocations to which they are exposed, the emotional reactions of some VREG clients may be so intense that it may be difficult for them to separate their emotional reactions from their cognitive reactions in general. However, such separation may be particularly difficult to achieve when the client is recounting or reliving prior traumatic racial situations.

When attempting to encourage the client to distinguish thoughts from feelings, the therapist may ask a client to articulate his or her thoughts when the therapist observes that the client is becoming tearful or exhibiting a facial expression typically associated with a negative emotion. Yet using such here-and-now techniques may not be appropriate for collectivistic clients because they may make them feel like specimens the therapist is attempting to dissect rather than fully integrated persons.

Yet many of the cognitive-behavioral techniques may be suitable for collectivistic and ALANA clients because they leave room for discussion of real external racial or cultural factors that may contribute to clients' self-defeating cognitions. If the client is unwittingly succumbing to actual ethnocentrism in the external world, then he or she will need assistance in overcoming these barriers so that he or she can still live a fulfilling life.

In addition, clients who constantly have been abused by institutional racism may need some prompting from therapists to develop rational thoughts about the abusive situations. While engaging in such prompting, it is important that the therapist relate to the client in an accepting and supportive manner. Furthermore, if the therapist intends to use role-playing as a therapeutic intervention in such situations, then the therapist may need to prepare clients for such activities. In the absence of explanatory information about why and how the process works, the client may refuse to participate in role plays because the process may seem artificial and may lead the client to wonder whether the therapist is trying to belittle the client. It is critical that the therapist be open-minded and receptive to the client's input about his or receptivity to "foreign" interventions. It is important to remember that different cultural groups may hold unique silent assumptions, and these assumptions may influence the client's perception of the therapist, the therapist's interventions, and the process more generally.

Be that as it may, it is important that therapists not use their own frame of reference in judging the "accuracy" of a client's reality. Therapists who do not understand the cultural and sociopolitical racial and socioeconomic realities of clients are not in a position to judge the accuracy of the client's life experiences as reflected in her or his cognitions. The data-gathering techniques of cognitive-behavioral approaches can be as helpful to the therapist in understanding the client's reality as they are to the client in understanding her or his own reality.

When using cognitive-behavioral techniques, therapists must understand the realities of their clients' day-to-day existences to determine the content of clients' homework assignments as well as the feasibility of their completing them. For example, mothers of low income whose lives are filled with stressful daily or hourly events may find the additional burden of completing homework more stressful than it is helpful (Cook & Fine, 1992).

Furthermore, clients whose primary language is not English or who are illiterate may be unable to complete homework assignments because they are incompetent in the therapist's language. Clients in these circumstances may be embarrassed to reveal such weaknesses to the therapist, particularly if he or she is of another socioracial group. Therefore, the therapist also must ensure that there are no language barriers that might interfere with a client's understanding of the homework assignments.

Nevertheless, cognitive-behavioral therapy may be uniquely appropriate for collectivistic and/or VREG clients in several respects. When implemented properly, the approach can be responsive to clients whose cultural orientations differ from the therapist's orientation in that clients are treated as partners in the process. As "co-therapists," clients can provide the therapist with access to their cultural worldviews. Therapists themselves are active participants in the process, which in itself may be more consistent with clients' expectations that the therapist do something concrete to "cure" them.

Also, the didactic instruction innate to the process helps prepare clients for the therapy process and provides opportunities for them to discuss their expectations for therapy and the therapist. The instructional process also permits the therapist to share her or his expectations as well. Perhaps more than either of the other theoretical orientations that we have covered in this chapter, the cognitive-behavioral approaches naturally offer a path by which the therapist can reveal herself or himself to the client, a path that may be traveled frequently when therapists' and clients' racial and/or cultural socialization has differed markedly.

Further Food for Thought

We have outlined some of the aspects of traditional theories where we think the opportunity for cultural and/or racial misinterpretation and misapplication is strong. Now, we invite you to answer the following questions about your own specific theoretical perspective and to consider the potential client-therapist cultural and racial impasses that your answers imply.

1. What assumptions about the causes of psychological distress and maladaptive behavior does your perspective advocate?
2. What specific methods and procedures are germane to your perspective?
3. For what types of problems is your approach an appropriate form of treatment?
4. What are the therapeutic or "healing" properties of your approach?

REFERENCES

Baptiste, D. A., Jr. (1990). The treatment of adolescents and their families in culturaltransition: Issues and recommendations. *Contemporary Family Therapy, 12,* 3–22.

Beck, A. T. (1967). *Depression: Clinical, experimental, and theoretical aspects.* New York: Hoeber Medical Division, Harper & Row.

Boyd-Franklin, N. (1989). *Black families in therapy: A multisystems approach.* New York: Guilford Press.

Casas, J. M. (1988). Cognitive behavioral approaches: A minority perspective. *Counseling Psychologist, 16*(1), 106–110.

Cook, D. A., & Fine, M. (1992). "Mother wit": Childrearing lessons from African American mothers of low income. In B. Swadener & S. Lubeck (Eds.), *Families and children "at promise": The social construction risk.* New York: SUNY Press.

Corey, G. (1985) *A case approach to counseling and psychotherapy.* Monterey, CA: Brooks/Cole.

Erikson, E. H. (1959). *Identity and the life cycle.* New York: Norton.

Hayashi, S., Kuno, T., Osawa, M., & Shimizu, M. (1992). The client-centered and person-centered approach in Japan: Historical development, current status, and perspectives. *Journal of Humanistic Psychology, 32*(2), 115–136.

Hill, C. E. (1989). *Therapist techniques and client outcomes: Eight cases of brief psychotherapy.* Newbury Park, CA: Sage Publications.

Kohut, H. (1971). *The analysis of the self.* New York: International Universities Press.

Lau, A. (1984). Transcultural issues in family therapy. *Journal of Family Therapy, 6,* 91–112.

Lerner, B. (1972). *Therapy in the ghetto: Political importance and personal disintegration.* Baltimore, MD: Johns Hopkins University Press.

Pannu, R. (1994). Being true to the self: A cultural perspective on Kohut's theory of self psychology. Unpublished paper, University of Maryland, College Park, MD.

Ridley, C. (1984). The clinical treatment of the nondisclosing Black client: A therapeutic paradox. *American Psychologist, 39*(11), 1234–1244.

Rogers, C. R. (1980). *A way of being.* Boston: Houghton Mifflin Company.

Rogers, C. R. (1986). Client centered therapy. In I. L. Kuthash & A. Wolf (Eds.), *Psychotherapist's casebook* (pp. 197–208). San Francisco, CA: Jossey-Bass.

Ryckman, R. M. (1978). *Theories of personality.* New York: D. Van Nostrand Company.

Sacco, W. P., & Beck, A. T. (1985). Cognitive therapy of depression. In E. E. Beckham & W. R. Leber (Eds.), *Handbook of Depression: Treatment, assessment, and research* (pp. 3–38).

Sue, S., Zane, N. & Young, K. (1994). Research on psychotherapy with culturally diverse populations. In A. E. Bergin & S. L. Garfield (Eds.) *Handbook of Psychotherapy and Behavior Change* (pp. 783–817). New York: John Wiley and Sons.

Tafoya, T. (1989). Circles and cedar: Americans and family therapy. *Journal of Psychotherapy and the Family, 6,* 71–98.

Triandis, H. C. (1994). *Culture and social behavior.* New York: McGraw-Hill.

Valdes, M. R. (1983). Psychotherapy with Hispanics. *Psychotherapy in Private Practice, 1*(1), 55–62.

Walker, A. (1992). *Possessing the secret of joy.* New York: Harcourt, Brace, & Javanovich.

CHAPTER

9 Beginning the Therapy Process

There are at least three points during the therapy process when the therapist is likely to wonder whether he or she should address race or culture as an issue with the client. They are (1) during the intake process and/or the beginning phase of therapy; (2) during the relationship establishment phase; and (3) throughout the course of therapy whenever the client's problems appear to have some race-related or cultural aspects. The beginning phase of therapy consists of four major components that have impact on the course of the therapy process. These are (1) establishment of a relationship; (2) client assessment; (3) clarification of client expectations; and (4) structuring or informing the client about the nature of the therapy process. On the surface, these may appear to be generic components of all therapy. However, when integrating race and culture into the therapy process, particular emphasis must be given to each of the four aforementioned components from the beginning. Moreover, more often than not, each component must be addressed a few times throughout the course of therapy.

Intake

Although it depends somewhat upon the client's level of racial identity development, usually the therapist's racial category per se does not become an overt issue for the client unless it differs from the client's racial category. However, Thompson and Jenal (1994) found evidence to suggest that clients may engage in some indirect testing of the therapist's loyalties even when the therapist is of the same racial classification as the client. Also, Tomlinson and Cheatham (1989) found some equivocal evidence to the effect that race and gender categories of clients were related to intake counselors' diagnostic judgments.

Moreover, as a matter of practice, therapists should develop the habit of asking clients about their racial and ethnic background during the initial sessions, even if they are ostensibly of the same group(s) as the therapist. Of course, the easiest way of obtaining this information is to solicit it via one's intake forms. However, forms generally cannot provide the qualitative information that the therapist can receive and offer by raising the question more directly.

Familiarity with the racial or cultural stereotypes commonly associated with the client's racial or ethnic groups often can provide the therapist with a point from which to explore the client's related self esteem issues. Moreover, noting the specific types of conflicts the client may have encountered vis-à-vis her or his racial or ethnic group memberships may provide information about why and how the client developed particular coping strategies.

For example, in the case of Marie, discussed in the previous chapter, Marie frequently remarked that her Asian American daughter was not included in the social activities of her peers at a predominantly White university, an exclusion she attributes to her daughter's studiousness: ". . . And then the other part is maybe improve family life and relations . . . and kind of help my daughter through her period of um she's not very happy as a, I mean she does well academically, but she feels she's out of it socially. . . . She's not, she doesn't feel accepted because they think she's a brain. And they kind of hurt her, you know, you're not one of them. . . ." (Hill, 1989, p. 130).

If the therapist had been familiar with (or acknowledged) the societal *racial* stereotype of Asians as "brainiacs," then she could have raised the issue of racial discrimination as a potential factor in her daughter's adjustment to college. Making the issue of race salient would have allowed the therapist to assess the quality of the daughter's as well as the mother's racial coping strategies, and offer remediation, if necessary.

Establishing a Relationship

As discussed in Part One, the sociopolitical implications of race and culture may have a profound impact upon the quality of the therapy relationship. We are using "relationship" here to mean what others (e.g., Gelso & Carter, 1985) have called the "therapeutic alliance," that is, the interpersonal process by which the therapist and client attempt to help the client achieve a post-therapy state that is better in some way than the one in which he or she entered therapy.

In their conceptualization of the relationship, Gelso and Carter differentiate between the "unreal" and the "real" components of the therapeutic alliance. *Unreality* refers to the transferential aspects of the interaction, and "[t]ransference entails a [client's] misperception or misinterpretation of the therapist, whether positive or negative" (p. 170). They contend that such misperception occurs from the moment of client-therapist contact and even before therapy begins. For them, the real component of the therapy relationship consists of "impersonal or nonintimate" (e.g., friendly conversation) as well as "intimate or personal" (e.g., genuine personal reactions or perceptions of the client) aspects. The real relationship also must appear at the inception of the therapy relationship, regardless of the therapist's theoretical orientation, or the relationship will not work.

Once the therapist and client attribute a racial classification to one another, they may consciously or unconsciously relate to each other based on their previous—actual or vicarious—experiences with members of the other person's socioracial group. In the language of psychoanalytic theory, racial and/or cultural transference and countertransference may be aroused. Racial sensitivities or cultural insensitivities may be heightened in therapy relationships because of the power differentials inherent in the client and therapist roles. The therapist has the greater power and, consequently, may impose his or her racial or cultural perceptions upon the client. Insensitivies may also be stimulated because the most vulnerable participant—the client—is expected to make himself or herself even more vulnerable to a potentially hostile stranger by revealing to him or her one's innermost thoughts and intimate details of one's life.

In exchange, the client risks that her or his psychological condition will be evaluated by the therapist after only brief contact, and with incomplete information. In one way or another the therapist's evaluations are documented and may remain with the client for the remainder of her or his life, forever influencing the manner in which the client is perceived by other mental health professionals. Then, too, the therapist's evaluations may shape the client's view of herself or himself and perhaps countless other people in the client's at-home community.

Client Dynamics

Sometimes racial differences between client and therapist can contribute to relationship barriers. With respect to Black clients and White therapists, Ridley (1984) uses the concept of "cultural [actually racial] paranoia" to describe the limited self-disclosure that might occur in such relationships. Terrell and Terrell (1981, 1984) offer the construct of "cultural" (actually racial) mistrust as a psychological explanation of why clients of color might terminate therapy prematurely.

In their counseling-simulation study, which was approximately equivalent to a first or informal intake session of therapy, Thompson, Worthington, and Atkinson (1994) found that African American women clients with low levels of cultural mistrust disclosed most to Black counselors and the same type of clients with high levels of mistrust disclosed the least amount to White counselors. Their findings seemed to confirm Terrell and Terrell's (1984) findings that high levels of cultural mistrust were associated with Black clients' premature termination from therapy. Consequently, these studies suggest that when the therapist and client are of different racial classifications, then the therapist would do well to at least inquire about the client's comfort in working with him or her. However, unless it is clear that the client is continuing to be nonresponsive to the therapist, it is usually better to raise such questions later in the initial session rather than immediately. The delay allows the client an opportunity to become somewhat more comfortable with the therapist as an individual rather than just as a symbol of a group. Nevertheless, the therapist should inquire about clients' racial preferences and expectations early enough to assure that the therapist and client have sufficient time to process (comprehend the implications of) the client's answer.

Be that as it may, trust is a crucial element in the therapy relationship. If a client has preconceived notions that members of the therapist's racial group cannot be trusted because they have oppressed or accorded inferior statuses to members of the client's socioracial group, then the client is not likely to trust the therapist automatically. Clients who consider their socioracial group to be superior to that of the therapist may also have difficulty entering into a trusting relationship with the therapist. Therefore, the therapist may have to prove that he or she is different from the client's in-group stereotype of members of the therapist's racial group.

It is not uncommon for clients of color to initially "test" the therapist to determine whether he or she can relate to the client's worldview regarding racial or cultural matters. For instance, a POC client might challenge a White therapist to see whether he or she understands the client's language or whether the therapist will be an oppressor rather than an advocate for the client. Similarly, a POC client might test a POC therapist to ascertain whether the therapist values the standards of the White culture more than the standards of his or her own cultural group. Often therapists who advise clients about how to "make it" in today's society (e.g., "I told my [Hispanic] son that I did not want him hanging around Mexican boys, and speaking Spanish."), based on their own or their ancestral racial or cultural accommodations, do not realize that they are communicating volumes to the client about the therapist's attitudes toward race, culture, and so forth. Moreover, by what the therapist says or does not say about her or his own group(s), clients often infer the therapist's feelings about the client's groups.

White clients who have never been exposed to successful People of Color may also test a POC therapist to ascertain his or her competence and intelligence. Questions that we have been asked that are examples of such tests are: "What's a doctor of philosophy degree?" "Does that mean you're a *real* therapist?" "Where did you go to school?" Moreover, if the therapist speaks accented English, it is not unusual for clients to have more difficulty understanding her or him than nonclients typically have. This difficulty is usually manifested as frequent requests that the therapist repeat himself or herself or expressions of apparent befuddlement. Interestingly, even therapists who are native-born Americans and speak unaccented American English quite proficiently sometimes have the experience of not being understood by clients who assume that they must be from another country due to the therapist's appearance. Clients in this category will typically ask the therapist many questions about his or her place of birth.

It is important that therapists not take such challenges to the therapy relationship personally. They should come to the therapy relationship prepared to explore clients' expectations of them as racial beings, and to engage in a process of proving that they accept clients wherever they are in their racial identity development. Also, they should be willing and capable of sharing their own racial identity development with their clients as necessary.

Furthermore, most clients will enter therapy behaving in a manner that conforms to their cultural socialization, often unbeknownst to themselves. If they are from collectivistic cultures as well, then they may also be experiencing ongoing ethnocentricism without being able to pinpoint cultural differences as the source of their distress. The therapist can begin the process of enhancing the client's cultural awareness and acceptance of her or his own culture by demonstrating awareness and acceptance of the client's culture.

Therapist Dynamics

As mentioned in previous chapters, therapists must be aware of the extent to which they engage in racial stereotyping, express prejudices, and/or need to be accepted by members of other races. Some therapists may find it difficult to like and trust clients of certain races, to believe in their inherent goodness, or even to have genuine communications with them. Due to internalized racial stereotypes, they may be unable to visualize their clients engaging in healthy lifestyles; which, in turn, biases their expectations for the outcome of therapy with certain clients.

Just as clients use defense mechanisms or coping strategies to alleviate their racial or cultural anxieties, so too do therapists. Thus, when faced with clients who elicit the therapist's unresolved racial and cultural conflicts, therapists may exhibit condescension toward clients of different races as a means of assuaging or overcompensating for feelings of anxiety or guilt derived from their groups' history of intra- and interracial interactions. Alternatively, due to the therapist's own negative experiences of racism or ethnocentricism, therapists may use their power to punish clients who symbolize the offending group to them.

Practically speaking, the moment that the therapist becomes aware of her or his client's racial classification, he or she should immediately engage in self-exploration to ascertain his or her reactions to the information. Even before the therapist meets the client, he or she should free associate to the client's racial information as revealed on the intake form and case notes, if they are available. The therapist should attempt to visualize specific aspects of the person related to race and/or racial stereotyping including skin color, body type, and so forth.

Skin color associations may have implications for how threatened one person—in this case, either the therapist or client—is by another person's race. For some individuals, the closer the imagined (or actual) skin color is to the color of the person imagining it, the more similar to themselves they will assume the other person is. Imagining skin color can assist the therapist in becoming aware of his or her own internalized skin color associations, and provides indirect information concerning society's treatment of people on the basis of their color.

In actuality, regardless of his or her racial classification per se, the lighter a person's skin color, the more societal advantages and privileges the person is likely to receive. Paler Hargrove (1994) cited Hughes and Hertel (1990) as reporting that among Black Americans, the socioeconomic distance between light- and dark-skinned people is as great as the distance between White and Black Americans. Moreover, Paler Hargrove (1993) found that although skin color may have different meanings within socioracial groups, in general, people of darkest skin colors relative to other members of their accorded groups are subjected to more negative racial socialization experiences, if they cannot "pass" for White (see Insight 9.1).

For the most part, therapists typically are taught to focus on the intrapsychic dynamics of the client when even the hint of racial tensions appears in the therapy interaction. They are also taught to locate the source of existing tensions in clients' racial and (occasionally) cultural categories rather than potentially modifiable psychological characteristics associated with membership in such categories. Consequently, problems related to race, culture, and social class are often avoided because category memberships seem permanent, and therapists think that related problems cannot be solved. Exercise 9.1 might be useful for deciding which areas might lead you to

INSIGHT 9.1
Skin Color Commentaries

In these excerpts from Lisa Paler Hargrove's (1993) skin color interviews, we see that skin color is a complex issue across groups, and people are not always consciously aware of how their skin color helps or hurts them in their social groups. The interviewer (LP) is a light-skinned woman who identifies as African American, Puerto Rican, and Jamaican American. The interviewee's name is fictitious.

Fine Shades of White

LP: How do you classify yourself racially?

Rosalina: Well, it's a big mess. My mother is Mexican, and she also has Native American blood in her and she's also French, and my father is White. So, if I have to pick one, normally I say Hispanic because that's the environment I was raised in because I was raised really with my mother.

LP: How would you describe your skin complexion?

Rosalina: I would say olive, but not really. I mean I had darker skin when I was younger, but as I get older and I'm not out in the sun as much, my skin gets lighter. So, I guess I would say "olive-ish."

LP: Are you self-conscious about your complexion?

Rosalina: No.

LP: Where do you learn your norms about what's healthy and what's unhealthy? For example, about pale skin versus tan skin?

Rosalina: Where? I guess I learned it from my mother, from my family.

LP: So is that more of an Hispanic thing? Would you consider your culturally defining group as Hispanic?

Rosalina: No, I would say more White or Anglo because I mean that's been my you know who I've predominantly gone to school with. My dad he was a good I mean he was a big influence although I didn't live with him my whole life my early childhood, I did. So, we were considered White.

LP: Okay, okay. How do White people look at skin color or complexion?

Rosalina: I don't know that I can make a generalization for all White people. Personally, it doesn't really it wouldn't effect how I would like whether or not I would befriend someone like for you know like the range of their skin color from light to dark but I don't know I don't think I understood your question, I don't think I'm answering you right

LP: It's okay. There's no right or wrong answer.

Rosalina: No, no I just don't think I'm giving you the kind of answer you wanted I'm not sure what you're looking for

LP: Well, I guess what I'm trying to look for is how not so much race within races in your own specific racial group how complexion how light versus medium versus dark effects how you look at another person, how it's affected your life—whatever skin color you define yourself as having, you define yourself as having olive skin that would be in the medium dark range as far as White people are concerned. How has that affected your life? That's the *broad* scope

Rosalina: Okay. Well as far as attraction goes, I'm more attracted to people with more olive to darker skin than like I would be like my boyfriend has brown hair and brown eyes and olive skin you know as opposed to like I can't find myself being attracted to a redhead with pale skin and freckles you know is that

LP: And why is that?

Rosalina: It's just not attractive to me I don't know why

LP: Uh can you describe any incidents positive or negative in which your complexion not race played an important role? For instance in getting a job choosing or attracting a partner. You mentioned that you're attracted to olive-skin people. Is that an advantage for *you* to have olive skin in the White community? Is that an advantage or a disadvantage?

Rosalina: Yes it's an advantage it's an advantage because people don't look at me and see that I'm of color. They think they look at me and see that I'm White unless I tell them I'm Mexican or unless I tell them I'm Native

(continued)

American and so they just see me with like a tan like in the summertime if I had a good tan, then they just see me as tan and that would be positive that's more I've found people to find that more attractive than the most comments I'll get is what a good tan I can get but no one's ever like a lot of times sometimes if um in the summer if I have a good tan then that's when people will ask me if I'm Hispanic or if I have any In other nationalities in me or whatever. (MmHmm) Ah it's never been it's never been negative I've never had a negative experience with it (MmHmm).

LP: So then it sounds like in your group of people the experience of having a *darker* white complexion has been positive

Rosalina: Yes

LP: Has there been any negative attributes to that?

Rosalina: For having a *darker* white complexion? (MmHmm) I don't think so. Not that I can think of . . .

The following excerpt from *A Question of Color*, a film by Kathe Sandler, reveals the pain of having dark skin in a society that devalues black. The filmmaker describes herself as a "Black American woman" from an interracial back-

ground. In her words, "I look White, but I identify myself as Black."

If You're Black Get Back

This first excerpt is from "Curtia" a medium-dark skinned young woman (perhaps in her early 20s).

"I happened to um start dating a guy that was you know very dark skinned, and you know I thought we made a real cute couple. I you know I was um feeling you know kind of taken by it all. And um he told me later in the relationship he was from uh Washington. And I was saying that I was going to school in Washington; and he should take me to meet his mother. And he said 'oh, no. I could never take you to meet my mother.' I said, 'why not?' And he said, 'Because you're too dark skin. She told me don't ever bring anyone into the house that was dark skin 'cause I'm too dark,' he said. And um because *he* was too dark. And that uh that he felt he should date lighter skinned women, even white women [soft laugh] to lighten his family up. [unseen interviewer: 'How did that make you feel?'] It made me feel lousy. Absolutely lousy.

---

inappropriately focus on the client's racial or cultural "problems" rather than your own conditions of racial or cultural encapsulation.

Additional areas for possible therapist self-exploration include: (a) amount and type of knowledge about the client's socioracial group; (b) previous vicarious (e.g., media exposure) and direct experiences, both positive and negative, with members of the client's racial group; (c) the influence of previous experiences on the therapist's feelings about the client; and (d) the influence of the therapist's prior experiences on his or her conceptualizations of members of the client's racial group.

Finally, the therapist should assess his or her level of comfort related to initially meeting the client. Thorough self-exploration will prepare the therapist for differentiating some of the real from the unreal aspects of the therapy relationship (Gelso & Carter, 1985).

The Process

The therapist should be aware that the client probably has unspoken, and perhaps unconscious, racial thoughts and assumptions about the therapist that are

EXERCISE 9.1

Self-Assessing Your Racial and Cultural Biases in the Therapy Relationship

Usher (1989) has pointed out that Pedersen's (1987) cultural bias assumptions might be useful for anticipating cultural (and racial) pitfalls in the counseling relationship. Here we use Pedersen's assumptions to raise questions that we hope will encourage you to explore potential personal pitfalls. In answering the questions, it might be useful to think about a particular client for whom the question(s) might be relevant.

Normal Behavior Assumptions

What do you consider to be "normal" therapist and client behavior during therapy?

How do you determine what is normal for a client?

Individualistic Orientation

Who or what is the focus of your counseling or psychotherapy?

If group goals are in conflict with the client's individual needs or desires, how do you resolve the conflict?

Fragmentation by Academic Disciplines

What academic disciplines other than the one(s) in which you were trained inform your practice?

How do you feel about integrating your and your client's religion and spirituality, parapsychology, and/or belief in unseen forces into the therapy process?

Dependence on Abstract Words

Is your typical mode of communication high context (abstract concepts gain meaning from the context in which they occur) or low context (abstract concepts have the same meaning across contexts)?

How do you assess the client's preferred type of context?

Overemphasis on Independence

At what age do you believe that a "child" should leave his or her parents and make a life independent of them?

How do you determine whether *independence* is excessive?

Client Support Systems

What do you think is the role of natural support systems in the therapy process?

What strategies do you use to include client's support systems as allies?

Linear Dependent Thinking

How comfortable are you with client reactions that have no clear beginning or end?

If a measured client characteristic and the client's perception of that characteristic are incongruent, how do you reconcile the two?

Discomfort with System Change

Can you describe an instance in which you intervened to change a system to fit the client's need rather than requiring him or her to change to fit the system?

How comfortable are you with challenging systems when such changes might benefit the client but hurt you or sociodemographic groups of which you are a member?

Neglect of History

What do you do when a client responds to your therapy interventions by discussing personal history or the history of her or his people?

What do you do to update your knowledge about the societal socioracial, cultural, and economic dynamics in the United States?

Dangers of Cultural Encapsulation

What do you do to broaden your racial and cultural perceptions?

What role do you play in promoting domination of clients by elitist groups of whatever origin or point of view?

analogous to the therapist's conceptualizations of the client. In establishing a relationship with the client, the therapist should have as central goals helping the client to feel comfortable with the therapist and understand the nature of the therapy relationship. The only way that a therapist will know what the client is thinking is to find ways of encouraging the client to express such thoughts during their conversation.

Nevertheless, rather than asking the client directly what he or she thinks of the therapist's race or culture, the therapist can tie race into the presenting problem and share aspects of his or her own experiences as a racial person. For instance, if a client presents with a career concern of not knowing what subject area to major in, the therapist may inquire about the client's familial racial or cultural values relative to his or her career decision-making. This inquiry could lead to the client's discussion of his or her family's value system as well as the therapist's relevant values. If the client is confused about entering or leaving a field in which there are very few members of his or her racial or cultural groups, the therapist should encourage the client to consider the possible repercussions of either decision.

To self-disclose about his or her own familial cultural socialization, a White therapist might say, "My family conformed to the typical White middle-class value system in which each person's wants and needs are considered to be more important than what particular family members might want or need for the person to do"; or a VREG therapist might say, "My family wanted me to strive to succeed for the good of my race (or family or culture), but that was confusing for me because I went to predominantly White schools where they valued individual achievement."

As the therapist and client talk about their mutual value systems, the therapist might ask the client if he or she has any concerns as to whether the therapist's value system might conflict with the client's values. The more that such give-and-take exchanges occur, the more genuine the relationship becomes and the more trust the client will have in the therapist's ability to recognize, empathize with, accept, and appreciate their racial and cultural similarities and differences.

Client Assessment

The assessment of the client begins with the therapist clarifying the nature of the client's presenting problem. A therapist must understand both the cultural and racial elements of a client's presenting problem. The therapist should not assume that two individuals presenting with the same problem necessarily experience the problem in the same way, that the problem has developed in a similar manner, or that the problem has similar meaning in the lives of both individuals.

Consider an example of two college students, both African American males, each presenting with a problem of feeling socially isolated on campus after transferring from a predominantly White community college to a predominantly White four-year college. In this example, assume that each student is equally adept at interacting with others and has a social history that includes continuous friendships from childhood, as well as successful interactions and extra-curricular involvements at the community college that he previously attended. Each student complains that the environment at the four-year college is not culturally diverse enough, either in terms of racial composition or cultural heterogeneity among the White students at the college.

The therapist might use a different approach in working with each of these students, depending on their expressed racial identities (see Chapter 5), their current coping styles, and the meaning that the problem has in their lives. One student might be trying very hard to fit in with his White roommates, but feels alienated from the African American students on campus who he perceives as segregating themselves. If asked to describe his philosophy of intergroup relating, he would say, "I believe in relating to people based on their common humanity." This client experiences his social isolation problem cognitively, but recognizes a void in his life and wants some answers that validate his experiences of the college and some strategies for getting his needs met.

In contrast, the other student resents living with White roommates, and experiences the African American students on the campus as apathetic and uninvolved in fighting the oppressive racial environment. He expresses a great deal of anger toward the college, and seeks an outlet for expressing his anger so that he can be effective in his efforts to lead the African American students in making environmental changes.

To select effective therapy interventions and appropriate outcome goals for each of these two students, it is necessary to assess thoroughly the racial and cultural aspects of their respective presenting problems. In each of these examples, the therapist needs to understand the racial identity attitudes and sociopolitical worldview of each student to decide how best to discuss the source of their isolation with them.

The first student exhibits a multicultural view of the world and integrated awareness with respect to expression of his racial identity statuses. Therefore, he would be alienated if the therapist suggested that he merely participate in the activities of the Black Student Association or only seek out African American resources on campus. Instead, he would probably relate best to a therapist who could explain to him the differences that exist among the African American students on campus, help him to discern those students who are more inclusive in their social involvements, and assist him in finding activities where he is likely to meet students of diverse cultural backgrounds. The second student has a Black liberationist worldview and uses Immersion and Emersion—an anti-White/pro-Black racial identity schema—to interact with his environment. He favors political approaches for negotiating the campus environment, and would probably feel best understood by a therapist who could empathize with his anger and frustrations.

Perhaps we should state our opinion that a therapist does not necessarily have to endorse the client's worldview or racial identity resolutions. However, he or she must understand, empathize, and be able to communicate with students who espouse diverse perspectives. Not assessing cultural worldviews and racial identity statuses could hinder the development of a productive therapeutic relationship. A thorough assessment also includes anticipating the interaction of the therapist's and the client's worldviews and racial identity statuses on therapy process. The therapist must maintain an observing ego that analyzes the tone of the racial interactions that occur between the therapist and client as they engage in the process and anticipate likely outcomes of therapy.

Another aspect of the assessment process includes determining the nature and quality of the systems in which the client functions. It is important to obtain information about the client's available and potential support systems, particularly for ALANA clients in predominantly White environments. As we have previously mentioned, many members of visible racial and ethnic groups or collectivistic cultures are committed to racial or cultural reference groups with whom they identify. Yet, in a society dominated by Whites, it is not always certain that ALANAs will have ready access to others from their own racial or cultural backgrounds.

Frequently, ALANAs who have achieved educational or occupational success often have had to sacrifice their cultural connections in order to take advantage of educational and career opportunities (Carter & Cook, 1992). As they attempt to regain balance in their lives, they may need assistance in locating people from their cultural group and reclaiming those aspects of their cultural identity that they may have mislaid.

Thus, in addition to assessing the availability of support systems for the client, it is also important to assess the nature and quantity of the conflicts the client experiences with respect to various systems. ALANA clients are frequently involved in social and legal systems that are founded on and maintained by principles of institutional racism. Therapists need to assess the client's skills in recognizing and coping with subtle and overt racism within such systems.

It could prove fruitless for a therapist to engage in assisting a client to resolve a particular problem, only to have the systems within which the client must function frustrate or negate the work that the client is doing in therapy. Therefore, the therapist needs to be able to incorporate the systems that are important to the client into his or her work. Effective incorporation means that the therapist attempts to utilize those systems that can support the counseling or therapy process and combats those systems that could undermine the therapeutic work.

Clarification of Expectations and Education

While most therapists enter the therapy process with particular theoretical orientations that guide their work with clients, few clients have similar guidelines for anticipating the course of therapy. Depending on whether the client has had previous experiences with therapy or is familiar with the field of psychology, his or her expectations for the process may range from none at all, to a reasonable facsimile, to totally erroneous.

Much of the cross-cultural counseling literature suggests that VREG clients expect counseling to be directive, with the therapist offering advice to the client. Certainly some evidence, as for example the case of Marie, suggests that some clients will harbor such expectations. Nevertheless, "directive" may have different meanings within cultural groups.

In addition to pertaining to the amount of advice giving, *directive* can also describe the therapist's activity level or degree of transparency; it can signify the amount of structuring or educating about the process that occurs; it can mean the amount of psychoeducation about the client's problem area the therapist provides; or it can even refer to the amount of activity (e.g., homework) the client is expected to perform between sessions.

Therefore, a therapist should not assume that he or she knows what the client expects without discussing the client's expectations with him or her. Once the therapist has an understanding of the client's expectations, the therapist can clarify his or her own intentions with the client. The therapist may need to educate the client as to the type of concerns that can be discussed, the frequency and duration of the sessions, the role of the therapist, the behaviors expected of the client, and the nature of the boundaries that govern their relationship. Racially and culturally responsive therapy should take into account the expectations of both the therapist and the client, and attempt to generate a mutually satisfying set of procedures that honor the cultures inherent to the therapy, the therapist, and the client.

Problems

Very often clients present problems whose racial or cultural dimensions are obvious to the therapist, but not necessarily to the client. Sometimes the client perceives racism as an aspect of his or her problem, but the therapist does not. Occasionally, the issues are more subtle and may not be obvious to either participant. The intricacy of identifying the racial/ethnic subtext of clients' problems is made even more difficult because both the therapist and client exist in a society that is attempting to be "color blind." In such a distorted society, to even admit that race is somehow an issue for you is to risk being labeled "racist" or "politically correct." Consequently, clients as well as therapists can be extremely reluctant to admit that they even consider such matters.

Thompson and Jenal (1994) have described four types of interactions that can occur when the therapist avoids discussing racial issues with African American clients. For the most part, these interactions parallel the racial identity reaction styles described by Helms (1984; 1992; see Chapter 11). Basic characteristics of the types of interactions are described in Table 9.1. The presence of the types of characteristics described by Thompson and Jenal should provide the therapist with information about whether the racial climate is positive and likely to facilitate growth or better adjustment or is negative and likely to contribute to deleterious outcomes.

Notice that the most facilitative type of relationship or events described by Helms—progressive—does not appear in the table. If the counselor is a reluctant participant and/or actively avoids discussing racial issues, then it is difficult to promote client growth with respect to such matters. However, the last type of regressive relationship described in Table 9.1, Thompson and Jenal's *Disjunctive* Type, illustrates that depending upon the client's level of racial identity development, he or she may be resilient in spite of inadequate counselor interventions. In their discussion of this type, Thompson and Jenal describe clients who are persistent about discussing the racial connotations of their issues in spite of the counselors' attempts to "universalize" the clients' concerns. Although Thompson and Jenal did not speculate on or measure the types of racial identity statuses that were operative in these relationships, the dynamics described by them suggest that clients were capable of using an *Internalization*

TABLE 9.1   Race-Related Counseling Process Relationship Types When the Counselor Is Race-Avoidant

Type	Description	
	Thompson et al.	*Helms*
Smooth-Parallel	Few or no disruptions during discourse. Benign disruptions such as requests for clarification of terminology. No mention of race in dyads with White counselors only. Difficulty discerning participants' racial identity.	Smooth, harmonious, conflict-free interactions. Participants are unwilling or unable to disturb the status quo.
Exasperated-Regressive	Uninterrupted spurts of conversation interrupted by breakdowns in client communication (e.g., staccato speech, sudden quietness). Hesitant use of words such as "Black" and "minority." "Tugging-match" quality of racial discussions.	Conflicted relationships marked by covert and overt fights about racial issues. Usually these are dysfunctional relationships in which participants' growth is stifled.
Constricted-Cross (Regressive)	An interaction riddled with frequent silences and disruptions and absence of client self-disclosure or willingness to participate in the process.	Most conflicted relationship type. Characterized by disharmony, mutual fear, covert and overt warfare. Least likely to promote growth.
Disjunctive-Regressive	Disruptions (e.g., lengthy explanations) initiated by the counselor. Client persistence in discussion race in spite of counselor avoidance.	See Exasperated type above.

The first term in the relationship-type pairs and descriptions in column 1 are adapted from Thompson et al. (1994). The second terms and descriptions are adapted from Helms (1992).

status in response to the counselors' *Conformity* (Pre-Encounter) or *Contact* statuses. A skill-building activity for the reader might be to read the full descriptions of the relationship types as described by Thompson and Jenal (1994) and Helms (1992; Chapter 11) for the purpose of "diagnosing" the clients' racial identity expressions or schemata.

Be that as it may, one could possibly work with clients without acknowledging the racial or cultural aspects of them or their issues. After all, traditional Western psychotherapists have done so since the beginning of "talk therapy" as a healing art. But in doing so, consider how much information the therapist has to ignore. Moreover, the client never has the benefit of using the therapy session to learn how to integrate the various parts of herself or himself into her or his life situation. In a similar vein, the therapist misses the opportunity to have an authentic relationship with someone who is both similar and not similar to the therapist in important ways.

The therapist's willingness to raise issues of race and culture communicates to the client that the therapy environment is a "safe" place for addressing such matters. Even if the client can see no immediate relevance of racial or cultural factors in the kinds of questions the therapist might raise, the therapist's willingness to discuss matters of race/ethnicity normalizes the topic. As a consequence, the client may be less reluctant to bring up such issues himself or herself when they appear relevant to the matters being addressed in therapy.

Conclusion

We believe that the manner in which the therapist initiates the therapy process can differentially influence how or whether the client actually reaches the end with him or her. Much literature suggests that POC clients frequently terminate therapy prematurely, or at least before their therapists think that they should (see Sue et al., 1994).

However, our experiences have been that when the proper foundation is laid, VREG clients remain in therapy for the duration. In fact, due to the valuing of extended families that is typical of the collectivistic cultures of many visible racial and ethnic groups, many VREG clients have difficulty letting go of the therapy relationship once they have bonded. Racially and culturally responsive therapists must invest a great deal of time and psychic energy in establishing a relationship wherein discussion of the cultural and racial identities of both the client and the therapist are salient. Through mutually disclosive relationships, the client and the therapist learn to recognize, evaluate, and integrate the racial and cultural aspects of the client, his or her presenting problem, and the social systems in which the client must function.

REFERENCES

Carter, R. T., & Cook, D. A. (1992). A culturally relevant perspective for understanding the career paths of visible racial/ethnic group people. In H. D. Lea & Z. B. Leibowitz (Eds.), *Adult career development: Concepts, issues, and practices* (pp. 192–217). Alexandria, VA: National Career Development Association.

Gelso, C. J., & Carter, J. A. (1985). The relationship in counseling and psychotherapy: Components, consequences, and theoretical antecedents. *The Counseling Psychologist, 13*(2), 155–243.

Helms, J. E. (1984). Toward a theoretical explanation of the effects of race on counseling: A Black and White model. *The Counseling Psychologist, 12*(4), 153–165.

Helms, J. E. (1992). *Black and White racial identity: Theory, research, and practice* (paperback). New York: Praeger.

Hill, C. E. (1989). *Therapist techniques and client outcomes: Eight cases of brief psychotherapy.* Newbury Park, CA: Sage Publications.

Hughes, M., & Hertel, E. R. (1990). The significance of color remains: A study of life chances, mate selection, and ethnic consciousness among Black Americans. *Social Forces, 68,* 1105–1120.

Paler Hargrove, L. K. (1993). Skin color interviews. Unpublished videocassette. University of Maryland, College Park, MD.

Paler Hargrove, L. K. (1994). The impact of skin color within the African American community. Unpublished paper, University of Maryland, College Park, MD.

Pedersen, P. (1987). Ten frequent assumptions of cultural bias in counseling. *Journal of Multicultural Counseling and Development, 15,* 16–22.

Ridley, C. R. (1984). Clinical treatment of the nondisclosing client: A therapeutic paradox. *American Psychologist, 39,* 1234–1244.

Sue, S., Zane, N., & Young, K. (1994). Research on psychotherapy with culturally diverse populations. In A. E. Bergin & S. L. Garfield (Eds.), *Handbook of Psychotherapy and Behavior Change* (pp. 783–817). New York: John Wiley and Sons.

Terrell, F., & Terrell, S. (1981). An inventory to measure cultural mistrust among Blacks. *The Western Journal of Black Studies, 5,* 180–185.

Terrell, F., & Terrell, S. (1984). Race of counselor, client sex, cultural mistrust level, and premature termination from counseling among Black clients. *Journal of Counseling Psychology, 31,* 371–375.

Thompson, C. E., & Jenal, S. T. (1994). Interracial and intraracial quasi-counseling interactions when counselors avoid discussing race. *Journal of Counseling Psychology, 41,* 484–491.

Thompson, C. E., Worthington, R., & Atkinson, D. R. (1994). Counselor content orientation, counselor race, and Black women's cultural mistrust and self-disclosures. *Journal of Counseling Psychology, 41,* 155–161.

Tomlinson, S. M., & Cheatham, H. E. (1989). Effects of counselor intake judgments on service to Black students using a university counseling center. Special issue: Counseling women and ethnic minorities. *Counseling Psychology Quarterly, 2,* 105–111.

Usher, C. H. (1989). Recognizing cultural bias in counseling theory and practice: The case of Carl Rogers. *Journal of Multicultural Counseling and Development, 17*(2), 62–71.

10 Racial and Cultural Nuances in the Psychotherapy Process

Because the existence of different cultural or sociopolitical experiences is generally implied by the societal usages of racial and ethnic classifications, it might be worthwhile to consider how such factors potentially influence the quality of the psychotherapy process as broadly defined. In this chapter, we present our conceptual frameworks for considering where and how race and culture enter the overall therapy process. In our discussion, we suggest specific cultural and racial dilemmas that might occur for the client and therapist as the process proceeds, and offer our own idiosyncratic resolutions for them, based (in most cases) on our own clinical experience rather than on empirical evidence. We call our resolutions "nuances" of psychotherapy. In addition to using the nuances to evaluate the quality of the overall process, therapists might also use them to assess the impact of the process on the client, that is, therapy outcome.

Conceptual Nuances

In our general conceptual model of therapy process and outcomes, we suggest that various types of outcomes are the result of what the client and therapist bring to the interaction (i.e., input), their complementary social roles, as well as what happens during therapy (i.e., process). Both the therapist's and client's psychological racial or cultural factors determine the quality of their interaction to a large extent.

For their part, therapists probably prefer techniques or interventions that are congruent with their racial and cultural views or philosophies of care giving. For their part, clients probably respond to the therapy situation in ways that are consistent with their cultural socialization regarding the solicitation of care. However, neither racial or cultural influences on therapists' styles of intervention nor clients' responses to such interventions have been examined to any great extent. Nevertheless, the participants' reactions to one another probably determine the consequences or outcomes of the process for the client. Figure 10.1 summarizes our overview of the process.

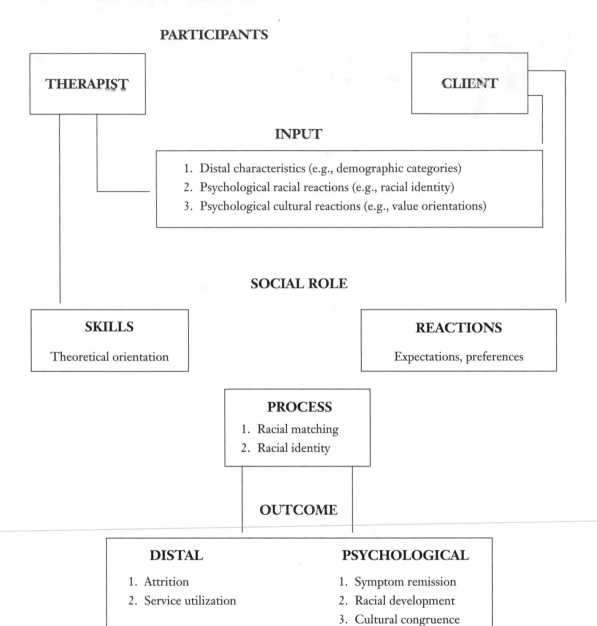

FIGURE 10.1   **A Conceptual Model of Race and Culture in the Therapy Process.**

Input

Therapists and clients each bring a set of distal or sociological and proximal or psychological racial and cultural characteristics to the therapy interaction (S. Sue & Zane, 1987). Recall that we have been using *distal* and *sociological* interchangeably to mean societal or cultural practices whose focus is nominal demographic or sociologically defined categories (e.g., racial classifications, social class) to which the person is assumed to belong, and from which the presence of psychological traits is inferred. Similarly, we have used *proximal* and *psychological* as synonyms for internalized principles of race and culture resulting from one's socialization experiences.

Presumably distal characteristics do not have a direct impact on the process, but may influence it indirectly if the therapist or client reacts to those visible aspects of the other. On the other hand, psychological characteristics ought to impact the process directly. Thus, both the therapist and the client bring to the interaction preexisting attitudes, customs, and predispositions acquired as a result of socialization into a certain socioracial or ethnic group(s), social class, and immigration or migratory cohort. Also, visible markers of each participant's nominal categories (e.g., skin color, attire) trigger for the other participant whatever attitudes, beliefs, and so forth that he or she has been socialized to hold toward people who resemble the other participant.

Therapist's Techniques. Usually the therapist's contribution to the process is defined as the techniques used to alleviate the client's symptoms or problems. Some theorists and organizations have begun to propose a variety of skills and procedures or techniques that should be included in service providers' armories. D. Sue and his associates (D. Sue et al., 1982) initiated the movement with a set of multicultural competencies, which were updated (D. Sue, Arredondo, & McDavis, 1992).

Sue et al. proposed that counselors who are "culturally skilled" should hold particular types of beliefs, possess certain knowledges, and be capable of using a variety of verbal and nonverbal therapy skills. Their criteria for culturally skilled counselors are summarized in Table 10.1.

Using Sue et al.'s multicultural competencies as their prototype, various researchers have attempted to operationally define such competencies. In fact, several paper-and-pencil measures have been developed for assessing therapists' levels of competencies (LaFromboise, Coleman, & Hernandez, 1991; Ponterotto, et al., in press; Sodowsky, 1994). Exercise 10.1 presents some sample items from a few of these measures. Also, the Office of Ethnic Minority Affairs of the American Psychological Association (APA) has produced a set of standards for providing services for VREG clients (see Appendix).

For the most part, neither the competencies nor the standards have been based on empirical investigations of the therapy process, but often are based on scholars' own experiences with clients of a particular group. Consequently, sometimes it may happen that a skill or knowledge base that worked with clients of one racial or cultural group does not work in the same way for clients of another group, even though the therapist may have been following the tenets of the various recommendations to the letter in each instance. Therefore, it might be wise to treat the competencies and

TABLE 10.1   Summary of Sue et al.'s (1982) Characteristics of Culturally Skilled Counselors[1]

Beliefs and Attitudes

1. Developed awareness and sensitivity to one's own racial and cultural heritage and concomitant respect and valuing of others' differences.
2. Awareness of one's own values and biases and of their potential effect on VREG clients, clients with collectivistic cultural orientations, and other potentially disempowering racial, class, gender and cultural characteristics.
3. Comfort with counselor and client differences and similarities with respect to racial and cultural beliefs.
4. Awareness of aspects of the client's and counselor's racial and cultural socialization that might necessitate referral of the client to a helper of his or her racial classification or cultural orientation.

Knowledges

1. Understanding of racism and ethnocentrism as it operates in the United States.
2. Possession of specific racial and cultural knowledge and information about the group(s) from which one's clients come.
3. General knowledge of traditional counseling and psychotherapy theories and practices and understanding of how they must be modified to best meet the needs of one's clients.
4. Awareness of institutional barriers, societal forces, and cultural traditions that impede clients' effective use of mental health services.

Skills

1. Ability to generate a diverse array of verbal and nonverbal interventions.
2. Capacity to communicate and interpret verbal and nonverbal messages "appropriately."
3. Competence in intervening in societal institutions and cultural systems on behalf of clients as appropriate.

[1]*Note:* We modified Sue et al.'s (1982) competencies somewhat to be consistent with our perspective.

standards as specifications of domains of concern rather than directions for how to do therapy that should be followed steadfastly.

Some studies suggest that VREG therapists may prefer to use active or structured interventions (e.g., questions, advice giving) and integrate societal factors in their diagnosis of clients' complaints (Berman, 1979a, 1979b). For example, in response to several vignettes of clients describing their problems, Berman found that White counselors in training were more likely than Black counselors in training to rely on individual or intrapsychic factors to "diagnose" clients' problems, whereas Black counselors in training were more likely than their White counterparts to use a combination of intrapsychic and environmental factors.

EXERCISE **10.1**

Practice in Assessing Your Multicultural Competencies

Several measures have been developed to permit measurement of Sue et al.'s (1982) multicultural competencies. Some of the measures use a self-report format (Sodowsky, Taffe, Gutkin, & Wise, 1994), whereas others require observer ratings (LaFromboise, Coleman, & Hernandez, 1991). We have rewritten sample items from these measures to give you an idea of how multicultural counseling competence is currently assessed.

Use the following scale to self-describe your own multicultural competence:

1 = Disagree
2 = Agree and disagree somewhat
3 = Agree

Items	Response Format (circle one)		
Knowledge			
1. I keep in mind research findings about VREG clients' preferences in counseling.	1	2	3
2. I know the impact of the current sociopolitical system on VREG clients.	1	2	3
Skills			
1. I am comfortable exploring sexual issues when I am working with VREG clients.	1	2	3
2. I use a variety of verbal and nonverbal communication strategies with VREG.	1	2	3
Beliefs and Awareness			
1. I believe that when I am working with VREG clients, my race may cause them to not trust me.	1	2	3
2. I am aware of the limitations placed on the counseling relationship due to cultural differences.	1	2	3

We don't have a scoring system for this exercise, but in case you hadn't guessed, higher scores are supposed to indicate higher levels of multicultural competence. You might examine the items and your responses to determine whether they correspond to your notion of multicultural counseling competence.

Also, Berman (1979a) found that Black counselors generally were more likely to use "expression" skills (e.g., directions, interpretations) than their White counterparts who were more likely to use more "attending" skills (e.g., questions, reflection of feeling). When Berman examined gender differences within her Black and White participants, she found the following: (a) White females used more reflection of feeling than the other socioracial-gender combinations; (b) questions predominated in White males' responses; (c) Black females tended to use both expressive and attending skills in equivalent amounts with direction-giving being their preferred strategy; and (d) direction-giving most typified Black males' predominant use of expressive skills.

Based on our own experiences, we have found that the category of skills defined as attending skills (e.g., minimal encouragers) often either do not exist in the cultures of VREG therapists in training or exist in a different fashion. Consequently, use of these skills often feels artificial to them. Two examples are the minimal encourager ("MmHmm"), and the reflection of feelings as distinguished from paraphrasing of content.

In some languages the word "MmHmm" does not exist (e.g., Chinese), or is considered disrespectful in certain circumstances (e.g., African American middle-class English), or the sentiment underlying it (e.g., "I'm listening.") is expressed in other ways (e.g., a head nod or joining in). Of course, the problem underlying usage of the reflection of feeling technique is that it is based on a basic premise of Eurocentric culture—mind-body dualism—that is, the notion that emotions and cognitions are separable, for instance (cf. Katz, 1985).

However, in most ALANA cultures, separation of feeling from content is not a meaningful distinction (cf. Helms, 1992), albeit perhaps for different culture-based reasons (see Chapter 7). Thus, in using either technique, the therapist not only must learn to perform the skill, but also must understand the cultural context in which the skill is appropriately expressed. Moreover, if VREG therapists actually represent their traditional ALANA or collectivistic culture of origin, then one might suppose that clients from the therapists' respective socioracial or sociocultural groups might find some traditional techniques rather unfamiliar as well.

Client Reactions.   The client's contribution to the process may involve a wide range of reactions assumed to occur in response to the therapist's interventions. Possible cultural or racial influences on the client's manner of reacting to therapy have been examined (or at least discussed) somewhat more frequently than their influence on therapists' behaviors. Yet here, too, primarily nominal methodologies have been used to examine relevant questions (Helms, 1994). That is, clients have been classified according to sociological categories, and psychological characteristics have been inferred from the imposed categories. With this caveat, a few studies do suggest that VREG clients may interpret structured interventions as relationship enhancing (Berman, 1979a, 1979b; Cannon & Helms, 1993).

With respect to Latino/Latina (Mexican American and/or Puerto Rican) client surrogates, some counseling-analogue studies in which clients listened to or watched therapist-client interactions have suggested that such clients might prefer directive rather than nondirective therapist styles (e.g., Borrego, Chavez, & Titley, 1982;

Pomales & Williams, 1989). However, Folensbee, Draguns, and Danish (1986) found that when Puerto Rican students actually participated in a simulation of a counseling interview, they rated counselors more positively in response to reflection of feelings than closed questions. The students also used more affect words and self referent pronouns in response to feeling reflections, suggesting that perhaps they became more individualistic in the feeling condition.

With African American surrogate clients who viewed a videotaped counseling simulation, Pomales, Claiborn, and LaFromboise (1986) found that therapist acknowledgement of race was related to positive evaluations when their Encounter (Dissonance) and Immersion racial identity attitudes were high. These findings join Thompson, Worthington, and Atkinson's (1994) conclusion that African American women client surrogates rated counselors most positively if they were also African American and responded to the racial content of the client's communications. Thompson et al. also interpreted their findings to indicate that client's racial identity development might influence their receptivity to racially neutral counseling.

Thompson et al.'s (1994) findings with African American client surrogates seem to parallel Dauphinais, Dauphinais, and Rowe's (1981) evidence that Native American high school (boarding) students rated tape-recorded counselors most positively if they had been led to believe that the counselor who conducted a culturally responsive (rather than a directive or nondirective) session was Native American rather than non-Native. Also, Gim, Atkinson, and Kim (1991) found that for Asian American client surrogates, counselors who attended to issues of cultural difference and were Asian American were rated more positively than counselors who ignored such issues (i.e., culture neutral).

Hill's (1989) case of "Marie" seems to be the only published analysis in which the researcher asked a VREG client in therapy how she felt about the techniques used by her therapist. According to Hill, immediately following her sessions, Marie (an Asian American female client) rated "Dr. M's" use of "Direct Guidance" and "[Self-] Disclosure" response modes as being "most helpful." However, in post-therapy interviews with the researcher (but not the therapist), Marie repeatedly expressed her dissatisfaction with the process because the therapist did not give her enough advice, and she felt that the advice that she had received was peripheral to her central concerns.

Thus, in general the available information about therapist techniques and client reactions is inadequate for definitely determining which techniques work best or are most preferred by clients of any socioracial classification or cultural orientation. Furthermore, for the most part, operational definitions of therapist's styles have been so simplistic (e.g., use of open versus closed questions) and inconsistent (e.g., sometimes open questions are considered directive and sometimes nondirective) that it is difficult to interpret the information that does exist.

Nevertheless, existing information does minimally support the idea that it is important for the counselor to be *capable* of discussing and managing racial issues with African American clients, and perhaps cultural issues with Latino/Latina, Native, and Asian American clients. However, an inherent bias in existing studies is that researchers typically have not examined psychological racial effects on clients' reactions to therapy for Asian, Latino/Latina, and Native Americans; nor psychological cultural effects for African Americans.

Social Roles

Expression of psychological racial or cultural factors (e.g., adaptations to racism or ethnocentrism) occurs in a manner consistent with one's ascribed role within the therapy process. Thus, the therapist expresses his or her psychological and cultural socialization by means of his or her skills and interventions; the client expresses his or her psychological socialization by reacting to whatever the therapist does in a manner that corresponds to his or her prior related socialization. Thus, for the client, relevant factors might include attitudes about help-seeking, expectations for therapy, and so forth; for therapists, such factors might include theoretical orientation, attitudes about help-giving, and so forth.

Culture probably defines the options that are available and/or desirable manifestations of the therapist and client roles. It seems possible that preference for or usage of one theoretical orientation rather than another might characterize members of different cultural groups whether they are therapists or clients. Be that as it may, although racial and cultural influences on clients' or therapists' expression of their respective therapy roles is an infrequent topic of investigation in the psychotherapy literature, when one does find such topics in the literature, race and culture are generally treated as distal considerations, if they are considered at all.

However, Helms (1984; 1990; 1995) proposed a therapy process model to explain qualitative differences in therapy sessions when race as sociopolitically defined is an implicit or explicit psychological variable. We think this therapy interaction model also can be interpreted to explain the differential effects of other cultural and sociopolitical variables such as language usage and acculturation when these variables are psychologically defined.

Therapy Interaction Process Model

The term *process* simply refers to the dynamics that occur when therapists and clients interact. Simply put, it is what the therapist and client actually do during the time they are together. When race or culture are recognized aspects of the therapy process, therapist techniques and client reactions may contribute to particular types of process dynamics.

In Chapter 6, we summarized Helms's racial identity schemas, defined as peoples' styles of expressing their internalized reactions to racism; that is, their racial identity ego statuses. The content of their reactions is alleged to differ according to whether their group was victimized by or benefitted from racism and racial oppression (see Tables 6.3 and 6.4). Helms contends that racial identity statuses *develop* or mature sequentially; that is, more sophisticated statuses gain the capacity to govern the person's styles of race-related information processing and/or behavioral expression by potentially evolving from less sophisticated or more primitive earlier statuses.

When interacting with others, therapists and clients (in this case) generally rely on the statuses that dominate their personality constellation to guide their actions and reactions. Thus, the therapist's expression of her or his underlying racial identity statuses influences his or her reaction to the client, and the client's underlying statuses, in turn, influence his or her reactions to the therapist. Therefore, each complementary response to the other person's observable expressions of his or her racial identity is an "event" (Helms, 1995). A series of events constitutes a relationship.

Relationships can differ qualitatively depending upon how the events most central to the person of less social power (e.g., the client) are negotiated. Based on their process and outcome characteristics, events can be classified as *parallel, regressive,* or *progressive.* Progressive and regressive events and relationships can also be crossed if the therapist's and client's racial identity expressions are diametrically opposed.

Parallel. Parallel events are those in which the therapist and client are expressing their racial identity similarly. Helms assumes that similarity of expression implies the same dominant racial identity statuses are functioning for both the client and therapist. In terms of process, parallel events are harmonious and relatively conflict free because the therapist and client intuitively understand one another. When most of a therapist and client's race-related interactions are parallel or the client's most salient issues are resolved in a parallel manner, then the entire relationship is classified as parallel.

An excerpt from one of Thompson's (1990) interviews can be used to illustrate parallel events.* The counselor ("Co") in this segment is a White female counseling graduate student, and the client (Cl) is an African American female undergraduate at the same educational institution as the counselor. Thompson et al. (1994) solicited African American undergraduates to discuss their issues of adjustment to college in either a "culturally" (in our view, racially) responsive or universal condition. The excerpt is from one of their responsive interviews.

> Co: Um you said you were tired of it all. You want to tell me more about how that affects you?
>
> Cl: Um . . . because I am by myself in conflict with a lot of reasons why they do some of the things that they do just because I think it's extreme. It's kind of I guess you can say ignorant in a way. It's not . . . it doesn't show a level of intelligence that we should be trying to portray . . . you know that we have. It's just not there.
>
> Co: Some of the things they do like . . .
>
> Cl: For instance, ah . . . we're watching a movie one night and a couple of friends were drunk and going [up] and down the hall punching White people, just to be punching White people. I thought, 'that doesn't need to be done.'
>
> Co: MmHmm.
>
> Cl: I mean that's just showing your ignorance, you know, that's not necessary, to prove anything, it doesn't mean anything. There are other ways to work around the same issue than violence. For one thing, it doesn't work.
>
> Co: No (empathetically [sic]). It sounds like you feel that there really are racial issues that need to be addressed.
>
> Cl: Yeah . . . MmHmm.

*Source: Thompson, C.E. (1990). Transcripts of race-approach condition interviews.

This sequence of events (i.e., speaking turns) seems to be parallel because although the therapist does not take the client beyond where she started with respect to racial issues, she does listen apparently empathically and is able to let the client know that she hears that race is an aspect of her circumstances. If the therapist wanted to move the interaction beyond its "parallelness," she might have encouraged the client to explore the meaning of "the same issue" (in the client's words) or the "racial issues" (in the therapist's words). Nevertheless, as this excerpt shows, parallel relationships may be helpful to the client as long as they do not force the client to move backward (e.g., pretend obliviousness) to her or his racial circumstances.

Regressive.   Regressive events are those in which the therapist attempts to force a more racially mature client to accept the therapist's less sophisticated interpretation of racial realities. Such events are typically characterized by disharmony and conflict. A series of events resolved in this manner contributes to regressive relationships overall.

The same counselor and client can be used to illustrate regressive events. When the topic changes to the area of intimate social relationships (see Chapter 6), the therapist seems to become less empathic.

> Co: Tell me more about your personal experience on this matter [the lack of compatible people with whom to form relationships].
> Cl: Um . . . since I've been here I haven't had any really just because, I guess, I don't know, I just kind of stay away, I don't get into anything. I haven't . . . there is one person I basically am talking to right now, you know he is White and just because . . .
> Co: Male?
> Cl: MmHmm. Male, yes. Is that what you are asking me?
> Co: Yeah, yeah. I was just wondering if you were talking about a friend that you talked to about this or someone you're thinking about.
> Cl: Thinking about.
> Co: Ok.
> Cl: Yes . . . and ah, it's not that I don't feel comfortable, it's figuring out what he feels, you know. I have that to work on and then if something should happen I know the flack I'm going to get. I kind of have to worry about how I'm going to deal with that. I've never had to deal with that in this environment. And even if it's worth, you know, my grieving point, then I'll know how I feel about that.
> Co: So you said you weren't really worried about that fact but it sounds like it would affect you.
> Cl: It will affect me . . . that's the thing, I know it will, or how it will affect him. I guess I'll have to work that one out when it gets there.
> Co: It sounds like a painful area to have to deal with making those decisions. I mean relationships are tricky anyway. I guess you'll have to make them in the context of race and who is going to think what about what you're doing.
> Cl: It's hard.

Notice that regressive events and relationships do not have to be obviously tense to the participants at the time. Rather they can involve the therapist's subtle redirection of the client's issues so that they no longer involve race. In this case, once the counselor makes sure that the client is talking about the difficulties she is encountering as she considers a dating-type relationship with a White male, her contributions to the discussion are rather abstract (e.g., "that fact," "it"). Moreover, she offers ambiguous and at worst bad advice," . . . you'll have to make [relationship] decisions in the context of race and who is going to think what about what you're doing."

Progressive. Progressive events are characterized by therapists who are acting in a manner that is more sophisticated with respect to racial identity expression (and presumably development) than their clients, and consequently, are capable of educating and assisting clients to develop racially in ways that are of benefit to the client. With respect to process dynamics, progressive events are often characterized by high levels of arousal and involvement on the part of both participants. As was the case for the other two types of relationships, progressive relationships are defined by an abundance of progressive resolutions of events or progressive resolution of a client's cardinal events. *Cardinal* here refers to internalized psychological reactions to race and/or racism that serve a guiding function in the particular person's life.

To illustrate progressive events, we resume Thompson's counselor-client counseling simulation where we left it when we were describing parallel events.

> Co: That maybe they are not being addressed in ways that you feel comfortable with . . .
>
> Cl: Right . . . not being addressed or just not being accepted. Some people just choose to look the other way or don't want to face it or see things for how they really are but, again my, my ah you know, I can't make someone else see something that they don't see or don't hear.
>
> Co: Right, I'm not sure if you're talking about making the Black students seeing what their actions are or helping White students to . . .
>
> Cl: Both
>
> Co: . . . confront their own racism.
>
> Cl: Both, helping Blacks to realize that they don't have to you know fight back in violent methods, you know and, and leave just because it's this way. And on the other hand, um . . . helping Whites to understand that we've got just as much intelligence as they do. We're here just as they are to get a education. To make better of ourselves. To have jobs, future, family, things like that and it means as much to us as it might to them.
>
> Co: MmHmm.

Notice that it is the therapist's introduction of "racism" that allows the client to open up about how she feels White people contribute to the problems that she and other Blacks have experienced in adjusting to college. However, once she has initiated it, she does not seem to know how to maintain the client's self-disclosure at the same level of intensity. When the client uses "we," she has obviously shifted into her version of a collectivistic orientation wherein what happens to "we" also happens to her. Perhaps the therapist could intensify the client's communication by attempting to draw her out with respect to what adverse experiences with racism she in particular has encountered on campus.

In Table 8.1, we summarized some of the characteristics of the three types of relationships. Notice that it is not the person's racial or ethnic classification per se that is alleged to determine the quality of events or relationships, but rather the combination of therapist and client dominant racial identity schema. Also, clearly from Helms's perspective, progressive relationships are considered more likely to promote positive client change. However, parallel relationships might also be effective to the extent that both participants either are operating from relatively mature statuses or are working on some mutually agreed upon goal.

In addition, although the racial identity interaction model was developed to describe qualitative differences in social interactions, including therapy relationships when race was an overt or covert aspect of the process, it seems possible that the model also may be useful when aspects of the therapist's and client's culture are evident. To use the model in this manner, however, it is important to recognize that acculturation also involves maturation or developmental progression. That is, a person learns the cultures of the environments in which he or she is socialized, and the longer he or she is immersed in those cultures, the better the person learns them. Thus, a person who expresses the culture(s) of his or her socialization is behaving "normally," even if his or her particular version of culture is not the societal norm. When a therapist (or other societal authority figure) implicitly or explicitly devalues a person's culture because it is not the same as the therapist's internalized culture and/or because the client's culture deviates from some societal standard, then the therapist sets up the dynamics for the same types of events and relationships that Helms (1995) proposes for race-related interactions.

Therapy Outcome

Of course, the entire reason for the therapist and client engaging in the therapy process is to effect an outcome or change in the client's condition or circumstances. Ideally, if the therapy proceeds as it should, then the client's presenting problem, symptoms, adjustment, or life circumstances are improved as a consequence of participating in the process.

As shown in Figure 10.1, outcome also can be conceptualized as distal ("socio") or proximal ("psycho"). In this case, distal outcomes are those that characterize the behavior of a group, such as attrition rates and service utilization. Proximal outcomes are individual-level consequences that pertain to the particular client, such as symptom remission, racial identity maturation, and cultural competence.

Although investigators sometimes have studied the effects of racial categories and occasionally ethnic group specific cultural dimensions on distal behaviors (see Sue et al., 1994), they rarely have examined the influence of race or culture on proximal outcomes. Consequently, when deciding upon racially or culturally appropriate outcomes for clients, the therapist and client may have to base their decisio jective information (e.g., what helps the client function better) rather than ~mpirical information or theoretical principles.

Conclusions

If we base our conclusions on "objective" information, then we cannot say with any certainty that the therapy process and outcome are meaningfully related to racial or cultural characteristics of the therapist and/or the client. Simply stated, researchers rarely have investigated therapist attitudes and behaviors or client reactions and symptoms when either the clients or therapists were members of VREGs or collectivistic cultures. Neither the available studies of therapist techniques nor client reactions have occurred to any great extent in real therapy interactions as opposed to simulations.

Consequently, what little we can say about racial or cultural influences on the therapy process, based on existing literature, must be said tentatively. In fact, if anything can be said with any certainty about race and culture and the psychotherapy process, it is that therapy researchers have been most thorough in their examination of the process when the clients under investigation were understood to be White, even though this "understanding" typically has not been acknowledged.

Yet enough ambiguities exist in the literature when race is acknowledged as a potential element to support the idea that "something" different may happen when therapists and clients are not racially congruent. However, the nominal definitions of race that typically have been used do not seem to be adequate for teasing out the various threads of the "something." Similarly, whereas evidence that clients sometimes prefer therapists of their own ethnic group implies that something related to culture (e.g., similar attitudes, language usage) may underlie such preferences, nominal classifications of culture do not permit one to understand what cultural dynamics are relevant. Therefore, it seems to us that cultural or sociopolitical differences and similarities might be a logical place to begin the search for more complex questions, if not answers. In a sense, our "practice nuances" are our attempt to suggest places where more formal inquiry might begin. Use Insight 10.1 to consider them.

Practice Nuances

As mentioned in Chapter 8, we believe that all of the major theoretical orientations on which counseling and psychotherapy are based can be adapted to permit the therapist to work effectively with clients of various racial and cultural groups. In modifying traditional theoretical approaches, a general rule of thumb is that the therapist should consider the assumptions and boundaries involved in a particular theoretical approach and determine the maximum degree of flexibility that he or she can employ and still maintain integrity in the therapy process. In learning to honor our clients' racial and cultural diversity, we have had to question many of the axioms that we were taught during our training as therapists, and adjust our methods to meet our clients at the intersections of their and our racial and cultural worldviews.

INSIGHT 10.1

Ignoring the Client's System

The following excerpt from Montalvo and Gutierrez (1989, pp. 49–50) illustrates the negative consequences that occur when the therapist minimizes the client's life circumstances for fear of being a "bad" therapist.

"In a shopping mall a therapist saw an ex-patient coming towards him. This woman had become a single parent through divorce, slipping, as do many, from a fairly comfortable working-class status into poverty. She was finally emerging from eight years of being trapped as a member of the permanent underclass and was now a computer programming student. As she approached him, he reflected on how he had helped her years ago. He would not put up with her feeling sorry for herself. He had told her that. When she complained bitterly, he had confronted her, pushing her to work seriously on her recovery. He

was glad he did not indulge her needs for dependence. To have done so would have been a disservice to her. She looked good now.

She interrupted his thoughts curtly, "Do you remember me?" "Yes, I do," he answered expecting a friendlier greeting. "You know, I always wanted to tell you something. You never gave me a break, you know that? You never understood what I was going through with the kids and no job. <u>You thought it was me, not what I was going through.</u>" (underline added) "Well, I'm sorry, but maybe my lack of pity did help you. I wanted you to take charge of your life," said the therapist. She replied, "But you wanted me to do it when I couldn't, and it would have helped if you would have understood that. I'm glad I moved on and found another therapist." She turned and walked away leaving the therapist with a disturbing vision [of himself].

With respect to the actual in-session therapy, as therapists in training, we were taught hard-and-fast rules regarding a variety of frequently occurring cultural themes including gift-giving, discussing religion in therapy, and the nature of the therapist's role with clients. However, as we realized that these rules were antithetical to the cultural values of some of our clients, we had to weigh the utility of the rules for our clients. Consequently, it has been necessary for us to become more flexible in our application of certain "tried-and-true" therapy methods so that we might sustain authentic relationships with our clients. In this section, we describe some of our racial/cultural nuances as they pertain to the therapy process.

Gift-Giving

Gift-giving and/or receiving traditionally have been taboos in therapy. Particularly in the psychoanalytic theoretical perspective, if a client gives the therapist a gift, the therapist is virtually required to interpret the actual act of giving the gift as well as the meaning of the gift itself. After the therapist discusses her or his interpretation with the client, it is customary for him or her to refuse the gift. Because it is assumed that the gift is intended to purchase the therapist's approval, the therapist's rationale for declining the gift is that by doing so, he or she discourages the client's attempt to ingratiate herself or himself with the therapist or to gain the therapist's approval and acceptance. More specifically, by refusing the gift, the therapist intends to discourage the client from trying to "buy" the therapist's (and symbolically other authority figures') approval, and show the client that the therapist is accepting the client for himself or herself.

From a racially and/or culturally sensitive perspective, it is important to consider the nature of gift-giving in the client's culture. Many members of visible racial and ethnic groups believe that a person should show his or her appreciation and/or respect for a person's help by giving that person a gift of gratitude. For example, in explaining the custom of gift-giving in traditional Native American cultures, Tafoya (1989) observes the following: "Native beliefs emphasize a circularity— if one has been given something, there is a sense that the recipient will respond in some manner. In traditional healing, the patient will give the Indian Doctor food, or blankets, money, tobacco, etc., and the circle is complete. . . ." (p. 86).

To decline such a gift would be insulting to the gift-giver and damaging to the relationship. However, the therapist can discuss the general meaning of gift-giving in the client's culture, and the specific meaning of giving a particular gift to the therapist. The timing of the gift also might have significance. For instance, holidays may be natural times for people to show others that they are important to them. The therapist may be perceived as an "extended family member" in some cultural groups; and thus, the client may consider gift-giving a natural aspect of such relationships. At the termination of therapy or after the client has undergone a particular major life event or survived a crisis, the client may be inclined to express his or her appreciation to the therapist in the form of a gift.

Generally, our stance on receiving gifts from clients is to accept them if they connote the client's cultural values in some manner, if they are given on a rare or occasional basis, and if they are not too extravagant (but to be perfectly honest, none of our clients has ever offered either of us an *extremely* extravagant gift). We do believe in discussing the meaning of the gift as a strategy for helping the client to express his or her feelings about the therapy relationship. Also, we think that it is inappropriate to make a client feel bad or guilty for having attempted to do something positive for the therapist.

As if receiving gifts is not provocative enough, we have supported some instances of the therapist giving a gift to the client at the termination of therapy. If the therapist and client have similar cultural values regarding gift-giving, it is a genuine expression of the relationship for the therapist to give the client a *token* gift at the time of termination. Also, if the client is forced to terminate therapy due to circumstances out of his or her control before the therapy is complete, then the therapist may decide to give the client a small gift at termination. The gift in this instance is intended to be a transitional object to help the client to carry the therapy with him or her into his or her new situation.

In deciding whether or not to give a client a gift at termination, the therapist should review the nature of the therapy relationship and consider how the client will interpret the intended gift as well as the therapist's giving of the gift. The gift should be of nominal monetary value and perhaps symbolize the therapy process in some manner. For instance, a journal is a gift that would encourage the client's continued growth.

Contact Outside of Therapy

Traditional therapy perspectives assert that the therapy relationship should be confined to the fifty-minute sessions that occur in the therapist's office. However, we believe that it is appropriate for the therapist to attend important public events in the client's life, such as graduations, weddings, recitals, and the like. For many VREG or collectivistic clients, their personal achievements are events that should be shared with the significant members of their community. The therapist often becomes such a figure in these clients' lives, particularly if for one reason or another, they have become separated from their primary cultural group.

Although we do not recommend socializing with the client outside of therapy, attending formal ceremonies that require limited interaction with the client sometimes is a way of showing support for the client and acknowledging difficult accomplishments. Thus, a therapist might attend a client's wedding ceremony, but decline the invitation to the reception. In such instances, the therapist probably should not buy the client another gift because the therapist's attendance at the event is considered to be the gift.

The social communities of VREG people can be very small in certain regions of the country or in certain societal institutions (e.g., schools, work settings). Due to the predominance of Whites in most areas, many ALANA people from traditional cultures must actively seek out other people of their own culture for their social networks. As a result, it is not uncommon that a therapist and client from the same cultural background could end up with shared friends, health care providers, beauticians or barbers, or religious associates. Under such circumstances, both the therapist and the client run the risk of frequently encountering each other outside of therapy.

When therapists encounter clients in social situations outside of therapy, it is typical that the therapist will speak only if he or she is first spoken to by the client. VREG clients may have difficulty resolving the disparity between the intimate nature of the therapist-client relationship during therapy and the distant nature of the therapist-client relationship outside of therapy.

The potentiality of qualitatively different types of social and therapy interactions should be an issue that the therapist discusses with the client in advance so that the client can understand that by maintaining a social distance, the therapist is trying to protect the client's confidentiality. In a frank discussion of the issue, the client and therapist can negotiate in advance how the client would like the therapist to respond to him or her in the event that they should meet in a social situation. However, the therapist should not be too surprised if ALANA or collectivistic clients attempt to introduce their therapist to other significant people in their lives. If clients are able to move beyond the apparent stigma of therapy within their cultural groups, then they are likely to adopt the therapist as part of their collective support system.

Multiple Roles of Therapist

Although the therapist may narrowly define his or her role with the client as one of establishing a relationship with the client for the purpose of resolving some prescribed emotional problem or assisting the client in changing her or his personality, the client may have other expectations. In many cultures, once an individual is identified as a "helper," the helpee may attempt to do his or her "one-stop shopping" with the therapist, that is, he or she may bring an assortment of problems to the therapist for resolution. Thus, clients may seek advice from therapists regarding medical problems, spirituality, financial concerns, or the problems of other members of their family. The therapist is considered to be the "wise one" who can help them resolve all of their life concerns.

Although it has become customary to give clients who attempt to involve their therapists in their lives the "dependent" label, it is important to consider how the client's cultural traditions influence his or her expectations for the therapy relationship. Therapists can discuss these expectations in advance and explain to the client what the appropriate limits of the relationship are. Generally, when the client understands the therapist's relationship boundaries and the reasons for them, he or she is not offended when the therapist must abide by them.

We do, however, suggest that therapists consider broadening their role with clients under certain circumstances. Many clients from oppressed groups could benefit from a therapist who takes on the role of an advocate for their clients. Clients who are in the social minority are typically at the mercy of various social institutions and systems; therapists can use their power to influence these systems on behalf of their clients. However, therapists must discern in which situations the client has the power to speak for himself or herself (with a little encouragement or urging), and in which situations he or she is absolutely powerless.

Discussing Religion in Therapy

Therapists-in-training are typically taught that they should not discuss religion with clients because such discussions are inherently value laden. Furthermore, there is concern that a client's religious beliefs may interfere with the process of therapy. Most of the major theoretical therapy orientations have as a goal assisting the client in becoming more self-directed, self-actualized, or self-empowered, whereas most religions or forms of spirituality have as a goal an individual's surrendering of his or her life to a higher or transcendent Power or Supreme Being.

Nevertheless, in actuality, the psychoanalytic approach in particular is rather akin to religion in that it requires the observant to surrender his or her being to the therapist by revealing the most intimate details of his or her life; as the client releases his or her defenses in response to the therapist, the therapist guides the client toward a healthier approach to life, in a manner not unlike that of a spiritual leader.

For many clients, their religious or spiritual beliefs or philosophies of life are strengths that have carried them through life's adversities. It is important that therapists understand their clients' religious beliefs just as they would assess any other defenses used by clients. Rather than viewing spirituality or religiosity as forces competing against the therapy process, therapists can use these beliefs in relating to their clients. (Cook & Wiley, in press).

For many ALANAs, their religious beliefs have assisted them in surviving the oppression that they have faced at the hands of White America. For others, their non-Christian beliefs have been the focus of ethnocentric oppression. Consequently, it would be inane for White therapists to believe that most ALANA clients would consider giving up their "Gods" and putting their complete trust in White therapists. Complete surrender of one's self contradicts many clients' historical cultural experiences of "God" or a spiritual force that protects one's people from the White "man," "master," or "devils."

Recall that Ghost Dancers came into being as a means of beseeching dead warriors to recapture and replenish the lands of the Native peoples while protecting worshippers from White men (see Chapter 4). If the therapist reacts to so central an issue as obliviously as did the therapist in this excerpt from Axelson (1993, p. 412), then it is not difficult to understand why a client would leave the process with feelings of disgruntlement.

> [Native American] Client: I know that I feel there is something around me that is good. I can take a piece of rock and say that it was formed from something I believe in. I can take a tree and feel good. I feel the obligation that is imposing on me to make me go to church; and I don't want to do that.
>
> ['non-Indian'] Counselor: You feel an obligation to go to church and somehow you want to resist the obligation. You're caught in the middle in giving in to it and fighting against it. You'd rather fight against it than do it . . .
>
> Client: Do you think I should? . . . go to church?
>
> Counselor: I'm wondering if going to church would help you, like anybody else, since you feel so reluctant. It just doesn't seem to be you.

Furthermore, if one were to examine the tenets of psychology and spirituality, it is apparent that there are many parallels in the two philosophical systems. For example, just as psychodynamic theorists believe in the process of re-parenting, most religious perspectives observe a "God" of the religion who can undo any past hurts and is the ultimate "parenting" force from whom individuals seek love and guidance.

Moreover, in person-centered therapy, the therapeutic principles of unconditional positive regard and empathic understanding are analogous to the all-loving, all-forgiving, all-knowing character of the Supreme Being to whom a person can release his or her worries and who believes in the innate power of individuals to become all that they can become. Also, the cognitive/behavioral intervention of reframing self-defeating cognitions is analogous to replacing self-doubt with spiritual beliefs regarding an individual's goodness and power to overcome obstacles and live life fully. Similarly, inducement of positive imagery is as much a spiritually based technique as it is a cognitive-behavioral intervention.

Be that as it may, most clients come to therapy as spiritual beings with some moral code by which they live their lives, and therapists, whether consciously or not, attempt to enhance their clients' spirituality or faith in themselves. Therefore, it makes sense to bring the client's religious or spiritual belief system into the therapy session and work with his or her beliefs openly rather than allowing them to become an implicit barrier to effective helping (Cook & Wiley, in press).

In doing so, however, the therapist should be aware that clients' religious expressions may also lie somewhere along a collectivistic-individualistic continuum. For example, most versions of spirituality-religion ascribe to some form of self-transcendence, but according to Worthington (1989, p. 569) "[for collectivistic religions,] transcendence of the self implies a merging of one's consciousness into a larger universal. For the theorist influenced by Western [individualistic] religions, transcendence of the self implies maintenance of individual identity but emphasis on aspects of existence outside the self [e g , other people, other cultures, other realms]."

If the therapist can discuss the client's spiritual-religious belief system with him or her, then the therapist may obtain valuable information about who else or what other spiritual forces may need to be included as a part or an adjunct to therapy (Boyd-Franklin, 1989). As an aid in promoting the discussion process and assessing the client's religious functioning, the criteria offered by Worthington (1989), paraphrased in Table 10.2, might be useful.

Self-Disclosure as a Therapy Tool

Although all theoretical approaches advocate client self-disclosure, whether therapist self-disclosure is endorsed varies across theoretical orientations. Psychodynamic therapists are the least self-disclosing, as they hope to foster transferential relationships with clients based on the clients' projections from previous relationships. In Rogers' (1980) later person-centered works, he advocated that therapists be more interactive and self-disclosive with clients than was the case in his earlier theorizing.

It is our belief that when working with ALANA clients, appropriate self disclosure is necessary to win the trust of clients. Self-disclosure is a natural part of relationship building. If you want clients to tell you *all* about themselves, then you must tell them *something* about yourself. But be appropriate and use good judgment. In general, a self-disclosure should not shift the therapy focus away from the client to the therapist. A guide to follow with respect to using racially or culturally enhancing disclosures is, ask yourself, "Is this disclosure for the good of the client or for the therapist? How will this disclosure affect the therapeutic relationship?"

For many ALANA clients, the process of therapy is so foreign that the therapist can demystify therapy by disclosing something about his or her own experiences with therapy. Also, self-disclosure can help to reduce the stigma associated with emotional problems if the therapist can share her or his own *past* experiences of being helped by the process. However, in such instances of sharing, the therapist should avoid overwhelming the client with too many dramatic incidents. Clients are reassured when they know that their guide has indeed encountered some of the same difficulties as they have, but has worked through them.

Self-disclosure is also particularly important for establishing cross-racial therapy relationships that feel safe to the client. Some clients are mistrustful of therapists who belong to a different socioracial group, because they hold stereotypic images of people from socioracial groups other than their own. Typically, stereotypes are negative and inhibit the development of a trusting relationship. However, even positive

2 An Adaptation of Worthington's (1989) Guidelines for Assessing Clients' Religion ...lity

Worthington contends that if it becomes evident at some time during the therapy that the solution to or maintenance of the client's religious or spiritual beliefs is an issue, then the therapist should thoroughly assess the client's beliefs. He offers the questions summarized below as relevant issues to consider in the assessment process.

1. Can a formal assessment be conducted?
   Formality can refer to the devices used to conduct the assessment (e.g., paper-and-pencil measure versus discussion) as well as the content of the assessment (e.g., exclusively religion vs. various sociodemographic domains).
2. Is it the content of the person's faith or the process ("faithing") of practicing one's faith that is relevant to the assessment situation?
   Content is the substance of a person's beliefs whereas faithing is the implementation of those beliefs.
3. What role does religion play in the client's life?
   A person can integrate religion into every aspect of his or her daily life or consider it a separate component. Religion may be used for life enhancement, for coping with stress, or as a psychological defense.
4. Where in the developmental process is the client with respect to religious identity relative to other domains of his or her life (e.g., cognitive, moral, and socioemotional)?
   Citing Strunk (1965) as his source, Worthington lists the following criteria for differentiating religious immaturity from maturity: "(a) the person should show social concern and involvement rather than withdrawal and social isolation; (b) the social involvement must arise from cognitive and spiritual awareness rather than being unthoughtful behavior; (c) religion should be integrated with social concern; (d) the spiritual awareness should include a personal conviction of a transcendental power greater than oneself."
5. How is the client's religion related to her or his diagnosis or presenting problem?
   Worthington (1989, p. 591) lists seven criteria intended to assist the therapist in distinguishing truly pathological expressions of religion from the therapist's misunderstanding or lack of knowledge about the client's particular form of religious or spiritual expression. However, the primary criterion seems to be whether observance of the religion "brings calm, peace, joy and love to the person."
6. What role does the client's religion serve in the development and maintenance of the client's problem?
   Here the therapist is interested in assessing the extent to which the problem has its origins or solutions in a person's religious or spiritual orientation.
7. How is "client" defined?
   Various aspects of the client's social and cultural network (family, religious organization, school) might be involved in the development, prevention, and remediation of the client's problem.
8. To what extent is the counselor competent to help with the client's personal issues and the religious implications of these issues for the client?

Some reasons why the therapist might choose to refer the client are as follows: (a) if the client's progress might be inhibited because the client and therapist's religious-spiritual beliefs are too similar or dissimilar; (b) the client's discussion of religion arouses the therapist's countertransference (unresolved) issues with respect to religion-spirituality; and (c) the client's religious-spiritual paradigm is so unfamiliar or antithetical to the therapist's belief system that the therapist cannot listen effectively or understand the client's concerns.

stereotypes may mar the relationship by requiring the client or therapist to conform to standards that do not fit.

Through self-disclosure, the therapist can reveal aspects of himself or herself that will make him or her more human in the client's eyes, thus dispelling the client's possible fantasies about the ways in which the therapist might intend the client harm. Moreover, relevant self-disclosure might contribute to the client's perception of the therapist as a "special" member of a certain racial group; or the client may come to consider that his or her beliefs about other racial groups are unfounded. In either case, in working for the good of the client, the therapist must win the trust of the client, and self-disclosure can be used to assist in this endeavor.

Therapist and Client Language Switching

Different cultural groups have their own idiosyncratic ways of speaking their native language and the marketplace version of their language. Even if the client's native language is English, he or she may have an at-home version of speaking the language that differs noticeably from his or her version of marketplace English. When individuals are the most relaxed and comfortable, they tend to revert to the language style of their primary cultural group.

Also, when clients are dealing with emotionally laden material that was internalized in a particular language or version of a language, they may also shift into the language in which the material was originally encoded. In the Thompson (1993) interview discussed previously, both the therapist and client language switch, but in opposite directions. The client uses her at-home language when she feels most uncomfortable about an issue. The therapist's shift is more subtle, but she becomes more formal when she is uncomfortable.

Various authors have noted language switching, as for example, bilingual (primarily Spanish-English) clients may shift from English to Spanish during times of stress, or may become "stuck" between the two languages. In such moments, a simple direction in the client's primary language (e.g., "en Espanol"; "in Spanish") might help him or her to complete the shift to one language or the other. If the therapist does not understand what the client says in the primary language, the client is usually willing to translate it once he or she gets unstuck. In anticipation of such moments, it is sometimes useful for the therapist and client to agree on a verbal prompt that can be used during moments of stress.

Few theorists or practitioners have noticed that this phenomenon of language switching also occurs among monolingual, multidialectical English speakers (e.g., Garner & Rubin, 1986). Newlon and Arciniega (1983) use the term "code switching" to refer to the process of mixing and combining words, styles, or phrasings from one culture with those of another. They offer as an example "Calo," allegedly a Mexican American communication style.

An excerpt from an interview informant in Garner and Rubin's (1986) study of conscious language or code switching among a sample of African American attorneys in the South is an example of how such switching might occur for this particular ethnic-group population: ". . . I'll say, 'Mr. Carter, I'm the solicitor. I'm prosecuting you for the case of rape against Mrs. Carter.' If he doesn't understand what I'm talking about . . . I can say, 'Look man, let me tell you what's goin' down. You got a situation here where this lady said that you took something from her and she didn't wanna' give it up to you . . .' " (p. 39).

Notice that when the attorney communicates in his or her version of at-home or culturally appropriate English (also called "formal" or "standard Black English"), it does not sound like the "street" English or "hip-hop" English that one hears spoken in television and media (see Garner and Rubin, 1986; Helms, 1992). Our cautionary advisory here is that the therapist should be aware of the stereotypes that he or she might hold about culturally congruent speech, and make sure that he or she is not expecting the client to conform to societal linguistic clichés and/or interpreting the client's speech according to societal stereotypes.

If the goal of therapy is to get clients to let down their defenses and be their true selves so that they can free associate or express themselves freely, then clients are most likely to engage in these processes in their native tongues. If the therapist and client belong to the same language and socioracial group(s), then the therapist can foster uncensored communication by speaking to the client in the therapist's and client's common dialect.

However, if the therapist and client are not of the same language group, then the therapist should not attempt to speak to the client in the client's at-home language even if both are of the same socioracial group, because it might be perceived as mimicry. If the therapist and client are of the same language group(s) but different socioracial groups, then the therapist might have to explain why he or she shares the client's private language.

When the therapist and client are of different language origins, and neither is at least partially competent in at least one of the other's languages, then a referral is in order. Sometimes referrals are not possible because of environmental constraints. In such cases, the therapist has to make use of an interpreter who is fluent in the client's primary language. Of course, this solution is not ideal and is subject to a variety of limitations as discussed by various authors (e.g., Lui & Yu, 1985; Marcos, 1979; Sabin, 1975), chief among which is the distortion of the client's communications.

Nevertheless, the reality of doing culturally responsive therapy is that sometimes the therapist, inadequate though he or she may be, is still better than the other alternatives available to the client at the time. Each therapist has to decide for himself or herself when such conditions prevail.

If the therapist and client are of different language origins, and both of them are at least minimally competent in the marketplace language ("standard" English in this case), then the therapist must learn to recognize some of the speech patterns of the client's at-home culture. This can be done by listening attentively to the client in an effort to discern when the client switches back and forth between the two cultural languages, as well as which emotions seem to accompany the shift. Even if the therapist does not understand the client's alternate language, he or she can comment on the ways in which the client's emotional status seems to differ in one language relative to the other. The client, in turn, can be asked to explain the meaning or significance of what or how something is expressed in his or her culture. In the Thompson (1993) regressive-events example, the therapist might have had an easier time communicating with her client if she had simply asked her client to explain what "talking to [a man]" means in the client's culture.

Also, to assuage the client's discomfort as he or she becomes conscious of his or her language switching, the therapist can also model language switching as it occurs in her or his culture. Learning to recognize and participate in language switching is very much like learning to dance. Initially the steps are awkward and the partners have to learn how to move with each other, but once they learn the steps and movements, they can move instinctively with (in some cultural groups) one another.

Termination Issues

When working with ALANA clients, termination can be a prolonged process and it may never be as complete as it is when working with White or individualistic clients in traditional therapy. Due to the values of collectivism and maintaining harmonious relationships in the cultures of most ALANAs, once the relationship has developed the therapist becomes a significant figure in the client's life. If the therapy relationship has been successful, then the client may believe that the therapist has agreed to a life commitment with the client. Therefore, the client may intend to know the therapist and contact her or him throughout the course of the client's life.

The therapist should be aware that assisting the client in "working through" his or her problem is only the first step toward disengaging. The client may not be ready to leave just because he or she has resolved the problem that brought him or her to the therapist in the first place. Consequently, the therapist needs to be prepared to alter the nature of the termination process so that leaving the relationship does not necessarily mean the end of the relationship. Otherwise, the client may postpone indefinitely his or her progress in therapy as a not-necessarily-conscious means of maintaining the connection with the therapist.

At the risk of being redundant, we need to point out again that the client's desire to maintain a connectedness with the therapist does not necessarily mean that the client is exhibiting dependency. Rather it probably means that the therapist has performed his or her social role well because the client feels comfortable about practicing his or her collectivistic cultural norms concerning maintenance of significant relationships. Nevertheless, the typical therapist cannot continue to see each of his or her clients forever, no matter how much he or she may care about the client's well being. Therefore, the therapist needs to plan a weaning process, which may include intermittent scheduling of appointments, briefer appointments, and an invitation for the client to keep in touch via letters or telephone calls.

Legal and Ethical Issues and Cultural Conflict

Some readers may have already reported us to their professional ethics boards for some of the therapeutic practices that we have recommended thus far. However, although we may have straddled the ethical boundaries a bit, we do not believe that we have actually crossed any of them. Perhaps our most distressing recommendation for traditionally trained psychologists is our suggestion that having contact with clients outside of therapy is appropriate. Some of them may argue that such behavior constitutes multiple relationships with clients.

Principle 1.17 of the American Psychological Association's (APA) "Ethical Principles of Psychologists and Code of Conduct," 1992, p. 1601), which pertains to multiple relationships, says in part: "In many circumstances and situations, it may not be feasible or reasonable for psychologists to avoid social or other nonprofessional contacts with persons such as patients, clients, students, supervisees, or research participants. A psychologist refrains from entering into or promising another personal, scientific, professional, financial, or other relationship with such persons if it appears likely that such a relationship reasonably might impair the psychologist's objectivity or otherwise interfere with the psychologist's effectively performing his or her functions as a psychologist, or might harm or exploit the other party."

Notice that the emphasis of the ethical principle is on *not doing harm*. Although we strongly endorse the principle of avoiding harming one's clients, we think that relationships outside of the therapy room per se need not harm the client. Rather, we view such interactions, when handled properly, as extensions of the therapeutic relationship. Be advised that we are not advocating that therapists be friends or social acquaintances with clients, and we definitely disapprove of sexual intimacies between therapists and clients. Nevertheless, we do contend that therapist-client relationships can be genuine with respect to race and culture, and that authenticity need not obliterate the boundaries of the participants' respective roles.

If the therapist is intending to become the "good parent" to the client, then in most cultures that we are aware of, such a parent would very proudly attend the child's graduation ceremony or other rites of passage. Important principles for the therapist to internalize are: Always work for the good of the client, set clear boundaries with the client, and accept responsibility for whatever relationship that you establish with your client.

The other place where incipient therapists sometimes have trouble with our therapy approach is our recommendation that therapists practice fluid terminations when necessary for the client's benefit. The applicable APA ethical principle is 4.09c, which reads as follows: "Prior to termination for whatever reason, except where precluded by the patient's or client's conduct, the psychologist discusses the patient's or client's views and needs, provides appropriate pretermination counseling, suggests alternative service providers as appropriate, and takes other reasonable steps to facilitate transfer of responsibility to another provider if the patient or client needs one immediately" (p. 1606). Our approach merely attempts to ensure that the client does not feel abandoned.

The ethical standards of most professional associations were derived from traditional theoretical perspectives. Strict adherence to such rigid guidelines may present cultural conflicts that can contribute to the client's terminating therapy prematurely, before he or she has had the opportunity to benefit from its potential curative properties. An inability to interpret guidelines in a manner that is congruent with the client's real-world circumstances may contribute to more confusion in clients' lives as they are forced to choose between the norms of their culture and the expectations of the therapist. However, we believe that the client is going to have to interact within his or her cultural groups long after the therapy relationship has ended. Therefore, in our opinion, therapists must prepare clients to function in a healthy manner within the clients' cultural frames of reference.

As we mentioned earlier, APA's Office of Ethnic Minority Affairs developed a set of standards for psychologists who provide services to visible racial/ethnic group clients (see Appendix). Office staff found that the general APA ethical standards did not adequately address the unique issues involved in responding effectively to clients' racial and cultural concerns. Neither we nor the Ethnic Minority staff advocate that therapists engage in unethical practices. However, they must consider what is ethical while keeping in mind the client's cultural context. Therapists cannot be ethical if they disregard the racial and cultural contexts in which they deliver services.

REFERENCES

Abramowitz, S. I., & Murray, J. (1985). Race effects in psychotherapy. In J. Murray & P. R. Abramson (Eds.), *Bias in psychotherapy* (pp. 215–255). New York: Praeger.

Andrews, G., & Harvey, R. (1981). Does psychotherapy benefit neurotic patients: A re-analysis of the Smith, Glass, and Miller data. *Archives of General Psychiatry, 38*, 1203–1208.

Atkinson, D. R. (1985). A meta-review of research on cross-cultural counseling and psychotherapy. *Journal of Multicultural Counseling and Development, October,* 138–153.

Axelson, J. A. (1993). *Counseling and development in a multicultural society* (2nd ed.). Pacific Grove, CA: Brooks/Cole.

Bergin, A. E. (1971). The evaluation of therapeutic outcomes. In A. E. Bergin & S. L. Garfield (Eds.), *Handbook of psychotherapy and behavior change* (pp. 217–270). New York: John Wiley.

Berman, J. (1979a). Individual versus societal focus: Problem diagnoses of black and white male and female counselors. *Journal of Cross-Cultural Psychology, 10*, 497–507.

Berman, J. (1979b). Counseling skills used by Black and White male and female counselors. *Journal of Counseling Psychology, 26*, 81–84.

Borrego, R. L., Chavez, E. L., & Titley, R. W. (1982). Effect of counselor technique on Mexican-American and Anglo American self-disclosure and counselor perception. *Journal of Counseling Psychology, 29*, 538–541.

Boyd-Franklin, N. (1989). Five key factors in the treatment of Black families. *Journal of Psychotherapy and the Family, 6*(1–2), 53–69.

Cannon, C. E., & Helms, J. E. (1993). An investigation of relationship factors in HIV counseling with Black, Latino, and White clients. Unpublished paper, University of Maryland, College Park.

Carter, R. T. (1990). Does race or racial identity attitudes influence the counseling process in Black and White dyads? In J. E. Helms (Ed.), *Black and White racial identity: Theory, research, and practice* (pp. 145–163). Westport, CT: Greenwood.

Carter, R. T., & Helms, J. E. (1992). The counseling process as defined by relationship types: A test of Helms's racial identity interaction model. *Journal of Multicultural Counseling and Development, 20*, 181–201.

Cook, D. A. & Wiley, C. Y. (in press). African American churches and Afrocentric spiritual traditions. In P. S. Richards & A. E. Bergin (Eds.) *Psychotherapy and religious diversity: A guide to mental health professionals.* Washington, DC: American Psychological Association Books.

Dauphinais, P., Dauphinais, L. & Rowe, W. (1981). Effects of race and communication style on Indian perceptions of counselor effectiveness. *Counselor, Education & Supervision, 21*, 72–80.

Ethical Principles of Psychologists and Code of Conduct (1992). *American Psychologist, 47*, 1597–1628.

Folensbee, R. W., Draguns, J. G., Jr., & Danish, S. J. (1986). Impact of two types of counselor intervention on Black American, Puerto Rican, and Anglo-American analogue clients. *Journal of
Counseling Psychology, 33,* 446–453.

Garner, T., & Rubin, D. L. (1986). Middle class Blacks' perceptions of dialect and style shifting: The
case of Southern attorneys. *Journal of Language and Social Psychology, 5,* 33–49.

Gim, R. H., Atkinson, D. R., & Kim, S. J. (1991). Asian-American acculturation, counselor ethnicity
and cultural sensitivity, and ratings of counselors. *Journal of Counseling Psychology, 38,* 57–62.

Glass, G. V., McGraw, B., & Smith, M. L. (1981). *Meta-analysis in social response.* Beverly Hills, CA:
Sage Publications.

Guidelines for providers of psychological services to ethnic, linguistic, and culturally diverse populations. (1993). *American Psychologist, 48,* 45–48.

Helms, J. E. (1984). Toward a theoretical explanation of the effects of race on counseling: A Black
and White model. *The Counseling Psychologist, 12,* 153–165.

Helms, J. E. (1990). Counseling attitudinal and behavioral predispositions: The Black/White interaction model. In J. E. Helms (Ed.), *Black and White racial identity: Theory, research, and practice*
(pp. 135–163). New York: Greenwood Press.

Helms, J. E. (1992). Why don't psychologists study cultural equivalence in cognitive ability tests?
American Psychologist, 47, 1083–1101.

Helms, J. E. (1995). An update of Helms's People of Color (POC) and White racial identity models.
In J. Ponterotto, L. A. Suzuki, & C. M. Alexander (Eds.), *Handbook of multicultural counseling*
(pp. 181–198). Beverly Hills, CA: Sage Publications.

Hill, C. E. (1989). *Therapist techniques and client outcomes.* Beverly Hills, CA: Sage Publications.

Katz, J. H. (1985). The sociopolitical nature of counseling. *The Counseling Psychologist, 13,* 615–624.

LaFromboise, T. D., Coleman, H. L., & Hernandez, A. (1991). Development and factor structure of
the Cross-Cultural Counseling Inventory—Revised. *Professional Psychology: Research and
Practice, 22,* 380–388.

Lui, W. T., & Yu, E. S. H. (1985). Ethnicity and mental health. In J. Moore & L. Maldonado (Eds.),
Urban ethnicity (pp. 211–247). Beverly Hills, CA: Sage Publications.

Marcos, L. R. (1979). Effects of interpreters on the evaluation of psychopathology in non-English-
speaking patients. *American Journal of Psychiatry, 136,* 171–174.

Montalvo, B., & Gutierrez, M. J. (1989). Nine assumptions for work with ethnic minority families.
In Saba, G., Karrer, B. M., & Hardy, K. V. (Eds.). (1990). *Minorities and family therapy.*
Binghamton, New York: Haworth Press.

Newlon, B. J., & Arciniega, M. (1983). Respecting cultural uniqueness: An Adlerian approach.
Individual Psychology Journal of Adlerian Theory, Research, and Practice, 39, 133–143.

Pomales, J., Claiborn, C. & LaFromboise, T. (1986). Effects of Black students' racial identity on perceptions of white counselors varying in cultural sensitivity. *Journal of Counseling Psychology, 33,*
57–61.

Pomales, J. & Williams, V. (1989). Effects of level of acculturation and counseling style on Hispanic
students' perceptions of counselor. *Journal of Counseling Psychology, 36,* 79–83.

Ponterotto, J. G., Rieger, B. P., Barrett, A., Harris, G., Sparks, R., Sanchez, C. M., & Magids, D. (in
press). Development and initial validation of the Multicultural Counseling Awareness Scale. In
J. Impara & G. R. Sodowsky (Eds.), *Ninth Buros-Nebraska Symposium on Measurement and
Testing: Multicultural Assessment.* Lincoln, NE: Buros Institute.

Rachman, S. J., & Wilson, G. T. (1980). *The effects of psychological therapy* (2nd ed.). New York:
Pergamon.

Rogers, C. R. (1980). *A way of being.* Boston: Houghton Mifflin.

Sabin, J. E. (1975). Translating despair. *American Journal of Psychiatry, 132,* 197–199.

Sattler, J. M. (1977). The effects of therapist-client racial similarity. In A. S. Gurman & A. M. Razin
(Eds.), *Effective psychotherapy: A handbook of research* (pp. 252–290). New York: Pergamon Press.

Sodowsky, G. R. (1994, November). *The Multicultural Counseling Inventory: Psychometric properties and
some uses in counseling training.* Paper presented at the meeting of the Ninth Buros-Nebraska
Symposium on Measurement and Testing: Multicultural Assessment, Lincoln, NE.

Sodowsky, G. R., Taffe, R. C., Gutkin, T. B., & Wise, S. (1994). Development of the Multicultural Counseling Inventory: A self-report measure of multicultural competencies. *Journal of Counseling Psychology, 41,* 137–148.

Strunk, O. P., Jr. (1965). Mature religion: A psychological study. In E. L. Worthington (1989), Religious faith across the life span: Implications for counseling and research. *The Counseling Psychologist, 17,* 590.

Sue, D. W., Arredondo, P., & McDavis, R. J. (1992). Multicultural counseling competencies and standards: A call to the profession. *Journal of Counseling and Development, 70*(4), 477–486.

Sue, D. W., Bernier, J. E., Durran, A., Feinberg, L., Pedersen, P., Smith, E. J., & Vasquez-Nutall, E. (1982). Position paper: Cross-cultural counseling competencies. *The Counseling Psychologist, 10*(2), 45–52.

Sue, S., & Zane, N. (1987). The role of culture and cultural techniques in psychotherapy: A critique and reformulation. *American Psychologist, 42*(1), 37–45.

Sue, S., Zane, N., & Young, K. (1994). Research on psychotherapy with culturally diverse populations. In A. E. Bergin & S. L. Garfield (Eds.), *Handbook of psychotherapy and behavior change* (pp. 783–817). New York: John Wiley & Sons.

Tafoya, T. (1989). Circles and cedar: Native Americans and family therapy. *Journal of Psychotherapy and the Family, 6*(1–2), 71–98.

Thompson, C. E. (1990). Transcripts of "race-approach" condition interviews. Personal Communication.

Thompson, C. E., Worthington, R., & Atkinson, D. R, (1994). Counselor content orientation, counselor race, and Black women's cultural mistrust level and self-disclosures. *Journal of Counseling Psychology, 41,* 155–161.

Worthington, E. L. Religious faith across the lifespan: Implications for counseling and research. *The Counseling Psychologist, 17,* pp. 555–612, copyright © 1989 by Sage Publications. Reprinted by Permission of Sage Publications, Inc.

CHAPTER

11 Racial and Cultural Themes in Career Counseling

Perhaps the interaction among personal characteristics, subjective culture, and systemic influences is most evident in the area of career development and the counseling and advising aimed at maximizing the client's options in these areas. Even the language that career theorists use in discussing appropriate strategies and interventions implies a greater degree of freedom in these areas than historically has been the case for any racial, cultural, and gender groups with the possible exception of White (English-speaking) males in this country. Thus, terminology such as "career choice," "career," and "career decision-making" implies a cornucopia of options from which the person has only to choose the one that most fulfills her or his personal needs and abilities.

In their presentation of a career development theory for disenfranchised groups, Carter and Cook (1992) noted the irrelevance of traditional career development theories for most of the U.S. population. They contend that such theories do not address the environmental systemic barriers that historically have limited the work options of Asian, African, Hispanic, and Native populations of both genders as well as White females.

In career counseling, the counselor needs to focus rather specifically on the sociopolitical implications of the client's racial classification for her or his work options as well as on those aspects of cultural socialization that can make the world of work a foreign and sometimes inhospitable environment for those whose psychocultural attributes do not match those of the work environments in which the client finds herself or himself or that he or she intends to enter.

Here, also, matters of internalized social class (psychosocial class) and external social class (socioeconomic status) barriers enter the process in full force, not only as an aspect of the client's quality of functioning, but also as a factor in the counselor's and client's manner of relating to one another. In particular, the counselor's interpretation of the client's options may be shaped by the social class socialization that has influenced this counselor's own career development. Moreover, internalized social class may interact with socioculture and sociorace to produce dynamics that are unfamiliar to the therapist or client.

In this chapter, we discuss some of the racial and cultural factors that counselors should consider when doing counseling with career themes. In general, our philosophy is that career counseling differs from other forms of psychotherapy only in that its career focus is typically more direct than is true of other forms of therapy. However, other forms of intrapsychic and/or interpersonal counseling and psychotherapy often have career issues as an underlying theme.

The specific focus of this discussion is the impact of sociorace, psychosocial class, and subjective culture (i.e., psychoculture) at the individual level (e.g., client's characteristics), the systemic level (e.g., impact of institutional racism), and the work environment. For our purposes, we consider three broad topic areas—theories of career development, career assessment, and career process. As is our custom, we attempt to explain how we think traditional perspectives must be modified to adequately service VREG and/or collectivistic populations as well as provide some information about alternative perspectives that have been offered to deal with the career concerns of members of these groups.

Consider the following case vignette:

> Patty is a 20-year-old Asian American student who is in her second year at a large public state university. She is majoring in chemistry with the intention of entering medical school when she graduates. After taking a heavy course load of "hard" science courses her first three semesters, she now has an overall GPA of 3.0. She knows that this is pretty low for a person intending to enter medical school, but explains that she has been "lazy" and will "just have to work harder." In exploring her interests, the intake counselor finds that Patty "really enjoys English and creative writing" and must be very good in this area because her two English courses account for her only *A* grades.

Imagine that Patty has been referred to you for career counseling. How would you proceed? What additional information would you seek from her? How would Patty's racial classification influence your assessment of her problem? What differential impact would her gender classification have on how you proceed? To what cultural factors would you attend?

Before we respond to our own questions, let us examine how traditional career theory proposes that one address Patty's concerns.

Traditional Career Theoretical Perspectives

Although the fact is rarely acknowledged, most career development theories were developed to explain the vocational process as it involves White, male, English-speaking, upper-middle class, individualistic career aspirants (see Osipow, 1975, and Zunker, 1981, for more extended discussions of this issue). This is, of course, the group with most freedom of choice as to which careers its members will pursue as well as the most viable career options. Nevertheless, some recent efforts have attempted to expand and/or reformulate these models so that they take into account the career life experiences of primarily White upper-middle class, English-speaking women (e.g., Betz & Fitzgerald, 1987). Therefore, our discussion will not focus much on the career issues of thc White socioracial group of either gender or social class. However, to the extent that members of these groups deviate from the norm of their group(s) on any of the sociodemographic categories (e.g., social class, cultural orientation), then our comments regarding VREGs and/or members of collectivistic cultures may pertain to them as well.

According to Leonard (1985), in evaluating the appropriateness of traditional vocational theories for VREG populations, it is useful to categorize the theories as either *personality* and *self-concept-based* or *developmental process-oriented.*

Personality and Self-Concept Theories

Personality- and self-concept-based theories attribute a person's vocational development and/or choices to intrapsychic processes such as needs and specific personality characteristics. Thus, this type of theory is individualistic even when it allows that people may engage in people-oriented vocational behavior because the reason they are hypothesized to do so is primarily for self-fulfillment. Exemplars of this approach are John Holland's (1973) personal occupational orientations and Anne Roe's (1956) psychoanalytic perspective.

Holland's Theory.   The basic premise of Holland's perspective is that an individual's career choice is an extension of her or his personality into the world of work. Both the work-seeker and the work environment are postulated to have *modal characteristics* or *styles.* Thus, a person seeks an occupation in those environments that match his or her personality style, and feels most satisfied with his or her career selection when the job and the environment are congruent. In general, *congruence* refers to the fit or correspondence between career-related aspects of the person (e.g., aptitudes, interests, skills) and some parallel attributes of the work environment (e.g., education, interests, skills).

Holland's modal personality and environmental styles are as follows: (a) **Realistic**—characterized by a preference for concrete rather than abstract work duties, objects rather than people, and individualistic rather than collectivistic work surroundings; (b) **Investigative**—an individualistic orientation characterized by a preference for abstract, creative, and analytic work tasks and work environments that permit independence; (c) **Artistic**—self-expressive style through the performance of artistic endeavors and creativity; personality characteristics may include introversion and a desire for independence; (d) **Social**—an interpersonally oriented and often extraverted style characterized by a preference for working with and for the benefit of people; (e) **Enterprising**—an extraverted, assertive leader-oriented style characterized by verbal facility, dominative tendencies, adventurousness, and the capacity to persuade and manipulate others for work-related purposes; and (f) **Conventional**—pragmatic, structured, and conservative with a preference for maintaining the status quo. Although persons and work environments may be characterized by more than one of these themes, Holland assumes that at least one of the themes is modal or generally governs the person's career behavior.

Thus, in Holland's framework, career decisions and level of attainment occur by means of self-evaluations. That is, the person consciously or unconsciously chooses those work environments that permit him or her to best express one's personality characteristics. Moreover, as Zunker (1981) points out, a variety of personality and aptitudinal dimensions are implicit in Holland's personality orientations or types. For example, Investigative individuals are presumably intelligent enough to perform analytic tasks, whereas Artistic people are presumably talented enough to express themselves creatively.

Therefore, a counselor using Holland's approach likely would begin by assessing either formally or informally Patty's modal personality and the degree of congruence between it and her current career choices. In this case, her choice of major and performance in related courses would be relevant. Patty's record to date suggests that she is an Artistic rather than an Investigative type. Thus, the traditional career counselor might encourage her to explore career options more obviously related to her expressed interests and aptitudes.

Roe's Theory.   At least originally, Roe's theory emphasized the importance of early childhood socialization experiences in determining later career choices. Roe's perspective is psychoanalytic, and consequently, emphasizes parent-child dynamics as crucial to the person's eventual career development. Thus, Roe (1972) argued that being born into a particular family at a specific time and place was a critical determinant of a person's work history.

More specifically, in Roe's framework, occupations are classified as people-oriented or nonpeople-oriented. She hypothesized that predilections toward people or social occupations were a function of the extent to which a person had been rewarded or punished for his or her social inclinations during early parent-child interactions. For example, a person raised in a warm and nurturing familial environment has had people orientations rewarded, and therefore would move toward work environments in which social needs could be reinforced. However, a person raised in cold or emotionally distant environments would not have had his or her social needs rewarded, and consequently would be attracted to work environments in which interpersonal contact is minimal. Examples of people-oriented occupations are social service, sales, and education. Examples of nonpeople-oriented occupations are Holland's realistic occupations (e.g., forest ranger, farming, mining) and technological jobs (e.g., laboratory technician, transportation, maintenance).

Thus, in Patty's case, the counselor would search for the source of her vocational confusion in the dynamics of her family. However, Roe's framework might be especially difficult to apply to Patty because it is based on a culture-specific (White male research scientists) definition of family. Thus, the counselor intending to use Roe's framework with Patty would have to be careful not to impose an inappropriate definition of culture on Patty and her family.

The Developmental Process Perspective

Developmental process theories describe career development as a sequential, stagewise process by which efficacious individuals explore their career options. Stages are assumed to be interrelated, elicited by psychosocial socialization, and to precipitate career-related crises that must be resolved in order for the person to achieve career maturity. However, depending upon the theorist, career maturity may be evidenced by a variety of presumably work-related characteristics. For example, relevant characteristics might include appropriate work habits (Havighurst, 1964). Although a variety of process theories exist (e.g., Havighurst, 1964; Ginzberg, Ginsberg, Axelrad, and Herma, 1951), Donald Super's (1988) version of this approach has had the most far-reaching effects.

Super proposed that the vocational self-concept develops by means of five developmental stages. In ascending order of maturity, these stages are as follows: (a) **growth** (from birth to age 14 or 15)—a period during which those attitudes, interests, and values that reflect the person's self-concept develop; (b) **exploratory** (from ages 15 to 24)—the initial narrowing of vocational options; (c) **establishment** (from ages 25 to 44)—trying out possibilities and making firmer decisions about desirable options; (d) **maintenance** (from ages 45 to 64)—ongoing adjustments to improve working conditions and maintain the status quo with respect to work; and (e) **decline** (at least age 65)—gradual disengagement from work.

Although they may occur at any time during the developmental process, certain developmental tasks are assumed to require resolution before the person can continue his or her progress toward developing a functional vocational self-concept. Moreover, certain tasks are generally more pertinent during certain developmental stages than others. For example, crystallization ordinarily occurs at the same time as the growth stage.

The general themes of the vocational developmental tasks are summarized in Table 11.1. Some relevant racial identity themes for ALANAs and Whites are also included in the table. However, just as it is the case that vocational tasks may actually occur during any of Super's developmental stages, it is also the case that any of the racial identity themes that we summarize can occur in conjunction with any of the developmental tasks. Also, we refer the reader to Helms and Piper (1994) for an analysis of the congruence between Super's vocational development stages and Helms's (1994) racial identity statuses.

If a career counselor were to use Super's model to conceptualize Patty's circumstances, then it appears that in terms of age, she is in the exploratory stage of vocational commitment. She has made a (perhaps) tentative choice about what she would like to do (go to medical school), although her choice might not correspond to her actual vocational characteristics. Therefore, a counselor using the process perspective might encourage her to engage in the activities that characterize crystallization; that is, more exploration of her vocational values, interests, and so forth.

Racial and Cultural Career Concerns

So far, nothing has been said about how racial and/or cultural dynamics might be expected to influence Patty's career choice. This is because most traditional vocational

TABLE 11.1   A Summary of Super's Developmental Tasks and Some Relevant ALANA and White Racial Identity Vocational Themes

Task	ALANA	White
Crystallization—Formulation of a general vocational direction by assessing personal resources, interest, values, and initial occupational planning	**Conformity** (PreEncounter)—Unconstricted view of occupational options because the person does not integrate information about race or culture into occupational planning	**Contact**—Obliviousness to racism and its role in the occupational world. So, person is unlikely to consider racial issues in initial occupational planning
Specification—Progression from tentative vocational inclinations toward a specific vocational objective	**Dissonance** (Encounter)—Floundering may occur if the person does not know what role racial and cultural factors play in fulfilling the desired objective	**Disintegration**—If the person is experiencing the confusion caused by racial moral dilemmas, then racial factors may become a consideration in pursuing a desired occupational direction
Implementation—Acquiring training related to occupational ideal and beginning employment	**Immersion/Emersion**—May have limited career options because of desire to remain with one's own group or because an activistic orientation makes others uncomfortable	**Reintegration**—may have limited career options because of desire to remain racially exclusive or because feelings of racial victimization serve as an excuse for not trying
Stabilization—Use of talents in relevant work environment to confirm appropriateness of one's vocational choice(s)	**Internalization**—May acquire skills and information about negotiating hostile or nonresponsive work environments. May also acquire a realistic sense of personal/social limitations within such environments	**Autonomy**—Informed positive realistic own-group racial commitment may inspire person to seek or work toward racial and cultural morality within the work environment
Consolidation—Progression in one's chosen career path by means of promotion, acquired status, and/or seniority or tenure	**Integrative Awareness**—Acquired capacity to form work-related coalitions with members of other groups to promote shared goals of fairness	**Immersion/Emersion**—May be involved in searching for an understanding of how personal racial characteristics influence the work environment

Note: This table was adapted from information presented in Carter and Cook (1992, p. 213), Zunker (1981, p. 11), and Helms and Piper (1994, p. 127).

INSIGHT **11.1**

"Career Choice" When There Is No Choice

In his biography of the lives of himself and several of his childhood friends, all of whom were socialized in a poor Black ghetto of Chicago, journalist Sylvester ("Vest") Monroe presents the following views of work through the eyes of himself and one of his "brothers":

> "I've [Monroe] known for a long time what I wanted to do," Vest said. "What I wanted to be. When we were kids, what did you want to be?"
>
> "I never thought about it," Half Man said. "I never wanted to be a fireman, policeman, cameraman, whatever. I guess that's why I been doing what I being doing. I never had one dream about what I wanted to be. I just went to do the chore."
>
> "How do you see your life five years from now? What would you like to be doing?"

"Still working," Half Man said. "Not having *whatever* (italics in original) I want, but the basic things of life. A new car, nice place to stay, and nice clothes. Always something to eat, you know. Also, a couple dollars in the bank. That's it. Living a middle-class life."

"He guessed that was as much as most of them [the rest of their friends] wanted—the ones, anyway, who hadn't got over like Vest had. Maybe none of them had exactly what they might have wished for, Half Man reckoned, but if you didn't want big, you didn't hurt bad. . . . [All of their friends] were happy, Half Man guessed, all of them except himself, and he was doing what he had always done in pursuit of happiness. He was working on it" (Monroe & Goldman, 1988, pp. 203–204).

theories have not considered such factors, although they are arguably implicitly present in each of them. Various critics have noted the absence of a deliberate focus on systemic factors as contributors to the career development of especially VREG populations (e.g., Carter & Cook, 1992; Leonard, 1985; Perry & Locke, 1985). Ordinarily in such critiques, *systemic factors* refers to institutional racism (see Chapters 4 and 5) as expressed through economic and educational discrimination against people of color.

In making the case against self-concept theory as the best approach for judging the vocational mental health of ALANAs and/or culturally distinctive populations, Carter and Cook (1992) note that the work-related self-concepts of members of such groups may appear to be impaired to outsiders, but may in fact represent healthy adaptations to institutional racism and ethnocentrism. For example, they point out that if a person, the person's family members, and/or other members of his or her relevant sociodemographic groups have had access only to menial jobs or have experienced long periods of unemployment, then the person may acquire either an externally induced negative career self-concept or atypical ways of viewing work according to traditional (read White middle-class) standards.

In Insights 11.1 and 11.2, Half Man and Dwayne's mother illustrate the more common strategies for surviving in a society that considers poor ALANA people expendable. One keeps on striving to maintain oneself and one's family legally even in the face of chronic depression and despair. Dwayne, on the other hand, illustrates one way in which work may be redefined. In his framework, work is whatever one needs to do to survive and acquire material goods and a reputation in one's community.

INSIGHT 11.2

A View of Work through Non-Middle-Class Eyes

French and Herndon (1995) present this portrait of multigenerational "vocational choice" through the eyes of a now-deceased street "gangsta" (Dwayne) from the lower socioeconomic class of inner city Washington, D.C.

"Dwayne's mother has always worked, but at low-paying jobs that have left her family on the financial edge. She often works extra shifts at the nursing home where she is an aide, and she cleans houses on the side. The hours add up to chronic fatigue. She falls asleep on the bus, on her feet, in the middle of conversation. Her children [three sons] kid her about it, but they don't really think it's funny. . . . 'I [Dwayne] have no knowledge of any of his [father's] background or family

members whatsoever. It's like I was born to my mother and the clan.' . . .

'We needed help, I went out there and did something to get the money. I went out there and did something to get the money. If you don't want to accept it, I drop the money on the floor and leave out the house. . . . She didn't want the money, but times came when you had to have it.'

"Dwayne says that he took his role of provider and protector so seriously that as soon as he was big enough, he fought any man who showed interest in his mother."

'I was the man of the house, . . . And it was almost like she was my woman. I never really had a father. I was the father.' (French & Herndon, 1995, p. 5).

From French, M. A., & Herndon, C. (1995, May 21) Bread's last jam. *The Washington Post*, Section F, Style, pp. 1, 4–6. © 1995, *The Washington Post*. Reprinted with permission.

Thus, Dwayne's work self-concept is collectivistic; it comes from the outside. He is okay if he "looks good" to others and has a reputation for being a "big man" in the community. Yet even in Dwayne's case, it is clear that his materialism is not expended entirely on himself. He shares his ill-gotten gains with his family of origin whether his mother wants him to or not. Moreover, although Dwayne's manner of sustaining his positive work self-concept (i.e., engaging in criminal activities) is objectionable as well as atypical of African American men, the themes by which it is defined are not. In his own way, Dwayne is pursuing the "American dream."

Carter and Cook (1992) note that VREG cultures often provide compensatory institutions that prevent their members from sustaining impaired vocational identity development. Such institutions permit them to satisfy their meaningful work-related needs in settings or through worker roles that are esteemed by the at-home cultural group(s).

For instance, they hypothesize that the Black Christian church serves as a "social equalizer" for its members. Regardless of their socioeconomic or vocational statuses in the external world, members of a church community can hold very powerful positions within the church. A pastor, deacon, or trustee (i.e., the highest-ranking leadership positions in some Christian denominations) of the church may hold a menial labor position in the work force. However, it is by his or (in rare instances) her high-status church position that the person defines himself or herself and is acknowledged by the in-group community.

Furthermore, work has been a critical part of the cultural socialization of all VREGs, but for many of them its practical purpose of preserving the culture is considered more important than its role in shaping the person's individual identity. In other words, work has been a pragmatic aspect of life for most VREG groups in that individuals contribute their skills and labor to their cultural societies and for the maintenance of their families (however family is defined).

As the first settlers of North America, Native Americans provided the initial cultural base for career development. According to Axelson (1985, p. 29): "Native American tribal cultures have historically been identified by the way they gathered their food (hunting and farming) and the areas in which they pursued their livelihood." However, what often is unacknowledged is the extent to which the indigenous people's work shaped present day agriculture and agribusiness in this country. "The native crops include tomatoes and potatoes; all the squashes and pumpkins; almost all the kinds of beans; peanuts, pecans, hickory nuts, black walnuts, sunflower seeds, cranberries, blueberries, strawberries, maple syrup, and Jerusalem artichokes; all the peppers, prickly pears, chocolate, vanilla, allspice, sassafras, avocados, wild rice, and sweet potatoes. <u>In the four hundred years since the European settlers began coming to North America, they have not found a single plant suitable for domestication that the Indians had not already cultivated</u>" (underline added). By the last decade of the twentieth century, crops of Indian origin constituted approximately one-third of the annual harvest of the United States" (Weatherford, 1991, pp. 127–128).

To the extent that they were permitted to do so, other VREGs replicated work as it existed in their cultures of origin when they immigrated to the United States. Thus, in addition to pure manual labor, immigrant groups of all socioracial groups often contributed their farming, hunting, and crafting skills to the wider society. VREGs and some White ethnic groups often were not permitted to use their business, artistic, scientific, and health care skills in the marketplace, and often sustained their communities through whatever work was accessible to them.

Carter and Cook (1992) note that it is ironic that African Americans, in particular, bear the stereotype of "laziness," and their consistently high unemployment rate is attributed to their "unwillingness" to work. Yet in their African ancestral cultures, members of the cultures used their skills and intellect to create many highly functional and exceedingly sophisticated societies. Moreover, when Africans were enslaved in the Americas (and other regions), their manual skills were exploited, whereas their knowledge and critical thinking skills were suppressed and misused (Axelson, 1985; see Chapter 4).

Also, as we discussed in Chapter 5, various Latino/Latina and Asian ethnic groups entered the American labor force due to the limited economic conditions of their homelands at the time and/or to escape political oppression. At various times, one or the other group was temporarily "welcomed" into the United States to meet the cheap labor needs of American industries. However, the welcome mat rarely meant that the new immigrants were treated well.

Furthermore, as the numbers of immigrants from the groups of color increased and/or the work for which they were recruited diminished, laws, regulations, and national policies were enacted to restrict the number of immigrants, prescribe their residential patterns, and determine citizenship eligibility (see Chapters 4 and 5).

Needless to say, members of these groups soon learned to enter those occupational domains that were open to them and were not a threat to the economic status of their White counterparts.

Carter and Cook (1992) recommend that because of the historical and enduring sociopolitical conditions of VREGs in the American labor force, career "choice" might be more aptly labeled career "path." However, oppressive restrictions imposed by White institutional racism may become barriers that inhibit the VREG person's progress down the available path. Yet it is these barriers that, while often central to the diminished quality of functioning of VREGs in the worlds of education and work, are virtually invisible to Whites. Highlen and Sudarsky-Gleiser (1994), citing Jones (1991) observe that "European-Americans [sic] 'believe that disparities in SES [socioeconomic status] are due primarily to a lack of motivation among African-Americans [sic], that there are no 'structural' impediments to SES advancement for African-Americans [sic], and the 'system' is an opportunity structure for anyone with the individual characteristics to get ahead" (p. 306).

Nevertheless, the "traditional" careers for VREGs (e.g., education and social science for African Americans; math and science for Asian Americans), to the extent that they are more fact than fiction, represent the career paths that they were permitted to follow under conditions of institutional racism. Consequently, it is patently unfair to assume that VREGs' career patterns are necessarily self-determined, even if they appear to be employed in "prestigious" occupations according to external standards.

Racial and Cultural Perspectives

Some theorists have proposed modifications of traditional career theories and/or alternate career perspectives to compensate for the lack of attention to career barriers in traditional theories. It might be useful to briefly describe some of them here. Although some of the perspectives were proposed for specific socioracial, cultural, and/or gender groups, we think that most of them can be applied to all groups. However, when applying them, the counselor ought to modify them to integrate the specific socioracial and sociocultural realities of the client who is the focus of the career intervention.

Gender and Socioracial or Sociocultural Considerations

Some theorists argue that special vocational circumstances exist for men (Leonard, 1985; Perry & Locke, 1985) and women (Yang, 1991) of color or collectivistic cultural orientation.

Traditional Asian Women.   Yang (1991) contends that the barriers to Chinese American women's career development can be categorized as follows: (a) "universal women's issues"—the experience of being socialized under conditions of gender segregation of occupations and the multiple psychological pressures that occur when a person attempts to juggle the roles of primary caretaker for family and friends and worker outside the home; (b) "cultural hurdles"—incompatibility between the cultural rules under which Chinese and other traditional Asian women are socialized (e.g., stability, interpersonal intimacy, social supportiveness of the family system) and the rules to which one must adapt (e.g., racism, devaluing of extended family, incompatible values) to survive in individualistically oriented work settings, and (c) "feminist-patriarchies socialization"—competitive (feminist) pressures for women to use their education in professional careers rather than in traditional voluntary social services versus the traditional (patriarchal) Chinese family system and the (patriarchal) world of work in the United States. With respect to resolution of any of these dilemmas, Yang notes, "When they [Chinese women] lose the moral support of one society, they may not be equipped to succeed in the other" (p. 356).

The implications for counselors of Yang's observations are that counselors should familiarize themselves with the work-related assumptions under which they were socialized as well as those of their clients and the society more generally. The counselor's awareness of the prevailing stereotypes for people of the client's sociorace and gender will make it easier to avoid imposing these stereotypes during counseling.

With respect to Chinese American women in particular, Yang (1991) recommends that the counselor assess the extent to which they have acculturated to traditional Anglo American culture, and assist the client in recognizing the personal and vocational implications of their multiple heritages and social conditioning. She advises that Anglo-acculturated Chinese women may have less difficulty fitting into individualistically oriented work environments than their more collectivistically oriented counterparts. Thus, acculturated women may learn easily or express more readily the levels of individualism, assertiveness, and independence necessary for survival in the world of work. Additionally, to the extent that their families are similarly acculturated, then the women should experience less person-environment incongruence.

The applicability of Yang's perspective to the particular case of Patty is probably obvious. The occupational stereotype of Asian people is that they generally enter scientific-technical occupations because such occupations do not require much competence in the English language. If this stereotype has any truth (and sometimes stereotypes do), then the counselor intending to intervene with Patty should be exploring the possible differential significance of her linguistic talents in the cultural, racial, gender, and social class environments that are most central to her vocational self-concept. In fact, such multitiered exploration is a good idea regardless of the sociodemographic characteristics of the vocational client.

ALANA Men. A few theorists have offered analyses of the systemic conditions of Black men and youths that contribute to their high rates of unemployment (e.g., Perry & Locke, 1985). However, many of the liabilities that limit the appropriateness of traditional theories for explaining the career development of Black men can pertain to Black women, Latinos/Latinas of color, and Native Americans of both genders as well. Perry and Locke (1985) contend that two major societal systems—the educational system and the economic system—circumscribe the career opportunities of Black men.

As Table 11.2 suggests with respect to occupational distributions, in fact the *patterns* of occupations are quite similar for African, Latina/Latino, and White Americans

TABLE 11.2   Occupational Distribution (%) of the Employed Civilian Labor Force by Gender and (Socio)race: 1991–1992

Occupation	Race and Gender						
	Black		White		Native American	Latino/Latina	
	Male	*Female*	*Male*	*Female*		*Male*	*Female*
Managerial and professional specialty	14.1	19.5	26.8	28.5	18.3	10.7	16.0
Technical, sales, and administrative support	17.3	38.2	21.1	44.6	26.8	14.7	38.4
Service	19.0	27.9	9.1	16.5	18.5	16.2	25.1
Precision, production, craft, and repair	14.8	2.1	19.5	2.0	13.7	20.6	1.1
Operators, fabricators, and laborers	31.3	12.0	18.9	7.2	19.4	29.9	16.6
Farming, forestry, and fishing	3.6	.3	4.7	1.1	3.3	8.0	1.1
Total (numbers in thousands)[1]	5,846	6,087	55,709	45,770	729	5,178	3,496

[1]Percentages and totals for employed persons 16 years and over are taken from the following sources: Bennett (1992), Garcia and Montgomery (1991), and Paisano (1993). Estimates according to gender were not available for populations not reported.

of both genders. For example, for all of the groups, the percentages of women in professions generally exceeds that of men in their groups. Nevertheless, the size of the percentages differs across occupational categories between and within groups. As evidence of these observations, notice in Table 11.2, for example, that the percentage of White males in the managerial and specialty occupations (26.8%) is almost double that of Black males (14.1%), almost two-and-a-half times that of Latinos (10.7%), and almost one-and-a-half times that of the gender-combined Native Americans (18.3).

However, within socioracial groups, a higher percentage of Black women (19.5%) than Black men (14.1%) were employed in managerial/professional occupations, which also was the case for Latinas (16%) and Latinos (10.7%), and White women (28.5%) and White men (26.8%). For the most part, it can be said that the size of White men and women's occupational percentages exceed those of the respective genders of Blacks, and Latinas/Latinos in the high status and high income occupations, but decrease as the status and/or income level of the occupations lessen.

Gender-separated statistics were not reported for Native Americans (Paisano, 1993). However, it appears that their combined occupational distributions sometimes parallel those of women of color and sometimes those of men of color. According to Paisano, Indigenous Americans were more likely than the "total population" (a figure that seemingly includes all socioracial groups) to be employed in service occupations, farming and related occupations, precision production, etc., and as operators, laborers, and so forth.

In comparing the occupational progress of Black and White Americans, Bennett (1992) summarized the following differences: (a) Although the percentage of Black adults (25 years and older) with a bachelor's degree increased from 8% in 1980 to 12% by 1992, the corresponding percentages of Whites increased from 18% to 22%, respectively; (b) The average annual labor participation rate of both Black and White men decreased between 1980 and 1992, but the annual labor participation rate of White men (76%) remained higher than that of Black men (70%) in 1992; (c) For Black and White women, the annual percentage of labor force participation was similar with the greater increase occurring for White women (from 51% to 58%) relative to Black women (from 53% to 58%). Thus, the employment trends suggest that although the two groups follow similar trends, the White group experiences greater advantage notwithstanding.

In addition, Bennett provides data in support of the hypothesis that Black people receive less compensation than their White counterparts for work in the same occupations. For example, she reports that in those occupations where salaries between Black and White men differed significantly, the range was from about $64.00 per $100.00 earned by White men (in farming, fishing, etc.) to $87.00 in the service occupations. Of the 3% of Black men and 9% of White men with a high school education employed as managers, executives, etc., Black men earned $60.00 per $100.00 earned by White men. Furthermore, of the college-educated Black men (26%) and White men (32%) employed as managers, executives, etc., Black men earned $70.00 for every $100.00 earned by their White counterparts.

Thus, Bennett's (1992) data suggest that differential educational levels cannot account for salary differences among Black and White men since even when their educational levels and occupational choices are similar, their salaries are not necessarily comparable. Her findings appear to confirm the foregoing systemic theorists' observations that institutional racism plays a major economic role in Black men's continuous occupational disadvantage. Nevertheless, earning a bachelor's degree seems to give Black men an economic advantage over Black men who are high school graduates.

According to Bennett, Black male college graduates earned incomes that were 66% higher than Black male high school graduates, and only 16% of college graduates earned annual salaries of less than $20,000 as compared to 55% of Black male high school graduates. Therefore, counselors working with young Black men trying to decide whether to pursue higher education would do well to encourage them to continue their education, institutional racism notwithstanding.

However, it should be noted that although critics of societal employment conditions generally focus on the plight of ALANA men, in fact, women of these groups are more likely to suffer economic deprivation. In support of this observation, Bennett

(1992) reports that although Black people (15%) were more than twice as likely to be "working poor" as White people (6%), there were more working-poor Black women (1.2 million) than working-poor Black men (.8 million). However, there were comparable levels of White women (3.3 million) and White men (3.5 million) among the working poor.

Working poor is defined as people who hold a job for which they receive an income that is below the poverty level. Paisano (1993) reported that 33.4% of the families of Indigenous Peoples headed by a man with no spouse were in poverty, as compared to 50.4% of those families headed by a woman with no spouse. Thus, the available statistical data suggest that vocational theorists and counselors should pay much more attention to the vocational development of ALANA women than is typically the case.

Systems Perspectives

Although calls for greater recognition of the significance of environmental factors have increased, vocational models incorporating such factors virtually do not exist. However, recently Carter and Cook (1992) proposed a systemic model for examining the vocational development of ALANA people; Ibrahim, Ohnishi, and Wilson (1994) proposed a general cultural diversity vocational model; and Helms (1994; Helms & Piper, 1994) suggested strategies for examining the impact of racial identity on vocational development.

Carter and Cook's Model.   According to these authors, the structure of American society includes boundaries or rules that regulate the quantity and quality of vocational participation and variety of occupational roles open to individuals and/or their socioracial groups and, occasionally, their cultural groups. These rules regulate individuals' interactions within society as well as subsystems within the society. Boundaries are communicated verbally and nonverbally.

For example, societal attitudes toward and beliefs about racial or cultural groups (e.g., positive or negative stereotypes) serve as feedback to members of the racial/cultural groups. This feedback may be communicated directly through the spoken word (e.g., "We have difficulty finding 'qualified' _____ [fill in the blank]") or nonverbally through official policies (e.g., educational tracking systems that place disproportionate numbers of African American and Latinos/Latinas in special education classes).

Furthermore, institutional inclusion or exclusion communicates the relevant occupational boundaries to the affected person and the groups of which he or she is a member. Such exclusion may be racial, cultural, socioeconomic, or a combination of all three. The exclusion of VREG workers from country clubs where business deals are frequently made is often an example of racial exclusion because many such organizations do not accept VREG members; cultural exclusion because golf is not a normative form of recreation in many cultural groups; and socioeconomic because many VREG workers may not have the financial resources to afford membership in such places, and if they can afford it, may have a socioeconomic history that would encourage viewing such large expenditures as frivolous. Thus, the distribution of socioeconomic resources and/or labor force participation (or lack thereof) is a means of enforcing sociopolitical boundaries.

In Carter and Cook's perspective, subsystems of the American society join or form alignments to enforce cultural values of the dominant culture and "collude to restrict access" of ALANAs through discriminatory practices. Relevant examples of collusion include inferior educational institutions for ALANAs; state, city, and local governments' allocation of fewer resources to ALANA communities; and an occupational world wherein the cultural standards for meritorious performance are often in conflict with ALANA and/or collectivistic values.

In essence, this systems perspective proposes a dynamic interaction among internal (e.g., physiological, mental) factors and external or environmental conditions (e.g., social roles, economics). Environmental conditions may be imposed by the subsystems within the societal, work, and family environments. A person may have the physical and mental capacity to pursue certain career options, but social or cultural-role requirements and economic factors may impede progress toward the desired goal. Moreover, if the boundaries of the work environment are not truly permeable, then even if a person appears to have circumvented them he or she may encounter invisible barriers (e.g., "glass ceilings" in corporations) that prevent the person from excelling in the nontraditional role.

In the case of Patty, Carter and Cook's perspective would suggest that it is important to identify the subsystems and the boundaries within and across systems that are likely to influence her career development. They suggest that the dynamics of family systems should be especially considered when assisting VREG clients to identify appropriate career paths. The familial experiences of one generation generally affect the progress and experiences of successive generations. Parents may direct their children toward career options that are similar to or better than their own, according to whatever survival knowledge they have acquired through their own work history. A familial history of exposure to racism and ethnocentrism in their various forms may lead children to believe that their vocational future will not be different from their parents' vocational past. Also, cultural traditions, language, lifestyles, norms, and values that are transmitted through the family may influence perceived occupational choices. Thus, in Patty's case, a counselor should explore the relevance of her family's work-related dynamics on her career decision-making process.

A Racial Identity Perspective

In a series of articles on vocational psychology and racial identity, Helms (1994; Helms & Piper, 1994) contends that vocational theory and research have been flawed by (a) theorists' inattention to racial (as distinguished from cultural) factors in career development, (b) the assumption that between-group socioracial comparisons would lead to meaningful information about the career development of any of the compared groups, and (c) the lack of race-specific constructs by which to interpret individual's vocational behavior. Nevertheless, Helms and Piper (1994) note that there is no prima facie reason why racial identity should be related to most of the person-level career variables in which racial effects have been investigated (e.g., interests, needs, work values, occupational choice).

Consequently, to help determine when racial identity (and other race-specific constructs) might be relevant to a person's career development, they introduced the notion of "racial salience." They define *racial salience* as "the extent to which a person conceives (correctly or incorrectly) of race as a significant definer of one's work options" (Helms & Piper, 1994, p. 129).

An example of racial salience for VREG career seekers might be the belief or awareness that certain careers are inaccessible to them because of their racial classification. An example of racial salience for Whites is the belief that certain menial jobs should be reserved for People of Color rather than for themselves. In either type of circumstances, "racial identity might serve as a mediator between the objective racial circumstances or stressors and the person's vocational behavior in response to the circumstances" (Helms & Piper, 1994, p. 129). That is, it might structure the person's interpretation of career-related events in her or his life.

Table 11.1 (see p. 205) summarizes some of the critical racial identity themes from a vocational perspective for ALANAs and Whites, respectively. Also, it suggests possible areas of correspondence between racial identity development and Super's developmental model of vocational self-concept.

The implication of the proposed interactive relationships between racial salience and racial identity for vocational counselors is that the counselor working with VREG clients has an obligation to explore with them the ways in which they have incorporated information about the racial history of their group into their vocational self-concepts. Interestingly, the counselor may find himself or herself teaching clients about the relevant history of their group as a means of expanding their options and/or helping them build self-protective skills in instances in which they choose to enter potentially hostile work environments.

Consider, for example, the case of an ALANA person who believes that racial segregation has prevented members of her or his group from entering certain occupations even when they had the requisite interests and abilities. Suppose also that this person's most salient racial identity status is Conformity expressed by means of denial or obliviousness. This person might attempt to enter the desired profession, secure in the knowledge that what has happened to other members of her or his socioracial group will not happen to him or her. In such a case, the counselor's task is not to discourage the client from seeking to enter the desired occupation, but rather it is to prepare the client for possible racial barriers that he or she might encounter "just in case."

Thus, in the case of Patty, assuming that Conformity is the racial identity status that she uses in making her career choices, the counselor would need to assess the extent to which she is aware of racial stereotypes concerning language usage and her group. In our experience, for example, it is not unusual to have American-born Asian American clients who speak what sounds like perfect American English to our ears complain that supervisors, students, and coworkers insist that they cannot understand them, or they do not speak clearly. Often poor evaluations and/or lack of promotions are based on the inadequate hearing of someone in an evaluative role.

In Patty's case, her academic record so far demonstrates unusual competence in English language. Moreover, if the counselor does not allow societal stereotypes internalized by Patty, the counselor, or the relevant racial and/or cultural groups to inhibit the exploration process, other evidence attesting to her linguistic skills will likely be uncovered. A variety of occupations in which she might make use of these skills is potentially available to her. In many of them, Asian Americans are underrepresented for racial as well as cultural reasons. Consequently, the counselor may need to assist Patty in discovering approximate role models (i.e., VREG people who are engaged in occupations similar to the one she is seeking to enter) and/or reframing her career choice so that it makes sense within the racial and cultural contexts in which she must function.

Helms and Piper (1994) advise that vocational counselors should be informed about the societal racial dynamics that may define the range of work environments available to clients; that is, the dynamics that might inhibit or facilitate clients' entry into particular occupations. However, they also suggest that racial identity theory, especially interaction theory, may be useful for explaining issues of environmental climate once the person obtains a position. Thus, they suggest that Helms's "perspective might be useful in explaining observed racial differences in workers' levels of expressed adaptation to the work environment (i.e., satisfaction) as well as the environment's (so to speak) perceptions and evaluations of the worker (i.e., satisfactoriness)" (Helms & Piper, 1994, p. 131).

Consequently, when counselors are confronted with clients who are dissatisfied with their work environment, whether the clients are supervisors or supervisees, they should explore the racial dynamics that might be occurring within the environment. Such exploration would be particularly indicated if the particular setting includes workers of different racial classifications and/or skin colors. In such instances, race is more likely to be a salient aspect of the interpersonal interactions that occur.

A Cultural Diversity Perspective

Although we probably no longer need to offer advisories to this effect, integration of racial factors into vocational theory and process is not necessarily the same thing as integrating cultural factors into these aspects of vocational psychology. Psychoculture pertains to the expression of one's socialization with respect to values, beliefs, interpersonal skills, and so forth—in fact, everything that one is. There is perhaps no setting that is more ripe for cultural discord than the work environment in the United States, and of course, the educational system that channels people into this environment.

Most work environments in the United States, particularly if they are economically successful (e.g., *Fortune* 500 companies) are individualistic in cultural orientation in addition to being governed by racial dynamics that protect the economic interests of Whites. Citing Terpstra (1974), Samovar and Porter (1991) suggest that the analysis of the culture in a business context should include the following eight major dimensions and accompanying array of specific factors:

1. Language (spoken, written, official, hierarchical, international, and so on);
2. Religion (sacred objects, philosophical systems, beliefs and norms, prayer, taboos, holidays, rituals);

3. Values and attitudes (toward time, achievement, work, wealth, change, scientific method, risk-taking);
4. Education (formal education, vocational training, higher education, literacy level, human resources planning);
5. Social organization (kinship, social institutions, authority structures, interest groups, social mobility and stratification);
6. Technology and material culture (transportation, energy systems, tools, science, invention);
7. Politics (nationalism, imperialism, power, national interests, ideologies, political risk); and
8. Law (common law, foreign law, international law, antitrust policy, regulations).

If one examines any of these dimensions from the perspective of a collectivist and/or a traditionalistic ALANA American, then it becomes clear that traditional Anglo American occupations and work environments may be built around cultural themes that are inconsistent with the cultural socialization under which members of many ALANA ethnic groups are conditioned. To illustrate this point, J. Helms frequently asks the students in her undergraduate cross-cultural psychology class to do Exercise 11.1. The reader might like to try the exercise before you continue. Generally, the students generate a list of model job-seeker actions such as:

Be on time for your interview.

Look directly at your interviewer.

Use a firm handshake.

Speak standard/proper English.

Be assertive and don't be afraid to list your assets.

Dress for success.

Of course the students are surprised to discover that their ideal interviewee characteristics would not necessarily be considered positive behaviors among members of various cultures within the United States. With respect to assertiveness for instance, Samovar and Porter (1991) note that maternal socialization for White Americans encourages speech that reflects excitement, assertiveness, and interest, whereas maternal socialization for traditional Navajos interprets such behavior as discourteous, mischievous, and self-centered. Thus, Navajo adults attempting to enter a traditional Anglo-defined work environment might be disadvantaged with respect to assertiveness skills relative to their White American counterparts.

Thomas and Alderfer (1989) note that acculturative stress—that is, the anxieties aroused by not knowing how to fit in—may be aggravated for workers from VREG cultures because the White-dominated culture of institutions is often implicit and unacknowledged. Thus, when VREGs do not automatically know the rules of the new culture that they have entered, their lack of cultural knowledge is used as a more general indictment of them and their cultures. Consequently, VREGs frequently find

EXERCISE **11.1**

How to Get a Job

Imagine that you are going to an interview for your ideal job. You *really* want this job! Describe what you should do in order to enhance your chances of being hired.

_____

_____

_____

_____

You might like to compare your list with the students' list on page 217. Do the two lists reflect common socialization with respect to what constitutes good worker behavior? Now, think about what you know about your own culture and cultures that are different from yours.

What, if anything, in your list would generate conflict for an individualistically oriented person?

_____

_____

What, if anything, in your list would generate conflict for a collectivistically oriented person?

_____

_____

themselves feeling alone and alienated in their efforts to manage the ensuing cultural conflicts within the organization. Moreover, they may not even have a name for or a way of communicating about the conflict.

It is possible to analyze each of the foregoing occupational cultural dimensions and the interviewee behaviors for potential cultural incongruities. We encourage vocational counselors to spend some time analyzing these factors with respect to the cultures of the clients with whom they work. Very often the counselor will find that it is necessary to teach nonacculturated and nonassimilated VREG clients and clients from collectivistic cultures the cultural "rules" of the work setting in which the client is attempting to function or intends to enter.

Career Assessment

Most of the traditional career theories have been implemented by means of career assessment devices, usually paper-and-pencil measures of career attitudes, behaviors, values, or beliefs (see Exercise 11.2). Many contemporary theorists have criticized the

EXERCISE **11.2**

Evaluating Career Development Measures for Racial or Cultural Bias

A variety of widely available measures have been developed to assess career characteristics associated with the traditional vocational theories that we discussed in this chapter. Here is a sampling of some of them.

Personality Vocational Measures

The California Occupational Preference Systems Interest Inventory, Revised Edition (Knapp & Knapp, 1980)—uses Roe's classification of occupations.

The Self-Directed Search Inventory (Holland, 1979) assesses Holland's occupational personality typology.

The Vocational Preference Inventory (Holland, 1978)—also assesses Holland's occupational personality typology.

Developmental Measures

The Career Development Inventory (CDI; Super, Thompson, Lindeman, Jordan, & Myers, 1981) assesses the career development process as described by Super.

The Career Maturity Inventory (CMI; Crites, 1978) based on Crites's hierarchical model of career development.

Evaluation

Try to locate one or more of these inventories (or another published inventory of your choice) in your local testing library or order them from the publisher. Get two copies of the same measure. Complete one version as yourself—that is, according to whatever racial, cultural, gender, and social class socialization defines you. Then complete the measure again as you think someone of another culture or racial classification or so forth might respond. Don't worry about being accurate.

Score separately or have the two versions of the completed profile scored separately. Do you notice any meaningful differences in the two versions? What do the profiles reveal about potential biases in the measures that you took?

---

utilitarianism of these measures because of their lack of inclusion of racial dynamics (Carter & Swanson, 1990; Helms, 1994) or attention to differential consequences of varied (from the norm group) cultural socialization (e.g., Fouad, 1994; Leong & Leung, 1994).

Furthermore, ALANA clients may be suspicious of tests because such devices are so often used to disempower them and to provide justification for maintaining discriminatory practices. Even so, most critics of these measures resolve the dilemma of needing some formal devices to assess clients, but having none that were designed to reflect the racial and cultural diversities of the clients' lives, by recommending creative usage of existing devices (e.g., Martin & Farris, 1994).

For example, in their discussion of appropriate usage of traditional vocational measures with Native American clients, Martin and Farris (1994) propose the following adjustments: (a) where feasible, translate the measures into the primary (i.e., at-home) language of the client being tested; (b) develop local norms so as to ascertain the client's at-home cultural socialization and the relations of that socialization to career achievement; and (c) augment traditional career measures with relevant acculturation measures.

Nevertheless, existing measures by themselves are not adequate if counselors intend to practice culturally and racially responsive vocational psychology. In addition to such measures and sometimes instead of them, it is important for counselors to use a broader definition of assessment than just standardized measures. Walsh and Betz (1990) identified four components of the vocational assessment process as globally defined.

Walsh and Betz's components are as follows: (1) **problem clarification**—interpreting the client's presenting problem in ways that suggest the type of additional information needed to resolve it; (2) **information gathering**—collection of relevant information about the person and his or her environmental contexts; (3) **understanding the problem**—using some theoretical framework to form hypotheses about the person and the person's circumstances based on the information that has been gathered; and (4) **coping with the problem**—determining whether the hypotheses result in useful solutions to the person's problems.

The information-gathering phase is especially important for ALANA and collectivistically oriented clients because one cannot rely on tests as the primary source of uncontaminated information about them. Thus, to assess a client whose culture is different from the counselor's culture, the counselor must start by becoming aware of the general norms of the client's culture. Having specific cultural information is imperative if the counselor is to have any chance of understanding the client holistically. Without such information, the counselor risks forming culturally biased hypotheses and interpretations of the client's attitudes and behaviors. Insight 11.3 illustrates what can happen if a client naively selects career or educational options that run counter to her or his at-home cultural socialization.

The counselor needs to be open to being educated, usually by the client, as to the cultural underpinnings that may influence the client's goals, motivations, problem-solving strategies, decision-making processes, and personal struggles. The client's cultural frame of reference is the one that the counselor should use in establishing and implementing applicable strategies. Furthermore, the counselor should obtain as much cultural and historical data as possible with respect to specific aspects of the client's culture and pay special attention to how work and careers are defined in the client's salient culture, in addition to identifying the variety of patterns of career development present in that culture.

Insights 11.2 and 11.3 show that even within socioracial groups of the same ostensible socioeconomic status, a variety of definitions and manifestations of work may exist. Gathering these types of information will aid the counselor in forming a more complete understanding of the client's worldview. In addition to gathering information about the racial and cultural factors that we have discussed, the vocational counselor should be prepared to investigate the function of social class status on the client's career aspirations or achievements.

Important issues to explore include the occupational history of the client's family, the family's status within its community, and the extent to which class and/or pres-

---

INSIGHT **11.3**

What Is Education Good For?

Most VREG people who have acquired an "outside" education can probably identify with these thoughts of Little Star.

"Traditionally educated Indians have had a difficult time working on their own reservations. When you get out of [Anglo] school you know so much and have so many solutions to reservation problems that you want to get things done and methods changed.

But you've been away a long time, and some things have already changed. So you start with the problems where they are now, not when you left. You spend a long time finding this out, maybe even talking to council members you joked about for years. You respect them for they know more about the situation than you. And you thought you knew everything.

If you want to get something done you either have to work thru the system or change the system. You talked about tribal government and structure, but when you're there you see that what actually gets done and the way it gets done has little to do with your Tribal Constitution and bylaws. A master's degree has nothing to do with leadership on the reservation, and you want to be a leader. You've forgotten how to work with your own people. . . .

You find yourself being as paternal as the BIA [Bureau of Indian Affairs] superintendent and maybe more patronizing. It's hard to realize that these people are the ones you've spoken of for so long as "my people." When you finally realize that they don't belong to you, but that you belong to your tribe then you're really on your way back. Then you can find what your spot in the circle of your tribal world. And just maybe you'll be an Indian again" (Little Star, 1991, pp. 388–389).

---

tige factors are related to the client's perceived and actual job opportunities. The counselor should attempt to determine what psychodemographic characteristics are salient in the client's vocational development. For example, what roles do social status and social mobility serve for the client? How rigid or flexible are gender roles within the client's culture? Are there certain jobs that women or men are simply not supposed to pursue?

Some formal or informal personality assessment might also be useful since such information can reveal how the client makes decisions as well as alert the counselor to any potential conflicts between the cultural dynamics of the client and the relevant work environment. Potentially useful personality characteristics to obtain information about include the client's manner of self-disclosing, his or her strategies for coping with racial discord, the significance to the client of education and achievement, career aspirations and expectations, and the quality of the client's social support network(s).

If the client is having difficulty obtaining a suitable job, then the counselor should attempt to assess whether the client's difficulties are due to inadequate job search strategies or particular barriers (e.g., geographic location) within the environment in which he or she is searching. Each possibility should be examined, and the counselor should use the obtained information to assist the client in changing those factors that are interfering with his or her progress toward gainful and/or fulfilling employment.

Career Process

The process—the actual *doing* of career counseling—requires attention to the personal and interpersonal racial and cultural dynamics that we have discussed in previous and subsequent chapters. Nevertheless, Fouad (1994) presents a very nice stepwise summary of the process as it involves Latino/Latina clients. We summarize it here with the proviso that her model can be used with clients from other socioracial or cultural groups as well. Just remember to fill the mold she presents with content that accurately and sensitively reflects the client's vocational concerns.

The first step in Fouad's framework is *establish a relationship.* This may seem like an obvious and easily achieved recommendation. But remember that a client's expectations for helping relationships is influenced by her or his cultural and perhaps racial socialization. When working with Latino/Latina clients, for example, Fouad gives examples of techniques a counselor may use to reduce interpersonal distance (e.g., handshakes, small talk) while maintaining a certain amount of formality (e.g., use of full names). However, an Anglo client or an Anglo-acculturated Latino/Latina client might view small talk and personal contact as intrusive. Thus, in one case, such behaviors would contribute to establishment of a strong working alliance, whereas in the other it might contribute to premature termination. Thus, it is important for the counselor to become adept at reading the client's cues. A client who seems to be avoidant at the beginning of a session may instead be implementing the norms of her or his culture.

The next step in the process is to *identify the client's career issues.* As one does so, one should integrate relevant aspects of the client's racial, cultural, gender, and social class socialization. Moreover, as one explores these venues, the counselor should always keep in mind the potential interactions between the person, and his or her salient cultural environments, and the occupational structure and level of institutional racism present in the fields the client wishes to enter.

The third step in Fouad's (1994; Fouad & Bingham, 1995) perspective is *cultural (and racial) analysis.* Here they emphasize the importance of attending to the impact of cultural (and racial) influences on the client's career concerns. However, Fouad warns counselors that clients may not always be able to *talk* about such issues because they may be outside of their awareness or they may simply be unwilling to discuss such matters. She suggests that sometimes special assessment techniques such as genograms, drawings, and checklists may be used to encourage clients to discuss such factors.

However, Fouad also warns that highly Anglo-acculturated clients may be insulted by the suggestion that culture has anything to do with their situation. Similarly, clients who interpret racial dynamics by means of immature or rigid racial identity statuses may resist information pertaining to racism and their particular circumstances. Nevertheless, just as one does with any other form of resistance, the counselor must attempt to entice the client into awareness rather than force-feeding him or her.

Goal setting is step four in the culture-race responsive vocational counseling process. Here the counselor attempts to use culturally appropriate (as revealed by the client) counseling skills to encourage culturally respectful goals. So, for example, direct negative comments or confrontation are generally inappropriate for collectivistically oriented clients as are goals that require them to desert salient cultural or racial communities.

The fifth step is the implementation of a race-culture appropriate *intervention*. Here traditional vocational assessment devices as previously discussed may be used if appropriate precautions are taken. Also, less traditional methodologies such as career fantasies, card sorts, and wish lists may be used. However, Martin (1991) noted that poor and nonassimilated ALANA clients may have limited occupational knowledge or they may lack the skills necessary to acquire and process the new information that is important to make vocational choices. In such cases, the counselor may need to think of activities by which the clients can acquire information and learn skills. Relevant activities might include "shadowing" someone employed in a field of interest, reviewing want-ads in newspapers to gain a sense of the educational requirements of various positions, and so forth.

Also, for clients from lower socioeconomic backgrounds, financial limitations and related familial pressures may limit a client's options. The vocational counselor should be prepared to assist clients in discovering realistic strategies for supporting themselves (and perhaps their families) as they move toward fulfilling their career goals.

The final steps, six and seven, in Fouad's (1994) analysis are *decision-making* and *implementation*. As the titles of the steps imply, at this point the counselor assists the client in making a culturally appropriate and racially informed decision. The client may implement the decision and leave counseling. If so, the counselor may initiate whatever follow-up activities are consistent with his or her normal practice.

However, the counselor should not be surprised if collectivistic and/or ALANA clients do not terminate once the career problem is resolved and/or "check in" periodically with the counselor of their own accord. Often the counselor's willingness and ability to work with the client's vocational problem in such an empathic manner is enough to bond the client to the counselor for some time.

REFERENCES

Axelson, J. A. (1985). *Counseling and development in a multicultural society.* Monterey, CA: Brooks/Cole.

Bennett, C. E. (1992, March). *The Black population in the United States: Population characteristics.* U. S. Department of Commerce Economics and Statistics Administration, Bureau of the Census.

Betz, N. E., & Fitzgerald, L. F. (1987). *The career psychology of women.* Orlando, FL: Academic Press.

Carter, R. T., & Cook, D. A. (1992). A culturally relevant perspective for understanding the career paths of visible racial/ethnic group people. In H. D. Lea & Z. B. Leibowitz (Eds.), *Adult career development: Concepts, issues and practices* (pp. 192–217). Alexandria, VA: National Career Development Association.

Carter, R. T., & Swanson, J. L. (1990). The validity of the Strong Interest Inventory for Black Americans: A review of the literature. *Journal of Vocational Behavior, 36,* 195–209.

Crites, J. O. (1978). *Career Maturity Inventory.* Monterey, CA: CTB/McGraw-Hill.

Fouad, N. A. (1994). Career assessment with Latinos/Hispanics. *Journal of Career Assessment, 2,* 226–239.

Fouad, N. A., & Bingham, R. P. (1995). Career counseling with racial/ethnic minorities. In W. B. Walsh & S. H. Osipow (Eds.), *Handbook of vocational psychology* (2nd ed.). Mahwah, NJ: Lawrence Erlbaum.

French, M. A., & Herndon, C. (1995, May 21). Bread's last jam. *The Washington Post, Section F: Style*, pp. 1, 4–6.

Garcia, J. M., & Montgomery, P. A. (1991). *The Hispanic population in the United States: March 1990, population characteristics*. U.S. Department of Commerce, Bureau of the Census.

Ginzberg, E., Ginsburg, S. W., Axelrad, S., & Herma, J. L. (1951). *Occupational choice: An approach to a general theory*. New York: Columbia University Press.

Havighurst, R. J. (1964). Youth in exploration and man emergent. In H. Borow (Ed.), *Man in a world at work* (pp. 215–236). Boston: Houghton Mifflin.

Helms, J. E. (1994). Racial identity and career assessment. *Journal of Career Assessment, 2*, 199–209.

Helms, J. E., & Piper, R. E. (1994). Implications of racial identity theory for vocational psychology. *Journal of Vocational Psychology, 44*, 124–138.

Highlen, P. S., & Sudarsky-Gleiser, C. (1994). Co-essence model of vocational assessment for racial/ethnic minorities (CEMVA-REM): An existential approach. *Journal of Career Assessment, 2*, 304–329.

Holland, J. L. (1973). *Making choices: A theory of careers*. Englewood Cliffs, NJ: Prentice-Hall.

Holland, J. L. (1978). *Manual for the Vocational Preference Inventory*. Palo Alto, CA: Consulting Psychologist Press.

Holland, J. L. (1979). *The self-directed search: Professional manual*. Palo Alto, CA: Consulting Psychologists Press.

Ibrahim, F. A., Ohnishi, H., & Wilson, R. P. (1994). Career assessment in a culturally diverse society. *Journal of Career Assessment, 2*, 276–288.

Jones, L. M. (1991). Racism: A cultural analysis of the problem. In R. I. Jones (Ed.), *Black psychology* (3rd ed.) (pp.609–635). Berkeley, CA: Cobb & Henry Publishers.

Knapp, L., & Knapp, R. R. (1980). *California Occupational Preference System Interest Inventory: Form R*. San Diego: Educational and Industrial Testing Service.

Leonard, P. Y. (1985). Vocational theory and the vocational behavior of Black males: An analysis. *Journal of Multicultural Counseling and Development*, July, 91–105.

Leong, F. T. L., & Leung, S. A. (1994). Career assessment with Asian-Americans. *Journal of Career Assessment, 2*, 240–257.

Martin, W. E. (1991). Career development and American Indians living on reservations: Cross-cultural factors to consider. *The Career Development Quarterly, 39*, 273–283.

Martin, W. E., Jr., & Farris, K. K. (1994). A cultural and contextual decision path approach to career assessment with Native Americans: A psychological perspective. *Journal of Career Assessment, 2*, 258–275.

Monroe, S., & Goldman, P. (1988). *Brothers: Black and poor—a true story of courage and survival*. New York: William Morrow Inc.

Osipow, S. (1975). The relevance of theories of career development to special groups: Problems, needed data, and implications. In J. Picou & R. Campbell (Eds.), *Career behavior of special groups—theory, research, and practice* (pp. 9–22). Columbus, OH: Charles E. Merrill.

Paisano, E. L. (1993, September). *We the . . . first Americans*. U.S. Department of Commerce Economics and Statistics Administration, Bureau of the Census.

Perry, J. L., & Locke, D. C. (1985). Career development of Black men: Implications for school guidance services. *Journal of Multicultural Counseling and Development, 13*(3), 106–111.

Roe, A. (1956). *The psychology of occupations*. New York: Wiley.

Roe, A. (1972). *The making of a scientist*. New York: Dodd, Mead.

Samovar, L. A., & Porter, R. E. (1991). *Communication between cultures*. Belmont, CA: Wordsworth Publishing.

Star, Little (1991). Going back. In P. Nabokov (Ed.), *Native American testimony: A chronicle of Indian-White relations from prophecy to the present* (pp. 388–389). Hudson, NY: Penguin Group.

Super, D. E. (1988). Vocational adjustment: Implementing a self-concept. *Career Development Quarterly, 36*, 351–357.

Super, D. E., Thompson, A. S., Lindeman, R. H., Jordan, J. P., & Myers, R. A. (1981). *Career Development Inventory*. Palo Alto, CA: Consulting Psychologists Press.

Terpstra, V. (1978). *The cultural environment of international business*. Cincinnati: South-Western.

Thomas, D. A., & Alderfer, C. P. (1989). The influence of race on career dynamics: Theory and research on minority career experiences. In M. Arthur, D. T. Hall, & B. Lawrence (Eds.). *Handbook of Career Theory*. New York: Cambridge University Press.

Walsh, W. B., & Betz, N. E. (1985). *Tests and assessment*. Englewood Cliffs, NJ: Prentice-Hall.

Weatherford, J. M. (1991). *How the Indians enriched America*. New York: Crown.

Yang, J. (1991). Career counseling of Chinese American women: Are they in limbo? *The Career Development Quarterly, 39,* 350–359.

Zunker, V. G. (1981). *Career counseling: Applied concepts of life planning*. Monterey, CA: Brooks/Cole.

12 Racial and Cultural Dynamics of Group Interventions

Group interventions and individual therapy require similar integration of socioracial and cultural issues. Therefore, therapists who conduct groups must consider that diverse racial and cultural dynamics may influence the character of the group. Potential racial or cultural insensitivities or misunderstandings in group members' communications as well as the racial and cultural themes inherent in the group leader's or facilitator's own behavior and attitudes toward clients can contribute to conflict and discord within the group.

Thus, group leaders must learn to monitor and manage their own racial and cultural interactions with each individual group member because these influence the quality of the group as a whole. Moreover, group leaders must be attuned to the underlying racial and cultural themes inherent in group members' interactions with the group leader and other members of the group, as well as their potentially diverse interpretations and expectations of the group as a form of helping or therapy.

Tsui and Schultz (1988) describe the therapeutic climate of the group as a form of social contact "wherein members often express and act out their innermost thoughts and feelings . . . [Therefore] unresolved bias is an important variable that can have a negative impact on the therapeutic work of the group" (pp. 136–137). Implicit in their observations are the principles that healthful change occurs in a climate of safety, and unacknowledged conflict may impede such change.

Thus, the group leader of racially or culturally heterogeneous groups must work to bring into group consciousness the unacknowledged, subtle sociopolitical and cultural norms that occur in interactions between people of different socioraces and/or geocultures. Also, the group leader must facilitate the development of a new set of norms that recognize cultural and sociopolitical differences in group members' socialization while simultaneously uniting group members (Tsui & Schultz, 1988). Unfortunately, much of the traditional group therapy literature is useful for teaching therapists how to promote change through the group processes from a universalistic cultural perspective, but ignores issues of racial and cultural diversity. Nevertheless, we have found some of the existing information useful in our group work, if we modify it to include racial and cultural considerations. Therefore, in this chapter we discuss Yalom's (1985) therapeutic factors as we modify them. Moreover, because conscious attention to racial and cultural parameters often makes implicit group conflict evident, some framework is needed for circumventing the potentially detrimental effects of the communication barriers that may result. We use Helms's (1990a) racial identity social interaction process model to discuss these issues.

Yalom's Therapeutic Factors

Yalom (1985) has described eleven therapeutic factors in group therapy that he considers to be intrinsic mechanisms of change. They are: (1) instillation of hope, (2) universality, (3) imparting of information, (4) altruism, (5) corrective recapitulation of the primary family group, (6) development of socializing techniques, (7) imitative behavior, (8) interpersonal learning, (9) group cohesiveness, (10) catharsis, and (11) existential factors. Yalom's factors are an appropriate starting point for discussing racially and/or culturally sensitive group interventions because his work has become the process framework by which most group therapy is conducted. We believe that the factors described by Yalom (1985) have the potential to be therapeutic under proper conditions.

However, unless the socioracial and/or cultural composition of the group is considered, these "therapeutic" factors may become counterproductive. It is important to be aware of the degree to which members of a group consider themselves to have equal opportunities for growth in their external world as they work together toward individual growth and change within the group. Due to societal constraints, members of visible racial/ethnic groups, individuals of lower socioeconomic levels, and/or women may believe that their growth opportunities are more limited than do group members who come from more privileged backgrounds.

Additionally, members of different cultural orientations may have internalized different socialization rules about the appropriate manner for coping with stress in group situations. The therapist has to work hard, but subtlely to make known the existing rules without making the group members feel inadequate (see Chapter 7). Thus, both types of issues (socioracial and cultural), together or independently, may influence the actual quality of Yalom's (1985) therapeutic factors in any particular counseling or therapy group session. In this chapter, we discuss client and leader socioracial and cultural considerations with respect to each of Yalom's factors. We also discuss racial identity theory as a framework for analyzing psychoracial group dynamics.

Instillation of Hope

Individuals who participate in group therapy must believe that they can be helped by the group experience. The group experience will be most helpful if group members come to the group with such hope in mind, and if that hope is reinforced by the group leader. Observations that other group members are growing also strengthens hope. In fact, Yalom (1985) relies heavily on group members to foster hope in one another by highlighting the successful achievements of current and past group members, and having group members share stressful incidents that they have overcome in their lives. As group members observe the struggle that others have transcended, they will believe that they too have hope of succeeding. This sharing process can be a great advantage of group therapy.

Client Characteristics.   The strength of one's faith in "patterning" one's life after another may be influenced by the observing person's belief that he or she has as much opportunity for success as the other group members. If group members are from backgrounds that are too diverse in terms of their sociopolitical statuses in society or their cultural orientations, then processes intended to instill hope instead may instill alienation and self-denigration. Group members who come from oppressed backgrounds may be reluctant to share their stressful life experiences because they are afraid of being looked down upon by other members of the group. In addition, members from collectivistic cultures may avoid expressing their inner worries to protect the harmony of the group and/or to avoid contributing to "loss of face" for their cultural in-group.

Leader Considerations.   The group leader needs to actively instill a sense of hope in group members. Foremost, group leaders must believe in the value of group interventions themselves. Too often, groups are used in agencies as a cost-effective approach to treatment and, consequently, groups are led by individuals who may not be intrinsically motivated to conduct groups. If the leader does not believe that group intervention is the treatment of choice for each member of her or his particular group, then he or she may minimize the importance of instillation of hope as a means of engaging group members and encouraging them to commit to the group process.

To instill hope, the group leader must be able to function in multiple roles. For one, the group leader must be capable of serving as a buffer between group members of widely diverse backgrounds and assist them in interpreting one another's dynamics. To do so effectively, the group leader should be aware of examples of individuals similar to the present group members who, either culturally or sociopolitically, have successfully overcome the kinds of obstacles that typify the members of the group. If the group leader has not had life experiences similar to those of the group members, then guests of similar backgrounds can be invited to speak to the group to normalize the experiences of group members.

Also, group leaders should openly acknowledge those societal constraints that impede the success of some members, but are not relevant in the lives of other members. The group leader can utilize his or her social power in the group to empower group members from oppressed groups by empathizing with the pain experienced by oppressed individuals and reinforcing the strengths of these individuals. However, as we discuss in the racial identity section later, the leader should be aware that he or she may lose social power if he or she is perceived as being over-identified with one faction of the group or another.

Universality

Related to the hope that one gains from the experiences of others, one also can experience a sense of relief in realizing that he or she is not alone—that others are experiencing similar difficulties. Yalom (1985) describes this universal connection as follows: "After hearing other members disclose concerns similar to their own, patients report feeling more in touch with the world and describe the process as a 'welcome to the human race' experience" (p. 8). This universality concept can be a powerful group tool with heteroracial and/or mixed cultural groups as well as homogeneous socioracial and sociocultural groups.

Client Considerations.   Members of different socioracial groups who hold stereotypic images of people of other socioracial groups (as well as their own) can gain a more realistic understanding of individuals of different races. This new understanding may facilitate personal growth by changing the racial attitudes that the client holds toward members of other groups as well as her or his own group.

Same-race groups, particularly visible racial/ethnic groups (VREGs), can offer individuals reality testing and validation of their experiences as members of their racial group, both in terms of shared or asynchronous cultural experiences, as well as shared or discrepant experiences as a member of an oppressed or oppressing racial group. Same-race groups can be used as interventions to support and empower ALANAs, as well as to help White people to explore their personal identities as White people in America (Regan & Scarpellini Huber, 1997).

Leader Considerations.   Group leaders can bridge the gaps in understanding or communicating that exist among individuals in racially heterogeneous groups. A group member initially may be focused only on her or his own pain around race, whether he or she is a White person who fears ALANAs or feels guilty about racism, or an ALANA who fears or is angry at White people and/or has been discriminated against by them.

The group leader can allow each person to share his or her emotional experience of being a particular "racial self" and can assist group members in empathically hearing each other out. While the experiences of group members may vary, there may be some universal themes in the emotional reactions of the group members. Group leaders might pull on the universal experiences of oppression in examining how people who are oppressed frequently oppress others, even members of their own racial groups. Despite the differences that exist among group members, it is crucial that the leader unite the group members around the universal aspects of their experiences.

Imparting Information

Groups can be helpful in providing group members with didactic information, interpersonal feedback from the group leader and members, and suggestions and advice about life problems. Structured groups, such as various types of life-skills training groups (e.g., stress management, assertiveness training), utilize didactic instruction as a major part of the group format. Psychoeducational groups—that is, groups that provide educational information and facilitate psychological awareness—are particularly useful as preventive interventions for providing traditionally underserved populations with skills to help them cope with stressful life circumstances. Didactic instruction is also useful in providing information to group members who are going through similar life transitions or circumstances.

Client Characteristics.   For individuals from cultural groups who are not familiar with traditional Western therapy approaches, didactic instruction in groups can prepare them for the group process and provide them with a more culturally congruent directive approach to therapy. The following description provided by Tsui and Schultz (1988) regarding Asian clients in groups may be applicable to other VREG or collectivistically oriented clients:

> Thrown into a strange culture in which traditional modes of behavior appear inappropriate, the Asian is being asked to manifest new behavior without even rudimentary education about the process of group therapy, the relationship of the group worker to the group, or what is expected of participants; nor is information available about what to expect or what will be gained from such participation. Usually, the Asian client is too polite to inquire since this might imply criticism of the attending authority—the group worker—and may wait to be drawn out by the leader, avoid self-disclosure with polite nods or smiles, or attempt to focus upon the trivial as a way of participating without violating cultural norms. In addition, the impact on the rest of the group may be profound" (p. 138).

Interpersonal feedback from group leaders and group members should be conducted within a cultural context. Various cultures have differing standards of appropriate interpersonal behavior. Thus, when group members are provided feedback, the discussion should include inquiries into the meaning of the individual's behavior in his or her own culture, as well as an interpretation of what it signifies in other cultures. African American and Latino men, for example, are frequently experienced as interpersonally threatening by members of other socioracial groups when exhibiting interpersonal behavior common to men of their respective cultures.

For example, what an African American man feels is often evident in his verbal expression, particularly if he is angry. Group members who have been socialized to separate emotions and behavior may be intimidated by such integration. Thus, group members may assist these men by providing them with an alternative cultural interpretation of African American and Latino men's behavior, ethnocentric though it may be. If the men as well as the other group members are helped to examine the cultural predispositions underlying their perceptions and reactions to one another's behavior, then all parties may learn to interpret others' reactions to them as cultural tensions when such interpretation is appropriate, rather than automatically assuming personal or interpersonal dysfunction.

Tsui and Schultz (1988) provide similar examples of the misinterpretations of Asians' behavior in groups. For example, Asian group members may be perceived as passive group members because they tend to be less vocal than other group members; what is interpreted as passivity may actually be a communication of respect for others, by waiting for them to speak first. Inaccurate feedback from fellow group members can initiate passive or aggressive reactions from the "attacked" group member, which may in turn create a negative reaction from the offending group members. Additionally, group members may project their own unwanted characteristics onto a group member and relate to the person on the basis of those projected characteristics rather than the actual person (Tsui & Schultz, 1988).

Suggestions and advice from group leaders and members should also be considered from a cultural perspective. Group members may become very frustrated if offered suggestions do not take into consideration the norms of their cultural group. Alternatively, group members could accept the culturally inappropriate advice, act upon it in the world external to the group, and receive negative repercussions from members of their cultural group. Either circumstance could result in the client's withdrawal from the group.

Leader Considerations. When group leaders provide didactic instruction in groups, they must avoid instructional materials that are racially or culturally biased or insensitive. Information provided to group members should be relevant to the lifestyles of all members and exceptions should be carefully acknowledged. It is important that group leaders elicit feedback from members as to the relevance of the information to their individual racial and cultural perspectives.

When group leaders facilitate group members' offering interpersonal feedback or suggestions and advice to each other, it would be helpful to have group members explore the cultural influences of their interpretations on other group members' behaviors and the advice that they are offering. Not only does a group member learn from the feedback from others, but the members offering feedback learn to examine the cultural derivations of their perceptions of others. Group members can then engage in a dialogue to determine how interpersonal feedback applies to a group member's culture and how it might apply in intercultural interactions.

Altruism

Members of groups can be helped through the process of helping others. According to Yalom (1985), "Psychiatric patients beginning therapy are demoralized and possess a deep sense of having nothing of value to offer others. They have long considered themselves as burdens, and the experience of finding that they can be of importance to others is refreshing and boosts self-esteem" (p. 14). The sense of being or having importance to others is what is meant by *altruism.* This phenomena of altruism may be applicable to any groups of individuals who have been relegated to a marginalized status in society, or have been the victims of internalized oppression, be it the elderly, battered women, urban adolescents, or individuals of low socio-economic statuses.

EXERCISE 12.1

An Inclusion Experience

This experience gives members a mind-set that group members are capable of reciprocal helping, prior to their even knowing anything about the other group members other than what is suggested to them by visible physical and demographic characteristics.

- In the beginning of the first session, ask the group members to close their eyes while you (the group leader) lead them through a brief relaxation exercise.

- Once they are relaxed, ask the group members to focus on their reasons for coming to the group, what they hope to

get out of the group, or how the group might help them.

- After group members have had adequate time to experience their responses to the aforementioned questions (approximately 5 to 10 minutes), ask them to open their eyes and look around at each individual group member, and *silently* consider how each person might be helpful to themselves as well as how they might help each of the other group members.

- Ask members to share as much about their experiencing as they feel comfortable about sharing.

Client Considerations. Group interventions can be therapeutic in providing members from social groups that are considered to have nothing to offer to society an opportunity to be contributing members of a group. However, if group members of more privileged positions in society are allowed to discount the help offered by socially less-privileged group members, then neither the oppressed nor privileged group members reap the therapeutic benefits of altruism.

Leader Considerations. Group leaders can work to make the group a "social equalizer" by recognizing that while group members may vary in their material or social status in society, each member comes to the circle with raw talent and personality characteristics that can benefit others. It should be made clear from the beginning that each member of the group has something to offer the others. If necessary, the group leader can spend time during screening interviews and in the initial sessions of the group helping group members to identify their individual intrapersonal and interpersonal strengths. Exercise 12.1 is an intervention that can be used to help group members gain respect for one another's capabilities.

The Corrective Recapitulation of the Primary Family Group

Yalom (1985) reports that, "Without exception, patients [or clients] enter group therapy with the history of a highly unsatisfactory experience in their first and most important group—the primary family" (p. 15). This statement alone could be considered culturally insensitive on a number of levels. First, the essence of culturally

EXERCISE **12.2**

Draw Your Culture

This is a warm-up exercise used by Regan and Scarpellini Huber (1997) in their White racial identity therapy groups. However, it should be appropriate for groups of any socioracial composition since it focuses on helping participants to perceive culture.

For this exercise, you will need some magic markers or crayons of different colors and some large sheets of newsprint, enough for each group member to have her or his own supplies.

Instructions: Participants are asked to draw their culture; that is, whatever symbolizes their culture to them. They may use as many colors as are available. Allow enough time for them to complete their drawings and still have time to process the pictures. When it appears that group members have completed their drawings, each group member should be asked to share the

meaning of his or her drawing with the rest of the group members.

Rules for the sharing activity are:

1. The quality of the drawing is irrelevant.
2. Everyone may ask questions or make comments about the presentations.
3. The sharing person should not be forced to disclose more than he or she is comfortable sharing.
4. The person's interpretation of her or his drawing must be respected.

This exercise is very useful in revealing the cultural dynamics present in the group at the beginning, and usually elicits a lot of complex reactions. So, the facilitator may use it to anticipate subsequent cultural and racial issues in the group.

---

sensitive therapy is that the therapist should look for the "exceptions" in her or his work with clients. Secondly, one must ask through whose eyes is a "highly unsatisfactory" experience determined?

For too long, traditional psychology and psychotherapy have based rigid theoretical and diagnostic standards on a select group of client characteristics of sociorace, gender, age, and sexual orientation. From these selected characteristics, sweeping generalizations are made about individuals whose lifestyles and worldviews are not consistent with the framework used to describe them. Not all group members will use the same criteria as the therapist to deem their primary family experiences to be *highly unsatisfactory*.

Finally, the description of the primary family as the first and most important group experience for an individual may (depending on how family is defined) negate the importance of extended family networks in many cultures. Different cultural groups may have alternate familial patterns and structures that differ from the nuclear family as portrayed in psychological literature (Katz, 1985).

Furthermore, Tsui and Schultz (1988) point out that Asian group members "may find the group's focus on process and analysis and the group worker's expectations of self-revelation quite shocking and antithetical to traditional values in which the Asian [family member] is never expected to disclose family or personal matters to outsiders" (p. 137). These observations may also pertain to African American clients. Exercise 12.2 might be useful for obtaining an idea about the variety of familial cultural orientations present in the group.

We are not suggesting that Yalom (1985) is totally off-base in concluding that early family conflicts are relived and can be corrected in group therapy. However, we advise that the therapist be tentative in her or his use of the impaired family-relations assumption. For instance, depending on the socioracial composition of the group, it is possible that societal conflicts may emerge to a greater degree than familial conflicts. Yet it is also possible that their families' manners of coping with racial and cultural conflicts may be expressed by clients.

Leader Considerations.   Group leaders must be careful not to interpret the corrective recapitualation of the primary family group from a biased cultural or racial perspective. For instance, how does the leader determine what is "corrective"? Might the leader try to "correct" a family pattern that does not need "correcting" from the client's cultural perspective? Group leaders can assess the nature of the "transferences" that occur in the group. There may indeed be a recapitualation of some primary social group; however, the primary social group may or may not be the nuclear family for every member of the group.

Development of Socializing Techniques

Group interventions provide members with social learning experiences—a safe place to develop basic social skills. Again, one must avoid cultural biases in determining what constitutes "basic social skills." For instance, Cheeks (1976) provided insights into the cultural biases inherent in traditional assertiveness skills training, and offered an alternative approach that is more fitting to the sociopolitical and cultural lives of Blacks in America.

More recently, Wood and Mallinckrodt (1990) provided guidelines for culturally sensitive assertiveness training for various visible racial/ethnic groups. Their guidelines include assessment and treatment strategies. General assessment strategies include "determining the etiology of the lack of assertiveness; using self-report inventories that avoid words, slang, or situations that may not be meaningful to the client; and developing norms for the cultural group for which the inventory will be used" (p. 5).

Wood and Mallinckrodt's general treatment strategies include adapting traditional strategies such as modeling and behavioral rehearsal, as well as innovative approaches such as "message matching," backup assertion, and discriminitive cue learning. Modeling and behavioral rehearsal strategies must be adapted to ensure that the responses modeled and rehearsed are most appropriate to the client's cultural circumstances. "Message matching" consists of helping clients to prepare assertive messages that are designed to be effective for specific racial and social classes, so that clients have a repertoire of assertiveness skills to use with a heterogeneous audience.

Backup assertion is a related skill "which involves expression of the assertive communication, followed by an inquiry to check out how the message was received" (p. 10). The inquiries help to identify any discrepancies between the intended message communicated by the client and the interpretation of the message by the receiver. Given the potential for such discrepancies in cross-cultural communications, this is a very useful technique. Finally, discriminative cue learning sensitizes clients to cultural, gender, and authority status communications to assist them in correctly perceiving relevant social characteristics of the situation and selecting the most effective assertive communication in a given situation.

Client Considerations. It could be helpful in mixed-race or same-race groups for group members to learn how others perceive their behavior and how they might adapt their behavior to be more responsive to race-related sociopolitical nuances. People of all socioracial groups might learn how people of other socioracial groups respond to their interactions with them. Moreover, if the group includes people of different cultural perspectives (e.g., collectivism-individualism), then the group might be used to teach people how to shift to the other cultural style when necessary.

Leader Considerations. Group leaders must examine their own cultural biases regarding what they deem to be "basic social skills." They should involve group members in the process of identifying a skill attainment level. They should consider the skills required to be successful within the cultures of individual group members, as well as the skills needed to succeed in a multicultural society. Both VREG as well as White group members should be encouraged to consider the skills that might facilitate their multicultural competence (LaFramboise & Rowe, 1983). Too often, the requirement that a person learn the skills to function effectively in another culture is limited to people of ALANA or nondominant cultural backgrounds.

Imitative Behavior

Due to the amount of time that group members and leaders spend together, and the social power ascribed to the leader and the members, individuals in groups frequently model their behavior after the leader and other members. Imitative behavior can be effective in modeling culturally sensitive and socioracially responsive behavior within the group.

Client Considerations. Imitative behavior is also helpful in assisting group members in working through issues related to racial oppression in society. Members of both oppressed and oppressor racial groups carry the marks of oppression in their intrapersonal and interpersonal dynamics. Racial scholars have described the self- and other-denigrating behaviors that ALANAs and Whites exhibit in reaction to their oppressed or oppressing statuses in society (Helms, 1990a).

Culturalists have described the ethnocentrism present in intergroup dynamics. For instance, leaders of African American women's groups have observed that self-esteem and competition issues have arisen in their groups around issues of skin color, hair texture, and body image (Boyd-Franklin, 1991; Gainor, 1992). Group members cannot "grow out of" internalized messages unless they have frank and honest emotional discussions of the pain that these messages have caused them.

Leader Considerations. In fostering imitative behavior, group leaders must be cognizant of differences in behavior across cultures and the implications of these differences when persons imitate behaviors that may be in conflict with their cultural group. In cross-cultural groups, leaders can model behaviors that recognize and value the differences that exist among members of the various cultural groups. Leaders can address the group using their own cultural voices and encourage group members to identify and openly express their cultural values and norms.

In mixed-race groups, ALANA as well as White leaders can confront behaviors resulting from internalized oppression or domination. In this respect, group leaders can model, self-disclosing about the ways in which they were socialized to think of themselves and others regarding internalized standards of physical attractiveness and competence.

To be maximally effective and provide a racially and culturally safe atmosphere, group leaders should model using supportive behaviors in response to open expressions of very vulnerable and rageful feelings (Gainor, 1992). Regan and Scarpellini Huber (1997) have described ways in which such modeling can take place in White groups aimed at helping group members to become nonracist White people.

Interpersonal Learning

The therapeutic factor of interpersonal learning in therapy groups consists of several components. Yalom (1985) has described the components of interpersonal learning accordingly:

". . . A regular interpersonal sequence occurs . . . [that consists of]

  a. Pathology display—the member displays his or her [inappropriate] behavior;
  b. Through feedback and self-observation, one
   (1) Becomes a better observer of one's behavior;
   (2) Appreciates the impact of that behavior upon
    (a) The feelings of others;
    (b) The opinions that others have of one;
    (c) The opinion one has of oneself" (p. 44).

Once the client becomes fully aware of this interpersonal sequence, he or she is able to take personal responsibility for his or her own interpersonal behavior. Yalom contends that the greater the affect associated with the awareness process, the better it is learned, and the more intellectualized the process, the less effectively it is learned.

"As a result of this [in-depth] awareness, the patient gradually changes by risking new ways of being with others" (p. 44). Factors hypothesized to promote change are as follows:

  "**a.** The patient's motivation for change and the amount of personal discomfort and dissatisfaction with current modes of behavior;
  b. The patient's involvement in the group—that is, how much the patient allows the group to matter;
  c. The rigidity of the patient's character structure and interpersonal style" (Yalom, 1985, p. 44).

As the person becomes more adept at analyzing and monitoring her or his own behavior and its consequences, then a number of other positive intrapersonal outcomes allegedly follow. These include abandonment of irrational fears, decreased social anxiety, and enhanced self-esteem. Yalom calls this improvement in internal status and positive interpersonal consequences an *adaptive spiral.* The therapist may encourage these adaptive changes by "offering specific feedback, encouraging self-observation, clarifying the concept of responsibility, encouraging risk taking, disconfirming fantasied calamitous consequences, reinforcement of transfer of learning, and so on" (p. 45).

Client Considerations. We have found group interventions to be a treatment of choice in helping individuals to learn how their racial and/or cultural attitudes are expressed and interpreted interpersonally. However, due in part to the horror stories of erratic group experiences during the hey-day of encounter-type groups in the sixties and early seventies, the anticipation of group therapy, in general, can be threatening to individuals (Corey & Corey, 1987). If you add to this anticipatory anxiety the idea that the reason for being in a group is to deal with racial issues, major hysteria can develop.

Racial issues are so volatile in this country that both ALANAs and Whites tend to develop elaborate defenses to avoid confronting each other on the reality of their experiences. For example, in our experiences as consultants with groups on cross-racial issues, one of the fears of some Whites is that ALANAs will unfairly "bash" them as racists, based on the history of their ancestors' treatment of ALANAs.

Furthermore, in response to this fear, some Whites may refrain from speaking honestly of their negative perceptions of the various visible racial/ethnic groups, so as not to reinforce their image as racists. Still others believe that by wallowing in free-floating guilt, they prove that they are not racists.

Some ALANA group participants anticipate that they will be expected to serve as experts in educating Whites about their respective racial groups. They may also feel that they must protect Whites by withholding the expression of their true feelings regarding the racial prejudice, discrimination, and injustice that they have experienced from Whites.

These are just some examples of the defenses used by Whites and ALANAs in racial consciousness groups. However, individuals may use a variety of responses to cope with racial information, some of which we will discuss in a subsequent section in this chapter on racial identity reactions in groups.

Whether or not a group is intended to alleviate racial discomfort or tensions, race is likely to be an interpersonal factor in the group experience. Using the interpersonal sequence described by Yalom (1985), it is possible to see how race can arise as an interpersonal dynamic. His analysis begins with a display of "pathology," which he considers to emanate from disturbed interpersonal relationships. One potential source of disturbed interpersonal relationships is racism, be it the attitudes of racial-group supremacy internalized by an oppressor or the attitudes of racial-group inferiority or rage internalized by an oppressed individual.

Within a therapy group, whether mixed-race or same-race, members display behaviors that are in part derived from their identities as persons of their racial and/or cultural group(s). These behaviors may be based on their cultural norms or socioracial status in society. Within the group, members can become aware of the relationship between their experiences of racial oppression or domination and the behavior that they exhibit in the group. Through feedback and self-observation, they can examine the impact of their behavior on the feelings and opinions of others, as well as their own opinions of themselves.

We take exception to Yalom's (1985) premise of individuals being responsible for shaping their own interpersonal worlds. Racial and cultural discrimination is an interpersonal reality for which oppressed groups are not responsible. However, while they do not have personal responsibility for, nor are they the creators of, acts of discrimination exhibited toward them, they do have a responsibility for developing adaptive coping strategies. The group can provide interpersonal education for individuals who are not aware of their oppressive behavior toward others, as well as for individuals who have developed maladaptive coping strategies in response to discrimination.

Yalom (1985) purports that the degree of meaningfulness of one's awareness is directly proportional to the degree of affect associated with the group experience. We have found in our experiences that the emotional experiences in race-related groups have to be carefully timed to allow for a level of trust to develop to withstand the impact of intense emotional expressions and to have enough time for the emotions to be experienced, processed, and worked through.

In the social microcosm of the real world, people must coexist in the world with other people who may have differing belief systems regarding race. Recognition of this reality and development of skills to cope with it are aspects of social learning that can take place within group interactions. The experiences of social learning within the group will help group members to move beyond their fears and anxieties about relating to members of different races and cultures. Also, functional learning will help group members to feel more comfortable with their own racial or cultural selves, thereby relieving them of the need to displace their reactions onto others.

Leader Considerations.   Group leaders should become knowledgeable about the impact of racism and ethnocentrism on Whites and ALANAs, so that they can facilitate interpersonal learning among group members. The leader must provide a safe environment for group members to express their raw feelings toward themselves as racial or cultural beings, and their attitudes toward individuals of other races or cultural groups. In permitting such self-expression, the group leader must be prepared to process in the here-and-now group members' feelings as they hear unpleasant comments from other group members.

Often group leaders will have to interpret group members' comments for one another to assure that group members are accurately hearing what is being stated rather than prematurely castigating each other for biased or prejudicial assumptions. Also, group leaders must assist group members in resolving embittered feelings, even in situations where racial attitudes or cultural beliefs among group members are not compatible.

At the outset of the group, leaders should make clear the expectation that group members can risk new ways of being with others within the group without being afraid. As group leaders observe racial insensitivities in interactions between group members, they can invite group members to share their experiences of the situation with each other. Group members would probably not risk such confrontational situations without prompting from the leaders, as most people have been socialized in many respects to avoid racial or cultural confrontations in social interactions. However, group leaders can create a safe environment for such risk-taking interactions by modeling the desired behaviors themselves.

Group members should be told at the beginning of the group that the roles of race and culture, as identity components of every individual, will be addressed in group interactions as relevant. During screening interviews, leaders should begin the discussion of racial and cultural dynamics by exploring how potential group members perceive themselves and others. Leaders can get a sense of group members' comfort level in discussing such issues and try to put them at ease by explaining the leader's philosophy of helping group members to develop an atmosphere of trust and support in examining race and culture in the group.

Leaders need to prepare group members for the reactions that their changed behavior may cause in their world outside of the group. The racial and cultural groups in which we are socialized are so ingrained with distorted perceptions of other racial and cultural groups that group members with newly developed behaviors and understandings about racial or cultural relations may become intolerant of the attitudes of others in their own group(s), or they may face ridicule from members of their own group(s) because they are violating group norms.

Group Cohesiveness

Yalom (1985) asserts that group cohesiveness is analogous to the "relationship" or therapeutic alliance in individual therapy. In group therapy, cohesiveness embodies group members' relationships with the leader(s), the other group members, and the group as a complete entity. Cohesiveness consists of relationships of perceived similarity of some kind, and mutual attraction, acceptance, support, and trust. Members of cohesive groups readily self disclose to one another and are influenced by each other. The greater the group members' attraction to the group, the greater the group attendance. Interestingly enough, group cohesiveness fosters the development and expression of hostility and conflict toward other group members and the group leader.

Client Considerations.   For racial groups who are in the minority in a social situation, such as African American students at predominantly White universities, cohesiveness in monoracial groups might develop easily if group members can be helped to perceive their similarities with respect to cultural background and racial alienation in the environment. The relationship that individual members develop with the group as a whole may serve to empower group members to deal with the alienating forces in the environment external to the group.

In interracial groups, leaders can foster cohesiveness by emphasizing the commonalities that group members share while simultaneously helping group members to accept their racial differences. Creating harmony in the midst of unspoken disharmony may require that clients be encouraged to express hostilities related to their racial or cultural differences as a means of achieving acceptance. Similarly, in same-race visible racial/ethnic groups, hostilities may occur (Gainor, 1992) as group members express their resentments toward each other based on their internalized oppression. Group members may attempt to "out-oppress" each other in competition over who has been more oppressed, or they may attack each other based on the pain that they have experienced from members of their own racial group (Gainor, 1992).

Moreover, because people may have cultural socialization experiences that are not the same as those of other people in their sociogroup (as we have noted in previous chapters), cultural factors (e.g., social class differences) may be used to create artificial barriers or similarities. Nevertheless, whether in same-race or interracial groups, or monocultural or nondominant culture groups, cohesiveness promotes an atmosphere in which group members can work through their divisions based on their prior racial and cultural experiences and attitudes.

Leader Considerations.   As group leaders attempt to foster cohesiveness in groups, they must consider the role of race and/or culture as either an impediment or an aid in the development of cohesiveness. For instance, obstacles may occur that depend on the racial identity attitudes of group members (see Chapter 5). Thus, a group member who perceives himself or herself in the racial minority of a mixed-race group may have difficulty developing an attraction toward the group and feeling accepted, supported, and trusting of them.

This feeling of alienation could also occur in a monoracial group in which one or more of the group members does not identify with his or her racial group. Counselors might mistakenly refer a client to a support group for members of the client's race when the client harbors negatively biased sentiments toward her or his societally ascribed sociogroup. It is important for the group leader to *assess* group members' perceptions of their similarities to other members, rather than merely assuming that certain similarities exist.

Group leaders must invest time in developing cohesiveness among group members early on in the group. They must also avoid colluding with the group to avoid the open expression of racial or cultural hostilities in the group. True growth will take place only if such negative emotions are worked through within the safe context of the group.

Catharsis

Catharsis can be a therapeutic factor in group therapy when group members experience and express both positive and negative feelings in the group *and also* experience some form of cognitive learning (Yalom, 1985). Yalom explains that charis provides "a sense of liberation, of acquiring skills for the future . . . [However,] the intensity of emotional expression is highly relative and must be appreciated not from the leader's perspective but from that of each member's experiential world. A seemingly muted expression of emotion may for a highly constricted individual, represent an event of considerable intensity" (p. 85).

Client Considerations. Yalom's (1985) conceptualization of catharsis could be particularly helpful for assisting group members in expressing their experiences with and attitudes toward people of different socioracial groups and learning new behaviors for interacting with members of the socioracial groups represented within the group. Furthermore, his explanation regarding variability in intensity of emotional expression acknowledges the existence of differences in emotional expression across cultures. However, because race and culture are so often confounded in U.S. society, it may be difficult for group members to recognize in themselves and others the distinction between the two. Thus, for example, what may be a cultural style for expressing emotion may be misinterpreted as a racial slight or slur.

Leader Considerations. The cognitive learning that is so crucial to the therapeutic value of catharsis must be promoted by the group leader. If left to the wherewithal of the group members, be they White or VREG people, the group may become a place where participants can vent their racial outrage and cultural pain without ever recognizing that they can have a role in combatting racism and ethnocentrism in their own lives and society. As Yalom (1985) warns, the therapeutic value of catharsis is not merely to "help group members rid themselves of suppressed, choked affect" (p. 85).

It should be noted that in addition to recognizing that anger may be expressed differently across cultures, group leaders should also be aware that in different cultures expressions of intimacy may vary in format and content. For example, physical contact (e.g., group hugs) may be experienced as a positive form of intimacy for some group members, but overwhelming or even immoral intimacy for others. Group leaders must take care to reinforce group members for their varied expressions of emotions and not allow their own cultural biases to determine what is considered restrictive or unleashed expressions of emotions.

Existential Factors

The last therapeutic factor described by Yalom (1985), existential factors, addresses the commonalities that group members experience in coming to terms with such meaning-of-life issues as the unfairness, injustices, and inescapable emotional pain that occur in life, including mortality, personal consequences for one's conduct in life, and the reality that one ultimately faces life alone.

Yalom (1985) provides an example of a group he conducted "composed of patients who lived continuously in the midst of extreme experience. All the members had a terminal illness, generally metastatic carcinoma; and all were entirely aware of the nature and implications of their illness" (p. 99). He described the therapeutic bonding circumstances of this group of individuals based on their shared grappling with existential issues of death as follows: "[Members were supportive of one another, they shared a] common bond of enmity toward the medical profession [and Yalom assisted them in] disentangling the threads of this anger. Some of the anger was displaced and irrational—anger at fate, envious anger at the living. . . . Some of the anger was entirely justified. . . . We attempted to understand the irrational anger and place it where it belonged. . . . We faced the justifiable anger and attempted to cope with it . . ." (pp. 99–100). In a similar manner, clients can be assisted in discovering the sources of their racial and cultural anger. The group leader can be their guide through the discovery process.

Client Considerations   The description of Yalom's (1985) shared-experience group could apply to a group for visible racial/ethnic group individuals who live continuously in the midst of extreme prejudice. Oppression due to institutional, individual, and cultural racism could be considered a source of existential distress. Racism engenders the feelings of unfairness, injustice, and inescapable pain of life, as well as the aloneness that ALANA individuals can feel when they experience instances of racism.

Moreover, given the violence that often accompanies verbal or symbolic expressions of racism, the fear of death may also be experienced by group members who have been victimized by extreme cases of racism. Efforts to respond to acts of racism and maintain one's self-esteem may force the person to reevaluate the manner in which he or she has conducted his or her life heretofore, as well as the import of the person's life to others.

Members of racially or culturally oppressed groups can benefit from the support of other group members who share a common bond of enmity toward the oppressor. Thus, the forms of anger expression that characterized Yalom's (1985) group might also appear in support groups for VREG individuals; that is, displaced and irrational anger, envious anger at Whites and perhaps other VREGs, and entirely justified or "rational" anger.

Group members can receive great benefit from confronting the existential nature of racism and learning life-skills for coping with it. In addition, it should be noted that Regan and Scarpellini Huber (1997) warn that parallel dynamics can occur in all-White groups as members become aware of the ways that they have been socialized to be racists.

Leader Considerations.   Group leaders must be aware of the pervasive and devastating effects of racism on an individual's mental health, regardless of the members' socioracial classification. In addition, leaders must work through their own issues and fears in confronting the impact of racism on their own lives, and be willing to engage in ongoing exploration of their own roles in perpetuating racism in America. Both Whites and some VREGs can reap the benefits of racism. Consequently, whereas some Whites may experience debilitating "White guilt," some VREGs may experience survivor guilt because they have been deemed "special" People of Color by White people, thereby reaping some privileges denied to other ALANAs.

Yet others in similar circumstances may experience no guilt whatsoever. Instead, they may consider their benefits to have been justly earned because they are superior in some way to their less-privileged counterparts. The group leader should be prepared to deal with either eventuality.

Racial Identity and Group Conflict

Once implicit racial or cultural issues occurring within a group are made explicit, it is likely that related conflicts will also move to the forefront of the group. According to

Mitchell and Mitchell (1984), group conflict occurs in cycles or episodes consisting of several components. The components are: (a) the person's "*entering state,*" which is influenced by "such variables as her or his behavioral predispositions, pressures from the social environment, conflict experiences with significant others, and previous conflict episodes with other group members" (p. 138); (b) a *catalyst,* some implicit or explicit event that elicits a particular reaction; (c) a consequential emotional reaction, which Mitchell and Mitchell call "frustration"; (d) "*conceptualization,*" each group member's (including the leader's) implicit interpretation of the episode of conflict; (e) "*behavior and interaction,*" the group members' reciprocally influential reactions to the situation based on their prior unspoken conceptualizations; and (f) the "*outcome,*" the condition of (e.g., emotional reactions, specific behaviors) participants at the conclusion of the episode of conflict. Mitchell and Mitchell contend that the same cycle may be repeated several times within a group with the same theme or different themes as its focus.

Racial Conflict within Groups

Racial identity process theory describes implicitly and explicitly how "race" can be a major potential source of conflict in most social interactions, particularly if they involve people of different races or racial identity orientations. Conflict or frustration in groups (and other social units) is one form of outcome that results when people's racial identity statuses are discordant, and the resulting discord persists without ever being properly resolved (Helms, 1984; Helms, 1990a; Helms, 1990b, Helms, 1995).

Thus, in Helms's model, using Mitchell and Mitchell's framework as a starting point for discussing racial dynamics in groups, group members' entering states include a typical racial identity constellation or profile as described in Tables 5.3 and 5.4. Each person's profile, or at least the ego statuses that are hypothesized to underlie the profile, in part, influences what the person perceives as racial stimuli or catalysts. Thus, the more immature the person's racial identity development, the more likely it is that he or she will respond to racial information at an unconscious level. Conversely, the more mature the person's development, the more likely it is that race will be an explicit issue in the group's climate.

In addition, one's racial identity status profile is hypothesized to influence how one interprets other people's responses to racial catalysts as well as one's own. In general, profiles that are predominated by less mature statuses contribute to simplistic (often stereotypic) interpretations of other people's racial circumstances, and obliviousness or lack of awareness of one's own contribution to the ensuing racial dynamics. Increasing developmental maturity among group members makes the group leader's growth-promoting task easier (if he or she is at least equivalently mature) because group members become more willing to confront the racial and cultural dynamics intrinsic to their group.

The conflict episode in Mitchell and Mitchell's (1984) terminology is approximately what Helms (1995) means by a racial "event." That is, she contends that a person's behavior reveals her or his underlying racial identity processes or ways of perceiving racial stimuli, and that behavior becomes a catalyst for the observing person's reactive racial-identity-related cognitive or interpretive, affective, and behavioral (CAB) responses. This cycle—catalytic behavioral expression, observer's reactive CAB response, initiator's rebuttal CAB reaction—shapes the climate of the group and is repeated throughout the course of the group, perhaps in different forms.

Moreover, the group leader participates in many such cycles with each of the group members, and the group members participate in many person-specific cycles with one another as well as with the group leader. Thus, the group leader has the facilitation task of monitoring all of the ongoing cycles, and intervening when necessary to prevent them from impeding the natural therapeutic factors of a group as described by Yalom (1985).

Types of Racial Identity Events

This monitoring task is not overwhelming if one recognizes that events can be classified according to the types of behaviors, interactions, and outcomes that they reveal. In fact, group members can eventually be taught to analyze their racial and cultural dynamics themselves (Regan & Scarpellini Huber, 1997). Helms (1995) contends that events can be classified as one of three types—parallel, regressive, and progressive, and one subtype—crossed. Crossed subtypes may be either progressive or regressive. Each of the types of events has distinguishable interpretive and behavioral characteristics and affective reactions, which contribute to predictable outcomes. Descriptions of the types are summarized in Table 9.1.

The type of event is determined by a combination of the manifest racial identity status of participants in the event, the level of racial identity immaturity-maturity evident in their CAB expressions, as well as the relative social statuses of the participants. In general, the group member(s) with greatest social status or power determines the quality or type of interaction. However, social status may be accorded on the basis of a variety of factors.

Some relevant factors (and remember that these may be influenced by each group member's cultural and/or racial socialization) include the following: (a) **social role**—for example, group leaders typically have more power than group members; (b) **numerical representation within the group**—generally members of the socioracial group in the majority within the group have the most power; (c) **sociorace**—Whites frequently have more power because they are members of the group that defines "appropriate" behavior; and (d) **gender**—men often have more power than women for similar reasons.

Also, it is possible for a person to possess a different quantity of social power in the group context than in the world external to the group. In addition, the person may acquire additional social power by banding together (that is, forming coalitions) with other group members who are perceived as similar on some critical dimension such as racial identity expression.

Parallel Expression.   An event (or coalition) is "parallel" with respect to racial identity if both or all participants' behavioral-affective responses to the racial catalyst appear to reflect the same racial identity status(es). Parallel events are typically placid, harmonious engagements whose tenor is determined by the statuses being expressed.

Thus, for example, events that are parallel with respect to early racial identity statuses (e.g., Contact-Conformity, Conformity-Conformity, Contact-Contact) are harmonious because participants "agree" to avoid addressing racial issues. However, an event that is parallel due to more sophisticated status expressions (e.g., Autonomy-Integrative Awareness, Autonomy-Autonomy, Integrative Awareness-Integrative Awareness) is probably harmonious because event participants collaborate in addressing racial issues, but these types of parallel events are probably relatively rare.

In any case, in Mitchell and Mitchell's terminology, parallel events and coalitions are probably more typically characterized by "accommodating" or "avoiding" CAB responses. *Accommodating* types are characterized by an abundance of appeasement, self-sacrifice, and acquiescence rather than assertive attention to the racial or cultural conflict; *avoiding*-type events involve obliviousness, withdrawal, and feigned indifference to racial catalysts.

Regressive Expression.

When regressive expression occurs, the person with the greater social power is responding to racial catalysts in a more simplistic fashion (e.g., avoiding, accommodating) than the person with less social power within the group context. Helms assumes that such interactions typically occur when the "statusful" person is less mature with respect to racial identity ego status development than the person with less status. For example, regressive expression might be expected to occur when the most and least powerful persons' respective CAB responses have strongly Contact-Reintegration or Reintegration-Autonomy implicit themes.

Confrontation or a "competing orientation" describes the manner of conflict resolution that typifies regressive events. Domination—winning over or convincing—and assertive lack of cooperation are cognitive, affective, and behavioral themes evident in regressive events. Moreover, if the events are also crossed, meaning that participants' racial identity CAB responses are diametrically opposed on every dimension, then events can be especially antagonistic and combative.

Progressive Expression.

Events are progressive when the CAB reactions of the person with most social power (e.g., the group leader) signify more complex racial identity development than those of the person (e.g., group member) with less status. Such events typically are invigorating, collaborative, and cooperative and incorporate complex attention to racial catalysts. Progressive events can also be crossed if the racial identity expressions of the participants are the antithesis of one another on the cognitive, affective, and behavioral dimensions, but the high-status person's manner of expression (and presumably underlying development) is the most sophisticated.

Helms contends that progressive events offer the best opportunities for growth. Mitchell and Mitchell's (1984) "collaborative" and "sharing (bargaining or compromising)" conflict resolution modes probably best pertain to progressive events. Both involve a large expenditure of psychic energy that is used to assure that the needs of the person of less status are met in ways that are most appropriate for that person's level of developmental maturity with respect to racial identity functioning.

In a group, it is useful if the group leader can quickly recognize and categorize the various types of events as they are happening. By doing so, he or she may rechannel detrimental interactions so that they do not become impediments to the healing properties of the group. An example of a nontherapy discussion group on racial topics might be useful for illustrating how such analyses might occur.

Talking about Race

In Table 12.1 is an excerpt from a group discussion about racial topics involving four volunteer research participants. Thus, it is not a therapy group and is perhaps more analogous to classroom discussions about race. Nevertheless, Helms (1990b) contends that one improves one's racial identity "diagnostic" skills by observing and analyzing events in everyday life. Therefore, this excerpt should be useful for instructional purposes.

The group leader, "Linda" (whose racial identity profile appears in Chapter 6), a White female university undergraduate, was randomly selected to be the leader when group members appeared for the discussion group. The other group members are "Steve" and "George," two White male university undergraduates, and "Rose," an Asian American female university undergraduate.

Racial identity profiles are not provided for the participants (other than Linda) because group leaders ordinarily do not have access to such information. Typically, one must formulate one's diagnosis from what a person says, how he or she says it, and others' CAB reactions rather than from external measures.

In Table 12.1, the group members are attempting to reach consensus as to whether Black athletes should be required to score a minimum of 700 on the Scholastic Aptitude Test (SAT) and have a minimum of a C-average in English, math, and science courses. Columns 1 and 2 in the table identify the speaker and speaking turn or number. Column 3 is the content of the speaking turn, and Column 4 is the racial identity theme(s) present in the comment.

Linda begins this interaction with what seems to be a Pseudo-Independent-Contact observation. Although she does not address the issue of race specifically, she is willing to discuss cultural limitations of tests, but does not know what they are. George's reaction to her comments is parallel with respect to Contact. That is, he not only avoids talking about race, but also culture. He neutralizes the issue. For the next 17 speaking turns (only a sample of which are shown in the table), each member of the group contributes to the parallel events or interaction, wherein neither race nor culture is discussed.

At speaking turn 21, Linda attempts to reassert her power as group leader and redirect the discussion. This time she lets it be known that the group is supposed to be discussing race, a point she has to make again before the rest of the group is willing to broach the topic, albeit indirectly. Her conflict resolution style is rather accommodating in that she uses self-blame to refocus the group. Consequently, they respond by engaging in a variety of reactions, which for the most part, can be characterized as some combination of Contact (avoidance) and Reintegration (stereotypic) expressive themes. When there is discord in the group, Linda is in the regressive role because the group has usurped her power as group leader by forming Contact (Conformity)—Reintegration coalitions with one another.

TABLE 12.1 A Segment of a Race-Explicit Discussion

Speaker	Turn	Comment	Theme
Linda	1	Do you think that the admission policy should be the same regardless of race? Why? Um, I think that the admission policy should be the same regardless of race. Basically my feeling is that as far as the athletes in general more of a question of (inaudible) athletes getting in who don't have a 700 on their SATs. I mean, that's why maybe more I think that than anything else you know aside from the racial issue but um I think that I think that it should be everyone should have the same requirements. I know I'm not giving a good reason. Cause I don't think it makes a difference. I think there are a lot of questions as whether it's a culturally biased exam and I think that they ought to have studies on it but unless they really proved that there is a cultural bias and can't adapt it to make it fit everybody then I don't think that there's any reason that somebody should be getting into college with less than a 700 SAT if that's what . . .	Pseudo-Independent, Contact
George	2	Yeah. Along that same lines, they shouldn't really be accepted because college is a form of higher education its not a form of higher sports education you know. Its uh, it should be intelligence first and athletics second. You have to have some kind of priorities for the school. A lot of schools tend to neglect that because the sports bring in more money to college than other things and that's where the problem comes in. It's not really a matter of bias its really a matter of money.	Contact
Steve	3	Yeah, its that. I disagree with you guys though because the only thing I think college should be a place for learning but with the big time athletics it is money . . . its a business. And basically what they're doing is. . . . I don't want to make a generalization because I know a lot of athletes who are actually scholar athletes . . . On the other hand there are a lot of people who aren't scholar athletes who are just plain athletes who have nothing to do with academics. Um, I don't think they should be . . . there should be a minimum like that simply because they're not here for academics. Nobody thinks they're here for academics. They're not going to win the Nobel Prize in anything but then again most (inaudible), like they're talking about starting a development league, like now if you pretty much want to play pro basketball, pro football, you have to go to college and you have to do well in college athletics. That's not fair to the people who they don't want to waste four years in college when the only reason they're here is they want to build their academic skills. They want to start a league . . .	Contact

(continued)

TABLE 12.1 Continued

Speaker	Turn	Comment	Theme
Linda	4	The athletic schools?	
Steve	5	Yeah, kind of like a minor league, kind of like a you know a farm system or something, but a big one. A real . . . a real thing. I think if that started up, then definitely you know there should be equal requirements but right now I don't think that most of the people here, even if they have over that they're not here for academics anyway. Their job . . . their goal, their dream for most of them, which isn't definitely true the whole, is to get into the very very high paying job in the pros. And um of course that's only true for the stars. But still, I mean the school really uses them. I mean the school really with all the time and everything that they put forward. I mean if you have a decent average when you on a big time athletic team then that's amazing. I mean I'm talked to some guys. That's absolutely amazing. Cause they take more time than anything. And, um, I think this school basically is taking advantage of them. They makes much bucks. The school makes millions and basically they give them a few thousand for scholarships.	Contact
Rose	6	Well, the purpose of (inaudible) is not that the school is making money or not the purpose is education and sports is just a minor part of the system that brings money in all the other controversies and lots of other things. So I think it should be equal and if they really have a big time going they really want to be an all star basketball player or does football player (inaudible) well try harder. Study harder. I mean, if they really have the goal, if you really believe in something that you can do and its going to take four years for you to get to the thing, well, try harder. I mean . . .	Conformity
Steve	7	But the thing . . . what I meant was its almost like they're never gonna do anything academically they don't care academically, some of them can't even make it academically. Um, why should someone be and if they're a star athlete, why should someone be hindered from succeeding in the field that they're good at because they're not good at something else? Namely academics. In other words, if someone is not a scholar is...completely not rock-dumb but just never was . . .	
Rose	8	Dumb but good in sports.	Conformity

TABLE 12.1 Continued

Speaker	Turn	Comment	Theme
Rose	17	No, that's really what we're talking about, IQ problems here. I mean if you have a little IQ I mean how are you going to think when you're playing? I mean seriously I mean you gotta have logic when you're playing even if you're a dumb jock and you want to play you need to know, hey, you know well look the guy's . . .	Conformity
Linda	21	I'm sorry, I don't mean to interrupt but I think that the um question deals and I guess it's my fault cause I kind of opened it up in the question of athletics, but I think it's really dealing specifically with the Black versus non-Black question of whether the test discriminates and should that be . . .	Autonomy
Steve	22	Oh, so we're talking about we're talking about the	
	23	Unintelligible Talking at once (lasts 6 seconds)	
Linda	24	I think I instigated when I said I think that all athletes should have the same SAT's. It shouldn't matter culturally. But the issue, I'll read it again: However several college coaches and Black educators have protested that this policy unfairly discriminates against Black athletes because the test may be culturally biased against them and they don't have the same educational opportunities as members of other racial groups. And I started by saying I think everyone should have it unless they prove the test biased that I don't think that there should be any I don't think they should put Blacks students in under the requirements that everybody has, the Black athletes.	Pseudo-Independent, Immersion
George	25	Yeah along that lines the same idea is that they have the same ability to learn as we do. We give them even better teachers they find in most cases than we have our own. They are taking the highest paid teachers are the ones that are going to these schools. I think that its the home that is ranking the students, not the schools where they try to make it seem like they're not getting a good education. They're getting a great education but they're not going there to learn. They're just going there for attendance, to hang out with their friends, or why not I think the problem is at their house. If they can't you know it's the parent's fault that they shouldn't be in college along that line because if the family doesn't raise you right, you don't belong in a society of higher education where you're going to hinder other people from getting their job done. You know?	Reingegration, Contact
Rose	26	(inaudible) I think it should be equal for everyone.	Conformity

(continued)

TABLE 12.1   Continued

Speaker	Turn	Comment	Theme
George	27	It's equal.	Reintegration, Contact
Steve	28	I don't remember the SAT. I don't understand how it could be culture biased. I mean its not, for God's sake.	Reintegration, Contact
Linda	29	I think it deals more with the English that they feel is culturally biased. I remember reading something to the effect of like the wording I mean it gets what they think the Black language as their speaking of I don't think it really exists or that it really should exist but things saying ain't things saying I don't even remember the rest of it but that's how they speak and that's this speaks on the SATs so it's biased against them for the examples they used on examples of what the White students could relate to or things like that. I think that's what the question I remember reading some article about it and I don't know if I necessarily think that people should go around learning to say "ain't" instead of you know "isn't" and if that's what they want I don't think they should be speaking . . . interruption	Reintegration, Pseudo-Independence
Steve	32	That's the whole issue with Spanish.	Contact
George	33	When people come to our country like a lot of the Japanese and such they learn to speak our language.	Reintegration
George	35	Yeah. They can speak our language better than we can.	Reintegration
Steve	36	That's true. They know it properly.	Reintegration, Contact
Rose	37	Grammar!	Conformity
George	38	Right, exactly. And you're telling me that because they're in their little society we have to bend for them.	Reintegration
Steve	39	And that is exactly what the bilingualists think they had in California where Spanish emigrants, well actually Mexican but who were speaking Spanish, wanted to have everything changed into both Spanish and English. I have no . . . I think that's a great idea, I mean . . .	Reintegration, Contact
Rose	40	And they're getting it, too.	Ambiguous

TABLE 12.1 Continued

Speaker	Turn	Comment	Theme
Steve	41	Right, yeah. I think . . . I think that you know it should be . . . you know, there should be something Spanish and English. That's great. But on the other hand, I don't think accommodations should be made like certain kinds of accommodations should be made like in other words your employer shouldn't be made to learn to speak Spanish to communicate.	Reintegration, Contact
Rose	42	just because . . .	
Steve	43	Right. Its the same thing here. I mean I know a lot of . . . there was a girl in my history class who's Japanese. She was amazing. I mean like she came and she like barely spoke English, but she got an A in that class. That impressed the hell out of me because she works like anything and she came and didn't know anything about language and these guys I don't think I mean come on they speak English to begin with, you know? I mean I don't think there is such a thing as a culture bias. If there is then you have to learn to adapt. I mean nobody can like hand something to you. I mean if you really want something and like I don't believe that people have like you you have a God-given right to do this like you have a right I mean there are certain things you do but on the other hand you don't have a right to be president of the United States. If you want to [be] President of the United States . . .	Reintegration
Rose	44	work for it . . .	
Steve	45	. . . you have to work for it. (inaudible) more advantages than you, but on the other hand that's just the way things are. If you want to be that you have to overcome what problem you have. And I mean I don't think that . . . I think that's going a little too far.	Reintegration

This transcript is an abridged version of a group discussion. The research project in which it occurred was funded by the Fund For Dispute Resolution, Washington, D.C.

Therapy Implications

Although the excerpt in Table 12.1 is not from a therapy group, we think that it is still possible to offer some guidelines for intervening to promote effective group dynamics where race and culture are potential therapy issues. Moreover, although racial identity theory was developed to assist therapists in managing racial dynamics in therapy, we think it has some implications for culture-based interventions as well.

First of all, the group leader must be aware of the racial sociopolitical and cultural issues for *each* of the major socioracial groups in the country. By awareness, we do not necessarily mean that the therapist has to be competent in each of the relevant groups, but rather that he or she be attuned to the crucial issues pertaining to the groups. This kind of information can be acquired through self-study, keeping up with current racial and cultural news events, and talking about these matters with members of one's own racial and cultural group members as well as racial and cultural out-group members. Without such information, it is impossible to intervene to promote growth, even if one's intentions are good. Notice how stereotypic Linda's explanation (turn 29) of cultural bias is, although her overall cognitive, affective, and behavioral reactions offer little doubt that she is the most "liberal" member of the group.

Second, it is important that the therapist intervene to stop efforts to avoid dealing with awkward topics as soon as he or she discovers that such avoidance is occurring. Where race and culture are concerned, our excerpt suggests that some strategies that group members may use to avoid discussing race in specific are as follows (speaking turn examples are in parentheses): (a) using "culture" (and other euphemisms) rather than "race" to depict out-group people without ever defining their concepts or terms (turn 1); (b) using "they" and "we" to refer to specific racial out-groups and the in-group respectively without ever saying directly who the speaker includes in such usages (turn 25); (c) shifting the group's focus away from the specific racial or cultural issue to one with which the group feels safer (turns 32 and 33); and (d) neutralizing the topic; that is eliminating all consideration of the racial or cultural aspects of an interaction (turn 2).

When the group leader hears any of these strategies, he or she should use direct confrontation (e.g., "George, when you say 'We give them even better teachers' . . . who are you talking about?") to focus the group on the relevant themes. Moreover, the group leader may have to pay special attention to group members who *may* be using an avoidant style (perhaps Rose in this case). However, as we discussed earlier, such interventions should be accompanied by ongoing monitoring of what is culturally appropriate for each group member.

Finally, we support Mitchell and Mitchell's (1984) recommendation that the group leader assist group members in understanding their potentially different interpretations of critical events. It is clear in the excerpt, for example, that group members frequently seem to be discussing something other than the issue on the table.

REFERENCES

Boyd-Franklin, N. (1991). Recurrent themes in the treatment of African-American women in group psychotherapy. *Women & Therapy, 11,* 25–30.

Cheeks, D. (1976). *Assertive Black . . . puzzled White.* San Luis Obisbo, CA: Impact.

Corey, M. S., & Corey, G. (1987). *Groups: Process and practice* (3rd ed.) Monterey, CA: Brooks/Cole.

Gainor, K. A. (1992). Internalized oppression as a barrier to effective group work with Black women. *The Journal for Specialists in Group Work, 17,* 235–242.

Helms, J. E. (1984). Toward a theoretical explanation of the effects of race on counseling: A Black and White model. *The Counseling Psychologist, 12,* 153–165.

Helms, J. E. (1990a). *Black and White racial identity: Theory, research, and practice.* Westport, CT: Greenwood Press.

Helms, J. F. (1990b). *Training manual for diagnosing racial identity in social interaction.* Topeka, KS: Content Communications.

Helms, J. E. (1995). An update of Helms's People of Color and White racial identity models. In J. Ponterotto, L. Suzuki, & C. Alexander (Eds.), *Handbook of Multicultural Counseling.* Thousand Oaks, CA: Sage.

Katz, J. H. (1985). The sociopolitical nature of counseling, *The Counseling Psychologist, 13,* 615–625.

LaFromboise, T., & Rowe, W. (1983). Skills training for bicultural competence: Rationale and application. *Journal of Counseling Psychology, 30,* 589–595.

Mitchell, R. C., & Mitchell, R. R. (1984). Constructive management of conflict in groups. *Journal for Specialists in Group Work, September,* 137–144.

Regan, A. M., & Scarpellini Huber, J. (1997). Facilitating White identity development: A therapeutic group intervention. In C. E. Thompson & R. E. Carter (Eds.), *Racial identity theory: Applications to individual, group, and organizational interventions* (pp. 113–126). Mahwah, New Jersey: Lawrence Erlbaum.

Trotzer, J. P. (1977). *The counselor and the group: Integrating theory, training, and practice.* Monterey, CA: Brooks/Cole.

Tsui, P., & Schultz, G. L. (1988). Ethnic factors in group process: Cultural dynamics in multi-ethnic therapy groups. *American Journal of Orthopsychiatry, 58,* 136–142.

Wood, P. S., & Mallinckrodt, B. (1990). Culturally sensitive assertiveness training for ethnic minority clients. *Professional Psychology: Research and Practice, 21,* 5–11.

Yalom, I. D. (1985). *The theory and practice of group psychotherapy.* New York: Basic Books.

13 Collaborating with Indigenous Healers and Helpers

Indigenous healers or helpers are designated individuals within a culture from whom people seek various forms of assistance, healing, and/or guidance. "Among other things, a healer is commonly a person to whom a sufferer tells things; and, out of his or her listening, the healer develops the basis for therapeutic interventions. The psychological healer, in particular, is one who listens in order to learn and to understand; and, from the fruits of this listening, he or she develops the basis for reassuring, advising, consoling, comforting, interpreting, explaining, or otherwise intervening" (Jackson, 1992; p. 1623).

Our focus so far in this book has been the traditionally recognized psychological helper or healer in Western cultures—the psychotherapist. However, in other parts of the world and among various subgroups within the United States, indigenous healers fulfill the role of psychotherapist although their clientele may know them by other labels. Western psychotherapists "generally [have] tended to emphasize the intrapsychic over the social, and cultural assimilation over cultural diversity as indices of adaptation and [mental] health" (de la Cancela & Martinez, 1983, p. 255). In contrast, the indigenous helpers of non-Western cultures emphasize supernatural or spiritual etiologies of emotional problems and subsequent healing practices more than Western individualistically oriented therapists do (Lefley, 1984).

Nevertheless, Western psychotherapy and indigenous therapies have many properties in common. For example, Dow (1986) contends that "symbolic healing" is the basic ingredient in Western psychotherapy and the non-Western indigenous healing practices. He describes the common characteristics of symbolic healing as follows: (a) The experiences of healers and healed are symbolized by culture-specific symbols derived from cultural myths; (b) the healer persuades the client who comes for healing that the problem can be defined in terms of the cultural myths; (c) the healer facilitates the client's emotional involvement with the healing symbols; and (d) the healer manipulates the healing symbols to help the patient interpret his or her own emotions. Dow uses the term "myth" to signify his contention that symbolic healing processes are based on experiential rather than objective reality.

Interestingly, the notion that therapy is effective within cultural groups when the therapist and client share a common mythology is relatively longstanding (Frank, 1974). With respect to Western psychotherapies more specifically, Calestro (1972; cited in Dow, 1986) proposes the following sequential evolution of myths:

"The therapist's beliefs regarding his [or her] efficacy as a curing agent generally derive from his [or her] training in and adoption of a particular school of psychotherapy. He [or she] is taught to believe that emotional distress or behavioral anomalies develop as a function of certain systematic and scientific principles. He [or she] is also taught that similar principles can be used in correcting psychological abnormalities. These beliefs, which are consistent with his [or her] assumptive world, make up the substance of his [or her] personal myth" (cited in Dow, 1986, p. 60).

Calestro further observes that the client or patient is able to change because he or she believes in the therapist's power to help.

Although Western psychotherapy consists of "mythic" properties that are similar in function and purpose to the properties of non-Western indigenous healers, Western therapists have dared to question the ameliorative capabilities of non-Western indigenous helpers (de la Cancela & Martinez, 1983; La Fromboise, 1988). Furthermore, whereas Western and non-Western healing practices share many critical elements, implementation of the elements may appear quite different to the client or therapist functioning outside of his or her regular cultural context. Thus, clients from non-Western cultures who are accustomed to other forms of helping may have to adapt to alternative practices when they are working exclusively with a Western therapist trained only in Western (indigenous) practices. Conversely, clients from Western cultures must adapt to the indigenous practices of non-Western therapists when receiving mental health services from them.

Nevertheless, there are similarities and differences in aspects of the etiology, diagnosis, and treatment of mental disorders between Western and non-Western psychotherapy (Lefley, 1984). For instance, sources of etiology for Western mental health systems include biogenetic, psychosocial, and interactional factors, in contrast to the supernatural, interpersonal, and interactional factors in non-Western healing systems. Observation and interview techniques are used for diagnosis in both cultural perspectives, but history taking and testing are used in Western culture and divination is used in non-Western cultures.

Regarding the treatment process per se, the therapeutic mode of interaction in Western systems is primarily therapist-patient verbal communication and the client's primary contribution to the process is talking. In contrast, non-Western systems integrate the therapist's communications with supernatural agents and the client's primary involvement is performance of the prescribed healing rituals (Lefley, 1984).

Given the cultural differences between Western and non-Western psychological healing and the significance of the client's belief in the efficacy of the treatment, many cultural psychologists have recommended that traditional psychotherapists collaborate with indigenous helpers of the client's culture in providing mental health services (Cook, 1993; de la Cancela & Martinez, 1983; Delgado, 1979; Ishiyama, 1990; LaFromboise, 1988; Lowrey, 1983; Rappaport & Rappaport, 1981). In this chapter, we provide a brief description of some of the less familiar types of indigenous helpers and therapies derived from non-Western cultures. We also briefly discuss contemporary forms of healing that make deliberate use of spiritual principles of healing. In both cases, our emphasis is on the collaborative relationships that can be formed between traditional psychotherapists and indigenous helpers (see also Chapter 7).

Types of Indigenous Helpers and Treatment and Practices

Indigenous helpers can be individuals or social networks that members of a culture typically seek out to obtain relief from emotional difficulties. Typically, indigenous helpers have gone through some form of apprenticeship or training to learn how to perform the healing practices that they provide. Moreover, some healers are believed by members of their group to have supernatural powers or to be able to commune with supernatural forces. Social networks typically consist of a group of individuals who are committed to some sort of helping mission, and whom members of the culture view as having particular skills to help them to solve certain problems. Social networks generally serve a variety of roles for members of the culture, including meeting their mental health needs as they are defined by the culture.

In non-Western cultures, indigenous practices for healing individuals' psychological disorders may consist of orientations that Westerners would consider to be highly mystical or supernatural. Indigenous healing practices vary in the degree to which they emphasize a person's capacity to achieve internal control over her or his emotional problems. Some supernatural orientations are internally focused or individualistic, whereas others locate the spiritual or curative force factors external to the person. Consequently, healers' practices—whether indigenous or Western—are primarily governed by their beliefs in the etiology of a person's problems; in our terminology, on whether the healers are individualistically or collectivistically oriented with respect to explaining, diagnosing, and treating mental health problems (see Chapter 7).

Mystical or Supernatural Beliefs and Practices

Those who believe that the etiology of mental health problems lies in the individual's suffering from "spirit-possession," such as *shamans* or *espiritistos*, use supernatural techniques to drive out or make peace with the "demons" or "evil spirits" (Lee, Oh, & Montcastle, 1992; Vontress, 1991). In a review of indigenous models of therapy in traditional Asian societies, Das (1987) described various types of spirit possession, each with particular manifestations and "prescriptions" or strategies for dealing with the different types of spirits. Similar types of possession are found in Hindu, Islamic, Japanese, and Puerto Rican cultures.

Hindu Cultures. The spirits of Hindu societies are known as *bhuta-preta*, and are believed to reside halfway between the human world and the world of ancestral spirits. Until they enter the ancestral world, the bhuta-preta find human bodies to infest and "make sick with their evil deeds" (Das, 1987). The treatment for the bhuta-preta spirit possession consists of rituals performed by the healer (e.g., scriptures, prayers), while the patient prays, eats consecrated food offerings, and recites a *mantra* at prescribed times.

Islamic Cultures. *Jinn*, the most common demons, may inflict themselves upon individuals or be instructed to do so by sorcerers who control the spirits (Das, 1987). The psychological healer, generally called a *pir*, uses ritualistic methods for helping jinn-inhabited patients, including wearing amulets and making offerings of small amounts of sugar and water that have been blessed by Allah (God) (Das, 1987).

Japanese Cultures. The shamans of the Japanese tradition are said to have the ability to make direct contact with supernatural beings while in a trancelike state (Nishimura, 1987). Women or men shamans can draw spirits into themselves and use their power over the spirit to help others who have been possessed by the spirits. Healing methods used by shamans include chants, prayers, and ritual offerings to spirits, as well as the use of modern medical techniques where appropriate.

Puerto Rican Cultures. The traditional healing practices of *espiritismo* or spiritism are based on the belief that "good" spirits may be called upon to ward off "bad" spirits (de la Cancela & Martinez, 1983). According to Koss (1987), the healer observes a patient, describes the patient's difficulties, then "captures" or "receives" the patient's problems into his or her body through visions. Treatment consists of prayers to transform the patient and exorcistic rites intended to expel the bad spirit. Herbal preparations are sometimes used to facilitate these processes.

Medical Traditions

Relative to the supernatural folk-healing approaches, the medical traditions emphasize promoting harmony between the various aspects of the person, although the proposed number and variety of aspects differ. The three versions of medical folk healing that we summarize are (a) Native American, (b) Asian Indian, and (c) Chinese.

Native American. As we mentioned in Chapter 7, the traditional healers in American Indian cultures believe that psychological disorders are derived from individuals being "out of harmony" with their social, physical, and spiritual environments. Healing, then, is holistic involving the physiological, psychological, environmental, social, and spiritual aspects (Lowrey, 1983). According to LaFromboise (1988), "A traditional American Indian healer is actually a doctor, counselor, priest, and historian. A healer is viewed as a safekeeper of ancient legends, which are maintained through the power of the spoken word. The healer uses the wisdom of spiritual legends for insight into human behavior and to explain emotional and behavioral problems" (p. 392).

Lowrey (1983) described the practices of a "diagnostician" who may do "hand trembling, crystal and star gazing and listening" (p. 70) to assess the source of the patient's disharmony, which is usually ascertained during a trance state. Specific healing ceremonies are then prescribed by the diagnostician who refers the patient to a medicine man or woman to perform the ceremony. Ceremonies include many "folk rites" and songs and prayers (Lowrey, 1983).

Asian Indian.   The Asian Indian medical tradition of *Ayurveda* also relies on a holistic treatment approach based on the belief in the inseparable connection of mind and body. The approach is collectivistic in that illnesses are defined by the contexts of familial, social, cultural, and cosmic forces (Das, 1987). Moreover, in the Ayurveda system, illness is assumed to occur when any of the three humors (wind, bile, and phlegm) becomes agitated and out of balance relative to the others. "The imbalance is believed to occur because of the excessive use, deficient use, or misuse of one of the following: (a) objects of the senses; (b) actions of the body, mind, and speech; and (c) time of the year (different seasons). Both physical and mental disturbances can upset the bodily humors and produce diseases with either predominantly psychological or physical symptoms depending on the manner in which the humors have been disturbed" (Das, 1987; p. 34).

According to Das (1987), Ayurveda distinguishes among three classes of primarily psychological disease: (1) psychogenic disorders referred to as *unmada*, which covers all mental disorders in which an individual loses the power to regulate his or her behavior according to the rules of society; (2) psychological disorders with predominantly physical symptoms; and (3) physical disorders with predominantly psychological symptoms. Ayurveda therapy includes physical treatment and psychological treatment (Das, 1987).

Purely, or at least primarily, psychological treatments are suggestion, exhortation, and prescribed meditation practices. Healers of mental disorders take an active role in patients' lives through advice, suggestion, and exhortation. Combined psychological and physical treatment can also involve pacification procedures such as applying external unguents or administering swallowing mixtures prepared from certain plants and metals that are used as tranquilizers and antidepressants. Ayurvedic treatment also consists of removal of the causes of psychological disorders and often takes the form of regulating the diet and conduct of the patient (Das, 1987).

Chinese.   The Taoist philosophy of the Chinese medical tradition also does not separate physical and mental mechanisms. Healing practices include meditation and relaxation accompanied by prescribed physical movements, all of which are therapeutic interventions for reducing anxiety and common emotional disorders (Das, 1987). Acupuncture and medicinal herbs may also be used to alleviate psychological distress.

Religious Spirituality

Although religious practices are also supernatural, our discussion of religious spirituality focuses more on the relationship that members of a culture have with their "God-figure" rather than the focus on evil spirits discussed in the mystical and supernatural practices section. Various religions propose that individuals should rely on a "higher (or universal) spiritual power" to direct them in their lives and that through prayer and other worship techniques, individuals can "call upon" this higher power for guidance and for emotional strength when problems arise. Psychological distress is considered to be related, in varying degrees, to an individual's failure to follow the edicts or life rules of his or her religion. Thus, the healing process involves calling on the higher power to heal believers of their distress, and religious helpers assist in this process through prayer and instructions for devout living.

Religious leaders vary in the extent to which they consider themselves to be healers. However, many often provide help that they perceive has therapeutic effects to their followers. Most religious leaders provide followers with interpretations of the appropriate "holy" books or writings wherein the particular religious way of life is prescribed, and the worship practices for communicating with the higher power are taught. The followers then can be involved in self-healing practices under the direction of the religious leader. Other religious leaders are considered to have "healing powers" that they actively invoke by practices such as "laying on of hands" and/or chanting to relieve followers of distress.

Perhaps it is obvious that the non-Western indigenous treatments are quite varied, and a service-provider could spend a virtual lifetime learning to practice any one of them effectively, which is why we recommend creative collaboration as necessary. Furthermore, specific cultural information about the client is necessary before one can even begin to initiate such collaboration.

With respect to developing collaborations with skilled practitioners of the mystical/supernatural approaches, medical approaches, or religious orientations to be described subsequently, the therapist must permit herself or himself to ask clients questions about their religious, spiritual, or moral socialization (Cook & Wiley, in press). Inquiries should solicit information about the formal practices and traditions in which the client was socialized, her or his feelings or attitudes about this socialization, as well as the client's present-day expectations, assumptions, and beliefs concerning who is qualified to deliver problem-solving services and in what manner such assistance should appear. In traditional Western therapy training programs, therapists are typically taught to avoid the topic of the client's religious/spiritual domain. However, we believe that breaking this cultural taboo is mandatory if one intends to deliver culturally relevant services.

In order to form effective collaborative relationships with religious helpers, it is important that therapists understand the premises of the relevant religion(s) and the role that particular religious or spiritual leaders serve in the client's framework. Brief descriptions of Asian Indian, Afro-Cuban, and African American religions and/or spirituality follow.

Asian Indian.   The basic premise of the Asian Indian Hindu religion is that an individual's life goal is to strive toward the realization of her or his unique self and the liberation of her or his spirit from the potentially everlasting cycle of birth to rebirth (Das, 1987). According to Das (1987), Hutchinson recommended the following goals for moving toward liberation of the self: (a) restraint or self-control, (b) observance of self-culture, (c) posture adjustment or control of the body, (d) regulation of breath, (e) restraint of the senses, (f) concentration of attention, (g) meditation, and (h) emancipation. Yoga techniques move individuals through "spiritual enlightenment and [consequently, toward] ultimate liberation" (Das, 1987).

Afro-Cuban.   de la Cancela and Martinez (1983) provide a brief description of a traditional healing "cult" in Afro-Cuban cultures—*santeria*—that involves the worship of African gods who are similar to Catholic saints. The rituals involved in worshipping the gods incorporate food and live animal sacrifices to the gods. *Santeros* (religious leaders) offer their followers direct advice for problem solving, emotional support, and explanations of irrational thoughts. Flexibility, eclecticism, and heterogeneity are inherent aspects of santeria that permit the healer to meet the different needs of followers (Sandoval, 1979, as cited in de la Cancela & Martinez, 1983).

African American.   In African American Christian cultures, as in most Christian, Jewish, and Islamic cultures in the United States, ordained ministers or clerics are viewed as indigenous helpers. In fact, many people in the United States, regardless of sociorace or culture, seek help from the ministers or spiritual leaders of their particular faiths rather than from mental health professionals because there is less stigma attached to religious helpers (Cook, 1993; Mollica, Streets, Boscarino & Redlich, 1986).

African American clergy, in particular, function as a major mental health resource to African American religious congregations and nonchurch members (Cook, 1993). African American ministers provide counseling on a variety of mental health and life issues including family, marital relations, spiritual conditions, drug and alcohol abuse, crisis situations, suicide, and a range of personal emotional problems, including those of individuals diagnosed by mental health professionals as experiencing some form of mental illness (Mollica et al., 1986).

African American ministers provide a therapeutic influence for members of their communities by reinforcing spiritual beliefs that reduce psychological distress (Crawford, Handal, & Wiener, 1989), offering worship services that include therapeutic aspects (Griffith, Young, & Smith, 1984), and providing formal and informal pastoral counseling services (Mollica et al., 1986; Wiley, 1991).

Behavior-Focused Psychotherapy

In actuality, the behavior-focused indigenous psychotherapies are a combination of what Western psychologists would call cognitive and behavioral therapies. The indigenous versions attempt to modify client attitudes as manifested in dysfunctional behavior of one kind or another (Cook & Wiley, in press).

Morita Therapy

Morita therapy is one type of behavior-focused indigenous psychotherapy (see Insight 13.1). According to Ishyama (1990), Morita therapists locate the cause of clients'

INSIGHT **13.1**

The Origin of Morita or Personal-Experience Therapy

Morita therapy was founded in 1920, 30 years after Western psychiatry was introduced in Japan. Its founder, Shoma Morita, was a Japanese professor of psychiatry at Jikei University in Tokyo.

Morita was born 18 years after Freud and died one year before him. Like Freud, Morita's therapeutic approach was allegedly inspired by his efforts to make sense of his own life experiences. In particular, two life experiences are said to have been critical catalysts for Morita's lifelong concern with the problems of life and death and parapsychological phenomena. The first happened at age 10 when he was terrified by a picture of hell that he saw in a Buddhist temple. The second began when Morita was about 16 years old. At that time, he began suffering from a variety of debilitating hysterical and psychosomatic symptoms (e.g., severe headaches, palpitations, mental and physical fatigue) as well as financial stressors. However, his symptoms abated when he stopped relying on medicines and health regimes and he devoted himself to his studies. From both sets of experiences, Morita allegedly learned to focus on personal life experiences as the solution to life's problems.

When Morita began his career, he attempted to use biological cures to treat clients with symptoms similiar to those that he had experienced during his youth. He called the constellation of symptoms *shinkeishitsu*, a Japanese term that apparently has no meaningful English translation. Nevertheless, Morita considered *shinkeishitsu* to be a common and ordinary hypochondriacal tendency—a natural aspect of the human condition. Nevertheless, he believed that *shinseishitsu* is responsible for a specific range of mental symptoms including obsessive-ruminative states and anxiety neuroses.

Morita therapy is considered to be a psychotherapy for "normal" people because of its emphasis on improving the dysfunctional symptoms that are common to human beings. Improvement occurs as the client is assisted in accepting that his or her symptoms or conditions are not abnormal or potentially life-threatening, and that he or she can and should live with them. Acceptance comes by means of personal experience.

Morita's "personal-experience therapy" (renamed *Morita* by his followers) is based on the principle that through personal experience, the client "can overcome [her or] his symptoms, gain insight into his [or her] disease, and realize his [or her] true self" (Kondo, 1976, p. 256). Treatment generally has three phases: (1) bed rest—the client is encouraged to withdraw from her or his former life and its distractions by staying in bed; (2) light work—the client engages in self-selected light work and keeps a daily diary that he or she shows to the therapist; and (3) readjustment to life—the client engages in increasingly more complicated self-selected work and learns to be more constructive in his or her daily life. "By being made to work, in spite of his [or her] symptoms, the [client] learns that he [or she] can accept the symptoms and live with them. This enables him [or her] to rid himself [or herself] of the vicious circle that is enslaving him [or her]" (Kondo, 1976, p. 257).

This overview of Morita therapy was adapted from Kondo (1976).

problems in their excessively negative self-focus, hypersensitivity, perfectionism, and the anticipatory anxiety resulting from these symptoms. Kondo (1976) advises that this complex constellation of symptoms was originally called *shinkeishitsu*, which approximately translates to "anxiety neurosis." Anticipatory anxiety often results in rather unproductive, mood-governed, and avoidant life-styles. In other words, the person feels incapable of functioning in his or her present environment because of her or his present mental and/or physical condition.

Therefore, the goals of therapy are to modify client attitudes and dismantle the self-perpetuating and symptom-aggravating cycle of unrealistic expectations and selective focus on subjective discomfort. Kondo (1976) contends that a guiding principle of Morita therapy is that the symptomatic help-seeker must learn to accept his or her symptoms as a legitimate aspect of herself or himself and abandon futile, anxiety-arousing attempts to rid oneself of them. In this framework, the therapist attempts to guide the client toward self-acceptance. Self-acceptance leads to the integration of the unconscious and conscious, the thinker and her or his thoughts, the feeler and his or her feelings.

Morita therapy may occur on a residential or outpatient basis and consists of many methods or interventions. However, in both settings, it often consists of didactic guidance, behavioral instructions, and encouragement intended to reduce self-focused attention and to foster the client's practice of more productive and self-enhancing attitudes in daily living. In the treatment process, the therapist confronts the client with new experiential data and he or she urges the client to examine one's perfectionistic tendencies and unrealistic thinking and attitudes (Ishyama, 1990).

Ishyama (1990) provides a description of the similarities and differences between Morita therapy and cognitive behavioral therapy. Both Morita and cognitive-behavioral therapies are based on the assumption that subjectively distorted information processing and unproductive attitudes are primary mediators of emotional and behavioral disorders. Whereas cognitive behaviorists tend to engage clients in discussions to alter cognitions (e.g., promote rational self-talk) that are assumed to regulate the clients' affective responses, Morita therapists contend that their "talk-therapy" helps clients to focus on identifying self-actualizing desires that have been neglected and assists them in choosing actions to fulfill those desires. Severe emotional symptoms in Morita therapy are treated by natural healing processes, that is, awakening the person's inner desires to live and be productive in whatever way has personal meaning.

Afrocentric Psychotherapy

NTU psychotherapy is a form of therapy based on Africentric principles of healing. Africentric principles are assumed to be rules for healthy functioning that have been handed down to African peoples via their classic African ancestors, although theorists seemingly differ in the extent to which they believe these principles are immutable across time and locale. Nevertheless, in general, Africentric frameworks or personality theories emphasize harmonious connectedness with one's spirituality as a guiding force for optimal functioning (e.g., Myers, 1988). Most also recommend active intervention

INSIGHT **13.2**

NTU Therapy: A Spiritual Psychotherapy

NTU (pronounced "in too"), a spiritually based psychotherapy, is an integration of ancient African and Africentric worldviews as nurtured by African Americans and principles of Western humanistic psychology. It is intended to be a universally applicable framework, although specific techniques might have to be modified to be culturally responsive to the unique aspects and needs of the "client system" (e.g., individuals, families, organizations).

The core principles of NTU are: (a) harmony—being flexibly in charge of one's life without controlling or fighting the unpredictable circumstances of one's life; (b) balance—aspects of life, nature, or oneself that appear to be dichotomous (e.g., masculinity-femininity) are present in all of nature and must be integrated into a unified whole; and (c) interconnectedness—NTU, a cosmic or spiritual universal force, connects all of life.

The first major goal of NTU therapy is to assist client systems to function harmoniously, genuinely, and in synchrony within their (especially) interpersonal contexts. The second goal is to assist the client system to function within the guidelines of *Nguzo Saba*, the seven principles of Kwanzaa (see also Chapter 4). *Nguzo Saba* are considered appropriate guidelines for healthy living.

The therapist does not rely merely on talking to the client to promote change, but rather uses a variety of techniques to encourage the client's healthy functioning. For example, to teach the principle of *Umoja* (unity), the therapist might use rituals such as libations, prayers, and Afrodrama. To teach *Ujamaa* (cooperative economics), appropriate techniques might include family budgeting, guided imagery, values clarification, and cooperative enterprises.

Moreover, the techniques are implemented within the context of a sacred, spiritual person-to-person therapy relationship. "The therapist appreciates that healing is natural, and it is *through* the therapist rather than being *caused* by the therapist that the healing occurs" (Phillips, 1990, p. 66). Thus, all interventions occur in the service of NTU, the spiritual healing force.

This Insight was summarized from Phillips (1990).

(e.g., education, guidance, community involvement) as a means of bringing the client into harmony with her or his interpersonal environment and herself or himself.

NTU (Phillips, 1990) describes the process by which such self-environment reconciliation can be promoted as involving the following not-necessarily linear phases: (a) Harmony—establishing a shared consciousness with the client is a primary objective; (b) Awareness—assisting the client in recognizing his or her own needs, strengths, limitations, and potentials; (c) Alignment—assuming responsibility for one's needs and actions; (d) Actualization—"trying on" new attitudes and behaviors in one's everyday life; and (e) Synthesis—intregrating knowledge, awareness, and realization on spiritual, mental, and physical levels. The ultimate outcome of NTU therapy is intended to be that "[the] client should be more keenly aware of self and others, engage life in a more authentic manner, and incorporate effective tools for clear identification, analysis, and resolution of future life difficulties" (p. 72).

Social Networks as Healing Sources

Various forms of social networks can be sources of collaboration for the mental health needs of clients. As discussed in Chapter 7, a wide variety of social groups can form a person's social network, including extended families and cultural institutions. The extended family is a primary caregiving network for most ALANA people. When one member of a family has a problem, the entire family takes the problem on as its own (LaFromboise, 1988). In fact, the extended family is so central to the well being of most collectivistic cultures that the therapist faced with a client from such cultures should immediately wonder what has gone awry in the extended family. Although the meaning of extended family may vary within groups, the family, kin, and friends may join forces to observe the individual, find reasons for her or his problematic behavior, and integrate the person back into the social life of the group.

With respect to American Indian communities in particular, La Fromboise (1988) notes that the informal resources and reciprocal exchanges of goods and services within such communities can diminish the impact of any disturbed individual group member's quality of functioning on the group as a whole. Thus, a benefit of the collective treatment of psychologically troubled individuals in tribal groups is that the individual is healed at the same time that the norms of the entire group are reaffirmed.

The goal of collectivistically oriented therapy is to encourage the client to transcend a predominant focus on her or his inner self by experiencing the self as being embedded in and reflected by the community. The inner motivations and unique experiences involving repression, self-esteem, ambivalence, or insight that typify individually oriented therapies are ignored, and symptoms are transformed into familiar culturally defined social categories rather than personal conditions. "New solutions to problems or new ways to see old problems become posssible through interconnectedness with the community" (LaFromboise, 1988; p. 392).

Other indigenous helping social networks include the American Indian "elders movement," consisting of older people who provide religious and personal counseling to members of the community (LaFromboise, 1988), and various ethnic political, social, professional, and religious organizations. According to LaFromboise (1988):

> "Over 200 Indian political organizations exist in the United States and Canada that provide psychological and social support, as well as support for advocacy within various levels of the government to bring about changes in everything from the treatment of American Indians in history books to increased funds for the economic development of American Indian resources" (pp. 391–392).

Other visible racial/ethnic groups (VREGs) have formed similar organizations to create a cultural community for their members, and to develop political strategies for counteracting institutional racism and ethnocentrism. For instance, in addition to the social aspect, fraternities and sororities also have a community service component that can be used for mental health collaboration. Given the low numbers of VREG members in various professions, group-focused organizations have been developed to address the unique concerns of underrepresented groups. These organizations can be a vital resource in collaborative efforts to reach out to ethnically diverse communities. Finally, religious institutions provide formal and informal healing services to members of their communities.

Spirituality and Social Networks

In the case of African Americans, mental health scholars and researchers have contended that African American churches can have a beneficial effect on the mental health of African Americans, in terms of both the therapeutic aspects of worship services (Griffith, English, & Mayfield, 1980; Griffith, Young, & Smith, 1984) and individual religious beliefs (Eng, Hatch, & Callan, 1985; Jacobson, 1992; Johnson, Matre, & Ambrecht, 1991; Taylor, 1988), as well as through formal and informal pastoral counseling and community service programs (Blue, 1991; Billingsley, 1989; Ganns, 1991; Griffith, 1982; Pope Curry, 1991; Staley, 1991; Wiley, 1991). Furthermore, both mental health professionals and the clergy have acknowledged the value of forming collaborative relationships in responding to the mental health needs of the community (Chalfant et al., 1990; Cook, 1992; Haughk, 1976; Maton & Pargament, 1987; Wiley, 1991).

Mental health professionals can assist churches in utilizing their resources (e.g., financial resources, personnel, physical facilities, communication networks) to provide effective social services. Because it might be useful to other therapists who are thinking about establishing a mental health program in a religious community, a church-based mental health model developed by D. Cook in collaboration with Dr. William Shaw, pastor of White Rock Baptist Church in West Philadelphia, is described in some detail in the following section.

Evolution of the Model

Discussions regarding the practice of mental health services in the church were initiated by Dr. Shaw while D. Cook was a member of his church. He identified areas in which he perceived that a psychologist would be most helpful to the church. Foremost were the problems for which individuals sought help from him that were beyond the scope of his training and expertise as a minister. Secondly, within the organizational structure of the church, there were layworkers who needed training in effective communication and basic helping skills so that they could perform assignments of reducing the isolation of individual members by reaching out to and being liaisons between the pastor and members of the church congregation. Finally, the pastor wanted to strengthen the church's impact in the surrounding African American community.

As Pastor Shaw articulated the church's needs, it became apparent that traditional mental health practices of counseling psychology were ideally suited for performing mental health interventions within the church setting. The primary service modes of counseling psychology—prevention, enhancement of personal development, and remediation—could be applied to address the problems identified by the pastor. Once the alliance between spiritual leader and mental health professional and a viable conceptual model for providing mental health services were in place, the next steps were to determine which church members could provide the requisite services and discover an acceptable way of introducing the practice to the church congregation.

Individuals from among the church membership with professional counseling training and experience were identified as volunteer service providers. The volunteer counselors were committed to contributing their time and services out of their spiritual and professional convictions to serve the community. Moreover, the congregation trusted the potential volunteer counselors' professional status and cultural and spiritual affiliations with the church.

In introducing and offering services to the church congregation, the pastor recommended that the psychologists change psychological jargon to be more consistent with the language of spirituality. Therefore, rather than calling it a "mental health counseling service," he suggested that the word *spiritual* rather than *mental health* was more consistent with the mission of the church, that *nurturing* was a more benevolent term than *counseling*, and that *ministry* was congruent with the form of services typically provided by the church. Thus, the "Ministry of Spiritual Nurturing" was formed.

The Reverend Dr. Christine Wiley (1991), a pastoral psychotherapist and assistant pastor of Covenant Baptist Church in Washington, D.C., developed a similar church-based counseling program—the Center for Holistic Ministry. Cook was unable to implement the complete Ministry of Spiritual Nurturing model in Philadelphia because she relocated. However, she has worked with other churches in implementing some aspects of the model, including the Center for Holistic Ministry.

The Ministry of Spiritual Nurturing

The conceptual model of the Ministry of Spiritual Nurturing consists of five major areas named to reflect the language of the church community. The areas are: (1) individual nurturing; (2) group nurturing; (3) reaching out/lending a helping hand; (4) church-community conferences; and (5) networking.

Individual Nurturing

The practice of individual nurturing involves providing brief counseling interventions of a developmental and remedial nature. Individual counseling or nurturing interventions include (a) an initial contact to assess the individual's concern; (b) brief problem-solving oriented counseling; (c) crisis intervention; (d) brief career counseling; and (e) referrals to an appropriate mental health professional outside of the church setting. Issues of confidentiality must be discussed with individuals and clear boundaries set as to the limits of the counseling relationship. The role of the volunteer counselors is primarily to assess an individual's mental health needs, to serve as a cultural liaison by acquainting individuals with the process of mental health care, and to link them to culturally responsive mental health services outside of the church.

When the professionals providing services are members of the congregation, they must conscientiously try to minimize dual relationships. For example, mental health professionals should not provide counseling for clients with whom they have personal relationships. However, in relatively large churches (over 1,000 active members), counselors' personal relationships may be limited to a relatively small number of individuals. In fact, the counselors' interactions with the majority of church members may resemble that of psychologists in university counseling centers who, on occasion, interact with students in individual counseling as well as in outreach and consultation capacities.

Group Nurturing

A variety of group counseling approaches comprises the group nurturing component of the Ministry of Spiritual Nurturing. Single session workshops, as well as time-limited and open-ended groups, may be used to provide preventive, developmental, and remedial interventions. Theme-oriented, structured skills training, discussion, and support groups can be provided for the church congregation and members of the surrounding community.

Groups designed to prevent the occurrence of various social and psychological problems can be conducted to reach a large segment of the community. For example, job skills training groups help in addressing the high unemployment rates in urban communities. Stress management and nutritional groups assist members in preventing health problems common to the African American community (such as hypertension). Improving family communication skills might lead to fewer broken homes, so groups can be designed with familial communication skills as a focus. Groups for adolescents could help prevent teen pregnancies, drug abuse, HIV/AIDS, school dropouts, and criminal behavior. Wiley (1991) has reported particular success with the group component of the Center for Holistic Ministry.

Groups that address developmental issues across the life span prepare individuals for various life transitions. Groups for people of specific ages may be particularly effective in a church setting because the environment can serve to reinforce the value of various age groups. For instance, to address elderly members' sense of loss as they perceive that they no longer make a difference in others' lives, leaders of groups for the elderly could collaborate with the church staff to ensure that the elderly members of the congregation are invited to be active participants in ongoing church services and programs. Similarly, psychologists who are conducting groups for youths and for parents could offer some sessions including both age groups to facilitate productive communication between the two groups.

Furthermore, other service providers have reported that remedial groups in which the members are trying to overcome some problem that they could not solve alone, such as twelve-step groups (e.g., Narcotics Anonymous, Alcoholics Anonymous), are frequently held in churches (Wiley, 1991). The instillation of hope is an important curative factor of groups (Yalom, 1985) in general, and in groups that require the person to relinquish self-control to a "higher power," the church is a natural conduit. The church setting may provide an additional source of hope as people generally connect faith, hope, and acceptance with the spiritual mission of churches.

Reaching Out/Lending a Helping Hand

Unlike the individual nurturing and group nurturing components of the Ministry of Spiritual Nurturing, which addressed services that counseling psychologists could provide directly, the "reaching out/lending a helping hand" component consists of outreach and consultative services that make use of helping auxiliaries within the church to assist in providing services. Church auxillaries consist of service organizations such as the Nurses' Aid Society, which cares for members who become ill during services, the Youth Ministry, which focuses on activities for the youth of the church, and the Brotherhood, which emphasizes the involvement of men in the activities of the church.

Mental health professionals can assist these auxillaries in planning programs and using their resources to reach out to the larger church congregation and the surrounding community. Moreover, the mental health professionals could recommend ways in which the auxillaries could provide more effective services. For example, the Nurses' Aid Society could be more proactive in providing preventive services such as blood pressure screening and developing a health-related newsletter that addresses issues particularly pertinent to the community.

Consulting therapists who intend to develop reaching out services should familiarize themselves with the overall structure of the church to ascertain how the various auxillaries and resources might best be used as service components of the church. Many services can be offered by layworkers of the church if they are given paraprofessional training, appropriate supervision, and consultation.

Church-Community Conferences

Mental health professionals can join forces with pastors to hold ongoing conferences with various constituents of the urban community to (a) respond to the psychological aftermath of community tragedies and disasters, (b) develop strategies for systemic change, and (c) serve as advocates for oppressed groups. Every day, the news media describe urban communities that are plagued by poverty, racism, gang violence, and crime. Innocent people are continually losing their jobs, their homes, their self-respect, and their lives. It has been argued that the flames of the Los Angeles riots of 1992 were fueled by the desperation among urban residents who face daily struggles to overcome the external barriers that impede their existence (Cook & Fine, 1995; Myers & King, 1983). Many African American churches are located in the heart of urban decay, and African American pastors still hold influential positions within the surrounding community.

When tragedies such as drive-by shootings, homicides, rapes, robberies, "carjackings," or homes destroyed by fire occur in the community, an organized vehicle for therapists and ministers to intervene and mitigate the aftermath of such intensely emotional and traumatic incidents is needed. Although exposure to repeated traumatic incidents seems to promote an inoculation effect, such that individuals appear to develop adaptive coping strategies, eventually those persons experiencing cumulative traumatic incidents may become susceptible to chronic post-traumatic stress reactions (Foreman, 1992). Therefore, church-community conferences can be offered to provide post-trauma services. Provisions of post-trauma interventions are particularly important for children and adolescents who live with the ongoing threat of violence in their daily lives (Cook & Fine, 1995; Huttman, 1991).

Networking

Direct service interventions alone will not solve the problems of the residents of urban communities. Psychologists, along with clergy and other community leaders, must identify the societal and community pressures that make inner city life such a hardship, and develop strategies for changing the system under which these people live. Mental health professionals oriented toward viewing people and their behavior in a sociocultural context, that is, as influenced by culture, sociorace, gender, sexual orientation, age, and sociohistorical perspectives, can be instrumental in examining the interaction of these factors in the circumstances of urban residents.

Help-givers can use this information to facilitate useful dialogues between the residents of inner cities and the social service and public officials who are making decisions about their lives. In addition, mental health professionals can provide training for other professions that is informed by a more culturally relevant perspective on the lives of city dwellers of various racial, cultural, and socioeconomic levels.

Finally, therapists can use their professional status in mainstream society to advocate for the good of oppressed individuals or groups. Through their involvement with African American people of various socioeconomic, occupational, and educational levels, they can gain a better understanding of the African American person's individual strengths and, at the same time, begin to correct the myths that society fosters in blaming the victims of oppression for their life circumstances. Mental health professionals' voices can be heard in places where the voices of many African American individuals cannot, particularly in the arenas of social services and public policy.

The focus of the description of the church-based intervention has been a model of intervention that works well in an African American community. Consequently, many of the interventions were designed to be congruent with the cultural characteristics of that group, and to address their particular physical health, mental health, and spiritual concerns. Nevertheless, we think that with slight modifications, the model can be adapted to be applicable to other ethnic, socioeconomic, and religious groups. In performing such adaptations, the important theme for the mental health practitioner is to remember to respect the integrity of the naturally existing systems that are already in place.

Implications for Therapy

Given the probable prevalence and prominence of indigenous helpers of some sort in many ethnic cultures, mental health professionals who are not familiar with and/or are uncomfortable with indigenous mental health practices should consider collaborating with indigenous helpers from the appropriate culture in treating clients. Of course, we have discussed only a small number of the indigenous healing practices that may exist in some form in the United States. However, therapists who are interested in expanding the varieties of expertise available to them via indigenous helpers may use clients as information resources. Therapists who are receptive to collaboration can facilitate the process by assessing the client's folk-healing beliefs as a regular part of the assessment process.

Western-trained psychotherapists may be quick to discount the efficacy of indigenous helpers (LaFromboise, 1988). However, we believe that therapists must be mindful of the elusiveness and ephemeral qualities of our own discipline as well as the prodigious numbers of people who lack faith in our healing capabilities. Indigenous helpers are accorded the same respect for their knowledge, training, and healing credentials within their cultures as traditional Western therapists expect to receive in their cultures. Furthermore, given the stigma often associated with the mental health professions, therapists would be wise to capitalize upon the trusting relationships and influence that indigenous healers have with members of their cultures by soliciting their assistance in reaching clients who lack faith in the therapy process (Cook, 1993). Exercise 13.1 might help the reader recognize the extent to which indigenous healers are an accepted part of daily existence even in Western cultures.

Collaborations with indigenous helpers may take many forms. Clients might receive treatment simultaneously from traditional Western therapists and indigenous helpers, or indigenous helpers might perform their healing practices before or after other therapists have provided their services (Lowrey, 1983). For instance, if a client presents with anxiety symptoms that he or she believes to be the result of evil spirits, it may be necessary for an indigenous helper to perform a ritualistic ceremony to ward off the evil spirits before the therapist can work with the client on anxiety-reduction practices. Thus, the belief systems of the client must be assessed if the therapist intends to provide quality care. Thorough assessment should include exploring the level and quality of clients' beliefs in folk-healing practices (Cayleff, 1986).

LaFromboise (1988) described examples of successful and unsuccessful collaborations between Western therapists and traditional Native American healers. She advised that for such collaborations to be successful, the psychologists or other mental health professionals must establish working relationships with healers in which issues of credibility, fees for service, professional efficacy, technical details of treatments, and patient expectations for each participant have been resolved.

In addition, it is important that Western therapists analyze the cultural assumptions inherent in their practices and their degree of consistency or inconsistency with the values and assumptions of the client's and indigenous healer's culture. Such analyses may address many of the confusions that can contribute to ineffective collaborations. LaFromboise (1988) contends that in psychology (and the other mental health disciplines), the focus of cultural analyses should be (a) the assumptions indigenous clients hold about the disciplines, (b) assumptions the discipline holds about indigenous clients and their cultures, and (c) the primary differences between Western and indigenous mental health interventions. Once the differences are evident, therapists can assess the potential for conflict in their own beliefs and those of the client's cul-

EXERCISE 13.1

Identifying Your "Indigenous" Healers and Helpers

Recall the last time that you or someone in your family was *seriously* ill and recovered. Describe the situation either in writing or on audiotape. Now, answer each of the following questions:

1. Describe the attributes of the healers or helpers that were called upon to make you (or the other person) better.
2. What was the role of listening in the healing process?
3. What was the role of speaking in the healing process?
4. What curative actions were performed during the healing process?
5. Describe any spiritual aspects of the healing process.
6. Describe any cognitive or emotional aspects of the healing process.
7. Why did healing occur?
8. What are the cultural "myths" upon which the healing process was based? If you do not believe that any myths were involved, provide the irrefutable evidence that healing occurred for the reasons you think.

By reviewing your answers, you can acquire a sense of the role of indigenous healers in your culture. You may also be able to figure out the extent to which mind, body, and spirit are interrelated aspects of your healthy functioning.

---

ture. The conflict assessment should include consideration of potential areas of compromise if compromise means the difference between helping a client and not helping a client.

The welfare of the client should always be the therapist's priority. Promoting the client's welfare may mean either modifying some of the boundaries posited by the therapist's theoretical orientation or refusing to endorse an indigenous cultural practice that is deemed physically or mentally harmful to the client. In this regard, de la Cancela and Martinez (1983) contend that therapists need to recognize that while there are some beneficial elements to many Latino/Latina folk-healing beliefs, some also have detrimental elements that are related to their "underlying ideology."

Two examples of potentially harmful underlying ideologies that de la Cancela and Martinez discuss are the client's "pathological use of faith" and the healer's "replication of existing social class relations." The use of faith is pathological when it is used to divert attention away from interpersonal and intrapsychic sources of a person's problems to "supernatural explanations;" and healers may rely on social class dynamics to foster passive dependency in their relationships with their clients.

In addition, Yamamoto, Silva, Justice, Chang, and Leong (1993) warn that specific healing practices may not be acceptable in the dominant culture that controls the legal and medical systems. An example that they describe is the practice of "coining" in some traditional Asian cultures. When coining is used to treat illness, the person's back and chest are oiled and her or his skin is massaged until it becomes warm. Then, according to Yamamoto et al., a coin is rubbed against the skin until the skin is bruised. Whereas coining and similar procedures might not be questioned when the

---

EXERCISE **13.2**

Making a Cross-Cultural Referral

Imagine yourself trying to convince someone who is not familiar with the healing processes in your culture to seek help from one of your cultural healers.

1. What aspects of the healing process might be difficult for the person to believe in?

2. What could you do to help convince the person that the healer can be helpful to him or her?

3. What would you tell him or her that your healer expects in return for his or her services?

---

adult person uses them on herself or himself or on other adults, the authors warn that the resulting bruises on a child can result in the child's parents being investigated for child abuse. Thus, therapists who intend to collaborate effectively with indigenous healers have a responsibility to investigate the ideologies and practices of the indigenous healers with whom they may collaborate, and to make decisions about collaboration with an open, yet discerning, mind. Exercise 13.2 suggests some factors to consider if one is considering collaboration with indigenous helpers.

Conclusion

The goals of using social networks, spiritual healing processes, and indigenous healers to provide mental health services are (a) to strengthen the emotional, psychological, and social resources of the relevant group and the individual members of the group, and (b) to train and empower the group members to become vital service providers in their communities. Obviously, social networks can come in many diverse forms, some of which have been described briefly in this chapter. Also, the term *indigenous healers* represents a diverse group of experts.

Nevertheless, by strengthening a natural support system within an extended family, tribe, or community in chaos, the community in turn may become strengthened. By interacting effectively through healing channels that are comfortable and familiar to the client, remediation of the mental health problem may occur more quickly. Moreover, if mental health professionals were to demonstrate cross-cultural competence as much as they preach it, then they would already know how to approach, respect, value, and accept the psychoracial, cultural, and religious perspectives of the indigenous helpers of the people to whom they are rendering services. If therapists fail to integrate the client's belief system into their practices, they may be jeopardizing the client's welfare, which is intricately connected to his or her beliefs about indigenous healers (Cayleff, 1986). To ignore the influence of indigenous healers is to neglect a vital resource in the promotion of mental health for clients regardless of their sociorace, culture, or religious persuasion.

REFERENCES

Billingsley, A. (1989, May). *The Black church as a social service institution.* Paper presented at a National Symposium for Grant Makers, Washington, DC.

Blue, L. C. (1991). Pastoral counseling and Black families. In L. N. June (Ed.), *The Black family: Past, present and future* (pp. 139–151). Grand Rapids, MI: Zondervan Publishing House.

Calestro, K. (1972). Psychotherapy, faith, healing, and suggestion. *International Journal of Psychiatry, 10,* 83–113.

Cayleff, S. E. (1986). Ethical issues in counseling gender, race, and culturally distinct groups. *Journal of Counseling and Development, 64,* 345–347.

Chalfant, H. P., Heller, P. L., Roberts, A., Briones, D., Aquirre-Hochbaum, S., & Farr, W. (1990). The clergy as a resource for those encountering psychological distress. *Review of Religious Research, 21,* 305–313.

Cook, D. A. (1992, December). *Identifying stressors of Black adolescents, parents, and extended family in an urban church setting: A pilot study.* Report submitted to the W. T. Grant Foundation, New York.

Cook, D. A. (1993). Research in African-American churches: A mental health counseling imperative. *Journal of Mental Health Counseling, 15,* 320–333.

Cook, D. A., & Fine, M. (1995). "Mother wit": Childrearing lessons from African American mothers of low income. In B. Swadener & S. Lubeck (Eds.), *Families and children "at promise": The social construction risk.* New York: SUNY Press.

Cook, D. A., & Wiley, C. Y. (in press). African American churches and Afrocentric spiritual traditions. In P. S. Richards & A. E. Bergin (Eds.) *Psychotherapy and Religious Diversity: A Guide to Mental Health Professionals.* Washington, DC: American Psychological Association Books.

Crawford, M. E., Handal, P. J., & Wiener, R. L. (1989). The relationship between religion and mental health/distress. *Review of Religious Research, 31,* 16–22.

Das, A. K. (1987). Indigenous models of therapy in traditional Asian societies. *Journal of Multicultural Counseling Development, 15,* 25–37.

de la Cancela, V., & Martinez, I. Z. (1983). An analysis of culturalism in Latino mental health: Folk medicine as a case in point. *Hispanic Journal of Behavioral Sciences, 5,* 251–274.

Delgado, M. (1979). Therapy Latino style: Implications for psychiatric care. *Perspectives in Psychiatric Care, 17,* 107–113.

Dow, J. (1986). Universal aspects of symbolic healing: A theoretical synthesis. *American Anthropologist, 88,* 56–69.

Eng, E., Hatch, J., & Callan, A. (1985). Institutionalizing social support through the church into the community. *Health Education Quarterly, 12,* 81–92.

Foreman, C. (1992). Disaster counseling. *American Counselor, 1,* 28–32.

Frank, J. D. (1974). Persuasion and healing: A comparative study of psychotherapy. New York: Schochen Books.

Ganns, J. A. (1991). Sexual abuse: Its impact on the child and the family. In L. N. June (Ed.), *The Black family: Past, present, and future* (pp. 173–184). Grand Rapids, MI: Zondervan Publishing House.

Griffith, E. E. H. (1982). The impact of sociocultural factors on a church-based healing model. *American Journal of Orthopsychiatry, 53,* 291–302.

Griffith, E. E. H., English, T., & Mayfield, V. (1980). Possession, prayer, and testimony: Therapeutic aspects of the Wednesday night meeting in a Black church. *Psychiatry, 43,* 120–127.

Griffith, E. E. H., Young, J. L., & Smith, D. L. (1984). An analysis of the therapeutic elements in a Black church service. *Hospital and Community Psychiatry, 35,* 464–469.

Haughk, K. C. (1976). Unique contributions of churches and clergy to community mental health. *Community Mental Health Journal, 12,* 20–28.

Huttman, E. (1991). A research note on dreams and aspirations of Black families. *The Journal of Comparative Family Studies, 22,* 147–158.

Ishiyama, F. I. (1990). A Japanese perspective on client inaction: Removing attitudinal blocks through Morita therapy. *Journal of Counseling & Development, 68,* 566–570.

Jacobson, C. K. (1992). Religiosity in a Black community: An examination of secularization and political variables. *Review of Religious Research, 31,* 16–22.

Jackson, S. W. (1992). The listening healer in the history of psychological healing. *The American Journal of Psychiatry, 149,* 1623–1632.

Johnson, G. D., Matre, M., & Ambrecht, G. (1991). Race and religiosity: An empirical evaluation of a causal model. *Review of Religious Research, 32,* 252–266.

Kondo, K. (1976). The origin of Morita therapy. In W. P. Lebra (Ed.), *Culture-bound syndromes in ethnopsychiatry and alternate therapies* (pp. 250–258). Honolulu, HI: University of Hawaii Press.

Koss, J. D. (1987). Expectations and outcomes for patients given mental health care or spiritist healing in Puerto Rico. *The American Journal of Psychiatry, 144,* 56–61.

LaFromboise, T. D. (1988). American Indian mental health policy. *American Psychologist, 43,* 388–397.

Lefley, H. P. (1984). Delivering mental health services across cultures. In P. B. Pederson, N. Sartorius, & A. J. Marsella (Eds.), *Mental health services: The cross-cultural context* (pp. 135–171). Beverly Hills, CA: Sage.

Lee, C. C., Oh, M. Y., & Montcastle, A. R. (1992). Indigenous models of helping in nonwestern countries: Implications for multicultural counseling. *Journal of Multicultural Counseling and Development, 20,* 3–10.

Lowrey, L. (1983). Bridging a culture in counseling. *Journal of Applied Rehabilitation Counseling, 14,* 68–73.

Maton, K. I., & Pargament, K. I. (1987). The roles of religion in prevention and promotion. *Prevention in Human Services, 5,* 161–205.

Mollica, R. F., Streets, F. J., Boscarino, J., & Redlich, F. C. (1986). A community study of formal pastoral counseling activities of the clergy. *American Journal of Psychiatry, 143,* 323–328.

Myers, H. F., & King, L. M. (1983). Mental health issues in the development of the Black American child. In G. J. Powell (Ed.), *Psychosocial development of minority group children* (pp. 275–306). New York: Brunner/Mazel.

Myers, L. (1988). *Understanding an Afrocentric Worldview: Introduction to an optimal psychology.* Dubuque, IA: Kendall/Hunt.

Nishimura, K. (1987). Shamanism and medical cures. *Current Anthropology, 28* (4,Suppl), S59–S64.

Phillips, F. B. (1990). NTU psychotherapy: An Afrocentric perspective. *The Journal of Black Psychology, 17*(1), 55–74.

Pope Curry, B. (1991). The role of the church in the educational development of Black children. In L. N. June (Ed.), *The Black family: Past, present, and future* (pp. 173–184). Grand Rapids, MI: Zondervan Publishing House.

Rappaport, H. & Rappaport, M. (1981). The integration of scientific and traditional healing: A proposed model. *American Psychologist, 36,* 774–781.

Staley, S. R. (1991). Single female parenting: A ministry perspective. In L. N. June (Ed.), *The Black family: Past, present, and future* (pp. 173–184). Grand Rapids, MI: Zondervan Publishing House.

Taylor, R. J., & Chatters, L. M. (1988). Church members as a source of informal social support. *Review of Religious Research, 30,* 193–203.

Vontress, C. E. (1991). Traditional healing in Africa: Implications for cross-cultural counseling. *Journal of Counseling and Development, 70,* 242–249.

Wiley, C. Y. (1991). A ministry of empowerment: A holistic model for pastoral counseling in the African-American community. *The Journal of Pastoral Care, 45,* 335–364.

Yalom, I. D. (1985). *The theory and practice of group psychotherapy.* New York: Basic Books.

Yamamoto, J., Silva, J. A., Justice, L. R., Chang, C. Y., & Leong, G. B. (1993). Cross-cultural psychotherapy. In A. C. Gaw (Ed.), *Culture, ethnicity, and mental illness* (pp. 101–124). Washington, DC: American Psychiatric Press.

PART THREE

Observing the Process

14 Using Race and Culture in Therapy Supervision

Supervision is the most logical starting point to begin the process of becoming a therapist who is capable of managing the subtle dynamics of race and culture in the counseling and psychotherapy process. It is through supervision that beginning therapists learn the basic skills involved in maintaining effective therapeutic interactions. Supervision is also the place where incipient therapists initiate the life-long process of developing and integrating their personal and professional identities (Bradley, 1989).

Thus, supervision may be considered the primary vehicle for influencing the therapeutic growth of beginning trainees and, for that matter, seasoned therapists who wish to update their (especially) racial and cultural therapy skills. Yet given the pervasive influence of supervision on trainee growth and development, our review of the supervision literature suggests that neither therapists' racial nor cultural responsiveness has been of much concern to supervisors and educators of counselors and therapists.

A Brief Historical Overview of the Issues

Our respective interests and examinations of racial and cultural issues in supervision coincided over 15 years ago when Cook (1983) began her dissertation research under the advisement of Helms. At that time, Cook's review of the literature revealed one theoretical article (Gutierrez, 1982) that explicitly addressed racial issues in therapy supervision. Moreover, studies or conceptualizations of cultural factors (as distinguished from racial factors) in the supervisory process were virtually nonexistent, which appears to be still the case.

The picture was about as bleak where empirical research was concerned. Cook discovered one published (Vander-Kolk, 1974) and one unpublished (Helms, 1982) empirical study of racial issues in the supervisory process. Cook's dissertation became a third study (Cook & Helms, 1988) and more than a decade later, Leong and Wagner's (1994) review described only one additional empirical study (Hilton, Russell, & Salmi, 1994), but several additional theoretical articles and book chapters with a "cross-cultural" focus. With perhaps the exception of Cook and Helms (1988), most of these earlier studies were based on an exclusively nominal definition of race in which one or more socioracial groups were compared on some presumably universalistic supervisory dimensions.

Fukuyama's (1994) qualitative study of VREG supervisees' phenomenological experience of supervision was probably the first attempt to allow supervisees to define the salient dimensions of race and culture in the process. So, in some sense it was a psychoracial or psychocultural study, although it is difficult to determine which. More recently, Ladany and associates (Ladany, Brittan-Powell, & Pannu, 1997; Ladany, Inman, Constantine, & Hofheinz, 1997) added two studies with an explicitly psychoracial focus to the empirical literature. They conducted studies of supervisees' racial identity and relevant aspects of the supervision process.

Empirical Studies

It might be useful to examine both the socioracial and the psychoracial studies of the supervisory process for what they can reveal about how or whether such factors are operative.

Socioracial Studies

ALANA supervisees as service recipients were the primary focus of the pioneering studies of racial issues in supervision. Efforts to document the experiences of ALANA supervisees paralleled efforts to describe the experiences of ALANA clients. In both cases, investigators intended to demonstrate to supervisors that they might need to consider using different or at least a variety of strategies when supervising trainees and/or their work with clients of different racial groups.

Vander-Kolk (1974) and Helms (1982) each found differences between Black and other VREG trainees' and White trainees' experiences of the supervision process. Vander-Kolk found that Black and White trainees entered the process with different expectations of their supervisory relationships. For example, prior to engaging in supervision, Black rehabilitation-counseling students, relative to White students, expected that their supervisors would be less empathic, respectful, and congruent.

Helms (1982) found differences between VREG practicum supervisees' self-evaluations of their counseling skills and their primarily White individual and group supervisors' evaluations of the supervisees' skills, with individual supervisors being the more negative of the two sets of evaluators. In Tables 14.1 and 14.2, Myrick and Kelly's (1971) subscales (Counseling Practices, Conceptualization Skills, and Personal/Professional Development) on which the three sets of evaluators (i.e., supervisee vs. individual [i.e., case] supervisor, group supervisor vs. supervisee, and group vs. case or individual supervisor) tended to differ are listed for VREG and White supervisees, respectively. In addition, items within subscales are also shown if they tended to be rated differently by the three sets of evaluators. One can get a clearer sense of the sources of conflict within the supervisor(s)-supervisee relationships by examining the item-level differences.

TABLE 14.1 Summary of Subscale and Process Items on which Supervisees, Individual Supervisors, and Group Supervisors Evaluated VREG Supervisees Differently

Type of Rating		
Supervisee vs. Individual Supervisor	**Group Supervisor vs. Supervisee**	**Group Supervisor vs. Individual Supervisor**
Better Personal/Professional Development		*Better Personal/Professional Development*
More keeping of appointments and assignment completion.		More keeping of appointments and assignment completion.
More ability to accept constructive criticism.		Better working relationships with other professionals.
Better Conceptualization Skills		*Better Conceptualization Skills*
More sensitivity to self-dynamics in supervision.		More sensitivity to self-dynamics in supervision.
Greater basic knowledge of counseling principles and methodology.		Greater application of a consistent counseling rationale.
More awareness of content/feelings in counseling.		
Better Counseling Practices	*Worse Counseling Practices*	*Better Counseling Practices*
More relaxed while counseling.		More relaxed while counseling.
More spontaneous in counseling.	Less spontaneity in counseling.	
More use of flexible verbal behavior.	Less expression of thoughts/feelings in counseling.	
More capable of expressing thoughts and feelings.		

Note: Subscales are Myrick and Kelly's (1971) Counseling Practices, Conceptualization Skills, and Professional Development. Items and subscales are listed if the ratings of the evaluator (supervisee, group supervisor, group supervisor) on the left tended to differ from ($p \leq .10$) the ratings of the evaluator on the right.

Comparison of the two tables reveals that the greatest number of differences occurred between VREG supervisees and their individual or case supervisor (column 1). The central themes underlying these differences seem to center around styles of self-expression, including language usage styles and expression of feelings, as well as differences in cultural value orientations involving such factors as time perspective, goal orientation, and interactions with other people.

TABLE 14.2   Summary of Subscale and Process Items on Which Supervisees, Individual Supervisors, and Group Supervisors Evaluated White Supervisees Differently

Type of Rating		
Supervisee vs. Individual	**Group vs. Supervisee**	**Group vs. Individual**
Better Counseling Practices	*Better Counseling Practices*	*Better Counseling Practices*
More ability to deal with content and feeling in supervision.		More awareness of content/feelings in counseling.
More verbally flexible in counseling.	More verbally flexible in counseling.	Less talking than clients.
		More relaxed in counseling.
		More confident in counseling.
		More spontaneous in counseling.
Better Conceptualization	*Better Conceptualization*	*Better Conceptualization*
Greater sensitivity to self-dynamics in supervision.		
Worse Personal/Professional Development	*Better Personal/Professional Development*	*Better Personal/Professional Development*
Less keeping of appointments and assignment completion.	More ability to accept constructive criticism.	More relaxed in supervision.
Better Conceptualization		
More awareness of content/feelings in counseling.		
More use of a consistent rationale in counseling.		

Note: Subscales are Counseling Practices, Conceptualization Skills, and Professional Development (Myrick & Kelley, 1971). Items and subscales are listed in the direction that the evaluator on the left (supervisee, group supervisor, group supervisor) tended to differ from (p ($\leq$ .10) the evaluator on the right.

Two of the socioracial studies examined supervisees' responses to explicitly cross-racial supervision (Cook, 1983; Hilton et al., 1994). Cook compared African, Latina/Latino, Asian, and Native American (ALANA) supervisees' perceptions of their cross-racial supervision relationships. Hilton et al. (1994) studied White women supervisees' experiences of supervision with African American and White supervisors under conditions of high or low levels of supervisor support.

Cook found differences between the ALANA groups. More specifically, she found that on average ALANA supervisees reported satisfaction with supervision if their supervisor of another sociorace exhibited a combination of conditional interest and liking during the relationship. However, differences in perceptions were found between the racial and gender groups (Cook & Helms, 1988). For example, Asian women supervisees were significantly more satisfied with their supervisory relationships than were Asian men, and Asian, Black, and Latino men were more satisfied than were Native American men.

Also, Cook found that directive supervision (e.g., offering continuous critical feedback to supervisees), provision of didactic information (e.g., supplying reading and background information), and expertise as a clinician (e.g., whether the supervisor maintained a caseload) were important themes in ALANA supervisees' perceptions of the supervisor role. Moreover, the directive and information-giving factors were positively related to supervisees' satisfaction with their supervisory relationship.

Hilton et al.'s (1994) study revealed that high support was related to more positive ratings of the supervisors' effectiveness and the quality of the supervisory relationship. However, White women supervisees' evaluations of supervisors did not vary according to the supervisor's race.

Psychoracial Studies

Fukuyama (1994), Ladany, Brittan-Powell, and Pannu (1997), and Ladany, Inman, et al. (1997) examined different aspects of the supervisory process. Fukuyama's study examined the quality of the process. Ladany et al.'s studies examined process and outcomes of supervision from a psychoracial perspective.

Fukuyama (1994) classified critical positive and negative incidents in "multicultural" supervision, provided by 10 former VREG interns from a university counseling center internship. Her positive category (i.e., events supervisees considered positive) included openness and support, culturally relevant supervision, and work in multicultural activities. The negative category (i.e., events supervisees considered negative) included lack of supervisor cultural awareness and the supervisor's questioning of the interns' abilities and/or interventions when interns used culturally relevant interventions.

Fukuyama also asked the VREG trainees to suggest ways to make supervision more multiculturally sensitive. The suggestions included: (a) initiate the discussion of multicultural issues early in the relationship, (b) provide more specific training to supervisors, (c) provide more supervisors from different backgrounds, (d) use all personnel sources in the agency for multicultural training, (e) caution supervisors not to over-interpret culture, (f) help clients deal with affects of racism, and (g) use intern seminars for further discussions of multiculturalism.

Ladany, Brittan-Powell, and Pannu (1997) examined whether supervisees' measured racial identity and their perceptions of supervisors' racial identity were related to their perceptions of the quality of the supervisory relationship. Ladany, Inman, et al. (1997) studied supervisees' abilities to conceptualize a multicultural case and their self-reported multicultural competence as functions of supervisee racial identity and supervisor focus. Although these two studies were quite extensive and included relatively large samples, we are only able to highlight some of their major findings related to racial identity and dyad types.

Racial Identity.   As previously discussed, racial identity can refer to person-level manifestations of racial socialization. Ladany, Brittan-Powell, and Pannu (1997) found that racial identity was related to self-reported multicultural competence for VREG and White supervisees, but the significantly related schemas were not analogous across VREG and White supervisee groups. For VREG supervisees, higher levels of dissonance (e.g., confusion) and awareness (i.e., racial self-actualization) were associated with higher levels of self-reported multicultural competence. On the other hand, for White supervisees higher levels of Pseudo-Independence (e.g., paternalistic liberalism) were associated with higher levels of self-reported multicultural competence (Ladany, Brittan-Powell, and Pannu, 1997).

Ladany, Inman, et al. (1997) did not find significant associations between racial identity and multicultural case conceptualization ability, or between self-reported multicultural competence and multicultural case conceptualization ability. However, they did find that if supervisors instructed them to focus on multicultural issues in their case conceptualizations, then supervisees did include racial factors in their conceptualizations of their client's treatment.

Dyad Types.   Helms's (1990; see Chapters 10 and 12) racial identity interaction model may have implications for supervision at the dyadic level. Her model examines the nature of relationships between individuals based on their manner of expressing their racial identity statuses. The model anticipates types of harmony and discord that may occur in the process when members of a dyad use ego statuses that are "parallel" or "crossed" (regressive or progressive).

A supervisor and supervisee are considered to be engaged in a *parallel interaction* if they are of the same or different socioraces, but consistently exhibit behavior primarily characteristic of similar ego statuses. In other words, they share analogous perspectives with regard to the participants' relevant racial groups.

Crossed dyads occur when two individuals primarily and consistently exhibit the characteristics of oppositional ego statuses most of the time that they are together. Crossed supervisory dyads would generally be characterized by participants' continuous engagement in conflicts emanating from their anti-other-race sentiments. However, crossed dyads can be "progressive" in that the racial identity of the person with the most power in the relationship is more advanced than that of the other person. They can also be "regressive" when the one in power is less developmentally advanced with respect to racial identity.

Ladany, Brittan-Powell, and Pannu (1997) found that the racial identity configuration of the supervisory dyad was significantly associated with supervisees' perceptions of the supervisory relationship. The worst ratings of the supervisory alliance occurred in supervision dyads in which the supervisees' measured racial identity status was more advanced than their perceptions of the racial identity of their supervisors (i.e., regressive relationships). Supervisees perceived that the supervisor had a greater influence on their multicultural competence when the supervisees' measured racial identity and the perceived racial identity statuses of supervisors were parallel or more advanced (i.e., progressive).

Furthermore, racial composition of the supervisory dyad was related to supervisees' perceptions of their supervisors' competence. For both VREG and White supervisees, being matched with a VREG supervisor was related to higher levels of perceived multicultural competence of supervisors as compared to being matched with a White supervisor. However, racial matching was not related to supervisees' evaluations of the quality of the supervisory alliance.

Conclusions

Together, the empirical studies suggest that examination of the socioracial (e.g., racial composition) and psychoracial (e.g., racial identity) aspects of supervision dyads might provide important information about what is occurring in the process. For example, it appears that explicit or measured psychoracial factors may have more pervasive influence on the supervisory process than sociorace—at least from supervisees' perspectives. However, it also seems possible that unmeasured psychoracial dimensions underlie what appear to between-group racial differences. Nevertheless, the emphasis in all of the previous multicultural supervision studies has been on supervisees as recipients of supervision services.

We're Advocating a Different Perspective

Over the years, our thinking about racial issues in supervision has evolved from merely focusing on the experiences of supervisees as racial beings to a consideration of racial and cultural dynamics among and between all individuals involved in supervision—the supervisor, the supervisee, and the client (Brown & Landrum-Brown, 1995; Cook, 1993; Cook, 1994; Cook & Paler Hargrove, 1997). In effect, we always try to entertain the possibility that each person directly or indirectly involved in supervision brings his or her own racial and cultural background into the process. Aspects of race and/or culture influence the intrapersonal and interpersonal dynamics of the supervision as well as the supervisees' quality of functioning in the therapy process in response to supervision.

One of the goals of racially and culturally responsive supervision is to "allow race [and culture] to enter the room" (Fukuyama, 1994; Regan, 1990); that is, to discuss the various implications of the supervisor's, the supervisee's, and the client's racial and cultural socialization, and the effects of the interactions among these dimensions on the supervision process (Cook, 1993). Although attention to cultural socialization is conceivably as important as acknowledgement of racial factors in promoting growthful supervisory relationships, culture is often more difficult to recognize because it may lack consensually agreed-upon visual cues to signal its presence.

Nevertheless, direct interactions that occur between the client and supervisee, the supervisee and supervisor, and the supervisor's vicarious exposure to the client (via audiotapes, videotapes, live observation, case notes) are all influenced by their racial and cultural predispositions. Since these racial and cultural dynamics are operative, even if they are not necessarily apparent, it is in the best interests of the therapeutic process that they be acknowledged, discussed, and integrated into the supervision process, just as any other identity issues would be (Cook, 1994; Cook & Paler Hargrove, 1997).

Supervisors are responsible for creating an atmosphere in which the supervisee is free to explore personal experiences, assumptions, and beliefs about racial and cultural matters with the intent of pinpointing areas of racial sensitivity and cultural vulnerability (Brown & Landrum-Brown, 1995; Peterson, 1991). Also, supervisors must be willing to examine and share their own racial and cultural perspectives, even if doing so makes them feel uncomfortable and vulnerable. The supervisors' perceptions, attitudes, and behaviors regarding race and culture may influence the supervisor-supervisee and therapist-client relationships, which, in turn, can influence the supervisor and supervisee's evaluations of one another's competence, as well as their conceptualizations of the client. Therefore, their openness to examining such matters provides a model for the supervisee to use in resolving his or her own professional conflicts, and for the client to use in resolving personal conflicts.

Members of a training committee of the Association of Counselor Education and Supervision (Borders, Bernard, Dye, Fong, Henderson, & Nance, 1991) have developed a curriculum guide for training counselor and therapist supervisors. The guide recommends that supervisors identify their own demographic characteristics, and those aspects of their cultural and perceptual frameworks that may be expected to affect the supervision relationship. The guide further suggests that supervisors learn to recognize supervisee differences, demonstrate respect for such differences, and address the differences during supervision. The supervisor's recognition of potential and actual racial-cultural conflict areas and use of appropriate interventions can assist counselors and therapists in recognizing their own racial and cultural contributions to the supervisory relationship (Borders et al., 1991) and the therapy process.

Here-and-Now Focus on Racial Issues

When the supervisor has established an atmosphere of openness with regard to examination and expression of race and culture, he or she can begin approaching race in the here-and-now with the supervisee, just as one does when teaching supervisees to conduct effective individual and group therapy (Sullivan, 1953; Yalom, 1985; see Chapter 11). In therapy, working in the here-and-now means that the therapist focuses his or her interventions on the interactive process between the therapist and the client rather than on the content issues of the therapy session (Zaslow, 1988). That is, the therapist focuses on the nature of the relationship rather than on the explicit words that are spoken (Yalom, 1985).

Within supervision, a here-and-now focus might mean examining the verbal and nonverbal communication patterns between the supervisee and client for what they might reveal about their therapy relationship. More specifically, working in the here-and-now in supervision or therapy consists of two aspects—experiencing and illumination of the process (Yalom, 1985).

Experiencing. The experiencing aspect of supervision refers to "what is going on here, right now" in the relationship for the supervisor and the supervisee, and the supervisee and the client, respectively. It refers to the ways in which the participants in the parallel dyads perceive each other, feel toward each other, and relate to each other. The racial characteristics of the individuals involved in the relationship are a factor in their respective here-and-now experiencings. Thus, feelings and events as they occur in the supervisory relationship become foci of the work in supervision. This focus includes the ways in which issues of race evolve and are managed in the supervision and therapy relationships.

During the experiential phase, supervisees can be helped to focus on their feelings toward clients at a very immediate and personal level (Yalom, 1985). Cook and Paler Hargrove (1997) have provided a case example of addressing racial issues in the here-and-now of supervision. In a retrospective of their supervision experience in which Cook was the supervisor and Paler Hargrove was the supervisee, they revealed how race can be experienced as an issue even when all members of the supervision triad are African American women.

Early in the supervision relationship, Cook noticed that Paler Hargrove tended to be rather formal in her interactions with a White client, but quite social in her interactions with a Black client. Paler Hargrove remained focused on therapeutic issues with the White client, but allowed the Black client to ramble in seemingly irrelevant story-telling.

During the supervision session, Cook intervened by playing segments of tapes of the two clients and asked Paler Hargrove to describe any differences in her interaction in the two tapes. Paler Hargrove did observe the difference, and admitted that she was far more anxious about her competency as a therapist with the Black client than with the White client. Cook encouraged Paler Hargrove to examine her feelings toward the Black client and her concerns about the client's impressions of her.

As a result of this experiencing process, the two of them were able to explore Paler Hargrove's conflicts about relating to a Black client as a therapist rather than as a "racial sister." Once Paler Hargrove's own racial impasse was made explicit (i.e., given a name), she was able to put into words a classic VREG supervisee fear—if she attempted to function in the therapist role, the client might accuse her of "acting White." The White supervisee version of this fear is that the client might blame her or him for the bad things and wrong-doings that other White people have committed.

Be that as it may, as the supervisee grows into the therapist role, it is not uncommon for a variety of personal attitudes and needs to surface and be examined (Zaslow, 1988). Exploration of attitudes about race and culture should be explicit aspects of the self-discovery process. To promote this process, the supervisor has to teach and model the use of emotions, cognitions, and the whole person in the here-and-now. Anything that happens during supervision plays a part in the supervisory and perhaps the therapy relationship. Thus, by learning to analyze the supervisor-supervisee process, the supervisee is able to move beyond a mere theoretical or intellectual understanding of the situation (Serok & Urda, 1987).

Discussions of race and culture can become a routine part of the exploration of the therapist-client interaction. Supervisors might ask their supervisees questions such as: At what point did you notice the client's race (or culture)? How does it feel when a person of my race makes such observations about your client? What do you think about what I just said? What do you usually do when you feel like this? How similar to your client's feelings about you is what you're feeling about me right now? Such questions represent verbalizations of the thoughts and feelings a supervisee (or supervisor) may not be able to acknowledge without assistance when he or she reads the identifying data on a client's intake form or when he or she sees the client for the first time.

The supervisor might also pose analogous questions to herself or himself. Sample questions are: What assumptions do I (the supervisor) make about the client because of his or her race? On what data are my assumptions based? How much influence does my worldview have on final decisions regarding conceptualizations and diagnoses of the client?

In response to such questions, the supervisor should be prepared to probe the supervisee for substantive rather than socially desirable superficial answers, and to personally engage in in-depth self-exploration. The supervisor should examine the supervisee's manner of responding to such questions for clues as to the supervisee's unspoken thoughts. Should the supervisee be resistant or reluctant to explore his or her racial attitudes, the supervisor can work toward helping the supervisee to become more open to personal exploration, just as a supervisor would if any other personal issues were affecting the supervisee's therapeutic work. By encouraging such an all-encompassing involvement, the supervisee-client and supervisor-supervisee relationships are intensified and enhanced (Serok & Urda, 1987).

Illumination.   The illumination component of the here-and-now process evolves from the interpersonal learning that occurs as a result of being encouraged to experience the present. As the supervisee and supervisor recognize, examine, and understand the influences of race on the supervision and therapy processes, they are better able to treat racial dynamics as welcome relatives rather than as intrusive guests in the interaction. Any issue that occurs during the course of supervision is considered relevant to the process and appropriate for further discussion (Serok & Urda, 1987).

By reflecting on the racial and cultural transactions that have just occurred in the therapy and supervision relationships, previously unacknowledged racial dynamics are illuminated or clarified. *Illumination* means that the supervisee has acquired a cognitive framework that permits her or him to generalize from present circumstances to subsequent interactions. Therefore, the framework that is developing in supervision can be applied to relevant therapy situations (Yalom, 1985). This framework may influence the supervisees' diagnosis or conceptualization of the client's problem, the therapist's expectations for the therapy process, the dynamics of the therapy relationship, and/or the therapy outcome.

As our previous review of the empirical literature suggests, supervisors should also be aware of their own issues and styles of processing (especially) racial information about the client and the supervisee. Given that the supervisor is in a position to influence, if not shape, the supervisee's therapeutic work with clients, the supervisor's attitudes and conceptualizations of the client are paramount.

In a situation in which the supervisee and client share the same racial or cultural backgrounds, and the supervisor does not, the supervisor should anticipate dynamics that might be stirred up in homoracial and heteroracial dyads. In the homoracial dyad, the supervisor should be prepared to anticipate and/or recognize supervisee-client racial or cultural dynamics that are not typical of the therapists' regular experience. Minimal preparation requires the supervisor to be aware of the societal racial climate's influence on members of the supervisee's, client's, and supervisor's racial groups and related behaviors.

Sometimes clients also make assumptions regarding the race of the supervisor who listens to the tapes of their therapy sessions. For example, Cook was the supervisor in a supervision triad in which the client's vicarious racial attitudes became an impediment to the flow of the supervisory process. In this particular situation, an African American client asked his African American therapist (i.e., the supervisee) to stop the tape recorder for a moment because the client wanted to be certain that he did not say anything that would jeopardize the supervisee's evaluation by the supervisor, who the client assumed was White.

Thus, failing to acknowledge racial attitudes and perspectives within the supervision triad does not mean that they do not exist, nor does it mean that they do not have an impact on the therapy and supervision. The separate internal processes of the members of the supervisory triad have implications for the development of authentic therapeutic as well as supervisory relationships (Peterson, 1991).

Racial Identity Interactions in Supervision

The power dynamics in supervision are such that the supervisor holds the most social power in the supervisory relationship. Due to the supervisors' professional credentials and their evaluative role and overriding responsibility for the clients' welfare, they are accorded greater social power in the supervisory relationship. Therefore, the supervisor's racial identity status(es) may shape the racial attitudes and behaviors of the supervisee and, indirectly, the client.

If the supervision dyad is progressive (i.e., growth-promoting) most of the time, the supervisor may help the supervisee to advance in his or her own racial identity development. In contrast, in a regressive dyad the supervisee might suppress his or her racial identity concerns. If the supervisee either expresses or suppresses his or her attitudes in supervision, he or she is likely to do the same in therapy and impose similar requirements on the client. Therefore, the supervisor is in a position to influence, either consciously or unconsciously, the degree to which each person involved in supervision is open about expressing her or his racial identity statuses.

Although both the supervisor and supervisee can initiate discussions of racial issues in supervision, the supervisor's response to such topics can determine the depth of the ensuing discussions. A supervisee may intuit (or in some instances a supervisor may give a direct message) that the supervisor does not recognize race as an important factor in therapy and supervision. Some of Regan's (1990) interviewees and Fukuyama's (1994) analysis of critical incidents suggest that supervisors may tend to minimize supervisees' efforts to attend to their client's racial concerns.

Examples of supervisor minimization strategies include: (a) insisting that such matters are superficial and not germane to the client's "real" problem, (b) simply refusing to talk about such matters, and (c) devaluing supervisees' competence if they choose to include such factors in their therapy. In response to such strategies, the supervisee may feel discouraged and reluctant to explore racial and cultural issues further for fear of receiving a negative evaluation.

Cook (1994) has applied racial identity theory to therapy supervision to describe some ways that racial issues are addressed or avoided in supervision. Table 14.3 provides a summary of VREG and White racial identity ego statuses and potential ways that supervisors and supervisees representing the different ego statuses might approach racial issues in supervision.

Many of the ego statuses of the VREG and White models are similar in their assumptions regarding individuals' struggles with their identities as racial beings and their responses to racism and related racial socialization. In those instances in which the characteristics of the statuses are similar for the two models, they are presented together.

For simplicity's sake, the ego statuses are listed in the order that Helms (1994) hypothesized that they evolve, and pure examples of the statuses are described. However, a supervisor or supervisee or client can express or be motivated by more than one ego status, and thus exhibit a variety of responses to race in supervision. The racial attitudes of one or the other participant in supervision, circumstances in the clinical agency, or other factors might trigger a particular racial identity ego status, making it more salient than others. For example, a White supervisee whose profile consists of both high Disintegration and Pseudo-Independence statuses might revert to use of a predominantly Disintegration status when interacting with a supervision partner, if that person is an ALANA who is strongly expressing the Immersion/Emersion ego status.

In racial identity interaction theory, the person with the most powerful social role (e.g., the supervisor) serves as the definer of the interaction. Ladany, Inman, et al.'s results (1997) suggested that parallel, regressive, and progressive supervisory dyads were related to supervisees' perceptions of their multicultural competence. The first combination in Table 14.3 (i.e., Contact-Conformity) is an example of a parallel dyad wherein both supervisor and supervisee are likely to be conforming to the societal rules for polite behavior regarding race.

Immersion/Emersion and Reintegration in Table 14.3 is an example of a crossed, parallel relationship. If this type of crossed dyad consists of a VREG supervisor and a White supervisee, each person might react to the other based on a history of White dominance and supremacy. For his or her part, the VREG supervisor might take advantage of holding position of power relative to a White person and use it arbitrarily. The supervisee, on the other hand, might discount or challenge the supervisor's competence and supervision interventions.

A White supervisor and VREG supervisee in a crossed dyad might engage in a process in which the supervisor demands that the supervisee perform according to traditional "White-normed" counseling theories and practices and then evaluates the supervisee according to these standards. The supervisee, in turn, might be engaged in

TABLE 14.3 Summary of Visible Racial and Ethnic Group (VREG) and White Racial Identity Ego Statuses and Potential Approaches to Racial Issues in Supervision (PARI)

Statuses and Potential Approaches to Racial Issues

Conformity (VREG)	*Contact (White)*

PARI: Ignores race of client, supervisee, and supervisor. Assumes theoretical approach generalizes to all individuals; focuses only on "common humanity."

Dissonance (VREG)	*Disintegration (White)*

PARI: Acknowledges client's race as demographic or descriptive characteristic; lacks awareness of assumptions being made about the client based on race. Ignores supervisee's and supervisor's race.

Immersion/Emersion (VREG)	*Reintegration (White) PARI:*

Recognizes own race as standard for "normal" behavior of client and "effective" performance of partner. Recognizes other-race clients, but cultural differences are seen as deficits or forms of "resistance." Holds biases toward theoretical approaches that represent own cultural perspective.

	Pseudo-Independence (White)

PARI: Discusses racial differences only if interacting with POC. Discusses cultural differences based on generalized assumptions about various racial groups. Recognizes cultural biases of theories; lacks working knowledge of how to adapt theories to VREG.

	Immersion/Emersion (White)

PARI: Acknowledges race of client, supervisee, and supervisor and their respective cultural assumptions and racial attitudes. Considers socio-political implications of race in therapy and supervision.

Internalization (VREG)	*Autonomy (White)*

PARI: Integrates personal cultural values and therapeutic and supervision values. Acknowledges race of client, supervisee, and supervisor and the cultural and socio-political influences on the therapeutic and supervisory relationships. Names cultural conflicts in supervision interactions without internalizing racial prejudices of other-race supervision partner.

Integrative Awareness (VREG)	

PARI: Recognizes race as an aspect of each person's identity and potential variability in racial identity attitudes. Acknowledges cultural assumptions of supervision partners and negotiates culturally sensitive approaches to supervision and therapy. Serves as advocates for oppressed groups in interactions with agencies and training program.

a struggle with the supervisor as he or she attempts to apply racially responsive and culturally sensitive theories and practices.

In any of these types of crossed dyads, but especially the latter, the supervisee is prone to be the loser because he or she is likely to receive negative evaluations for her or his work. Thus, one cannot help wondering whether this was the case in some of the previously discussed empirical literature (e.g., Helms, 1992).

However, differential supervisor-supervisee power dynamics can lead to progressive acknowledgement of the import of racial factors. That is, supervisors and supervisees of more developmentally advanced racial identity evolution may be more capable of mutual acknowledgement of race than those in dyads where developmental disparities exist. Advanced development should foster greater inclusion of the client's, supervisee's and supervisor's racial concerns.

For example, persons who primarily use the Conformity and Contact ego statuses to interpret racial events may merely acknowledge their client's racial classification. Such an approach could contribute to intellectualized and externally focused interactions around issues of race. In contrast, in instances where Internalization and Autonomy statuses are dominant for the supervisor and supervisee, their racial discussions might more readily include a "here-and-now" focus on the ways in which race is influencing the supervisory relationship. As supervisors and supervisees are able to advance toward here-and-now interactions regarding the racial issues in their relationships, they will move toward greater degrees of race-related genuineness and authenticity as therapists and supervisors.

Implications for Research

Racial identity models potentially provide an unlimited source of ideas for future research in heterogeneous racial and cultural supervision. The multiple racial (and cultural) dynamics and variables that are purportedly involved in supervision are potentially rich catalysts for process and outcome research. Measures of racial identity expressions (Helms, 1990, 1996) can be used to examine the relationship between supervisors' and supervisees' racial identity attitudes and numerous other variables relevant to the supervision process. Similarities or differences in a supervisor's or supervisee's racial identity perspectives may relate to characteristics of the supervisory relationship or the supervisee's perceptions of the supervisor's credibility (e.g., expertness, trust, and attractiveness).

However, it might be difficult to conduct needed investigations if one waits for a suitable supply of VREG supervisees or supervisors to populate a single setting. Cook's (1983; Cook & Helms, 1988) study of supervisees remains the largest and most socioracially diverse sample of ALANA supervisees to date. Ladany, Inman, et al. (1997) also obtained a large heteroracial sample and developed some ingenious strategies for comparing racial identity across socioracial groups.

Nevertheless, if one lacks the resources or stamina to lure research participants across multiple sites as both of these sets of researchers did, then other alternatives are still available. The most obvious, of course, is intensive case studies. Supervisors and/or supervisees could be asked to respond several times to theoretically relevant measures, or sessions could be monitored or analyzed over the course of the supervisory period.

Helms (1982) also recommends that in those sites in which only one or two VREG supervisees or supervisors per year are available, a researcher might collect data over several years and combine them across VREG socioracial groups. In studies of single cases or combined samples, one should be careful to protect the confidentiality of one's research participants, even if doing so means not releasing one's findings until one's research participants can no longer be subjected to institutional recriminations. Also, once the researcher is ready to disseminate research findings based on combined socioracial samples, he or she must be able to explain on what dimensions the included groups are similar enough to yield meaningful results.

Noticing When and How Culture Appears

The cultural orientation or predisposition of each of the participants in the process—supervisor, supervisee, and client(s)—may also be invisible, but is a meaningful dynamic in supervision. Hardy (1989) coined the phrase "the theoretical myth of sameness (TMOS)" to describe the general philosophy in family training programs that "all families [or clients] are virtually the same" (p. 18). We think Hardy's points about therapy supervision pertain to the therapy process more globally as well as to the supervisor-supervisee relationship, regardless of whether the therapist-client relationship involves families, other kinds of groups, or individual clients.

Hardy contends that TMOS comes in two versions: (a) the conventional ideology found in most traditional therapy literature and training programs, and (b) the contemporary ideology that is evolving in reaction to the conventional perspective. To paraphrase Hardy, the conventional TMOS assumes (usually implicitly) that VREG and White clients are the same and that everyone must learn to be competent in individualistic culture. Clients are clients regardless of their prior racial or cultural socialization. Accordingly, " . . . programs [or supervisors] adopting this view emphasize the importance of theory comprehension and skill acquisition without punctuating differences that might be attributable to race, culture, ethnicity, and/or gender" (Hardy, 1989, p. 20).

The contemporary TMOS, which Hardy attributes primarily to VREG therapists, recognizes that VREG and White clients may not be the same. Although Hardy praises this perspective for alerting therapists to the possibility that clients' racial and cultural dynamics deserve attention, he also criticizes it because VREGs are often treated as though they are monolithic (e.g., Blacks, Latinos, etc.). Thus, he asserts that "[r]arely, does this view attempt to examine the differences *within* [racial and cultural] groups that are attributable to geographic and socio-economics, for example" (p. 21).

We think that both types of myths are operative in therapist training programs in general and supervisory processes in particular. However, the conventional TMOS is the more prevalent and has the most pervasive influences on virtually every aspect of the supervision including (a) supervisees' perceptions of and satisfaction with their supervisory relationships, (b) supervisors' evaluations of supervisees, (c) conceptualizations of clients' cultural dynamics, and (d) comprehension of the processes that ensue when supervisor-supervisee-client cultures are incongruent. Unfortunately, information about the influence of culture on any of these aspects of supervision must be inferred from previously cited studies of racial influences in supervision (e.g., Cook, 1993; Cook & Helms, 1988; Helms, 1982). Exercise 14.1 demonstrates some of the cultural dimensions we used in making our inferences about culture.

Supervisees' Perceptions.   From Cook's studies, it appears that ALANA supervisees are more satisfied with supervision when supervisors are perceived as giving them direction and advice. This is consistent with a collectivistic orientation wherein the person of higher social status is expected to be a guide or teacher. Thus, it is tempting to speculate that supervisors provided the kinds of information that VREG supervisees needed to adjust to a culturally unfamiliar process. Nevertheless, it is not clear that supervisors and supervisees interpreted the supervisors' perceived structuring activities similarly—that is, that both parties interpreted such supervisor behaviors as positive.

Supervision Evaluations.   Helms's (1982) study suggests that VREG supervisees may be penalized if supervisors perceive that they are acting in ways that are contrary to the supervisors' cultural expectations. Relative to the supervisees themselves and in most cases the group supervisors as well, individual or case supervisors perceived VREG supervisees as behaving in ways that would violate individualistic cultural values in some instances, but conform to them in others.

For example, case supervisors' evaluations of supervisees' expression of content and feelings during counseling and sensitivity to self-dynamics in supervision were more negative than the supervisees' own ratings. Also, group supervisors were relatively more critical of supervisees' expression of feelings and spontaneity in counseling (see Tables 14.1 and 14.2).

These differences in perceptions are consistent with Sue and Sue's (1977) hypothesis that verbal communication, particularly when feelings are involved, is incongruent with the values of many VREG cultures—at least at the levels supervisors may expect. Also, the supervisors' lower evaluations of VREG trainees' keeping of appointments is consistent with the notion of different time perspectives across cultural groups.

However, the supervisors' relatively negative evaluations of supervisees' acceptance of criticism, interrelationships with others, and consideration of supervisors' opinions seem to indicate a style of behavior that is contrary to the collectivistic orientations and ensuant respect for authority that are alleged to characterize most of the VREG groups. Individual supervisors' evaluations tended to be more negative generally than those of the supervisees or their group supervisors. The findings also seem to contradict Fukuyama (1994) and Cook's (1983) findings, which suggested that these were the kinds of supervisory dimensions valued by VREG supervisees.

Yet when supervisees were White, they and their individual supervisors seemed to share similar perceptions of the supervisees' competencies for the most part. In fact, in one case (keeping appointments), supervisors rated supervisees more positively than they rated themselves. Moreover, the most differences for White supervisees occurred

EXERCISE **14.1**

Assessing Your Cultural Style
in the Supervisory Process

The following exercise is adapted from a measure that Cook (1983) developed to assess supervisees' perceptions of cultural barriers in the supervisory process according to Sue and Sue's (1977) cultural barriers model. Next to each of the items below are three columns labeled "I expect to," "My culture expects me to," "My supervisor expects me to." In column 1, write the number that describes how you typically behave in an individual supervisory session; in column 2, describe what is normative for your culture; and in column 3, describe what you think is expected of you by a supervisor of your choice. Use the following scale and write the number on the line under the appropriate column that best describes what you think.

1	2	3	4	5	6	7
Completely false	False	Somewhat false	Neither true nor false	Somewhat true	True	Completely true

	I expect to	My culture expects me to	My supervisor expects me to
1. Communicate my feelings nonverbally.	___	___	___
2. Be reluctant to discuss my personal problems.	___	___	___
3. Talk about my work (clients) rather than myself.	___	___	___
4. Like my supervisor to support me by touching me (e.g., hug me, shake my hand, pat my back).	___	___	___
5. Use standard ("proper") English when I talk to my supervisor.		___	
6. Look at my supervisor directly whenever I am listening to her or him.	___	___	___

Now you can get a sense of the reasons for possible tensions in your supervisory relationship by comparing the numbers across the three columns. The greater the differences between numbers across columns within a row, the greater the possibilities for conflict in supervision. If differences occur only between columns 1 and 2, then the conflict is primarily intrapsychic. That is, you are in conflict with your culture. If differences occur only between columns 1 and 3 or columns 2 and 3, then the conflict is primarily extrapsychic. You may be having difficulty conforming to supervisory expectations for either individual or cultural reasons. In any case, you may wish to share your responses to this exercise with your supervisor (or supervisee) to encourage discussion if you are experiencing tensions in your supervisory relationship.

when individual and group supervisors' ratings were compared (see Table 14.2). In all cases, group supervisors rated the supervisees more positively with respect to a variety of competencies, suggesting that they perceived them as being more well-rounded than individual supervisors did.

Thus, it seems that the individual and group supervisory process may be a different phenomenological experience for VREG supervisees relative to their White counterparts. Helms's (1982) study also suggests that differences in perceptions of the persons involved in the process may have other consequences. For example, VREG supervisees' perceptions of their level of counseling practice skills were positively related to whether they thought that they could be recommended for a counseling position. Their group supervisors' perceptions of the VREG supervisees' counseling practice and conceptualization skills were positively related to whether the supervisors' would recommend them for a counseling position. In both cases, higher levels of perceived competence were related to greater readiness for a counseling position. However, where individual supervisors were concerned, none of their evaluations of VREG supervisees was related to their willingness to recommend the supervisees for a counseling position.

For White supervisees, none of their perceived competencies was significantly related to their self-perceived readiness for a counseling position, but their perceived conceptualization skills tended to be negatively related. However, case supervisors' perceptions of White supervisees' conceptualization skills were positively related and their perceived personal/professional development tended to be positively related to individual supervisors' willingness to recommend them for a counseling position. None of the counselor evaluation subscales was related to group supervisors' willingness to recommend White supervisees for a counseling position.

The obtained patterns of relationships may have some differential cultural implications for supervising VREG and White supervisees. It appears that VREG supervisees may enter the process with fairly concrete goals—namely, to improve their counseling skills so that they can obtain a job in their field. Thus, they may view the supervisor's focus on peripheral topics (e.g., self-exploration) as tangential to their goals unless they are given specific information about why and how such exploration will move them closer to *their* goals.

Furthermore, since individual supervisors are the primary source of recommendations for counseling positions, perhaps individual supervisors should develop in advance specific criteria for defining meritorious supervisee performance when the supervisee is from a different socioracial or cultural group. Such information should be communicated to the supervisee early in the process so that he or she knows to what standards he or she must conform. Regular assessments of the supervisee's progress should occur so that the supervisee can monitor her or his own progress and the supervisor can determine whether the goals are still appropriate.

For White supervisees, the Helms (1982) study suggests that supervisees and supervisors may perceive the same competency dimensions as important, but not necessarily with the same consequences. Interestingly, structuring the process and self-presentation appeared to be important characteristics for both case supervisors and White supervisees to a lesser extent. For example, the better able White supervisees believed they were at conceptualizing therapy-related processes, the less ready for a job they perceived themselves to be, but perceptions of supervisees' conceptualization skills were related to their greater readiness for a counseling position for case supervisors.

Perhaps conforming to cultural norms of individualism by becoming introspective during the supervisory process makes White supervisees doubt themselves more, but makes supervisors respect them more. Thus, individual supervisors may have the delicate responsibility of helping White supervisees to develop professionally (e.g., self explore) in order to fulfill the supervisors' expectations, while bolstering their self-esteem.

Implications for Cultural Research

Similarities and differences in the supervisors', supervisees', and clients' cultural orientations might contribute to qualitatively different processes and outcomes. One approach researchers might use to differentiate psychocultural constructs from psychoracial constructs is to perform content analyses of recalled critical incidents in supervision or in session. Both culture- and/or race-related statements made during supervision sessions or memorable moments could be analyzed for the purpose of discovering the strategies and interventions supervisors and supervisees use to cope with culture and race during supervision. Intensive examination of supervisory interactions including process (e.g., who initiated the discussions), response styles (e.g., avoidance), and manifestations of power dynamics (e.g., the supervisor's and supervisee's manner of responding to each others' statements) are still unexplored supervisory terrain.

Implications for Training

The price of ignoring race or culture in supervision may be greatest for those with the least sociopolitical and contextual power. If supervisors do not assist supervisees in addressing racial issues in therapy, clients may be denied opportunities to explore basic parts of their identities and may never discover the influence of their racial identities on the qualities of their interpersonal relationships. If supervisees are permitted to ignore culture, then the client may never learn that he or she has a culture that influences how he or she is perceived and treated by others or how he or she perceives and treats others.

Given that supervision is intended to assist supervisees in integrating their personal and professional identities (Bradley, 1989), if race and culture are ignored, supervisees may not develop fully integrated professional identities. That is, they may not acquire the capacity to be aware of their reactions to clients from various socioracial groups or to recognize their own cultural biases in conceptualizing their clients. Moreover, as long as race and culture are permitted to be invisible guests in the supervisory process, clients' reactions to the racial and cultural aspects of their therapists will remain powerful but unacknowledged forces in the therapy process.

Supervisees who approach supervision with an awareness of the possibilities of racial and cultural issues in therapy and supervision may have to cope with their feelings

of frustration, and perhaps anger, if they realize that their supervisors are not addressing salient aspects of their personal and professional identity development. Finally,
supervisors who ignore racial issues in supervision may unknowingly develop negative
reputations within the institutional supervisee community for being racially and culturally insensitive and for providing inadequate supervision.

Racial identity models can provide a relatively nonthreatening focus for discussing racial differences in supervision. Such models may also be adapted to pertain to cultural processes. The models permit examination of individual differences
rather than encouraging sweeping generalizations about different racial groups—
generalizations that can contribute to alienation and defensiveness when people discuss racial issues.

The individual focus of racial identity theory assumes that each individual has
developed not-necessarily conscious perspectives with respect to herself or himself as
a racial being, members of her or his racial group, and members of other racial groups.
It also acknowledges that these perspectives are developed, in part, from unjust circumstances in this country over which the individuals (regardless of racial category)
have had no control. However, just as counselors promote "development" in other
areas of service-recipients' identities, individuals can also be encouraged to discuss
their racial attitudes by means of principles of "growth and development" rather than
"blame."

After discussing their individual racial identity orientations and the potential
impact of them on the supervisory relationship, supervisors and supervisees can examine the contribution of their racial attitudes on their conceptualizations of their
clients. They can each question themselves about whether certain assumptions about
clients are based on the supervisor's and supervisee's racial socialization and their
racial and cultural worldviews. It is also appropriate to discuss supervisors', supervisees', and clients' racial expectations and predispositions as possible influences in the
structuring of the therapy and/or supervisory processes.

The racial and cultural value systems of the supervisor, supervisee, and client,
and the sociopolitical histories of their respective racial groups may implicitly affect
their perceptions of therapy and supervision (Cook, 1983; see Chapter 5). Supervision
should include discussion of strategies that supervisors and supervisees can use to
make these elements explicit. Supervisees can be encouraged to use the client's reactions to the therapist's racial appearance as a race-related intervention. Exploring
these idiosyncratic internal processes can facilitate the development of authentic therapeutic and supervisory relationships. Furthermore, analysis of racial and cultural
interactions in supervision can provide a cognitive framework that supervisees may
generalize to therapy.

Conclusion

The unspoken assumptions regarding the racial and cultural natures of the participants in supervision and therapy may influence every aspect of supervision. Thus,
establishment of the supervisory relationship, expectations for supervision, assign-

ment of clients, conceptualizations of clients and treatment planning, recommendations for client referrals, and evaluation of supervisees are all potentially influenced in some manner by racial and/or cultural factors.

Supervisors who are committed to competent training must be willing to bear their own awkwardness and discomfort in dealing with race and culture as they teach their supervisees to "break the silence." By being willing to reveal and openly discuss their own racial identity attitudes and cultural orientations, supervisors teach supervisees that a good therapist does not have to be infallible. If supervisors and therapists are to achieve authenticity in therapeutic and supervisory relationships, then they must try to relate to whole persons, rather than facades from which the racial and cultural selves have been erased.

Many contemporary therapy modalities require therapists' total involvement in their work with clients (Serok & Urda, 1987). Race and culture are critical components of total involvement. The supervisor's acknowledged expressions of racial and cultural relativism in the supervisory relationship can serve as a model for supervisees to adapt in their therapy relationships. Race and culture do not have to continue to be avoided. Nor do race and culture have to be treated as distasteful ordeals that one must bear. Instead, each can become a personal attribute that one learns to accentuate and appreciate in oneself as well as others. In other words, race and culture can become positive focuses of growth and development in supervision like other aspects of supervisees' personal and professional identities. The supervisor can be the catalyst in this developmental process.

REFERENCES

Borders, L. D., Bernard, J. M., Dye, H. A., Fong, M. L., Henderson, P., & Nance, D. W. (1991) Curriculum guide for training counseling supervisors: Rationale, development, and implementation. *Counselor Education & Supervision, 31,* 58–80.

Bradley, L. J. (1989). *Counselor supervision: Principles, process, practice.* (2nd ed.). Muncie, IN: Accelerated Development.

Brown, M. T., & Landrum-Brown, J. (1995). Counselor supervision: Cross-cultural perspectives. In J. Ponterotto, J. M. Casas, L. Suzuki, & C. Alexander, (eds.). *Handbook of Multicultural Counseling.* Thousand Oaks, CA: Sage Publications, pp. 263–286.

Cook, D. A. (1983). *A survey of ethnic minority clinical and counseling graduate students' perceptions of their cross-cultural supervision experiences.* Unpublished doctoral dissertation, Southern Illinois University, Carbondale.

Cook, D. A. (1993, February). *The use of "here-and-now" techniques in addressing issues of race in therapy supervision.* Symposium presentation at the Columbia Teacher's College Cross-Cultural Roundtable, New York.

Cook, D. A. (1994). Racial identity in supervision. *Counselor Education & Supervision, 34,* 132–141.

Cook, D. A., & Helms, J. E. (1988). Visible racial/ethnic group supervisees' satisfaction with cross-cultural supervision as predicted by relationship characteristics. *Journal of Counseling Psychology, 35,* 268–273.

Cook, D. A., & Paler Hargrove, L. (1997). The supervisory experience. In C. E. Thompson & R. T. Carter (eds.). *Racial identity theory: Applications to individual, group, and organizational interventions.* Mahwah, NJ: Lawrence Erlbaum, pp. 83–96.

Fukuyama, M. A. (1994). Critical incidents in multicultural counseling supervision: A phenomenological approach to supervision research. *Counselor Education & Supervision, 34,* 142–147.

Gutierrez, F. (1982). Working with minority counselor education students. *Counselor Education & Supervision, 21*, 218–226.

Hardy, K. V. (1989). The theoretical myth of sameness: A critical issue in family therapy training and treatment. *Journal of Psychotherapy and the Family, 6*(1–2), 17–33.

Helms, J. E. (1982). *Differential evaluations of minority and majority counseling trainees' practicum performance.* Unpublished manuscript, Southern Illinois University, Carbondale.

Helms, J. E. (1990). *Black and White racial identity: Theory, research, and practice.* Westport, CT: Praeger.

Helms, J. E. (1994). Racial identity and career assessment. *Journal of Career Assessment, 2*, 199–209.

Helms, J. E. (1996). Toward a methodology for measuring and assessing "racial" as distinguished from "ethnic" identity. In G. R. Sodowsky & J. C. Impara (Eds.), *Multicultural assessment in counseling and clinical psychology* (143–192). Lincoln, NE: Buros Institute of Mental Measurements.

Hilton, D. B., Russell, R. K., & Salmi, S. W. (1994). The effects of supervisor's race and level of support on perceptions of supervision. *Journal of Counseling & Development, 73*, 559–563.

Ladany, N., Brittan-Powell, C., & Pannu, R. (1997). The influence of supervisory racial identity interaction and racial matching on the supervisory working alliance and supervisee multicultural competence. *Counselor Education & Supervision, 36*, 285–305.

Ladany, N., Inman, A., Constantine, M., & Hofheinz, E. (1997). Supervisee multicultural case conceptualization ability and self-reported multicultural competence as functions of supervisee racial identity and supervisor focus. *Journal of Counseling Psychology, 44*, 284–293.

Leong, F. T., & Wagner, N. M. (1994). Cross-cultural counseling supervision: What do we know? What do we need to know? *Counselor Education & Supervision, 34*, 117–131.

Myrick, R. D., & Kelly, R. D., Jr. (1971). A scale for evaluating practicum students in counseling and supervision. *Counselor Education and Supervision, 10*, 330–356.

Peterson, F. K. (1991). Issues of race and ethnicity in supervision: Emphasizing who you are, not what you know. *The Clinical Supervisor, 9*, 15–31.

Regan, A. (1990, February). *Cross-cultural issues in the supervision of practicum and research.* Symposium presentation at the Columbia Teachers' College Cross-Cultural Roundtable, New York.

Serok, S., & Urda, L. V. (1987). Supervision in social work from a Gestalt perspective. *The Clinical Supervisor, 5*, 69–85.

Sue, D. W., & Sue, S. (1977). Barriers to effective cross-cultural counseling. *Journal of Counseling Psychology, 24*, 420–429.

Sullivan, H. S. (1953). *The interpersonal theory of psychiatry.* New York: W. W. Norton.

Vander-Kolk, C. (1974). The relationship of personality, values, and race to anticipation of the supervisory relationship. *Rehabilitation Counseling Bulletin, 18*, 41–46.

Yalom, I. D. (1985). *The theory and practice of group psychotherapy.* New York: Basic Books.

Zaslow, M. R. (1988). A model of group therapist development. *International Journal of Group Psychotherapy, 38*, 511–519.

15 Race and Culture in Therapy Research

Perhaps nowhere is the confusion of racial and cultural factors in psychology more evident than in the counseling and psychotherapy empirical literature. However, the confusion is particularly intriguing because researchers and theorists apparently believe that by becoming "multicultural" in their research orientations, they have contributed considerable information to the understanding of the impact of race and culture on the human condition. In fact, in describing multiculturalism as the fourth major movement in counseling and psychotherapy theory and research, Pedersen (1991) implies that willingness to consider the impact of a variety of cultural factors on the quality of human functioning and knowledge of such factors are synonymous.

In fact, however, counseling and psychotherapy researchers have yet to contribute much pragmatic information to the race and culture knowledge base with respect to the therapy process. The lack of meaningful information is evident at every phase of the process, including assessment of therapist and client characteristics, process dynamics, and therapy outcome (see Figure 10.1). Helms (1994a) attributes the lack of a definitive mental health focus on race and culture to researchers' premature replacement of these specific emotionally laden areas of concern with a safer, undifferentiated consideration of the mental health concerns of various "culturally diverse" or "multicultural" collective-identity groups.

A benefit of the contemporary all-inclusive multicultural or pluralistic approach to mental health theory and service delivery was that it did permit theorists, practitioners, and researchers in the mental health fields to consider broadening the parameters of effective service delivery to include populations for whom the White Western male models were not necessarily appropriate. By insisting that every person has some form of cultural diversity and that all forms are equally important (or not important), everyone could be included in what was originally a quest for racial group empowering and culturally responsive human services.

However, rather than helping to expand practitioners' knowledge base with respect to the differential influences of race and culture on the therapy process, present-day multicultural researchers have helped perpetuate the ongoing obfuscation of such factors. By treating all forms of human diversity as though they are of equal salience and import to the person as well as the societies in which the person must function (Ridley, Mendoza, Kanitz, Angermeier, & Zenk, 1994), race and culture are minimized.

Thus, an unintended effect of multicultural scholarship is that because it intends to be all-inclusive; race and culture—the original catalysts for the multicultural movement—have all but been eliminated as relevant domains of scientific inquiry.

As evidence of the lack of race and culture-focused therapy research, Ponterotto and Casas (1991) reviewed studies of "North American racial/ethnic minority groups" published over a six-year period (1983–1900) in four major counseling journals. They found that only 184 (or 10.2%) of the total of 1,800 published articles focused on groups so defined, and of those only about 5% (91) of the total had an empirical focus. African American clients or client surrogates were the most frequently studied population (36.3%). The next most frequently occurring empirical studies were Black-White comparisons (15%), followed by studies of Hispanic (7.5%) and Native American (7.5%) clients or client surrogates.

In this chapter, we recommend that counseling and psychotherapy researchers resume deliberate consideration of the effects of racial and cultural factors on the therapy process via empirical investigations of racial and cultural psychological issues or characteristics that have been hypothesized to describe members of specific groups. Several scholars have reviewed the existing research in this topic domain (e.g., Atkinson, 1983, 1985; Helms, 1990a, 1990b; Sue, Zane, & Young, 1994). Therefore, instead of repeating their efforts and achievements, we use our racial and cultural perspectives to consider conceptual and theoretical barriers that have inhibited mental health researchers' efforts to understand the dynamics of race and culture in the therapy process as outlined in our therapy model. In other words, we attempt to delineate specific areas of therapy process and outcome where some efforts to examine racial or cultural factors have occurred, but with less than satisfactory results. We conclude with some proposals for future research directions.

Conceptual Barriers

Although it is not commonly acknowledged, counseling and psychotherapy theorizing and researching take place within specific racial and cultural contexts—those of White American men. Virtually all of the traditional commonplace theoretical counseling and psychotherapy perspectives reflect European or Western views of the world, and these views have been embraced by White American mental health specialists to explain the dynamics of all peoples within the country's boundaries. In addition, most of the influential university professors, journal editors, and psychotherapy researchers have been White American men. For example, according to Focus, "In the past 13 years none of the Editors of the 27 journals published by APA [American Psychological Association] have been ethnic minority persons. Only 5% (1.8% are women) of Consulting Editors currently on the boards of APA journals are ethnic minority persons and only 2% (< 1% are women) of the ad hoc reviewers are ethnic minority persons" ("Division 45 Resource Survey," 1994, p. 23).

Therefore, the relative absence of a deliberate focus on the impediments and benefits of race or culture is to be expected because racial and cultural group memberships typically have not been insurmountable sources of tension for White people, and especially for White men. Despite protestations to the contrary, White men as a group are the most politically and economically powerful socioracial and gender group in the country. In the fields of counseling and psychotherapy in particular, this power often is manifested in their overrepresentation in gatekeeper roles. Gatekeepers not only control access to economic resources (e.g., research grants), but also determine what questions are asked and how they are asked. Therefore, the same racial and cultural factors that shape therapist-client and supervisor-supervisee dynamics probably also influence the decision-making processes of gatekeepers.

With respect to racial factors in particular, Helms (1993) notes that VREG researchers may not be permitted to publish work derived from their own life experiences if these experiences diverge too much from those of the relevant gatekeeper (e.g., professor, journal editor). As shown in Table 15.1, she uses White racial identity theory to describe potential impasses that occur with respect to research conceptualization and dissemination.

Although he was not concerned with the psychotherapy process per se, Lonner (1994) noted that with respect to culture, gatekeepers can be extremely resistant to the process of acquiring knowledge about groups other than the "dominant majority [White] group." Thus, he uses the following quote to describe the resistance of two eminent social psychologists: " 'It takes more intellectual resources than we have just to understand our own current culture. . . . We just don't have time to read about

TABLE 15.1 Summary of the Influence of White Identity on White Researchers' Cross-Cultural Scholarship

Identity Status	Assumption	Implication
Contact	Universalism of White culture	If they are included at all, data from People of Color in predominantly White samples are not analyzed separately. Results are assumed to pertain to people regardless of race.
Disintegration	Ambivalence regarding study of race	Diversity research is permitted only if it conforms to standards of excellence of White research despite reality constraints.
Reintegration	Ethnocentrism	Whites are the standard for normal behavior or behavioral norms. A study is deficient unless Whites are used as a control group.
Pseudo-Independence	Liberalism	When racial group differences are found, principles of cultural disadvantage are used to explain People of Color, but Whites are not explained.
Immersion-Emersion	Reeducation	White culture and sociopolitical history are explicitly used to design studies and explain Whites' behaviors.
Autonomy	Pluralism	Scholar recognizes inherent cultural assumptions of one's work and does not impose them on nongroup members.

This table is reprinted from Helms (1993), p. 243.

[other cultures]' . . . Because of this, they say they will not read articles dealing with other [than European American] cultures, even if they are theoretically interesting and methodologically sophisticated" (p. 240).

Lonner's psychologists were justifying their ethnocentrism regarding cultures outside of the United States. Nevertheless, their comments suggest that although they may not have respected these "other cultures," at least they seemed aware that other *national* cultures exist. However, as we observed in earlier chapters, the fact that many cultures co-exist within the borders of the United States has remained a continuing point of denial and contention (e.g., Rowe, 1994). For example, in responding to Helms's (1992) speculation that African American cultural socialization might account for Black-White differences in performance on cognitive ability tests, Rowe illustrated his cultural obliviousness as follows: "Helms imagined that these [African American] children possess all kinds of 'African-centered' [cultural] values (e.g., 'immaterial forces over linear thinking,' . . . One is left with the impression that people of black [sic] skin are culturally, cognitively, and socially different from people of white [sic] skin" (Rowe, 1994, p. 215).

Ethnocentrism has permitted psychotherapy research producers and consumers to remain oblivious to the ways in which White cultural perspectives govern the process of scientific inquiry. Two immediate consequences of the relative lack of race- and culture-focused inquiry in counseling and psychotherapy research are that the terminology for discussing such dynamics has been ambiguous at best and conceptualizations of relevant racial and cultural constructs and research designs have been incredibly simplistic.

Conceptualization of Racial and Cultural Factors

Part of the difficulty in investigating the effects of race and/or culture on the therapy process is the absence of a meaningful vocabulary for discussing racial as distinguished from cultural factors. Thus, it is not unusual to find terms such as "culture," "culturally deprived," "multicultural," "minority," "social class," and "ethnic group" all used to mean something about racial-group classification, i.e., nominal race. Moreover, the same terms also have been used with imprecise cultural referents. Westbrook and Sedlacek (1991) noted the tendency of applied researchers and scholars to substitute a multitude of variants of "culture" for "ethnicity" (by which they presumably meant *racial classification*). In their critique of psychotherapy research, Ridley et al. (1994) complained that because so many theorists and researchers use "cultural sensitivity" to mean so many different things, it is a virtually meaningless construct for describing therapist skills and techniques, or for that matter, clients' reactions to particular skills and techniques.

One consequence of using the same terms to mean race and culture is that both concepts become conceptually nebulous and inextricably intertwined. Consequently, researchers can delude themselves into believing that they have investigated one or the other when, in fact, neither has been investigated. Furthermore, because all of the existing race-culture terms tend to be euphemisms for various demographic categories, researchers have been able to avoid developing techniques and strategies for examining the internalized effects of race and culture on the therapy process.

In addition, the pluralistic version of multiculturalism that now dominates psychotherapy investigations relies on conceptualizations of "culture" that are so broad as to be impossible to investigate or implement. Thus, it is by no means clear that the same competencies required to deliver effective services to clients for whom internalized racial or cultural characteristics are primary are equally appropriate for clients for whom other socialization (e.g., gender, generation, religious affiliation) experiences are more central aspects of their personhood.

Several critics (e.g., Betancourt & Lopez, 1993; Helms, 1994a) of existing race-culture-focused empirical research suggest that a first step toward contributing meaningful information to the race and culture psychotherapy knowledge base is to be more definitive with respect to language usage. Thus, racially and culturally responsive theorists and researchers must assume the responsibilities themselves for (a) conceptualizing racial and cultural factors consistently and precisely in each research endeavor that they undertake; (b) incorporating these well-defined racial and/or cultural psychological dimensions into their research efforts instead of or in addition to demographic categories; and (c) developing racially and/or culturally congruent measures and assessment strategies for investigating the characteristics of the various socioracial and cultural groups whose psychologies have been neglected.

Helms (1994a, 1994b) developed a definitional typology for classifying operational definitions of race in counseling research. The typology might be useful for considering the race-culture conceptual issues in therapy assessment, process, and outcome. Accordingly, generalizing from Gotanda's (1991) analysis of racial factors in the legal system, Helms proposed the following categories of operational definitions: (a) nominal classification, (b) cultural referent, and (c) supposition of shared sociopolitical experiences.

Nominal Classification. When nominal or demographic classification is used to define race or culture, participants (therapists and/or clients, in this instance) are assigned to one or another hypothetically mutually exclusive racial (e.g., Black or White) or cultural (e.g., ethnic classification) category on the basis of pseudo-biological characteristics (e.g., self or researcher racial or ethnic designation). Psychological characteristics (e.g., strength of preferences for counselors of the same racial or ethnic group as oneself) are then assumed to be related to racial group membership, which is assumed to reflect some underlying psychological personality characteristic (e.g., racial attitudes).

Cultural Referent. Race is sometimes used to refer to a cultural orientation or style (e.g., Afrocentric, Eurocentric). Typically, when used in this manner, race refers to a culture assumed to have been handed down to successive generations by ancestors of a particular national origin, tribe, continent, or other collective-identity group. In this usage, *racial-cultural* refers to a complex mixture of customs, traditions, beliefs, and so forth that are assumed to be associated with racial-group membership due to shared culture-specific socialization experiences.

By way of examples of race used as culture in counseling psychology, Katz (1985) proposed some characteristics of White western European culture assumed to influence the therapy process whereas Sue and Sue (1990) did the same for lower social class Asian, Black, Latino/Latina, and Native Americans. From their perspectives, dimensions such as collective versus individualistic orientation, competition versus cooperation, and so forth might reflect different cultural orientations.

Shared Political Experiences. Psychologists have often followed the common societal practice of using "race/ethnicity" to allude to a group's shared social and political history of domination or subjugation and economic exploitation or deprivation. As we discussed in Chapter 2, for theoretical and research purposes, we use the term "sociorace" because it takes into account the evidence that such categories are reified social fictions without denying the fact that people who have been differentially classified or labeled according to their alleged racial-group- or ethnic-group-related *physical characteristics* have been exposed to different political and economic constraints within society.

Assessment

Attempts to determine what characteristics clients and (occasionally) therapists bring to their interactions have generally focused on pre-therapy preferences and/or expectations for therapist racial or ethnic group characteristics where clients are concerned and diagnostic predispositions where therapists are concerned. With few exceptions, most of these studies have used nominal definitions of race or ethnic group.

Client Factors. In racial preference studies, usually some "racial" characteristic (e.g., demographic categories) is identified and related to self-reported preferences. This category of preference studies is distinguished from the (subsequently described) racial-preference process and outcome studies in that the preferences typically are not linked to particular relationship issues or post-therapy or therapy analogue symptoms. Also, more often than not, the "clients" in such research are not people seeking help for mental health problems. With few exceptions (e.g., Helms & Carter, 1991), most of this literature has explored VREG people's preferences for White versus own-group therapists.

Thus, for example, Haviland, Horswill, O'Connell, and Dynneson (1983) studied 62 Native American college students and found that they had stronger preferences for Native rather than non-Native counselors for both personal and educational–vocational problems regardless of blood quantum and percentage of life lived on a reservation. Preferences were assessed by means of Likert-type rating scales. Also, Haviland et al. found that students' reported willingness to use a counseling center with a Native staff member was enhanced when their same socioracial group preferences were high.

Several critical reviews of this most-researched "therapy" topic exist (Atkinson, 1983; Harrison, 1975; Sue et al. 1994). In general, reviewers have concluded that preference studies have yielded contradictory findings, with clients or client surrogates sometimes preferring therapists of their own race or ethnic group, and sometimes not. Different explanations for observed discrepancies have been offered including:

(a) reviewer racial biases (Sue & Zane, 1987); (b) lack of attention to within-group heterogeneity (Parham & Helms, 1981); and (c) differential group-specific preferences (Atkinson, 1983).

The reason why researchers have expended so much energy and so many resources in investigating ALANA clients' preferences for racially or ethnically similar counselors or therapists is not readily apparent. However, it is tempting to speculate that the impetus for VREG researchers may have been to demontrate the need for VREG therapists so that they would be trained and employed in greater numbers; whereas the impetus for White researchers may have been to demonstrate the universalism of their skills and thereby ensure their place in the mental health fields. Nevertheless, preferences and expectations are not synonymous (Harrison, 1975). So, information about clients' preferences actually indicates nothing about what a client seeking help believes will characterize his or her therapist. Nor do preference studies of the type described so far reveal anything about how clients can be expected to behave if they do encounter a therapist of the disfavored group.

Studies of racial and cultural expectations also have not provided much information about what attitudes, values, and so forth (i.e., client input) clients bring to the therapy process, perhaps because the number of expectation studies with a race-culture focus are so few in number. In addition, this small pool of studies suffers from an overemphasis on racial-group comparisons. Nevertheless, the existing literature does suggest that when other sociological characteristics (e.g., social class) are controlled, asking clients about their expectations may yield important information for determining how the therapist should proceed. For example, Acosta (1979) found that about half of their lower socioeconomic status Mexican American (49%) and Anglo American (48%) psychiatric outpatient sample expected their therapists to ask questions primarily.

Therapist Factors. Interestingly, therapists' racial-cultural pre-therapy characteristics rarely have been the focus of scientific inquiry. In the overwhelming majority of those studies in which therapist characteristics ostensibly were examined, in actuality, therapist reactions to clients of another (socio) race or ethnic group were the real focus. Thus, a relatively large body of studies has examined the extent to which therapists differentially diagnose clients due to clients' racial or ethnic classifications.

Although reviewers of the existing racial assessment studies reach contradictory conclusions (e.g., Sattler, 1977; Abramowitz & Murray, 1983), there is some evidence that suggests that clients who come from racial or ethnic groups different from those of the therapist or assessor, may receive more severe psychiatric diagnoses than clients who are members of the therapist's racial or ethnic groups. Many of these assessment studies use vicarious participation analogues in which clinicians respond to video- or audiotaped simulations or written descriptive reports of clients differing only in racial or ethnic characteristics. By far, the preponderance of existing assessment-bias literature focuses on African American clients and White therapists.

Using approximations of the analogue as just described, the following results have been reported: (a) Li-Repac (1980) found that Chinese American therapists relative to White American therapists were significantly less likely to evaluate Chinese clients as depressed, inhibited, and socially inept, but more likely to evaluate White clients as seriously disturbed; (b) Stevens (1981) found that school psychologists evaluated African American and Mexican American 8-year-old boys as more hyperkinetic than Anglo-American boys; and (c) Strickland, Jenkins, Myers, and Adams (1988) found a racial classification and level of psychopathology interaction such that African American clients received more severe diagnoses from graduate student clinical psychologists than did White American clients.

Although again reviewers differ as to whether clinicians' diagnoses are evidence of therapist racial, ethnic, or cultural biases, some archival studies are at least suggestive of differential racial or ethnic group effects. For example, Baskin, Bluestone, and Nelson (1981) found that White and Asian therapists diagnosed Black psychiatric outpatients as schizophrenic more often than did Black or Latino therapists. Moreover, in general, Black women relative to other racial groups were much more likely to be diagnosed as schizophrenic rather than depressed relative to their women counterparts of other races. E. Jones (1982) reported similar results in his Black-White outpatient comparison study, whereas Craig (1982) did not find race-related differences in psychiatric referrals.

Conclusions. Whether one considers assessment of client or therapist pre-therapy characteristics, the one identifiable theme common to both is inconsistent and often contradictory findings. Some explanations for observed inconsistencies have been offered. Neighbors, Jackson, Campbell, and Williams (1989) attributed the discrepancies to two types of errors that diagnosticians potentially make: (a) incorrectly assuming that VREG and White clients are inherently different, or (b) assuming that VREG and White clients are necessarily similar. The dissimilarity error means that therapists evaluate the same symptoms differently (e.g., perceive greater psychopathology) when clients are of different racial or ethnic groups. The similarity error is that the same problem or disorder may be misdiagnosed because the clinician expects it to be manifested similarly in different cultural groups. Thus, for example, depression may be misdiagnosed in groups with no clear mind-body distinctions.

Lopez (1989) further concluded that bias can occur in opposite directions. He suggested that clinicians may "underpathologize" VREG clients' problems, that is, severely underestimate the seriousness of their concerns, or they may "overpathologize," that is, assume that rational responses to dysfunctional conditions or circumstances (e.g., racial oppression) are dysfunctional.

Also, an additional explanation for clinicians' presumably different reactions to clients of different races or ethnic groups that neither Neighbors et al. (1989) nor Lopez (1989) explicitly covers is race- or culture-specific disorders—that is, the extent to which clients express their distress through culture-specific syndromes and/or have racially or culturally prescribed styles for seeking help that are unfamiliar to clinicians (see Chapter 13). Thus, for example, African American women clients may express greater levels of emotionality than they necessarily feel when they are interacting with White therapists as a means of ensuring that the therapist will take their problems seriously.

Of course, whatever "errors" characterize diagnosticians' reactions to dissimilar clients can also characterize therapists' reactions to them. To the extent that the therapist's perceptions of the client are distorted, then his or her therapeutic interventions are also likely to be misguided. As for clients, although the research examining their pre-therapy characteristics appears to be rather superficial, it seems reasonable to assume that their misperceptions of their therapists may parallel those their therapists have of them. Thus, for example, clients too may think their therapists are more similar to themselves than the therapists actually are, and react accordingly.

With respect to clients and therapists, it is clear that the nominal approach for assessing racial or cultural factors has been rather sterile. Greater attention to the sociopolitical or cultural characteristics of both parties would presumably provide more information that could be used to develop appropriate interventions to benefit the client without violating the cultural integrity of the therapist.

Process Issues

In their review, Ponterotto and Casas (1991) asserted that counseling studies of race and ethnicity tended to examine simplistic counselor and client therapy process variables with counselor and client racial (classification) similarity and counseling process being the topic most frequently examined.

As is true of most of the previously discussed counselor preference studies, counseling and psychotherapy process studies have tended to use nominal operationalizations of race or culture and analogue methodologies.

Racial Matching. The terms "racial matching" or "ethnic matching" describe situations in which the therapist or client are of the same racial or ethnic groups. In psychotherapy research, racial or ethnic group matching is usually determined by client self-report or researcher designation. Thus, with a couple of exceptions (Carter & Helms, 1992; Thompson, Worthington, & Atkinson, 1994) racial matching studies typically have not assessed sociopolitical (e.g., racial identity) or cultural (e.g., individualism) characteristics of therapy participants. Most therapy that occurs, and consequently most therapy research, involves therapists and clients of the same sociorace—White. Thus, the interactions are racially homogenous, congruent, or matched.

One could argue that most of the existing counseling and psychotherapy literature has implicitly identified effective and ineffective process dimensions for racially congruent therapist and client combinations. Nevertheless, researchers have not seemed to realize that by studying primarily White therapist-client dyads, they have in effect studied process dimensions within the context of White racially matched therapist and client interactions.

Rather than summarizing the extensive body of research literature that has attempted to identify necessary and sufficient conditions of counseling and psychotherapy process any more than we have in previous chapters, it is probably more efficient to refer the reader to some of the historical overviews and critical reviews of this extensive literature. In addition to those previously cited, several excellent reviews and meta-analyses of this literature exist including a series of handbooks by Garfield and Bergin (1978), Bergin and Garfield (1994), and Brown and Lent (1984).

However, unless a researcher indicates that the racial classifications of his or her sample were other than White, then those aspects of clients and/or therapists that have been alleged to define effective process may not be effective if the therapist and client are not both White. In other words, if either participant is a VREG person, then it is yet to be proven whether the therapy works in the same ways as it does if both are White.

Whenever researchers have purposefully investigated the impact of racial or cultural matching on the therapy process, the focus of such inquiry typically has been the reactions of VREG clients. More often than not, in such studies, White therapists have been compared to VREG therapists of the same VREG or cultural group as the clients. Typically, the purpose of such studies is to determine whether VREG clients react differently to therapist members of their own group than they do to White therapists (Abramowitz & Murray, 1983; Atkinson, 1985; S. Sue et al., 1994; Sattler, 1977). Therapists from more than one VREG are rarely compared to one another, and White clients' reactions to VREG therapists are seldom investigated.

Furthermore, almost no recent racial-ethnic matching studies exist in which the clients or client surrogates actually interact with therapists for any of the socioracial groups of color. Exceptions are E. Jones (1978), Carter and Helms (1992), and Thompson et al.'s (1994) therapy process and therapy-process analogue studies of African American clients. Jones compared Black and White female clients' reactions to White male therapists, and Thompson et al. compared Black female surrogate clients' reactions to racially responsive or universalistic White female therapists. Both found evidence to suggest that process dynamics may be qualitatively different when the process involves Black female clients. Carter and Helms (1992) classified counseling analogue dyads according to racial identity relationship types, and compared counselor intentions and client reactions among parallel, regressive, and progressive dyads. They also found qualitative differences in the three types of relationships. Otherwise, little can be said about racial or ethnic matching and therapist techniques or client reactions.

It is possible to conceptualize process as a distal variable. For example, therapist theoretical orientations or type of treatment modality imply particular process dimensions, but do not explicate them. There is some evidence, albeit contradictory, that clients may be assigned to different treatment modalities according to race or ethnic group (e.g., Sattler, 1977). However, strictly speaking, such studies are not matching studies because investigators typically have not identified the racial or ethnic classifications of the referring therapists.

Conclusions. Nominal examination of therapist and client characteristics has not been very useful for identifying psychological or proximate effects of race and culture on therapist techniques or client reactions. Racial classification is unchangeable and does not vary of its own volition. Moreover, participants' classifications do not portend particular behaviors. Thus, studying racial and cultural matching actually offers very little useful information about the management or expression of such factors in the therapy process.

Also, researchers' operational definitions of the concept of racial or ethnic matching have been rather arbitrary. Hence, investigators have attempted to determine the circumstances under which White therapists can work effectively with ALANA clients, but rarely have they attempted to ascertain the same information for ALANA therapists providing services either to White clients or to ALANA clients (for overviews, see Atkinson, 1985; Helms, 1990b; and Sue, Zane, and Young, 1994). Furthermore, much of the existing racial matching literature focuses on issues that presumably are relatively tangential to therapy process or outcome.

Thus, by means of analogue methodologies primarily, investigators have examined whether VREG clients prefer therapists similar to themselves, and whether therapists diagnose clients differently and/or refer them to different forms (e.g., less desirable) of treatment according to racial classification. However, in the final analysis, it is not clear that many of the preferred independent or dependent variables used in counseling and psychotherapy race-culture research reveal very much about what actually occurs during the helping process.

Outcome Issues

Outcome refers to the consequences of therapy for the client. As indicated earlier, outcome can be distal or proximal. However, the most frequently used outcome variables have been client satisfaction or evaluations of the interpersonal attractiveness of the therapist. In general, outcome studies in which racial matching was used as a "process" variable have revealed contradictory results. Sometimes ALANA clients appear to be most satisfied with therapists of their own socioracial or ethnic classification and sometimes racial/ethnic group matching does not seem to matter.

Whenever so much variability in results occurs, it is evidence that investigators probably have not yet identified the critical variables. In this case, we think the variables that should be investigated are the psychological impact of race (e.g., racial identity), racism (e.g., cultural mistrust), ethnocentrism, and culture (e.g., value orientations) on culturally congruent outcomes. It is intriguing that there seem to be no studies of outcome in which improvement in the client's racial or culture-related symptomatology were the focus. In previous chapters, we discussed measures or strategies that might be used to define race and culture as internal conditions of the person. Also, many of the racially culturally responsive interventions that we recommended are certainly fruitful topics for outcome as well as process research.

Nevertheless, to conduct pragmatic race-culture research (by implication therapy) effectively, more information is needed about the factors that actually constitute "good" outcomes for the various socioracial and cultural groups that have been examined. It seems logical to us, for example, that collectivistic clients might not necessarily consider becoming individualistic a desirable outcome, and conversely, individualistic clients might not want to become collectivistic.

Similarly, it seems that individually oriented outcome measures might not necessarily be appropriate for clients from other cultural perspectives. Most standard psychotherapy outcome measures were developed by researchers who were socialized in individually oriented cultures, and the resulting measures probably reflect those origins. "Marie" (see Chapter 9) did not change on some of the individualistically oriented measures of affect and symptomatology (e.g., the Pd scale of the MMPI) that Hill (1989) used to assess her, but did change on others albeit in a negative, but perhaps more culturally congruent, direction (e.g., greater depression and hysteria). At the time of her therapy, Marie's mother was dying. Without going into a great deal of detail, it seems that by the end of therapy, Marie was expressing her sadness over her impending loss in a manner that was even more consistent with traditional Asian American cultural emotional expression than when she entered—she was somaticizing her distress. Was this a good or a bad outcome?

Although we cannot answer that question, we can note that racial matching per se probably had little to do with her outcomes. Marie's therapist was African American and Hill, the researcher who analyzed the case, is White American. Neither of them seemed aware of the cultural aspects of process and outcome as they related to Marie. We think that such obliviousness to culture and race has generally characterized psychotherapy practice and research as it is traditionally practiced.

Future Research Directions

In an analysis of the study of racial factors in the therapy process, Helms (1990b) identified the following areas as requiring empirical investigation: (a) suppositions that visible racial/ethnic group clients' (VREG; Cook & Helms, 1988) racial or cultural characteristics are impediments in the therapy process; (b) the effectiveness of therapists' attitudes and techniques during the therapy process, especially in response to racial material; and (c) the quality of the interaction between therapists and clients when racial factors are either blatant or subtle issues. These areas are also germane for investigators who intend to explicate cultural influences on therapy process and outcome.

As we have repeatedly stressed, psychotherapy research has rarely involved the examination of either therapist or client socioracial or cultural constructs as influences on the therapy process or outcome (see Helms, 1990b, for an overview). In previous chapters we discussed some methodologies for undertaking investigations, and in Insight 15.1, we present some of the studies and other scholarship that we think used innovative and potentially fruitful methodologies. The cited studies illustrate that it might be possible to operationalize socioracial constructs as independent variables in many different ways, but also suggest that it might be important to analyze or select one's dependent variables for socioracial and cultural relevance as well.

As previously mentioned, information about what the therapist should do in response to racial, ethnic, or cultural material during the therapy process is severely lacking. This vacuum is due, in part, to the shortage of theoretical frameworks specific to the therapy process for investigating such matters. It might also be due in part to: (a) the small numbers of any single group of VREG or collectivistic clients or therapists in any treatment setting, (b) the lack of standard measures for researchers to use

---

INSIGHT **15.1**

Some Research Approaches We Like

Below we list a few of the studies and/or methodological resources that we think treat race or some aspect of culture as psychological variables, which, of course, is why we like them. Although it may not be obvious, this type of research and scholarship requires major effort and commitment. Unfortunately, scholars who do this kind of work may not necessarily be appreciated for their efforts.

Berman, J. (1979). Counseling skills used by Black and White male and female counselors. Journal of Counseling Psychology, 26, 81–84.

> Although this study was completed a while ago, it is still a good model for examining issues of expressed collectivism-individualism within the counseling process.

Fong, M. L., & Borders, L. D. (1985). Effects of sex role orientation and gender on counseling skills training. *Journal of Counseling Psychology, 32,* 104–110.

> This study treats gender as a nominal and a psychological variable, and illustrates that the latter may influence counselor's skill acquisition and effectiveness.

Matsumoto, D. (1994). *Cultural influences on research methods and statistics.* Pacific Grove, CA: Brooks/Cole.

> This is an easily understandable primer in which the author illustrates how cultural process can influence the research process, and provides strategies for negotiating such influences. We think it can also be used to consider psychological influences of race.

Thompson, C. E., & Carter, R. T. (Eds.) (1997). *Racial identity theory: Applications to individual, group, and organizational interventions.* Mahwah, NJ: Lawrence Erlbaum.

> We like this one because it contains many different authors writing about their applications of racial identity theory in a variety of settings. Although it is not a book about research per se, each chapter could be the source of many research ideas.

Thompson, C. E., & Jenal, S. T. (1994). Interracial and intraracial quasi-counseling interactions when counselors avoid discussing race. *Journal of Counseling Psychology, 41,* 484–491.

> This is an excellent example of how to combine experimental and qualitative methodologies to study racial dynamics in the counseling process. It moves beyond merely treating counselor-client racial classifications as the source of race-related tensions, and it is an empirical study.

Tsoi Hoshmand, L. L. S. (1989). Alternate research paradigms: A review and teaching proposal. *The Counseling Psychologist, 17*(1), 3–79.

> This is the most thorough overview that we've seen concerning how to do and how to teach qualitative research methodologies to counseling psychologists and other applied psychologists. As you might have guessed, we think that there is a plethora of research questions concerning race and culture that might be best addressed via qualitative methodologies.

---

in comparing therapists' use of race and/or culture-focused interventions, and (c) the lack of methodologies and conceptualizations that allow researchers to assess race and culture as active, experiential processes rather than mere demographic categories.

Ridley et al. (1994) provided a conceptual rationale for integrating racial and cultural material into the therapy process. In doing so, they raised some provocative questions that are worthy of further empirical investigation. These include: (a) whether all of a client's potential social identities are equivalently important to her or him and consequently, should be an integral part of the therapy process from its inception; (b) the extent to which therapists' "cultural" characteristics influence their capacity to adequately diagnose clients' cultural concerns; and (c) whether quality of use of the proposed conceptual framework fosters differential therapy outcomes.

In an effort to provide a measure of therapist's skills, Sodowsky, Taffe, Gutkin, and Wise (1994) developed a self-report measure for assessing therapists' culturally related behavior based on Sue et al.'s (1982) counseling competencies. An implicit assumption of the measure is that the same competencies are required to deliver responsive services to nontraditional clients regardless of gender, race/ethnicity, residency status, and so forth. Therefore, investigations of the validity of the competencies as measured are needed. In other words, it is premature to require a general set of multicultural competencies without investigating their usefulness in practice and training. Investigators should attempt to determine: (a) whether therapists actually use the assessed competencies if left to their own devices; and (b) if they do, whether such behavior contributes at all to better therapy process or outcomes.

Furthermore, to reiterate our major theme, we think that researchers ought to attempt to discover whether the proposed competencies are equally useful across racial, ethnic, and cultural groups, and perhaps of equal importance, if they can be learned by therapists regardless of their racial or cultural orientations. Berman's (1979) studies of counselor skills suggest that one should not be surprised to discover that different competencies may be necessary for various groups.

Both the sample-size concerns and the lack of information concerning clients' and therapists' experiences of the process can be remedied to some extent by expanding the range of methodologies that are used to investigate racial and cultural factors in process and outcome. Qualitative methodologies are especially good at providing in-depth information about small samples. Hoshmand (1989) summarized a variety of qualitative techniques that might be valuable under such circumstances. Moreover, although he does not address cultural factors per se, models such as Martin's (1989) cognitive mediation model seem to be the type of conceptual framework that could encourage investigators to search for the ways in which clients and therapists interpret their environments. However, even if investigators do not decide to pursue alternate research paradigms, we think that it is time to consider a moratorium on racial preference vicarious participation analogue studies. There is very little that they can reveal about process or outcome.

Finally, we contend that because they are immutable, racial or ethnic classifications per se should fall outside of the domain of counseling and psychotherapy theory, research, and practice. The knowledge that a client of a particular racial classification may (or may not) prefer a therapist of another racial classification or ethnic designation has little if any pragmatic value because the only option available to a therapist of the undesired race or ethnic group is to refer the client elsewhere, if possible. Moreover, even if a researcher can select therapists or clients by racial classification, such procedures have no obvious analogy in real-life therapy situations. In other words, it is quite unlikely that the therapist can control or manipulate either the therapist's own racial classification or the client's. Nor would such procedures reveal anything substantial about either participant's internalized racial or cultural dynamics.

REFERENCES

Abramowitz, S. I., & Murray, J. (1983). Race effects in psychotherapy. In J. Murray & P. Abramson (Eds.), *Bias in psychotherapy*, (pp. 215–255). New York: Praeger.

Acosta, F. X. (1979). Pretherapy expectations and definitions of mental illness among minorities and low-income patients. *Hispanic Journal of Behavioral Sciences, 1*(4), 403–410.

Atkinson, D. R. (1983). Ethnic similarity in counseling psychology: A review of research. *The Counseling Psychologist, 11,* 79–92.

Atkinson, D. R. (1985). A meta-review of research of cross-cultural counseling and psychotherapy. *Journal of Multicultural Counseling and Development, October,* 138–153.

Baskin, D., Bluestone, H., & Nelson, M. (1981). Ethnicity and psychiatric diagnosis. *Journal of Clinical Psychology, 37,* 491–498.

Bergin, A. E., & Garfield, S. L. (Eds.). (1994). *Handbook of psychotherapy and behavior change* (4th ed.). New York: John Wiley & Sons.

Berman, J. (1979). Counseling skills used by Black and White male and female counselors. *Journal of Counseling Psychology, 26,* 81–84.

Betancourt, H., & Lopez, S. R. (1993). The study of culture, ethnicity, and race in American psychology. *American Psychologist, 48,* 629–637.

Brown, S. D., & Lent, R. W. (Eds.). (1984). *Handbook of counseling psychology.* New York: John Wiley.

Carter, R. T., & Helms, J. E. (1992). The counseling process as defined by relationship types: A test of Helms's interactional model. *Journal of Multicultural Counseling and Development, 20*(4), 181–201.

Cook, D. A., & Helms, J. E. (1988). Visible racial/ethnic group supervisees' satisfaction with cross-cultural supervision as predicted by relationship characteristics. *Journal of Counseling Psychology, 35,* 268–273.

Craig, T. J. (1982). Racial patterns in liaison psychiatry. *Journal of the National Medical Association, 74,* 1211–1215.

Division 45 Resource Survey. (1994). *Focus, 8*(2), 23.

Garfield, S. L., & Bergin, A. E. (1978) (Eds.). *Handbook of psychotherapy and behavior change* (2nd ed.). New York: Wiley.

Gotanda, N. (1991). A critique of "Our Constitution is Color-Blind." *Stanford Law Review, 44*(1), 1–73.

Harrison, D. K. (1975). Race as a counselor-client variable in counseling and psychotherapy. A review of the research. *The Counseling Psychologist, 5*(1), 124–133.

Haviland, M. G., Horswill, R. K., O'Connell, J. J., & Dynneson, V. V. (1983). Native American college students' preference for counselor race and sex and the likelihood of their use of a counseling center. *Journal of Counseling Psychology, 30,* 267–270.

Helms, J. E. (1990a). *Black and White racial identity: Theory, research, and practice.* Westport, CT: Greenwood Press.

Helms, J. E. (1990b). Three perspectives on counseling and psychotherapy with visible racial/ethnic group clients. In F. C. Serafica, A. I. Schwebel, R. K. Russell, P. D. Isaac, & L. B. Myers (Eds.), *Mental health of ethnic minorities* (pp. 171–201). New York: Praeger.

Helms, J. E., & Carter, R. T. (1991). Relationships of White and Black racial identity attitudes and demographic similarity to counselor preferences. *Journal of Counseling Psychology, 38,* 446–457.

Helms, J. E. (1992). Why is there no study of cultural equivalence in cognitive ability testing? *American Psychologist, 47,* 1083–1091.

Helms, J. E. (1993). I also said, "White racial identity influences White researchers." *The Counseling Psychologist, 21,* 240–243.

Helms, J. E. (1994a). How multiculturalism obscures racial factors in the therapy process. *Journal of Counseling Psychology, 41,* 378–385.

Helms, J. E. (1994b). The conceptualization of racial identity and other "racial" constructs. In E. Trickett, R. J. Watts, & D. Birman (Eds.), *Human diversity* (pp. 285–311). San Francisco: Jossey-Bass.

Hill, C. E. (1989). *Therapist techniques and client outcomes: Eight cases of brief psychotherapy*. Newbury Park, CA: Sage.

Hoshmand, L. L. S. T. (1989). Alternate research paradigms: A review and teaching proposal. *The Counseling Psychologist, 17*(1), 3–79.

Jones, E. E. (1978). Effects of race on psychotherapy process and outcome: An exploratory investigation. *Psychotherapy: Theory, Research, and Practice, 15*, 226 236.

Jones, E. E. (1982). Psychotherapists' impressions of treatment outcome as a function of race. *Journal of Clinical Psychology, 34*, 722–731.

Katz, J. (1985). The sociopolitical nature of counseling. *The Counseling Psychologist, 13*, 615–624.

Li-Repac, D. (1980). Cultural influences on clinical perception: A comparison between Caucasian and Chinese-American therapists. *Journal of Cross-Cultural Psychology, 11*, 327–342.

Lonner, W. J. (1994). Culture and human diversity. In E. J. Trickett, R. J. Watts, & D. Birman (Eds.). *Human diversity: Perspectives and people in context*. San Francisco: Jossey-Bass.

Lopez, S. R. (1989). Patient variable biases in clinical judgement: Conceptual overview and methodological considerations. *Psychological Bulletin, 106*, 184–203.

Martin, J. (1989). A rationale and proposal for cognitive-mediational research in counseling and psychotherapy. *The Counseling Psychologist, 17*(1), 111–135.

Neighbors, H. W., Jackson, J. S., Campbell, L., & Williams, D. (1989). Seeking professional help for personal problems: Black Americans' use of health and mental health services. *Community Mental Health Journal, 21*, 156–166.

Ottavi, T. M., Pope-Davis, D. B., & Dings, J. G. (1994). Relationship between racial identity attitudes and self-reported multicultural counseling competencies. *Journal of Counseling Psychology, 41*, 149–154.

Parham, T. A., & Helms, J. E. (1981). The influence of Black students' racial identity attitudes on preference for counselor's race. *Journal of Counseling Psychology, 28*, 250–257.

Pedersen, P. (1991). Multiculturalism as a generic approach to counseling. *Journal of Counseling and Development, 70*, 6–12.

Ponterotto, J., & Casas, J. M. (1991). *Handbook of racial/ethnic minority counseling research*, Springfield, IL: Charles C. Thomas.

Ridley, C. R., Mendoza, D. W., Kanitz, B. E., Angermeier, L., & Zenk, R. (1994). Cultural sensitivity in multicultural counseling: A perceptual schema model. *Journal of Counseling Psychology, 41*, 125–136.

Rowe, D. C. (1994). No more than skin deep. *American Psychologist, 49*(3), 215–216.

Sattler, J. M. (1977). The effects of therapist-client racial similarity. In A. S. Gurman & A. M. Razin (Eds.), *Effective psychotherapy: A handbook of research* (pp. 252–290).

Sodowsky, G. R., Taffe, R. C., Gutkin, T. B., & Wise, S. L. (1994). Development of the Multicultural Counseling Inventory (MCI): A self-report measure of multicultural competencies. *Journal of Counseling Psychology, 41*, 137–148.

Stevens, G. (1981). Bias in the attribution of hyperkinetic behavior as a function of ethnic identification and socioeconomic status. *Psychology in the School, 18*(1), 99–106.

Strickland, T. L., Jenkins, J. O., Myers, H. F., & Adams, H. E. (1988). *Journal of Psychopathology and Behavioral Assessment, 10*(2), 141–151.

Sue, D. W., Bernier, J. E., Durran, A., Feinberg, L., Pedersen, P., Smith, E. J. & Vasquez-Nuttall, E. (1982). Position paper: Cross-cultural counseling competencies. *The Counseling Psychologist, 10*, 45–52.

Sue, D. W., & Sue, D. (1990). *Counseling the culturally different: Theory and practice* (2nd ed.). New York: John Wiley.

Sue, S., & Zane, N. (1987). The role of culture and cultural techniques in psychotherapy: A critique and reformulation. *American Psychologist, 42*(1), 37–45.

Sue, S., Zane, N., & Young, K. (1994). Research on psychotherapy with culturally diverse populations. In A. E. Bergin & S. L. Garfield (Eds.), *Handbook of psychotherapy and behavior change* (4th ed.) (pp. 783–817). New York: John Wiley & Sons.

Thompson, C. E., Worthington, R., & Atkinson, D. R. (1994). Counselor content orientation, counselor race, and Black women's cultural mistrust and self-disclosure. *Journal of Counseling Psychology, 41,* 155–161.

Vontress, C. E. (1970). Counseling Blacks. *Personnel and Guidance Journal, 48,* 713–719.

Westbrook, F. D., & Sedlacek, W. E. (1991). Forty years of using labels to communicate about nontraditional students: Does it help or hurt? *Journal of Counseling and Development, 70,* 20–28.

16 Answers to Questions We've Been Asked

As educators and consultants with acknowledged interests in the applied implications of racial and cultural factors and human development, we often are asked specific questions about how to manage such factors in the therapy process. Because each of us has answered each of these questions many times and in many places, we think that they must represent critical areas of concern for many practitioners. Also, responding to these questions here provides us with an opportunity to address those issues that did not seem to fit in prior chapters.

Therefore, in this chapter, we use a question-and-answer format to discuss our efforts to clarify the ambiguous areas of race and culture in the counseling and psychotherapy process. However, although most of the time our perspectives are virtually identical, in this chapter, you will find that occasionally we do have differences of opinion. In those cases, we present both perspectives with our initials so that you can tell which of us holds which viewpoint(s).

Questions and Answers

What should a therapist do when the client's cultural values differ from the therapist's cultural values?

First of all, the therapist needs to be sure that he or she is truly attempting to cope with cultural incongruence as opposed to racial dynamics or cultural distortion. In previous chapters, we attempted to make the distinction between racial and cultural influences on therapist's and client's quality of functioning. Chapters 3 through 7 should be especially useful in helping the therapist to differentiate the two types of internalized systemic influences.

If the impasse in the therapy relationship is attributable to racial rather than or in addition to cultural dynamics, then the therapist must assess the extent of his or her own relevant racial knowledge base as it pertains to the therapist's and client's socioracial groups. The therapist should also assess his or her own as well as the client's typical manner of racial identity expression. Also, sometimes it is useful to attempt to classify the dynamics of the relationship (e.g., parallel, regressive) using the racial identity social interaction model. Such classification permits the therapist to form hypotheses about the sources of the tensions within the relationship, and Chapters 6 and 7 might be useful in this regard.

Nevertheless, because racial tensions within the therapy relationship sometimes are indirect manifestations of the therapist's and client's socialization experiences with respect to race in the external world, the therapist must attempt to assess the impact of these societal forces on the client. Communicating an awareness of and empathy toward the client's racial circumstances can do wonders for resolving racial discord within the therapeutic alliance.

Up to this point, we have not dealt with the issue of "cultural distortion." We use the term *cultural distortion* to mean both the tendency of clients (and therapists) to exhibit exaggerated versions of naturally occurring cultural themes in their environments as well as maladaptive behavior that may be erroneously attributed to cultural socialization. Either the therapist or client might engage in cultural distortion. Montalvo and Gutierrez (1989) provide several excellent examples of these two forms of distortion.

Most cultures in the United States are at least somewhat patriarchal, although the male dominance may be expressed in different ways. Consequently, pathological dominance may be confused with "normal" expressions of dominance. An area where such confusion typically occurs is family dynamics and child abuse. Montalvo and Gutierrez present an example of a Latina wife and mother who lures her daughter back into an incestuous relationship with the girls' father because, due to the form of tyrannical patriarchy that characterized the mother's family of origin, she is unable to recognize or resist dysfunctional expressions of machismo.

Also, we are aware of Asian clients whose families conceal the fathers' abusive behavior to "save face," a distortion of a cultural norm. Also, the families of some African American clients we have encountered justify the abusers' behavior because, "It would be wrong for a Black woman (or child) to 'bring down' a high-achieving Black man." Obviously, such rationales represent distortions of the male role in families in African American culture as well as a family-wide internalization of societal racial stereotypes of the Black man (Perry & Locke, 1985).

However, if the therapist has resolved or ruled out racial factors as the source of the therapy "cultural" impasse, then we have several suggestions for how he or she might cope with the differences between his or her cultural values and those of the client. In our opinion, the therapist should do the following:

1. Clarify for himself or herself what specific cultural values are in conflict, and what the nature of the conflict seems to be.
2. Attempt to listen objectively to what the client is saying. Objective listening means that the therapist tries to temporarily set aside his or her cultural frame of reference so that he or she can "hear" the client's frame of reference in his or her comments. Hear them out first.
3. Seek consultation with members of the client's cultural group to discover whether the client's expression of a cultural principle that seems weird to the therapist is in fact atypical of the client's group. The therapist may also need to seek consultation from professional members of his or her own cultural group

to discover whether or not the therapist can be flexible with respect to his or her own cultural values, and whether such flexibility is advisable under the circumstances.

4. Weigh the relative usefulness of the therapist's and client's relevant cultural values for adaptive functioning within the client's cultural context.

5. Consider what the client may have to give up or lose if he or she replaces his or her own cultural values with the therapist's values.

6. Consider whether the therapist can ethically and legally support the client's continued expression of her or his cultural norms. If endorsement of the client's cultural self-expression would violate the therapist's legal or ethical standards and/or would place the client in legal jeopardy, then the therapist must inform the client of the exact nature of his or her cultural indiscretion. Thus, if the therapist continues to see the client, he or she should inform the client about the therapist's own relevant values, societal values, and the applicable laws in the jurisdictions in which the therapy is occurring.

7. Assist the client in weighing the gains and losses to himself or herself if he or she continues to operate in a manner that is contrary to the legal regulations in the relevant jurisdictions or catchment areas.

8. Define one's own bottom line in advance as much as possible. Such definition means that the therapist must know when he or she can no longer continue to work with a client whose values are markedly different from those of the therapist.

9. Moreover, if the client's behavior constitutes a reportable legal violation under the laws that govern the therapist's behavior, then the therapist must report it. In doing so, the therapist should try to explain to the client why it is necessary for him or her to respond in this manner. Afterward, if the client is still speaking to the therapist, then he or she might try to help the client negotiate the relevant legal or social system.

When should the therapist talk about race in therapy? Do you think therapists should always talk about race with clients?

The short answer to the second question is, "No, we do not believe that the therapist should *always* talk about race with clients." However, when or whether race should be discussed with clients depends on the particular circumstances as well as what is meant by "talking about" it. If we exclude total disregard, then talking about or discussing race can range from a bare mention of the topic to intensive analysis of the racial dynamics of the client's circumstances within and outside of the therapy relationship.

Sometimes the manner in which race becomes an issue in the therapy relationship dictates the level of intensity necessary as well as whether it should be a focus of the therapy. Obviously, if a client indicates on an intake form that race in some form is an aspect of her or his problem, then the therapist should bring it up during therapy, even if the client does not. Sometimes clients are reluctant to initiate such discussions because they are afraid of the therapist's reactions to them if they do. In such cases, the client's readiness to explore the topic typically determines the depth at which it can and should be explored.

Also, when the client's problem is a race-related problem involving someone of the therapist's race, then the therapist should initiate a discussion that focuses on the client's potential symbolic reactions to the therapist as a representative of the relevant group. While it might not be necessary to immediately disabuse the client of idealized perceptions of the therapist that permit the client to confide in someone of the therapist's socioracial group, it is necessary to try to counteract negative stereotypes about the therapist (if they are not accurate) that potentially inhibit the client's self-expression. Often it is possible to determine when it might be appropriate for the therapist to initiate a race-related focus. Examples are when the client precedes relevant topics with a speech disfluency (e.g., "umm") or apologizes upon realizing that he or she has said something negative about the therapist's group.

At other times, the client's needs to express racial concerns are less obvious but no less central. For example, if the client seems to be holding back and no other obvious explanation is evident, then race may be an issue. Particularly if the therapist and client are of different socioraces, then the client may not be able to say that she or he does not want to work with a person of the therapist's race. So, instead of stating her or his position directly, the client may passively resist by not participating in the process.

Also, when the therapist begins asking questions about the therapist's credentials or training and/or her or his racial classification as soon as the client sits down, often such inquiries are the client's not-so-subtle attempt to alert the therapist to the fact that the therapist's race is an issue for the client. Rather than taking the client's racial discomfort personally and becoming defensive, the therapist should provide the client with an opportunity to express her or his race-related concerns. If it becomes obvious that the implicit tensions cannot be resolved well enough to permit the relationship to proceed in a healthful manner, then the therapist should make appropriate referrals.

When the client seems to be making unwarranted seemingly race-related assumptions about the therapist's background or presumed unexpressed thoughts, then it might be time to discuss race. For example, a client of mine (*JH*) intended to compliment me by expressing how strong she thought I was for having survived life on the streets. Since her description of me represented her projections (and stereotypes) of Black women rather than my reality, it became the catalyst for helping her to understand why her efforts to be friendly were rebuffed by African American women in her office at work.

Be that as it may, as the therapist is working with the client, she or he should be alert to the possibility that race has become an issue for the client, and be continuously ready to intervene to alleviate its negative impact on the client and the therapy relationship. Race may not necessarily be invited into the therapy session, but it is always a potential guest.

How does a therapist teach a client about racism?

Well, we are pretty direct about that, especially if the client is being victimized by racism or engaging in self-blame for circumstances that are beyond her or his control because of racism. We share with the client similar examples from our own experience or we use examples from the client's situation to provide alternative inter-pretations of events. Then we assist the client in assessing the advantages and disad-vantages to the client and/or (if appropriate) his or her group of remaining in the stressful situation.

If the client must remain in the situation for whatever reason, then we attempt to teach him or her coping strategies and survival skills. Usually what we teach in this regard are those strategies that have worked for us, and we are continually learning and adapting new strategies from our everyday life experiences. However, a useful step for most clients who are being disempowered by racism is to assist them in recogniz-ing and refuting the negative self-referent messages that they are internalizing from the situation.

But aren't you afraid the client will attribute everything to racism?

Not if the therapist performs the educational task properly. The therapist should teach the client that racism is not an excuse for passivity no matter how overwhelm-ing it may seem to be at the moment. Just because racism exists does not mean that it cannot be overcome in some manner, although different clients may need to take alternate paths in order to avoid succumbing to it. So, the therapist must be careful to guide the client toward various paths rather than imposing them upon the client.

Also, in working with clients' race-related problems, the racial aspect of the problem is rarely the entire problem. Therefore, the therapist should attempt to teach the client to distinguish race-related aspects of the problem from nonrace-related aspects of the problem(s). Furthermore, since sometimes clients who are rebounding from "Conformity" or "Contact" (obliviousness) racial identity tend to perceive everything as racist, we warn the client about this possibility in advance.

How should a therapist work with a client whom she or he keeps encountering in social settings?

Actually, we already addressed this issue in Chapter 10. So, we will briefly reiterate our answer here. If the therapist knows in advance that the possibility for running into the client in nontherapy places exists, the therapist should discuss the possibility of chance encounters with the client. The discussion should include the following: (a) the client's thoughts and feelings about encountering the therapist in other more public settings; (b) the boundaries and limits the therapist must maintain in such sit-uations; and (c) the therapist's policies and procedures for maintaining the client's confidentiality.

Under these circumstances, it is important for the therapist to explain to collec-tivistically oriented clients and clients unfamiliar with the therapy process why the therapist cannot be their friend outside of therapy. The explanation should not be some distant justification based on esoteric ethical standards because the client prob-ably will not understand such explanations. Instead, the therapist should personalize the relevant standard so that the client can understand how it pertains to her or his situation in particular. Here, too, it is often important to discuss with the client the difficulties that will likely arise for the client and therapist if they bring up therapy issues during a social gathering.

How should a therapist tell a White client that the client is being racist?

White therapists could be fairly direct about this because most White people do not think that White people are experts on racism, and thus, they do not expect them to address it in a therapeutic setting. The tendency of Whites to consider race and racism as less relevant to White people than it is to People of Color probably means that the therapist will have to use many examples and explain why he or she thinks each is an example of (White) racism. Even so, the therapist may find that the client discounts the therapist's interpretations if they are incongruent with the client's level of racial identity development.

Alderfer (1994), a White male psychologist and consultant who typically writes about race relations from an Immersion-Emersion perspective, warns applied psychologists of the following: "White people do not easily discuss race relations. For most whites [sic], the range of feelings goes from uncomfortable to severely uncomfortable. The most common behavioral pattern [for them] is avoiding the issue, if at all possible. When that response is not feasible, the next line of defense is to deny the presence of racial dynamics" (Alderfer, 1994, p. 215).

To break through such a strong racially and societally reinforced defensive system, White therapists must be able to be very empathic without endorsing the client's racism. Effective empathy in this instance requires that the therapist be capable of being open and honest with the client about those racial and racism socialization experiences that they share. Such self-revelation will allow the client to see that the therapist understands and shares the White socialization experiences that have led the client to be oblivious to his or her personal racism. It will provide for the client a model of how nondefensive consideration of racial dynamics in the client's environments could manifest itself. Of course, to help the client resolve his or her issues of racism, the therapist must be equally vigilant about recognizing and demolishing his or her own racism issues (Helms, 1992).

Therapists of Color who intend to inform a White client of his or her racism may want to avoid using the word "racist" unless the client uses it first to describe himself or herself. On some not-necessarily conscious level, most White people feel threatened by being "revealed" as a racist by a Person of Color, even if they are. Perhaps the intimidation arises from uncertainty about what constitutes racism and consequently, confusion about whether or not one has those characteristics; or perhaps the label makes it difficult to maintain the self-protective defensive mechanisms to which Alderfer (1994) alludes.

Nevertheless, if a Person of Color, presumably a victim of the mysterious forces of racism, uses the racism label, it is considered more insulting than it is if used by a White person. In a peculiar turn of events, White people often consider an ALANA person's use of the racism label more impactful than a White person's usage. Most White people so accused feel an obligation to defend themselves against the ALANA accuser, whereas the White accuser is discounted (Alderfer, 1994; Helms, 1992).

VREG therapists may not be accustomed to being in the power position in VREG-White interactions and may be inclined to enjoy their unusual status. However, an effective therapist does not want so much power in the therapy relationship (although it might come in handy in life more generally) because it inhibits the client's motivation to work on his or her issues. Moreover, lest the VREG therapist become too euphoric about the possibility of relationship power, we should warn him or her that power in this case does not mean that the White client will accept the Therapist of Color's "racism" diagnosis. It merely means that those clients who are "accidental" racists will feel more obligated to resist the diagnosis than they would if the therapist were White. Depending on his or her dominant racial identity status, the client may express resistance by becoming defensive (Pseudo-Independence) or by exhibiting debilitating shame or guilt (Disintegration) or anger and denial (Contact).

Moreover, many White clients will have difficulty acknowledging their own racism to an ALANA therapist because they believe that the ALANA therapist cannot possibly care about them if the therapist "sees" the clients' racism. The Therapist of Color will need to respect these feelings if she or he wishes the client to change her or his racism.

What if, as a Therapist of Color, I really do not like this racist client?

If you can find one, get supervision from a therapist who is resolving her or his own issues of racial identity in a manner that would permit you to participate in a progressive interaction with him or her. Otherwise, if you and the client are committed to remaining in a therapy relationship, then consider this to be your opportunity to learn to work effectively with clients whom you do not like. A lot of clients enter therapy with mental health problems (e.g., narcissistic personalities, character disorders) that may make them "unlikable," at least initially. For example, narcissistic clients are not particularly likable. Racism is one of those types of mental health problems. However, an effective therapist stays with even unlikable clients in the hope that when they feel safe with you they can begin to give up the symptoms of disorder.

When a client invites the therapist to an important event in his or her life, should the therapist go?

We answered this one in Chapter 10. However, in general, we believe that you should make an appearance at such events, if you can. Also, as we said previously, on occasion, at the end of therapy, under certain circumstances, it might be appropriate for the therapist to give or receive small tokens. For example, when the therapist must terminate therapy prematurely, he or she might give the client a transitional object (e.g., a journal or calendar) or when a client is graduating or relocating, the therapist might give him or her something to remind him or her of their work (e.g., a paperweight).

What should a therapist do if a client brings you a gift?

The therapist must talk to the client about what the gift means to the client and his or her cultural group. Whether the therapist accepts a one-time gift depends on the circumstances and whether the therapist can accept it in the cultural spirit in which it was given. If the client frequently brings the therapist gifts, then he or she still needs a cultural framework for interpreting the meaning of the client's behavior. Also, the therapist needs to think about what aspects of the therapy process the gift-giving symbolizes, and whether it is appropriate for the therapist to encourage or discourage it. The decision should be based on whether keeping or returning the gifts is best for the client's improvement.

Suppose the client brings in other family members and wants the therapist to see them, too?

In responding to this question, we are assuming that the question refers to individual therapy rather than couples or other forms of family therapy. Whether or not the therapist agrees to provide therapy for the client's family members depends on a number of factors including the nature of the therapy issues and the longevity of the relationship with the initiating client. If the issues of the initiating client and the incoming clients are too overlapping and interdependent for the therapist to differentiate, then the therapist should use the initial contact and her or his relationship with the client to refer the family members to another "trusted" therapist or appropriate resource.

Also, if the relationship with the first client is long-standing and providing services to other family members would give even the appearance that the therapist was not being objective with the other family member clients, then a referral is in order. However, in each of these instances, with the client's permission, it is often possible to establish a long-distance collaborative relationship with the referral therapist in which each therapist attends to different aspects of the family's concerns.

Then, too, for collectivistic clients or clients expressing collectivistic concerns, one of us (*JH*) will often encourage clients to bring in other relevant family or group members to assist in solving the client's problems. However, in such instances, it is necessary to make it clear to all participants that the invited parties are present to assist the client. Nevertheless, sometimes therapists who use this approach will find that other members of the client's collective group(s) are also in need of services. In such instances, a referral may be in order.

My client usually does not get to the important issues until the last fifteen minutes of our session. What should I do?

Well, you did not mention anything about this client's *culture*. It is hard to give an all-purpose answer to this one. So, here are some ways we would think about what to do.

Consider how time is conceptualized in the client's culture. Remember that in some cultures time, especially in social relationships, is defined by phenomenological experiences rather than by numbers on a clock. Clients who operate from this perspective may not really begin to share their concerns until they "feel" the time is right. Moreover, if this style of interacting with the therapist has been going on for awhile, then it is possible that the client believes that he or she is doing what is expected of her or him in this situation.

Therefore, the therapist should also determine the client's familiarity or lack of familiarity with the therapy process as it is typically practiced, as well as how it is typically practiced by the therapist who is asking the questions. Clarify whether he or she knows the "rules" by which the therapy will proceed. Strange though it may seem, many clients do not automatically know that therapy sessions typically last for 50 minutes. On the other hand, some clients may know that 50 minutes is standard for traditional therapists, but may assume that such rules are suspended if the client and therapist share a common socioracial or ethnic group or cultural orientation.

Consider whether trust is established and expressed in the same way in the client's cultural group as it is in traditional therapy and/or in the therapist's primary cultural group(s). The client's desire to remain in the therapist's presence longer than absolutely necessary might be considered a compliment in her or his culture, even if it is not considered such in the therapist's culture.

Ask yourself whether it will be possible to shape the client to conform to the traditional 50-minute hour and why it is necessary to do so. Fluid time is so ingrained for some clients that any other kind of intimate relationship feels artificial to them. If forced to always conform to the therapist's particular version of time-appropriate behavior, such clients may eventually drift away from therapy without really being sure why they have done so. Nevertheless, therapists who work in service-providing agencies often *must* conform to agency standards for billable hours. If these standards are truly rigid, then the therapist should explain them to the client so that he or she will understand why the therapist continually rushes the client out of the session just as he or she is getting comfortable.

If the therapist has some schedule flexibility, then he or she can consider whether creative scheduling alternatives might work better for the client who seems slow to warm up. For example, instead of weekly 50-minute sessions, the therapist might offer double sessions on alternate weeks.

The point of all of our suggestions is that we do not think that the 50-minute session should be cast in iron. Rather the length of sessions (insofar as possible) should be driven by the therapist's conceptualization of what will work best for the client.

Can White people counsel ALANAs?

It is probably not difficult to guess our answer to this one. In a sense, at least 20% of this book has been our effort to suggest ways in which White individualistically oriented therapists can provide effective therapy to VREG clients and/or clients from collectivistic cultural orientations. Nevertheless, our short answer to this question is: White therapists and counselors can counsel ALANAs, if the White counselor is continually working on resolving his or her own issues of racial identity, racism, and ethnocentrism *and* the ALANA client is willing. We also think it might be helpful if the therapist reads our book, but we could be biased in that regard.

If there is a VREG counselor in an agency, should White counselors automatically refer VREG clients to that person?

Just because there is a Therapist of Color in an agency does not mean that he or she is necessarily suitable for working with each and every VREG client. Remember a person's color, socioracial group, or ethnic classification actually reveals nothing about his or her racial knowledge and attitudes or cultural orientation. However, it may be even more necessary for VREG therapists to continually examine their own level of racial identity development and acculturative and assimilationist issues because colleagues and clients will be more likely to expect it of them.

Nevertheless, we not only expect White therapists to be capable of assessing their client's racial and cultural dynamics, we also expect them to use the same skills to assess the racial and cultural competence of their colleagues regardless of their color. In our opinion, a therapist who makes a referral merely because a client and therapist are of matching colors is engaging in unethical practice.

My client who is the same race as I am thinks that people of my skin color are better than people of his skin color. Should we discuss this in therapy?

As we discussed in Chapters 4 and 5, skin color historically has been a stable, visible characteristic through which racism can be communicated and regulated. Consequently, although it is not always evident, all of the socioracial groups express skin color biases toward in-group members to some extent. In virtually all of the groups, people with whiter or lighter skin colors are accorded preferential treatment because "white" skin relative to the subjugated populations was the color of the oppressor or colonialists.

Therefore, the therapist should discuss with the client the general origins of the message that some skin colors are necessarily better than others as well as the particular messages that he or she has internalized. The discussion should include exploration of how previous experiences might be related to the client's expectations of how he or she will be treated by the therapist.

The therapist asking this question is being idealized by the client because of the therapist's skin color. Therefore, the therapist should recognize that he or she holds considerable power over the client because of the client's beliefs that the therapist's skin color makes him or her an innately superior person. Therefore, the therapist's racism educational efforts should not only include discussion of the various societal manifestations of racism, but also its various manifestations within the therapy relationship. Discuss with the client the ways in which he or she is likely to react to the therapist and the therapy process because of the client's internalized racism.

Moreover, with clients who have experienced skin color abuse, the therapist should expect to see evidence of self-esteem deficits, poor self-concept, depression, and suppressed anger. As with racism more generally, the therapist must be attuned to the pain that likely accompanies the message that "you are inferior because of your appearance." The therapist can often assist the client in overcoming feelings of skin color inferiority by not reinforcing the stereotypes with which the client is familiar.

Would you ever point out to a VREG person that he or she is being a racist?

This question and the following question are two of those infrequent places where we disagree. So, we will each speak for ourselves.

DC: Yes, I would point out that the person is being a racist with respect to other People of Color. Also, if the VREG person is being bigoted, I would try to make him or her aware of that as well.

JH: Yes, I would try to help the person see the ways in which her or his attitudes, behaviors, and feelings were examples of (personal) racism. Also, since some VREGs do benefit from institutional racism even though they do not control it, sometimes I would try to help these "accidental" beneficiaries of racism to recognize their benefits. I would also feel some obligation to educate them about the ways in which systems can punish VREG people who are even perceived to be expressing racism toward Whites.

Can an ALANA be racist?

DC: I think he or she can be racist toward other ALANAs who do not have as much power as he or she does (e.g., a supervisee of another sociorace). However, I do not think ALANA people can be racist toward Whites because they do not have enough power, but they can be bigots toward (White) people who have more power than they.

JH: I think ALANA people can be personally or individually racist toward members of other socioracial groups, including White people. However, I do not think that informing people of racial mistreatment or preferring to associate with members of one's own racial group are examples of racist behavior, if one is an ALANA person. Nor do I think that ALANA people can be institutionally or culturally racist because they do not have enough power. Also, if an ALANA person expresses personal racism toward a White person, then I think the consequences for doing so are more severe than they are for White people who express racism because ALANA people do not control the legal and societal institutions that administer punishment.

What should a therapist do if we did not address her or his critical issues anywhere in this book?

Write to us. Do not phone us because we are both working women and cannot spare the time or money to return your calls. If you send us your questions, we will not respond to them individually, but if we ever revise this book, we will attempt to answer the questions that we missed in this edition. By that time, we might have learned a little more than we know now about how to perform racially and culturally responsive therapy.

REFERENCES

Alderfer, C. P. (1994). A White man's perspective on the unconscious processes within Black-White relations in the United States. In E. J. Trickett, R. J. Watts, & D. Birman (Eds.), *Human diversity* (pp. 201–229). San Francisco: Jossey-Bass.

Helms, J. E. (1992). *A race is a nice thing to have: A guide to being a White person or understanding the White people in your life* . Topeka, KS: Content Communications.

Montalvo, G., & Gutierrez, M. J. (1989). Nine assumptions for work with ethnic minority families. In Saba, G., Karrer, B. M., & Hardy, K. V. (Eds.). (1990). *Minorities and family therapy.* Binghamton, New York: Haworth Press.

Perry, J. L., & Locke, D. C. (1985). Career development of Black men: Implications for school guidance services. *Journal of Multicultural Counseling and Development, July,* 106–111.

APPENDIX A

Ethical Principles of Psychologists and Code of Conduct

CONTENTS

INTRODUCTION

PREAMBLE

GENERAL PRINCIPLES

Principle A: Competence

Principle B: Integrity

Principle C: Professional and Scientific Responsibility

Principle D: Respect for People's Rights and Dignity

Principle E: Concern for Others' Welfare

Principle F: Social Responsibility

ETHICAL STANDARDS

1. **General Standards**

1.01 Applicability of the Ethics Code

1.02 Relationship of Ethics and Law

1.03 Professional and Scientific Relationship

1.04 Boundaries of Competence

1.05 Maintaining Expertise

1.06 Basis for Scientific and Professional Judgments

1.07 Describing the Nature and Results of Psychological Services

1.08 Human Differences

1.09 Respecting Others

1.10 Nondiscrimination

1.11 Sexual Harassment

1.12 Other Harassment

1.13 Personal Problems and Conflicts

1.14 Avoiding Harm

1.15 Misuse of Psychologists' Influence

1.16 Misuse of Psychologists' Work

1.17 Multiple Relationships

1.18 Barter (With Patients or Clients)

1.19 Exploitative Relationships

1.20 Consultations and Referrals

1.21 Third-Party Requests for Services

1.22 Delegation to and Supervision of Subordinates

1.23 Documentation of Professional and Scientific Work

1.24 Records and Data

1.25 Fees and Financial Arrangements

1.26 Accuracy in Reports to Payors and Funding Sources

1.27 Referrals and Fees

2. **Evaluation, Assessment, or Intervention**

2.01 Evaluation, Diagnosis, and Interventions in Professional Context

2.02 Competence and Appropriate Use of Assessments and Interventions

2.03 Test Construction

2.04 Use of Assessment in General and With Special Populations

2.05 Interpreting Assessment Results

2.06 Unqualified Persons

2.07 Obsolete Tests and Outdated Test Results

2.08 Test Scoring and Interpretation Services

Copyright 1992 by the American Psychological Association, Inc. 0003-066X/92/$2.00

American Psychologist, Vol. 47, No. 12, 1597–1611

2.09 Explaining Assessment Results
2.10 Maintaining Test Security

3. Advertising and Other Public Statements
3.01 Definition of Public Statements
3.02 Statements by Others
3.03 Avoidance of False or Deceptive Statements
3.04 Media Presentations
3.05 Testimonials
3.06 In-Person Solicitation

4. Therapy
4.01 Structuring the Relationship
4.02 Informed Consent to Therapy
4.03 Couple and Family Relationships
4.04 Providing Mental Health Services to Those Served by Others
4.05 Sexual Intimacies With Current Patients or Clients
4.06 Therapy With Former Sexual Partners
4.07 Sexual Intimacies With Former Therapy Patients
4.08 Interruption of Services
4.09 Terminating the Professional Relationship

5. Privacy and Confidentiality
5.01 Discussing the Limits of Confidentiality
5.02 Maintaining Confidentiality
5.03 Minimizing Intrusions on Privacy
5.04 Maintenance of Records
5.05 Disclosures
5.06 Consultations
5.07 Confidential Information in Databases
5.08 Use of Confidential Information for Didactic or Other Purposes
5.09 Preserving Records and Data
5.10 Ownership of Records and Data
5.11 Withholding Records for Nonpayment

6. Teaching, Training Supervision, Research, and Publishing
6.01 Design of Education and Training Programs
6.02 Descriptions of Education and Training Programs

6.03 Accuracy and Objectivity in Teaching
6.04 Limitation on Teaching
6.05 Assessing Student and Supervisee Performance
6.06 Planning Research
6.07 Responsibility
6.08 Compliance With Law and Standards
6.09 Institutional Approval
6.10 Research Responsibilities
6.11 Informed Consent to Research
6.12 Dispensing With Informed Consent
6.13 Informed Consent in Research Filming or Recording
6.14 Offering Inducements for Research Participants
6.15 Deception in Research
6.16 Sharing and Utilizing Data
6.17 Minimizing Invasiveness
6.18 Providing Participants With Information About the Study
6.19 Honoring Commitments
6.20 Care and Use of Animals in Research
6.21 Reporting of Results
6.22 Plagiarism
6.23 Publication Credit
6.24 Duplicate Publication of Data
6.25 Sharing Data
6.26 Professional Reviewers

7. Forensic Activities
7.01 Professionalism
7.02 Forensic Assessments
7.03 Clarification of Role
7.04 Truthfulness and Candor
7.05 Prior Relationships
7.06 Compliance With Law and Rules

8. Resolving Ethical Issues
8.01 Familiarity With Ethics Code
8.02 Confronting Ethical Issues
8.03 Conflicts Between Ethics and Organizational Demands
8.04 Informal Resolution of Ethical Violations
8.05 Reporting Ethical Violations
8.06 Cooperating With Ethics Committees
8.07 Improper Complaints

Introduction

The American Psychological Association's (APA's) Ethical Principles of Psychologists and Code of Conduct (hereinafter referred to as the Ethics Code) consists of an Introduction, a Preamble, six General principles (A-F), and specific Ethical Standards. The Introduction discusses the intent, organization, procedural considerations, and scope of application of the Ethics Code. The Preamble and General Principles are *aspirational* goals to guide psychologists toward the highest ideals of psychology. Although the Preamble and General Principles are not themselves enforceable rules, they should be considered by psychologists in arriving at an ethical course of action and may be considered by ethics bodies in interpreting the Ethical Standards. The Ethical Standards set forth *enforceable* rules for conduct as psychologists. Most of the Ethical Standards are written broadly, in order to apply to psychologists in varied roles, although the application of an Ethical Standard may vary depending on the context. The Ethical Standards are not exhaustive. The fact that a given conduct is not specifically addressed by the Ethics Code does not mean that it is necessarily either ethical or unethical.

This version of the APA Ethics Code was adopted by the American Psychological Association's Council of Representatives during its meeting, August 13 and 16, 1992, and is effective beginning December 1, 1992. Inquiries concerning the substance or interpretation of the APA Ethics Code should be addressed to the Director, Office of Ethics, American Psychological Association, 750 First Street, NE, Washington, DC 20002-4242.

This Code will be used to adjudicate complaints brought concerning alleged conduct occurring on or after the effective date. Complaints regarding conduct occurring prior to the effective date will be adjudicated on the basis of the version of the Code that was in effect at the time the conduct occurred, except that no provisions repealed in June 1989, will be enforced even if an earlier version contains the provision. The Ethics Code will undergo continuing review and study for further revisions; comments on the Code may be sent to the above address.

The APA has previously published its Ethical Standards as follows:

American Psychological Association. (1953). *Ethical standards of psychologists*. Washington, DC: Author.

American Psychological Association. (1958). Standards of ethical behavior for psychologists. *American Psychologists, 13*, 268–271.

American Psychological Association. (1963). Ethical standards of psychologists. *American Psychologists, 18*, 56–60.

American Psychological Association. (1968). Ethical standards of psychologists. *American Psychologists, 23*, 357–361.

American Psychological Association. (1977, March). Ethical standards of psychologists. *APA Monitor*, pp. 22–23.

American Psychological Association. (1979). *Ethical standards of psychologists*. Washington, DC: Author.

American Psychological Association. (1981). Ethical principles of psychologists. *American Psychologists, 36*, 633–638.

American Psychological Association. (1990). Ethical principles of psychologists. (Amended June 2, 1989). *American Psychologist, 45*, 390–395.

Request copies of the APA's Ethical Principles of Psychologists and Code of Conduct from the APA Order Department, 750 First Street, NE, Washington, DC 20002-4242, or phone (202) 336-5510.

Membership in the APA commits members to adhere to the APA Ethics Code and to the rules and procedures used to implement it. Psychologists and students, whether or not they are APA members, should be aware that the Ethics Code may be applied to them by state psychology boards, courts, or other public bodies.

This Ethics Code applies only to psychologists' work-related activities, that is, activities that are part of the psychologists' scientific and professional functions or that are psychological in nature. It includes the clinical or counseling practice of psychology, research, teaching, supervision of trainees, development of assessment instruments, conducting assessments, educational counseling, organizational consulating, social intervention, administration, and other activities as well. These work-related activities can be distinguished from the purely private conduct of a psychologist, which ordinarily is not within the purview of the Ethics Code.

The Ethics Code is intended to provide standards of professional conduct that can be applied by the APA and by other bodies that choose to adopt them. Whether or not a psychologist has violated the Ethics Code does not by itself determine whether he or she is legally liable in a court action, whether a contract is enforceable, or whether other legal consequences occur. These results are based on legal rather than ethical rules. However, compliance with or violation of the Ethics Code may be admissible as evidence in some legal proceedings, depending on the circumstance.

In the process of making decision regarding their professional behavior, psychologists must consider this Ethics Code, in addition to applicable laws and psychology board regulations. If the Ethics Code establishes a higher standard of conduct than is required by law, psychologists must meet the higher ethical standard. If the Ethics Code standard appears to conflict with the requirements of the law, then psychologists make known then commitment to the Ethics Code and take steps to resolve the conflict in a responsible manner. If neither law nor the Ethics Code resolves an issue, psychologists should consider other professional materials[1] and the dictates of their own conscience, as well as seek consultation with others within the field when this is practical.

The procedures for filing, investigating, and resolving complaints of unethical conduct are described in the current Rules and Procedures of the APA Ethics Committee. The actions that APA may take for violations of the Ethics Code

---

[1]Professional materials that are most helpful in this regard are guidelines and standards that have been adopted or endorsed by professional psychological organizations. Such guidelines and standards, whether adopted by the American Psychological Association (APA) or its Divisions, are not enforceable as such by this Ethics Code, but are of educative value to psychologists, courts, and professional bodies. Such materials include, but are not limited to, the APA's *General Guidelines for Providers of Psychological Services*, (1987), *Specialty Guidelines for the Delivery of Services by Clinical Psychologists, Counseling Psychologists, Industrial/Organizational Psychologists, and School Psychologists* (1981), *Guidelines for Computer Based Tests and Interpretations* (1987), *Standards for Educational and Psychological Testing* (1985), *Ethical Principles in the Conduct of Research With Human Participants* (1982), *Guidelines for Ethical Conduct in the Care and Use of Animals* (1986), *Guidelines for Providers of Psychological Services to Ethnic, Linguistic, and Culturally Diverse Populations* (1990), and *Publication Manual of the American Psychological Association* (3rd ed., 1983). Material not adopted by APA as a whole include the APA Division 41 (Forensic Psychology)/American Psychology—Law Society's *Specialty Guidelines for Forensic Psychologists* (1991).

include actions such as reprimand, censure, termination of APA membership, and referral of the matter to other bodies. Complainants who seek remedies such as monetary damages in alleging ethical violations by a psychologist must resort to private negotiation, administrative bodies, or the courts. Actions that violate the Ethics Code may lead to the imposition of sanctions on a psychologist by bodies other than APA, including state psychological associations, other professional groups, psychology boards, other state or federal agencies, and payors for health services. In addition to actions for violation of the Ethics Code, the APA Bylaws provide that APA may take action against a member after his or her conviction of a felony, expulsion or suspension from an affiliated state psychological association, or suspension or loss of licensure.

Preamble

Psychologists work to develop a valid and reliable body of scientific knowledge based on research. They may apply that knowledge to human behavior in a variety of contexts. In doing so, they perform many roles, such as researcher, educator, diagnostician, therapist, supervisor, consultant, administrator, social interventionist, and expert witness. Their goal is to broaden knowledge of behavior and, where appropriate, to apply it pragmatically to improve the condition of both the individual and society. Psychologists respect the central importance of freedom of inquiry and expression in research, teaching, and publication. They also strive to help the public in developing informed judgments and choices concerning human behavior. This Ethics Code provides a common set of values upon which psychologists build their professional and scientific work.

This Code is intended to provide both the general principles and the decision rules to cover most situations encountered by psychologists. It has as its primary goal the welfare and protection of the individuals and groups with whom psychologists work. It is the individual responsibility of each psychologist to aspire to the highest possible standards of conduct. Psychologists respect and protect human and civil rights, and do not knowingly participate in or condone unfair discriminatory practices.

The development of a dynamic set of ethical standards for a psychologist's work-related conduct requires a personal commitment to a lifelong effort to act ethically; to encourage ethical behavior by students, supervisees, employees, and colleagues, as appropriate; and to consult with others, as needed, concerning ethical problems. Each psychologist supplements, but does not violate, the Ethical Code's values and rules on the basis of guidance drawn from personal values, culture, and experience.

General Principles

Principle A: Competence

Psychologists strive to maintain high standards of competence in their work. They recognize the boundaries of their particular competencies and the limitations of their expertise. They provide only those services and use only those techniques for which they are qualified by education, training, or experience. Psychologists are cognizant of the fact that the competencies required in serving, teaching, and/or studying groups of people vary with the distinctive characteristics of those groups. In those areas in which recognized professional standards do not yet exist, psychologists exercise careful judgment and take appropriate precautions to protect the welfare of those with whom they work. They maintain knowledge of relevant scientific and professional information related to the services they render, and they recognize the need for ongoing education. Psychologists make appropriate use of scientific, professional, technical, and administrative resources.

Principle B: Integrity

Psychologists seek to promote integrity in the science, teaching, and practice of psychology. In these activities psychologist are honest, fair, and respectful of others. In describing or reporting their qualifications, services, products, fees, research, or teaching, they do not make statements that are false, misleading, or deceptive. Psychologists strive to be aware of their own belief systems, values, needs, and limitations and the effect of these on their work. To the extent feasible, they attempt to clarify for relevant parties the roles they are performing and to function appropriately in accordance with those roles. Psychologists avoid improper and potentially harmful dual relationships.

Principle C: Professional and Scientific Responsibility

Psychologists uphold professional standards of conduct, clarify their progressional roles and obligations, accept appropriate responsibility for their behavior, and adapt their methods to the needs of different populations. Psychologists consult with, refer to, or cooperate with other professional and institutions to the extent needed to serve the best interests of their patients, clients, or other recipients of their services. Psychologists' moral standards and conduct are personal matters to the same degree as is true for any other person, except as psychologists' conduct may compromise their professional responsibilities or reduce the public's trust in psychology and psychologists. Psychologists are concerned about the ethical compliance of their colleagues' scientific and professional conduct. When appropriate, they consult with colleagues in order to prevent or avoid unethical conduct.

Principle D: Respect for People's Rights and Dignity

Psychologists accord appropriate respect to the fundamental rights, dignity, and worth of all people. They respect the rights of individuals to privacy, confidentiality, self-determination, and autonomy, mindful that legal and other obligations may lead to inconsistency and conflict with the exercise of these rights. Psychologists are aware of cultural, individual, and role differences, including those due to age, gender, race, ethnicity, national origin, religion, sexual orientation, disability, language, and socioeconomic status. Psychologists try to eliminate the effect on their work of biases based on those factors, and they do not knowingly participate in or condone unfair discriminatory practices.

Principle E: Concern for Others' Welfare

Psychologists seek to contribute to the welfare of those with whom they interact professionally. In their professional actions, psychologists weigh the welfare and rights of their patients or clients, students, supervisees, human research participants, and other affected persons, and the welfare of animal subjects of research. When conflicts occur among psychologists' obligations or concerns, they attempt to resolve these conflicts and to perform their roles in a responsible fashion that avoids or minimizes harm. Psychologists are sensitive to real and ascribed differences in power between themselves and others, and they do not exploit or mislead other people during or after professional relationships.

Principle F: Social Responsibility

Psychologists are aware of their professional and scientific responsibilities to the community and the society in which they work and live. They apply and make public their knowledge of psychology in order to contribute to human welfare. Psychologists are concerned about and work to mitigate the causes of human suffering. When undertaking research, they strive to advance human welfare and the science of psychology. Psychologists try to avoid misuse of their work. Psychologists comply with the law and encourage the development of law and social policy that serve the interest of their patients and clients and the public. They are encouraged to contribute a portion of their professional time for little or no personal advantage.

Ethical Standards

1. General Standards

These General Standards are potentially applicable to the professional and scientific activities of all psychologists.

1.01 Applicability of the Ethics Code

The activity of a psychologist subject to the Ethics Code may be reviewed under these Ethical Standards only if the activity is part of his or her work-related functions or the activity is psychological in nature. Personal activities having no connection to or effect on psychological roles are not subject to the Ethics Code.

1.02 Relationship of Ethics and Law

If psychologists' ethical responsibilities conflict with law, psychologists make known their commitment to the Ethics Code and take steps to resolve the conflict in a responsible manner.

1.03 Professional and Scientific Relationship

Psychologists provide diagnostic, therapeutic, teaching, research, supervisory, consultative, or other psychological services only in the context of a defined professional or scientific relationship or role. (See also Standards 2.01, Evaluation, Diagnosis, and Interventions in Professional Context, and 7.02, Forensic Assessments.)

1.04 Boundaries of Competence

(a) Psychologists provide services, teach, and conduct research only within the boundaries of their competence, based on their education, training, supervised experience, or appropriate professional experience.

(b) Psychologists provide services, teach, or conduct research in new areas or involving new techniques only after first undertaking appropriate study, training, supervision, and/or consultation from persons who are competent in those areas or techniques.

(c) In those emerging areas in which generally recognized standards for preparatory training do not yet exist, psychologists nevertheless take reasonable steps to ensure the competence of their work and to protect patients, clients, students, research participants, and others from harm.

1.05 Maintaining Expertise

Psychologists who engage in assessment, therapy, teaching, research, organizational consulting, or other professional activities maintain a reasonable level of awareness of current scientific and professional information in their fields of activity, and undertake ongoing efforts to maintain competence in the skills they use.

1.06 Basis for Scientific and Professional Judgments

Psychologists rely on scientifically and professionally derived knowledge when making scientific or professional judgments or when engaging in scholarly or professional endeavors.

1.07 Describing the Nature and Results of Psychological Services

(a) When psychologists provide assessment, evaluation, treatment, counseling, supervision, teaching, consultation, research, or other psychological services to an individual, a group, or an organization, they provide, using language that is reasonably understandable to the recipient of those services, appropriate information beforehand about the nature of such services and appropriate information later about results and conclusions. (See also Standard 2.09, Explaining Assessment Results.)

(b) If psychologists will be precluded by law or by organizational roles from providing such information to particular individuals or groups, they so inform those individuals or groups at the outset of the service.

1.08 Human Differences

Where differences of age, gender, race, ethnicity, national origin, religion, sexual orientation, disability, language, or socioeconomic status significantly affect psychologists' work concerning particular individuals or groups, psychologists obtain the training, experience, consultation, or supervision necessary to ensure the competence of their services, or they make appropriate referrals.

1.09 Respecting Others

In their work-related activities, psychologists respect the rights of others to hold values, attitudes, and opinions that differ from their own.

1.10 Nondiscrimination

In their work-related activities, psychologist do not engage in unfair discrimination based on age, gender, race, ethnicity, national origin, religion, sexual orientation, disability, socioeconomic status, or any basis proscribed by law.

1.11 Sexual Harassment

(a) Psychologists do not engage in sexual harassment. Sexual harassment is sexual solicitation, physical advances, or verbal or nonverbal conduct that is sexual in nature, that occurs in connection with the psychologist's activities or roles as a psychologist, and that either: (1) is unwelcome, is offensive, or creates a hostile workplace environment, and the psychologist knows or it told this; or (2) is sufficiently severe or intense to be abusive to a reasonable person in the context. Sexual harassment can consist of a single intense or severe act or of multiple persistent or pervasive acts.

(b) Psychologist accord sexual-harassment complainants and respondents dignity and respect. Psychologists do not participate in denying a person academic admittance or advancement, employment, tenure, or promotion, based solely upon their having made, or their being the subject of, sexual-harassment charges. This does not preclude taking action based upon the outcome of such proceedings or consideration of other appropriate information.

1.12 Other Harassment

Psychologists do not knowingly engage in behavior that is harassing or demeaning to persons with whom they interact in their work based on factors such as those persons' age, gender, race, ethnicity, national origin, religion, sexual orientation, disability, language, or socioeconomic status.

1.13 Personal Problems and Conflicts

(a) Psychologists recognize that their personal problems and conflicts may interfere with their effectiveness. Accordingly, they refrain from undertaking an activity when they know or should know that their personal problems are likely to lead to harm to a patient, client, colleague, student, research participant, or other person to whom they may owe a professional or scientific obligation.

(b) In addition, psychologists have an obligation to be alert to signs of, and to obtain assistance for, their personal problems at an early stage, in order to prevent significantly impaired performance.

(c) When psychologists become aware of personal problems that may interfere with their performing work-related duties adequately, they take appropriate measures, such as obtaining professional consultation or assistance, and determine whether they should limit, suspend, or terminate their work-related duties.

1.14 Avoiding Harm

Psychologists take reasonable steps to avoid harming their patients or clients, research participants, students, and others with whom they work, and to minimize harm where it is foreseeable and unavoidable.

1.15 Misuse of Psychologists' Influence

Because psychologists' scientific and professional judgments and actions may affect the lives of others, they are alert to and guard against personal, financial, social, organizational, or political factors that might lead to misuse of their influence.

1.16 Misuse of Psychologists' Work

(a) Psychologists do not participate in activities in which it appears likely that their skills or data will be misused by others, unless corrective mechanisms are available. (See also Standard 7.04, Truthfulness and Candor.)

(b) If psychologists learn of misuse or misrepresentation of their work, they take reasonable steps to correct or minimize the misuse or misrepresentation.

1.17 Multiple Relationships

(a) In many communities and situations, it may not be feasible or reasonable for psychologists to avoid social or other nonprofessional contacts with persons such as patients, clients, students, supervisees, or research participants. Psychologists must always be sensitive to the potential harmful effects of other contacts on their work and on those persons with whom they deal. A psychologist refrains from entering into or promising another personal, scientific, professional, financial, or other relationship with such persons if it appears likely that such a relationship reasonably might impair the psychologist's objectivity or otherwise interfere with the psychologist's effectively performing his or her functions as a psychologist, or might harm or exploit the other party.

(b) Likewise, whenever feasible, a psychologist refrains from taking on professional or scientific obligations when preexisting relationships would create a risk of such harm.

(c) If a psychologist finds that, due to unforeseen factors, a potentially harmful multiple relationship has arisen, the psychologist attempts to resolve it with due regard for the best interests of the affected person and maximal compliance with the Ethics Code.

1.18 Barter (with Patients or Clients)

Psychologists ordinarily refrain from accepting goods, services, or other nonmonetary remuneration from patients or clients in return for psychological services because such arrangements create inherent potential for conflicts, exploitation, and distortion of the professional relationship. A psychologist may participate in bartering *only* if (1) it is not clinically contraindicated, *and* (2) the relationship is not exploitative. (See also Standards 1.17, Multiple Relationships, and 1.25, Fees and Financial Arrangements.)

1.19 Exploitative Relationships

(a) Psychologists do not exploit persons over whom they have supervisory, evaluative, or other authority such as students, supervisees, employees, research participants, and clients or patients. (See also Standards 4.05–4.07 regarding sexual involvement with clients or patients.)

(b) Psychologists do not engage in sexual relationships with students or supervisees in training over whom the psychologist has evaluative or direct authority, because such relationships are so likely to impair judgment or be exploitative.

1.20 Consultations and Referrals

(a) Psychologists arrange for appropriate consultations and referrals based principally on the best interests of their patients or clients, with appropriate consent, and subject together relevant considerations, including applicable law and contractual obligations. (See also Standards 5.01, Discussing the Limits of Confidentiality, and 5.06, Consultations.)

(b) When indicated and professionally appropriate, psychologists cooperate with other professionals in order to serve their patients or clients effectively and appropriately.

(c) Psychologists' referral practices are consistent with law.

1.21 Third-Party Requests for Services

(a) When a psychologist agrees to provide services to a person or entity at the request of a third party, the psychologist clarifies to the extent feasible, at the outset of the service, the nature of the relationship with each party. This clarification includes the role of the psychologist (such as therapist, organizational consultant, diagnostician, or expert witness), the probable uses of the services provided or the information obtained, and the fact that there may be limits to confidentiality.

(b) If there is a foreseeable risk of the psychologist's being called upon to perform conflicting roles because of the involvement of a third party, the psychologist clarifies the nature and direction of his or her responsibilities, keeps all parties appropriately informed as matters develop, and resolves the situation in accordance with this Ethics Code.

1.22 Delegation to and Supervision of Subordinates

(a) Psychologists delegate to their employees, supervisees, and research assistants only those responsibilities that such persons can reasonably be expected to perform competently, on the basis of their education, training, or experience, either independently or with the level of supervision being provided.

(b) Psychologists provide proper training and supervision to their employees or supervisees and take reasonable steps to see that such persons perform services responsibly, competently, and ethically.

(c) If institutional policies, procedures, or practices prevent fulfillment of this obligation, psychologists attempt to modify their role or to correct the situation to the extent feasible.

1.23 Documentation of Professional and Scientific Work

(a) Psychologists appropriately document their professional and scientific work in order to facilitate provision of services later by them or by other professionals, to ensure accountability, and to meet other requirements of institutions or the law.

(b) When psychologists have reason to believe that records of their professional services will be used in legal proceedings involving recipients of or participants in their work, they have a responsibility to create and maintain documentation in the kind of detail and quality that would be consistent with reasonable scrutiny in an adjudicative forum. (See also Standard 7.01, Professionalism, under Forensic Activities.)

1.24 Records and Data

Psychologists create, maintain, disseminate, store, retain, and dispose of records and data relating to their research, practice, and other work in accordance with law and in a manner that permits compliance with the requirements of this Ethics Code. (See also Standard 5.04, Maintenance of Records.)

1.25 Fees and Financial Arrangements

(a) As early as is feasible in a professional or scientific relationship, the psychologist and the patient, client, or other appropriate recipient of psychological services reach an agreement specifying the compensation and the billing arrangements.

(b) Psychologists do not exploit recipients of services or payors with respect to fees.

(c) Psychologists' fee practices are consistent with law.

(d) Psychologists do not misrepresent their fees.

(e) If limitations to services can be anticipated because of limitations in financing, this is discussed with the patient, client, or other appropriate recipient of services as early as is feasible. (See also Standard 4.08, Interruption of Services.)

(f) If the patient, client, or other recipient of services does not pay for services as agreed, and if the psychologist wishes to sue collection agencies or legal measures to collect the fees, the psychologist first informs the person that such measures will be taken and provides that person an opportunity to make prompt payment. (See also Standard 5.11, Withholding Records for Nonpayment.)

1.26 Accuracy in Reports to Payors and Funding Sources

In their reports to payors for services or sources of research funding, psychologists accurately state the nature of the research or service provided, the fees or charges, and where applicable, the identity of the provider, the findings, and the diagnosis. (See also Standard 5.05, Disclosures.)

1.27 Referrals and Fees

When a psychologist pays, receives payment from, or divides fees with another professional other than in an employer-employee relationship, the payment to each is based on the services (clinical, consultative, administrative, or other) provided and is not based on the referral itself.

2. Evaluation, Assessment, or Intervention

2.01 Evaluation, Diagnosis, and Interventions in Professional Context

(a) Psychologists perform evaluations, diagnostic services, or interventions only within the context of a defined professional relationship. (See also Standard 1.03, Professional and Scientific Relationship.)

(b) Psychologists' assessments, recommendations, reports, and psychological diagnostic or evaluative statements are based on information and techniques (including personal interviews of the individual when appropriate) sufficient to provide appropriate substantiation for their findings. (See also Standard 7.02, Forensic Assessments.)

2.02 Competence and Appropriate Use of Assessments and Interventions

(a) Psychologists who develop, administer, score, interpret, or use psychological assessment techniques, interviews, tests, or instruments do so in a manner and for purposes that are appropriate in light of the research on or evidence of the usefulness and proper application of the techniques.

(b) Psychologists refrain from misuse of assessment techniques, interventions, results, and interpretations and take reasonable steps to prevent others from misusing the information these techniques provide. This includes refraining from releasing raw test results or raw data to persons, other than to patients or clients as appropriate, who are not qualified to use such information. (See also Standards 1.02, Relationship of Ethics and Law, and 1.04, Boundaries of Competence.)

2.03 Test Construction

Psychologists who develop and conduct research with tests and other assessment techniques use scientific procedures and current professional knowledge for test design, standardization, validation, reduction or elimination of bias, and recommendations for use.

2.04 Use of Assessment in General and With Special Populations

(a) Psychologists who perform interventions or administer, score, interpret, or use assessment techniques are familiar with the reliability, validation, and related standardization or outcome studies of, and proper applications and uses of, the techniques they use.

(b) Psychologists recognize limits to the certainty with which diagnoses, judgments, or predictions can be made about individuals.

(c) Psychologists attempt to identify situations in which particular interventions or assessment techniques or norms may not be applicable or may required adjustment in administration or interpretation because of factors such as individuals' gender, age, race, ethnicity, national origin, religion, sexual orientation, disability, language, or socioeconomic status.

2.05 Interpreting Assessment Results

When interpreting assessment results, including automated interpretations, psychologists take into account the various test factors and characteristics of the person being assessed that might affect psychologists' judgments or reduce the accuracy of their interpretations. They indicate any significant reservations they have about the accuracy or limitations of their interpretations.

2.06 Unqualified Persons

Psychologists do not promote the use of psychological assessment techniques by unqualified persons. (See also Standard 1.22, Delegation to and Supervision of Subordinates.)

2.07 Obsolete Tests and Outdated Test Results

(a) Psychologists do not base their assessment or intervention decisions or recommendations on data or test results that are outdated for the current purpose.

(b) Similarly, psychologists do not base such decisions or recommendations on tests and measures that are obsolete and not useful for the current purpose.

2.08 Test Scoring and Interpretation Services

(a) Psychologists who offer assessment or scoring procedures to other professionals accurately describe the purpose, norms, validity, reliability, and applications of the procedures and any special qualifications applicable to their use.

(b) Psychologists select scoring and interpretation services (including automated services) on the basis of evidence of the validity of the program and procedures as well as on other appropriate considerations.

(c) Psychologist retain appropriate responsibility for the appropriate application, interpretation, and use of assessment instruments, whether they score and interpret such tests themselves or use automated or other services.

2.09 Explaining Assessment Results

Unless the nature of the relationship is clearly explained to the person being assessed in advance and precludes provision of an explanation of results (such as in some organizational consulting, preemployment or security screenings, and forensic evaluations), psychologists ensure than an explanation of the results is provided using language that is reasonably understandable to the person assessed or to another legally authorized person on behalf of the client. Regardless of whether the scoring and interpretation are done by the psychologist, by assistants, or by automated or other outside services, psychologist take reasonable steps to ensure that appropriate explanations of results are given.

2.10 Maintaining Test Security

Psychologists make reasonable efforts to maintain the integrity and security of tests and other assessment techniques consistent with law, contractual obligations, and in a manner that permits compliance with the requirements of this Ethics Code. (See also Standard 1.02, Relationship of Ethics and Law.)

3. <u>Advertising and Other Public Statements</u>

3.01 Definition of Public Statements

Psychologists comply with this Ethics Code in public statements relating to their professional services, products, or publications or to the field of psychology. Public statements include but are not limited to paid or unpaid advertising, brochures, printed matter, directory listings, personal resumes or curricula vitae, interviews or comments for use in media, statements in legal proceedings, lectures and public oral presentations, and published materials.

3.02 Statements by Others

(a) Psychologists who engage others to create or place public statements that promote their professional practice, products, or activities retain professional responsibility for such statements.

(b) In addition, psychologists make reasonable efforts to prevent others whom they do not control (such as employers, publishers, sponsors, organizational clients, and representatives of the print or broadcast media) from making deceptive statements concerning psychologists' practice or professional or scientific activities.

(c) If psychologists learn of deceptive statements about their work made by others, psychologists make reasonable efforts to correct such statements.

(d) Psychologist do not compensate employees of press, radio, television, or other communication media in return for publicity in a news item.

(e) A paid advertisement relating to the psychologist's activities must be identified as such, unless it is already apparent from the context.

3.03 Avoidance of False or Deceptive Statements

(a) Psychologists do not make public statements that are false, deceptive, misleading, or fraudulent, either because of what they state, convey, or suggest or because of what they omit, concerning their research, practice, or other work activities or those of persons or organizations with which they are affiliated. As examples (and not in limitation) of this standard, psychologists do not make false or deceptive statements concerning (1) their training, experience, or competence; (2) their academic degrees; (3) their credentials; (4) their institutional or association affiliations; (5) their services; (6) the scientific or clinical basis for, or results or degree of success of, their services; (7) their fees; or (8) their publications or research findings. (See also Standards 6.15, Deception in Research, and 6.18, Providing Participants With Information About the Study.)

(b) Psychologists claim as creditional for their psychological work, only degrees that (1) were earned from a regionally accredited educational institution or (2) were the basis for psychology licensure by the state in which they practice.

3.04 Media Presentations

When psychologists provide advice or comment by means of public lectures, demonstrations, radio or television programs, prerecorded tapes, printed articles, mailed material, or other media, they take reasonable precautions to ensure that (1) the statements are based on appropriate psychological literature and practice, (2) the statements are otherwise consistent with this Ethics Code, and (3) the recipients of the information are not encouraged to infer that a relationship has been established with them personally.

3.05 Testimonials

Psychologists do not solicit testimonials from current psychotherapy clients or patients or other persons who because of their particular circumstances are vulnerable to undue influence.

3.06 In-Person Solicitation

Psychologists do not engage, directly or through agents, in uninvited in-person solicitation of business from actual or potential psychotherapy patients or clients or other persons who because of their particular circumstances are vulnerable to undue influence. However, this does not preclude attempting to implement appropriate collateral contacts with significant others for the purpose of benefiting an already engaged therapy patient.

4. Therapy

4.01 Structuring the Relationship

(a) Psychologists discuss with clients or patients as early as is feasible in the therapeutic relationship appropriate issues, such as the nature and anticipated course of therapy, fees, and confidentiality. (See also Standards 1.25, Fees and Financial Arrangements, and 5.01, Discussing the Limits of Confidentiality.)

(b) When the psychologist's work with clients or patients will be supervised, the above discussion includes that fact, and the name of the supervisor, when the supervisor has legal responsibility for the case.

(c) When the therapist is a student intern, the client or patient is informed of that fact.

(d) Psychologists make reasonable efforts to answer patients' questions and to avoid apparent misunderstandings about therapy. Whenever possible, psychologists provide oral and/or written information, using language that is reasonably understandable to the patient or client.

4.02 Informed Consent to Therapy

(a) Psychologists obtain appropriate informed consent to therapy or related procedures, using language that is reasonably understandable to participants. The content of informed consent will vary depending on many circumstances; however, informed consent generally implies that the person (1) has the capacity to consent, (2) has been informed of significant information concerning the procedure, (3) has freely and without undue influence expressed consent, and (4) consent has been appropriately documented.

(b) When persons are legally incapable of giving informed consent, psychologists obtain informed permission from a legally authorized person, if such substitute consent is permitted by law.

(c) In addition, psychologists (1) inform those persons who are legally incapable of giving informed consent about the proposed interventions in a manner commensurate with the persons' psychological capacities, (2) seek their assent to those interventions, and (3) consider such persons' preferences and best interests.

4.03 Couple and Family Relationships

(a) When a psychologist agrees to provide services to several persons who have a relationship (such as husband and wife or parents and children), the psychologist attempts to clarify at the outset (1) which of the individuals are patients or clients and (2) the relationship the psychologist will have with each person. This clarification includes the role of the psychologist and the probable uses of the services provided or the information obtained. (See also Standard 5.01, Discussing the Limits of Confidentiality.)

(b) As soon as it becomes apparent that the psychologist may be called on to perform potentially conflicting roles (such as marital counselor to husband and wife, and then witness for one party in a divorce proceeding), the psychologist attempts to clarify and adjust, or withdraw from roles appropriately. (See also Standard 7.03, Clarification of Role, under Forensic Activities.)

4.04 Providing Mental Health Services to Those Served by Others

In deciding whether to offer or provide services to those already receiving mental health services elsewhere, psychologists carefully consider the treatment issues and the potential patient's or client's welfare. The psychologist discusses these issues with the patient or client, or another legally authorized person on behalf of the client, in order to minimize the risk of confusion and conflict, consults with the other service providers when appropriate, and proceeds with caution and sensitivity to the therapeutic issues.

4.05 Sexual Intimacies With Current Patients or Clients

Psychologists do not engage in sexual intimacies with current patients or clients.

4.06 Therapy With Former Sexual Partners

Psychologists do not accept as therapy patients or clients persons with whom they have engaged in sexual intimacies.

4.07 Sexual Intimacies With Former Therapy Patients

(a) Psychologists do not engage in sexual intimacies with a former therapy patient or client for at least two years after cessation or termination of professional services.

(b) Because sexual intimacies with a former therapy patient or client are so frequently harmful to the patient or client, and because such intimacies undermine public confidence in the psychology profession and thereby deter the public's use of needed services, psychologists do not engage in sexual intimacies with former therapy patients and clients even after a two-year interval except in the most unusual circumstances. The psychologist who engages in such activity after the two years following cessation or termination of treatment bears the burden of demonstrating that there has been no exploitation, in light of all relevant factors, including (1) the amount of time that has passed since therapy terminated, (2) the nature and duration of the therapy, (3) the circumstances of termination, (4) the patient's or client's personal history, (5) the patient's or client's current mental status, (6) the likelihood of adverse impact on the patient or client and others, and (7) any statements or actions made by the therapist during the course of therapy suggesting or inviting the possibility of a post-termination sexual or romantic relationship with the patient or client. (See also Standard 1.17, Multiple Relationships.)

4.08 Interruption of Services

(a) Psychologists make reasonable efforts to plan for facilitating care in the event that psychological services are interrupted by factors such as the psychologist's illness, death, unavailability, or relocation or by the client's relocation or financial limitations. (See also Standard 5.09, Preserving Records and Data.)

(b) When entering into employment or contractual relationships, psychologists provide for orderly and appropriate resolution of responsibility for patient or client care in the event that the employment or contractual relationship ends, with paramount consideration given to the welfare of the patient or client.

4.09 Terminating the Professional Relationship

(a) Psychologists do not abandon patients or clients. (See also Standard 1.25e, under Fees and Financial Arrangements.)

(b) Psychologists terminate a professional relationship when it becomes reasonably clear that the patient or client no longer needs the service, is not benefiting, or is being harmed by continued service.

(c) Prior to termination for whatever reason, except where precluded by the patient's or client's conduct, the psychologist discusses the patient's or client's views and needs, provides appropriate pretermination counseling, suggests alternative service providers as appropriate, and takes other reasonable steps to facilitate transfer of responsibility to another provider if the patient or client needs one immediately.

5. Privacy and Confidentiality

These Standards are potentially applicable to the professional and scientific activities of all psychologists.

5.01 Discussing the Limits of Confidentiality

(a) Psychologists discuss with persons and organizations with whom they establish a scientific or professional relationship (including, to the extent feasible, minors and their legal representatives) (1) the relevant limitations on confidentiality, including limitations where applicable in group, marital, and family therapy or in organizational consulting, and (2) the foreseeable uses of the information generated through their services.

(b) Unless it is not feasible or is contraindicated, the discussion of confidentiality occurs at the outset of the relationship and thereafter as new circumstances may warrant.

(c) Permission for electronic recording of interviews is secured from clients and patients.

5.02 Maintaining Confidentiality

Psychologists have a primary obligation and take reasonable precautions to respect the confidentiality rights of those with whom they work or consult, recognizing that confidentiality may be established by law, institutional rules, or professional or scientific relationships. (See also Standard 6.26, Professional Reviewers.)

5.03 Minimizing Intrusions on Privacy

(a) In order to minimize intrusions on privacy, psychologists include in written and oral reports, consultations, and the like, only information germane to the purpose for which the communication is made.

(b) Psychologists discuss confidential information obtained in clinical or consulting relationships, or evaluative data concerning patients, individual or organizational clients, students, research participants, supervisees, and employees, only for appropriate scientific or professional purposes and only with persons clearly concerned with such matters.

5.04 Maintenance of Records

Psychologists maintain appropriate confidentiality in creating, storing, accessing, transferring, and disposing of records under their control, whether these are written, automated, or in any other medium. Psychologists maintain and dispose of records in accordance with law and in a manner that permits compliance with the requirements of this Ethics Code.

5.05 Disclosures

(a) Psychologists disclose confidential information without the consent of the individual only as mandated by law, or where permitted by law for a valid purpose, such as (1) to provide needed professional services to the patient or the individual or organizational client, (2) to obtain appropriate professional consultations, (3) to protect the patient or client or others from harm, or (4) to obtain payment for services, in which instance disclosure is limited to the minimum that is necessary to achieve the purpose.

(b) Psychologists also may disclose confidential information with the appropriate consent of the patient or the individual or organizational client (or of another legally authorized person on behalf of the patient or client), unless prohibited by law

5.06 Consultations

When consulting with colleagues, (1) psychologists do not share confidential information that reasonably could lead to the identification of a patient, client, research participant, or other person or organization with whom they have a confidential relationship unless they have obtained the prior consent of the person or organization or the disclosure cannot be avoided, and (2) they share information only to the extent necessary to achieve the purposes of the consultation. (See also Standard 5.02, Maintaining Confidentiality.)

5.07 Confidential Information in Databases

(a) If confidential information concerning recipients of psychological services is to be entered into databases or systems of records available to persons whose access has not been consented to by the recipient, then psychologists use coding or other techniques to avoid the inclusion of personal identifiers.

(b) If a research protocol approved by an institutional review board or similar body requires the inclusion of personal identifiers, such identifiers are deleted before the information is made accessible to persons other than those of whom the subject was advised.

(c) If such deletion is not feasible, then before psychologists transfer such data to others or review such data collected by others, they take reasonable steps to determine that appropriate consent of personally identifiable individuals has been obtained.

5.08 Use of Confidential Information
for Didactic or Other Purposes

(a) Psychologists do not disclose in their writings, lectures, or other public media, confidential, personally identifiable information concerning their patients, individual or organizational clients, students, research participants, or other recipients of their services that they obtained during the course of their work, unless the person or organization has consented in writing or unless there is other ethical or legal authorization for doing so.

(b) Ordinarily, in such scientific and professional presentations, psychologists disguise confidential information concerning such persons or organizations so that they are not individually identifiable to others and so that discussions do not cause harm to subjects who might identify themselves.

5.09 Preserving Records and Data

A psychologist makes plans in advance so that confidentiality of records and data is protected in the event of the psychologist's death, incapacity, or withdrawal from the position or practice.

5.10 Ownership of Records and Data

Recognizing that ownership of records and data is governed by legal principles, psychologists take reasonable and lawful steps so that records and data remain available to the extent needed to serve the best interests of patients, individual or organizational clients, research participants, or appropriate others.

5.11 Withholding Records for Nonpayment

Psychologists may not withhold records under their control that are requested and imminently needed for a patient's or client's treatment solely because payment has not been received, except as otherwise provided by law.

6. Teaching, Training Supervision, Research, and Publishing

6.01 Design of Education and Training Programs

Psychologists who are responsible for education and training programs seek to ensure that the programs are competently designed, provide the proper experiences, and meet the requirements for licensure, certification, or other goals for which claims are made by the program.

6.02 Descriptions of Education and Training Programs

(a) Psychologists responsible for education and training programs seek to ensure that there is a current and accurate description of the program content, training goals and objectives, and requirements that must be met for satisfactory completion of the program. This information must be made readily available to all interested parties.

(b) Psychologists seek to ensure that statements concerning their course outlines are accurate and not misleading, particularly regarding the subject matter to be covered, bases for evaluating progress, and the nature of course experiences. (See also Standard 3.03, Avoidance of False or Deceptive Statements.)

(c) To the degree to which they exercise control, psychologists responsible for announcements, catalogs, brochures, or advertisements describing workshops, seminars, or other non-degree-granting educational programs ensure that they accurately describe the audience for which the program is intended, the educational objectives, the presenters, and the fees involved.

6.03 Accuracy and Objectivity in Teaching

(a) When engaged in teaching or training, psychologists present psychological information accurately and with a reasonable degree of objectivity.

(b) When engaged in teaching or training, psychologists recognize the power they hold over students or supervisees and therefore make reasonable efforts to avoid engaging in conduct that is personally demeaning to students or supervisees. (See also Standards 1.09, Respecting Others, and 1.12, Other Harassment.)

6.04 Limitation on Teaching

Psychologists do not teach the use of techniques or procedures that require specialized training, licensure, or expertise, including but not limited to hypnosis, biofeedback, and projective techniques, to individuals who lack the prerequisite training, legal scope of practice, or expertise.

6.05 Assessing Student and Supervisee Performance

(a) In academic and supervisory relationships, psychologists establish an appropriate process for providing feedback to students and supervisees.

(b) Psychologists evaluate students and supervisees on the basis of their actual performance on relevant and established program requirements.

6.06 Planning Research

(a) Psychologists design, conduct, and report research in accordance with recognized standards of scientific competence and ethical research.

(b) Psychologists plan their research so as to minimize the possibility that results will be misleading.

(c) In planning research, psychologists consider its ethical acceptability under the Ethics Code. If an ethical issue is unclear, psychologists seek to resolve the issue through consultation with institutional review boards, animal care and use committees, peer consultations, or other proper mechanisms.

(d) Psychologists take reasonable steps to implement appropriate protections for the rights and welfare of human participants, other persons affected by the research, and the welfare of animal subjects.

6.07 Responsibility

(a) Psychologists conduct research competently and with due concern for the dignity and welfare of the participants.

(b) Psychologists are responsible for the ethical conduct of research conducted by them or by others under their supervision or control.

(c) Researchers and assistants are permitted to perform only those tasks for which they are appropriately trained and prepared.

(d) As part of the process of development and implementation of research projects, psychologists consult those with expertise concerning any special population under investigation or most likely to be affected.

6.08 Compliance With Law and Standards

Psychologists plan and conduct research in a manner consistent with federal and state law and regulations, as well as professional standards governing the conduct of research, and particularly those standards governing research with human participants and animal subjects.

6.09 Institutional Approval

Psychologists obtain from host institutions or organizations appropriate approval prior to conducting research, and they provide accurate information about their research proposals. They conduct the research in accordance with the approved protocol.

6.10 Research Responsibilities

Prior to conducting research (except research involving only anonymous surveys, naturalistic observations, or similar research), psychologists enter into an agreement with participants that clarifies the nature of the research and the responsibilities of each party.

6.11 Informed Consent to Research

(a) Psychologists use language that is reasonably understandable to research participants in obtaining their appropriate informed consent (except as provided in Standard 6.12, Dispensing With Informed Consent). Such informed consent is appropriately documented.

(b) Using language that is reasonably understandable to participants, psychologists inform participants of the nature of the research; they inform participants that they are free to participate or to decline to participate or to withdraw from the research; they explain the foreseeable consequences of declining or withdrawing; they inform participants of significant factors that may be expected to influence their willingness to participate (such as risks, discomfort, adverse effects, or limitations on confidentiality, except as provided in Standard 6.15, Deception in Research); and they explain other aspects about which the prospective participants inquire.

(c) When psychologists conduct research with individuals such as students or subordinates, psychologists take special care to protect the prospective participants from adverse consequences of declining or withdrawing from participation.

(d) When research participation is a course requirement or opportunity for extra credit, the prospective participant is given the choice of equitable alternative activities.

(e) For persons who are legally incapable of giving informed consent, psychologists nevertheless (1) provide an appropriate explanation, (2) obtain the participant's assent, and (3) obtain appropriate permission from a legally authorized person, if such substitute consent is permitted by law.

6.12 Dispensing With Informed Consent

Before determining that planned research (such as research involving only anonymous questionnaires, naturalistic observations, or certain kinds of archival research) does not require the informed consent of research participants, psychologists consider applicable regulations and institutional review board requirements, and they consult with colleagues as appropriate.

6.13 Informed Consent in Research Filming or Recording

Psychologists obtain informed consent from research participants prior to filming or recording them in any form, unless the research involves simply naturalistic observations in public places and it is not anticipated that the recording will be used in a manner that could cause personal identification or harm.

6.14 Offering Inducements for Research Participants

(a) In offering professional services as an inducement to obtain research participants, psychologists make clear the nature of the services, as well as the risks, obligations, and limitations. (See also Standard 1.18 Barter [With Patients or Clients].)

(b) Psychologists do not offer excessive or inappropriate financial or other inducements to obtain research participants, particularly when it might tend to coerce participation.

6.15 Deception in Research

(a) Psychologists do not conduct a study involving deception unless they have determined that the use of deceptive thickness is justified by the study's prospective scientific, educational, or applied value and that equally effective alternative procedures that do not use deception are not feasible.

(b) Psychologists never deceive research participants about significant aspects that would affect their willingness to participate, such as physical risks, discomfort, or unpleasant emotional experiences.

(c) Any other deception that is an integral feature of the design and conduct of an experiment must be explained to participants as early as is feasible, preferably at the conclusion of their participation, but no later than at the conclusion of the research. (See also Standard 6.18, Providing Participants With Information About the Study.)

6.16 Sharing and Utilizing Data

Psychologists inform research participants of their anticipated sharing or further use of personally identifiable research data and of the possibility of unanticipated future uses.

6.17 Minimizing Invasiveness

In conducting research, psychologists interfere with the participants or milieu from which data are collected only in a manner that is warranted by an appropriate research design and that is consistent with psychologists' roles as scientific investigators.

6.18 Providing Participants With Information about the Study

(a) Psychologists provide a prompt opportunity for participants to obtain appropriate information about the nature, results, and conclusions of the research, and psychologist attempt to correct any misconceptions that participants may have.

(b) If scientific or humane values justify delaying or withholding this information, psychologists take reasonable measures to reduce the risk of harm.

6.19 Honoring Commitments

Psychologists take reasonable measures to honor all commitments they have made to research participants.

6.20 Care and Use of Animals in Research

(a) Psychologists who conduct research involving animals treat them humanely.

(b) Psychologists acquire, care for, use, and dispose of animals in compliance with current federal, state, and local laws and regulations, and with professional standards.

(c) Psychologists trained in research methods and experienced in the care of laboratory animals supervise all procedures involving animals and are responsible for ensuring appropriate consideration of their comfort, health, and humane treatment.

(d) Psychologists ensure that all individuals using animals under their supervision have received instruction in research methods and in the care, maintenance, and handling of the species being used, to the extent appropriate to their role.

(e) Responsibilities and activities of individuals assisting in a research project are consistent with their respective competencies.

(f) Psychologists make reasonable efforts to minimize the discomfort, infection, illness, and pain of animal subjects.

(g) A procedure subjecting animals to pain, stress, or privation is used only when an alternative procedure is unavailable and the goal is justified by its prospective scientific, educational, or applied value.

(h) Surgical procedures are performed under appropriate anesthesia; techniques to avoid infection and minimize pain are followed during and after surgery.

(i) When it is appropriate that the animal's life be terminated, it is done rapidly, with an effort to minimize pain, and in accordance with accepted procedures.

6.21 Reporting of Results

(a) Psychologists do not fabricate data or falsify results in their publications.

(b) If psychologists discover significant errors in their published data, they take reasonable steps to correct such errors in a correction, retraction, erratum, or other appropriate publication means.

6.22 Plagiarism

Psychologists do not present substantial portions or elements of another's work or data as their own, even if the other work or data source is cited occasionally.

6.23 Publication Credit

(a) Psychologists take responsibility and credit, including authorship credit, only for work they have actually performed or to which they have contributed.

(b) Principal authorship and other publication credits accurately reflect the relative scientific or professional contributions of the individuals involved, regardless of their relative status. Mere possession of an institutional position, such as Department Chair, does not justify authorship credit. Minor contributions to the research or to the writing for publications are appropriately acknowledged, such as in footnotes or in an introductory statement.

(c) A student is usually listed as principal author on any multiple-authored article that is substantially based on the student's dissertation or thesis.

6.24 Duplicate Publication of Data

Psychologists do not publish, as original data, data that have been previously published. This does not preclude republishing data when they are accompanied by proper acknowledgment.

6.25 Sharing Data

After research results are published, psychologists do not withhold the data on which their conclusions are based from other competent professionals who seek to verify the substantive claims through reanalysis and who intend to use such data only for that purpose, provided that the confidentiality of the participants can be protected and unless legal rights concerning proprietary data preclude their release.

6.26 Professional Reviewers

Psychologists who review material submitted for publication, grant, or other research proposal review respect the confidentiality of and the proprietary rights in such information of those who submitted it.

7. Forensic Activities

7.01 Professionalism

Psychologists who perform forensic functions, such as assessments, interviews, consultations, reports, or expert testimony, must comply with all other provisions of this Ethics Code to the extent that they apply to such activities. In addition, psychologists base their forensic work on appropriate knowledge of and competence in the areas underlying such work, including specialized knowledge concerning special populations. (See also Standards 1.06, Basis for Scientific and Professional Judgments; 1.08, Human Differences, 1.15, Misuse of Psychologists' Influence; and 1.23, Documentation of Professional and Scientific Work.)

7.02 Forensic Assessments

(a) Psychologists' forensic assessments, recommendations, and reports are based on information and techniques (including personal interviews of the individual, when appropriate) sufficient to provide appropriate substantiation for their findings. (See also Standards 1.03, Professional and Scientific Relationship; 1.23, Documentation of Professional and Scientific Work; 2.01, Evaluation, Diagnosis, and Interventions in Professional Context; and 2.05, Interpreting Assessment Results.)

(b) Except as noted in (c), below, psychologists provide written or oral forensic reports or testimony of the psychological characteristics of an individual only after they have conducted an examination of the individual adequate to support their statements or conclusions.

(c) When, despite reasonable efforts, such as examination is not feasible, psychologists clarify the impact of their limited information on the reliability and validity of their reports and testimony, and they appropriately limit the nature and extent of their conclusions or recommendations.

7.03 Clarification of Role

In most circumstances, psychologists avoid performing multiple and potentially conflicting roles in forensic matters. When psychologists may be called on to serve in more than one role in a legal proceeding—for example, as consultant or expert for one party or for the court and as a fact witness—they clarify role expectations and the extent of confidentiality in advance to the extent feasible, and thereafter as changes occur, in order to avoid compromising their professional judgment and objectivity and in order to avoid misleading others regarding their role.

7.04 Truthfulness and Candor

(a) In forensic testimony and reports, psychologists testify truthfully, honestly, and candidly and, consistent with applicable legal procedures, describe fairly the basis for their testimony and conclusions.

(b) Whenever necessary to avoid misleading, psychologists acknowledge the limits of their data or conclusions.

7.05 Prior Relationships

A prior professional relationship with a party does not preclude psychologists from testifying as fact witnesses or from testifying to their services to the extent permitted by applicable law. Psychologists appropriately take into account ways in which the prior relationship might affect their professional objectivity or opinions and disclose the potential conflict to the relevant parties.

7.06 Compliance With Law and Rules

In performing forensic roles, psychologists are reasonably familiar with the rules governing their roles. Psychologists are aware of the occasionally competing demands placed upon them by these principles and the requirements of the court system, and attempt to resolve these conflicts by making known their commitment to this Ethics Code and taking steps to resolve the conflict in a responsible manner. (See also Standard 1.02, Relationship of Ethics and Law.)

8. Resolving Ethical Issues

8.01 Familiarity With Ethics Code

Psychologists have an obligation to be familiar with this Ethics Code, other applicable ethics codes, and their application to psychologists' work. Lack of awareness or misunderstanding of an ethical standard is not itself a defense to a charge of unethical conduct.

8.02 Confronting Ethical Issues

When a psychologist is uncertain whether a particular situation or course of action would violate this Ethics Code, the psychologist ordinarily consults with other psychologists knowledgeable about ethical issues, with state or national psychology ethics committees, or with other appropriate authorities in order to choose a proper response.

8.03 Conflicts Between Ethics and Organizational Demands

If the demands of an organization with which psychologists are affiliated conflict with this Ethics Code, psychologists clarify the nature of the conflict, make known their commitment to the Ethics Code, and to the extent feasible, seek to resolve the conflict in a way that permits the fullest adherence to the Ethics Code.

8.04 Informal Resolution of Ethical Violations

When psychologists believe that there may have been an ethical volition by another psychologist, they attempt to resolve the issue by bringing it to the attention of that individual if an informal resolution appears appropriate and the intervention does not violate any confidentiality rights that may be involved.

8.05 Reporting Ethical Violations

If an apparent ethical violation is not appropriate for informal resolution under Standard 8.04, or is not resolved properly in that fashion, psychologists take further action appropriate to the situation, unless such action conflicts with confidentiality rights in ways that cannot be resolved. Such action might include referral to state or national committees on professional ethics or to state licensing boards.

8.06 Cooperating With Ethics Committees

Psychologists cooperate in ethics investigations, proceedings, and resulting requirements of the APA or any affiliated state psychological association to which they belong. In doing so, they make reasonable efforts to resolve any issues as to confidentiality. Failure to cooperate is itself an ethics violation.

8.07 Improper Complaints

Psychologists do not file or encourage the filing of ethics complaints that are frivolous and are intended to harm the respondent rather than to protect the public.

APPENDIX B

Guidelines for Providers of Psychological Services to Ethnic, Linguistic, and Culturally Diverse Populations

Introduction

There is increasing motivation among psychologists to understand culture and ethnicity factors in order to provide psychological services. This increased motivation for improving quality of psychological services to ethnic and culturally diverse populations is attributable, in part, to the growing political and social presence of diverse cultural groups, both within APA and in the larger society. New sets of values, beliefs, and cultural expectations have been introduced into educational, political, business, and health care systems by the physical presence of these groups. The issues of language and culture do impact on the provision of appropriate psychological services.

Psychological service providers need a sociocultural framework to consider diversity of values, interactional styles, and cultural expectations in a systematic fashion. They need knowledge and skills for multicultural assessment and intervention, including abilities to

- recognize cultural diversity;
- understand the role that culture and ethnicity/race play in the socio-psychological and economic development of ethnic and culturally diverse populations;
- understand that socioeconomic and political factors significantly impact the psychosocial, political, and economic development of ethnic and culturally diverse groups;

These guidelines were published by the APA Office of Ethnic Minority Affairs in July 1991. Copyright 1991 by the American Psychological Association. They are reprinted here for the general information of the membership.

Correspondence concerning this article should be addressed to L. Philip Guzman, American Psychological Association, 750 First Street NE, Washington, DC 20002-4242.

- help clients to understand/maintain/resolve their own sociocultural identification; and
- understand the interaction of culture, gender, and sexual orientation on behavior and needs.

Likewise, there is a need to develop a conceptual framework that would enable psychologists to organize, access, and accurately assess the value and utility of existing and future research involving ethnic and culturally diverse populations.

Research has addressed issues regarding responsiveness of psychological services to the needs of ethnic minority populations. The focus of mental health research issues has included

- the impact of ethnic/racial similarity in the counseling process (Acosta & Sheehan, 1976; Atkinson, 1983; Parham & Helms, 1981);
- minority utilization of mental health services (Cheung & Snowden, 1990; Everett, Proctor, & Cartmell, 1983; Rosado, 1986; Snowden & Cheung, 1990);
- relative effectiveness of directed versus nondirected styles of therapy. (Acosta, Yamamoto, & Evans, 1982; Dauphinais, Dauphinais, & Rowe, 1981; Lorion, 1974);
- the role of cultural values in treatment (Juarez, 1985; Padilla & Ruiz, 1973; Padilla, Ruiz, & Alvarez, 1975; Sue & Sue, 1987);
- appropriate counseling and therapy models (Comas-Diaz & Griffith, 1988; McGoldrick, Pearce, & Giordano, 1982; Nishio & Bilmes, 1987);
- competency in skills for working with specific ethnic populations (Malgady, Rogler, & Costantino, 1987; Root, 1985; Zuniga, 1988).

The APA's Board of Ethnic Minority Affairs (BEMA) established a Task Force on the Delivery of Services to Ethnic Minority Populations in 1988 in response to the increased awareness about psychological service needs associated with ethnic and cultural diversity. The populations of concern include, but are not limited to, the following groups: American Indians/Alaska Natives, Asian Americans/Pacific Islanders, Blacks/African Americans, and Hispanics/Latinos. For example, the populations also include recently arrived refugee and immigrant groups and established U.S. subcultures such as Amish, Hasidic Jewish, and rural Appalachian people.

The Task Force established as its first priority development of the Guidelines for Providers of Psychological Services to Ethnic, Linguistic, and Culturally Diverse Populations. The guidelines that follow are intended to enlighten all areas of service delivery, not simply clinical or counseling endeavors. The clients referred to may be clients, organizations, government and/or community agencies.

Guidelines

Preamble: The Guidelines represent general principles that are intended to be aspirational in nature and are designed to provide suggestions to psychologists in working with ethnic, linguistic, and culturally diverse populations.

1. Psychologists educate their clients to the processes of psychological intervention, such as goals and expectations; the scope and, where appropriate, legal limits of confidentiality; and the psychologists' orientations.
   a. Whenever possible, psychologists provide information in writing along with oral explanations.
   b. Whenever possible, the written information is provided in the language understandable to the client.
2. Psychologists are cognizant of relevant research and practice issues as related to the population being served.
   a. Psychologists acknowledge that ethnicity and culture impact on behavior and take those factors into account when working with various ethnic/racial groups.
   b. Psychologists seek out educational and training experiences to enhance their understanding and thereby address the needs of these populations more appropriately and effectively. These experiences include cultural, social, psychological, political, economic, and historical material specific to the particular ethnic group being served.
   c. Psychologists recognize the limits of their competencies and expertise. Psychologists who do not possess knowledge and training about an ethnic group seek consultation with, and/or make referrals to, appropriate experts as necessary.
   d. Psychologists consider the validity of a given instrument or procedure and interpret resulting data, keeping in mind the cultural and linguistic characteristics of the person being assessed. Psychologists are aware of the test's reference population and possible limitations of such instruments with other populations.
3. Psychologists recognize ethnicity and culture as significant parameters in understanding psychological processes.
   a. Psychologists, regardless of ethnic/racial background, are aware of how their own cultural background/experiences, attitudes, values, and biases influence psychological processes. They make efforts to correct any prejudices and biases.
      Illustrative Statement: Psychologists might routinely ask themselves, "Is it appropriate for me to view this client or organization any differently than I would if they were from my own ethnic or cultural group?"
   b. Psychologists' practice incorporates an understanding of the client's ethnic and cultural background. This includes the client's familiarity and comfort with the majority culture as well as ways in which the client's culture may add to or improve various aspects of the majority culture and/or of society at large.
      Illustrative Statement: The kinds of mainstream social activities in which families participate may offer information about the level and quality of acculturation to American society. It is important to distinguish acculturation from length of stay in the United States and not to assume that these issues are relevant only for new immigrants and refugees.

c. Psychologists help clients increase their awareness of their own cultural values and norms, and they facilitate discovery of ways clients can apply this awareness to their own lives and to society at large.

Illustrative Statement: Psychologists may be able to help parents distinguish between generational conflict and culture gaps when problems arise between them and their children. In the process, psychologists could help both parents and children to appreciate their own distinguishing cultural values.

d. Psychologists seek to help a client determine whether a "problem" stems from racism or bias in others so that the client does not inappropriately personalize problems.

Illustrative Statement: The concept of "healthy paranoia," whereby ethnic minorities may develop defensive behaviors in response to discrimination, illustrates this principle.

e. Psychologists consider not only differential diagnostic issues but also the cultural beliefs and values of the client and his/her community in providing intervention.

Illustrative Statement: There is a disorder among the traditional Navajo called "Moth Madness." Symptoms include seizure-like behaviors. This disorder is believed by the Navajo to be the supernatural result of incestuous thoughts or behaviors. Both differential diagnosis and intervention should take into consideration the traditional values of Moth Madness.

4. Psychologists respect the roles of family members and community structures, hierarchies, values, and beliefs within the client's culture.

a. Psychologists identify resources in the family and the larger community.

b. Clarification of the role of the psychologist and the expectations of the client precede intervention. Psychologists seek to ensure that both the psychologist and client have a clear understanding of what services and roles are reasonable.

Illustrative Statement: It is not uncommon for an entire American Indian family to come into the clinic to provide support to the person in distress. Many of the healing practices found in American Indian communities are centered in the family and the whole community.

5. Psychologists respect clients' religious and/or spiritual beliefs and values, including attributions and taboos, since they affect world view, psychosocial functioning, and expressions of distress.

a. Part of working in minority communities is to become familiar with indigenous beliefs and practices and to respect them.

Illustrative Statement: Traditional healers (e.g., shamans, curanderos, espiritistas) have an important place in minority communities.

b. Effective psychological intervention may be aided by consultation with and/or inclusion or religious/spiritual leaders/practitioners relevant to the client's cultural and belief systems.

6. Psychologists interact in the language requested by the client and, if this is not feasible, make an appropriate referral.

a. Problems may arise when the linguistic skills of the psychologist do not match the language of the client. In such a case, psychologists refer the client to a mental health professional who is competent to interact in the language of the client. If this is not possible, psychologists offer the client a translator with cultural knowledge and an appropriate professional background. When no translator is available, then a trained paraprofessional from the client's culture is used as a translator/culture broker.

b. If translation is necessary, psychologists do not retain the services of translators/paraprofessionals who may have a dual role with the client, to avoid jeopardizing the validity of evaluation or the effectiveness of intervention.

c. Psychologists interpret and relate test data in terms understandable and relevant to the needs of those assessed.

7. Psychologists consider the impact of adverse social, environmental, and political factors in assessing problems and designing interventions.

   a. Types of intervention strategies to be used match the client's level of need (e.g., Maslow's hierarchy of needs).

   Illustrative Statement: Low income may be associated with such stressors as malnutrition, substandard housing, and poor medical care; and rural residency may mean inaccessibility of services. Clients may resist treatment at government agencies because of previous experience (e.g., refugees' status may be associated with violent treatments by government officials and agencies).

   b. Psychologists work within the cultural setting to improve the welfare of all persons concerned, if there is a conflict between cultural values and human rights.

8. Psychologists attend to, as well as work to eliminate, biases, prejudices, and discriminatory practices.

   a. Psychologists acknowledge relevant discriminatory practices at the social and community level that may be affecting the psychological welfare of the population being served.

   Illustrative Statement: Depression may be associated with frustrated attempts to climb the corporate ladder in an organization that is dominated by a top echelon of White men.

   b. Psychologists are cognizant of sociopolitical contexts in conducting evaluations and providing interventions; they develop sensitivity to issues of oppression, sexism, elitism, and racism.

   Illustrative Statement: An upsurge in the public expression of rancor or even violence between two ethnic or cultural groups may increase anxiety baselines in any member of those groups. This baseline of anxiety would interact with prevailing symptomatology. At the organizational level, the community conflict may interfere with open communication among staff.

9. Psychologists working with culturally diverse populations should document culturally and sociopolitically relevant factors in the records. These may include, but are not limited to:

   a. number of generations in the country

   b. number of years in the country

c. fluency in English
d. extent of family support (or disintegration of family)
e. community resources
f. level of education
g. change in social status as a result of coming to this country (for immigrant or refugee)
h. intimate relationship with people of different backgrounds
i. level of stress related to acculturation.

REFERENCES

Acosta, F. X., & Sheehan, J. G. (1976). Preference towards Mexican American and Anglo American psychotherapists. *Journal of Consulting and Clinical Psychology, 44,* 272–279.

Acosta, F., Yamamoto, J., & Evans, L. (1982). *Effective psychotherapy for low income and minority patients.* New York: Plenum Press.

Atkinson, D. R. (1983). Ethnic similarity in counseling psychology: A review of research. *The Counseling Psychologist, 11,* 79–92.

Cheung, F. K., & Snowden, L. R. (1990). Community mental health and ethnic minority populations. *Community Mental Health Journal, 26,* 277–291.

Comas-Diaz, L., & Griffith, E. H. (1988). *Clinical guidelines in cross-cultural mental health.* New York: Wiley.

Dauphinais, P., Dauphinais, L., & Rowe, W. (1981). Effects of race and communication style on Indian perceptions of counselor effectiveness. *Counselor Education and Supervision, 20,* 37–46.

Everett, F., Proctor, N., & Cartmell, B. (1983). Providing psychological services to American Indian children and families. *Professional Psychology: Research and Practice, 14,* 588–603.

Juarez, R. (1985). Core issues in psychotherapy with the Hispanic child. *Psychotherapy, 22,* 441–448.

Lorion, R. P. (1974). Patient and therapist variables in the treatment of low income patients. *Psychological Bulletin, 81,* 344–354.

Malgady, R. G., Rogler, L. H., & Costantino, G. (1987). Ethnocultural and linguistic bias in mental health evaluation of Hispanics. *American Psychologist, 42,* 228–234.

McGoldrick, M., Pearce, J. K., & Giordano, J. (1982). *Ethnicity and family therapy.* New York: Guildford Press.

Nishio, K., & Bilmes, M. (1987). Psychotherapy with Southeast Asian American clients. *Professional Psychology: Research and Practice, 18,* 342–346.

Padilla, A. M., & Ruiz R. A. (1973). *Latino mental health: A review of literature* (DHEW Publication No. HSM 73-9143). Washington, DC: U.S. Government Printing Office.

Padilla, A. M., Ruiz R. A., & Alvarez, R. (1975). Community mental health for the Spanish-speaking/surnamed population. *American Psychologist, 30,* 892–905.

Parham, T. A., & Helms, J. E., (1981). The influence of Black students racial identity attitudes on preferences for counselor's race. *Journal of Counseling Psychology, 28,* 250–257.

Root, Maria P. P. (1985). Guidelines for facilitating therapy with Asian American clients. *Psychotherapy, 22,* 349–356.

Rosado, J. W. (1986). Toward an interfacing of Hispanic cultural variables with school psychology service delivery systems. *Professional Psychology: Research and Practice, 17,* 191–199.

Snowden, L. R., & Cheung, F. K. (1990). Use of inpatient mental health services by members of ethnic minority groups. *American Psychologist, 45,* 347–355.

Sue, D., & Sue, S. (1987). Cultural factors in the clinical assessment of Asian Americans. *Journal of Consulting and Clinical Psychology, 55,* 479–487.

Zuniga, M. E. (1988). Assessment issues with Chicanas: Practical implications. *Psychotherapy, 25,* 288–293.

INDEX

Abourezk, James, 41
Abraham, F. Murray, 41
Accommodating responses, 245
Acculturation, 21, 35, 101
    African Americans, 122–124
    Asian Americans, 118–120
    definition of, 37, 109
    Latina/Latino Americans, 120
    Native Americans, 110, 118–121
    White Americans, 124–126
    See also Culture
Acupuncture, 258
Adages, 3
Adaptive spiral, 237
Advocates, 189, 268
Affect versus intellectualization, 236,
    238, 241
Affirmative action, 17
Affluent guilt, 26
Africa, 11–12
African Americans, 74
    acculturation, 122–124
    authors as, 2, 3
    census (1990), 57
    children's racial
        misclassification, 16
    churches, 207, 265–269
    culture, 113–116
    culture of poverty, 23–24
    family structure, 143
    history quiz, 53
    indigenous healers, 260
    institutional and cultural racism, 39
    intermarriage, 49–50
    laziness stereotype, 208, 209
    as major socioracial group, 11–12
    men, 206, 207
    Ministry of Spiritual Nurturing,
        266–269
    model of personality, 80
    occupational distribution, 211
    primary reference group, 23
    sociopolitical history of, 48–53
    therapy orientations, 133
    and White American history, 51–52
    women, 135
    worldviews, 167
    See also ALANAs; VREGs

Afrocentric psychotherapy, 262–263
Afrocentric theories, 17
Afro-Cuban cultures, 260
Age cohorts, 8
Agriculture, Native Americans, 208
ALANAs, 39
    books and films, 66
    Carter and Cook's model of
        vocational development,
        213–214
    as collectivistic cultures, 22–23
    cultural labels, 28–30
    definition of, 10
    feelings and content, 178
    men, 210–213
    occupations of men, 210–213
    preference for term, 28
    racial labels, 27–28
    racist versus bigoted, 326
    support systems, 168, 188, 221
    termination issues, 195
    theoretical orientations, 133
    Whites counseling, 325
    See also Physical characteristics;
        specific sociracial
        groups; VREGs
Alcoholics Anonymous, 27, 267
Aleuts, 45
Allmuseri, 48
Allocentrism, 114
Altered state of consciousness in
    person-centered therapy,
    148
Alternative cultural formulation,
    104, 105
Altruism, 231–232
Amadeus (film), 41
Ambiguity, 104
American Arab Anti-Discrimination
    Committee, 41
American culture, 19, 21, 30, 38,
    70, 108
    See also American dream; United
        States; White Americans
American dream, 39, 45, 207
American Historical Association, 38
American Psychological Association
    (APA), 9, 300

"Ethical Principles of
    Psychologists and Code of
    Conduct," 196, 327
    Office of Ethnic Minority Affairs,
        175, 197
Anal stage, 141
Ancestors. See Ethnicity
Anglocization, 124
Angola, 48
Answers to questions, 316–326
Anticipatory anxiety, 237, 262
Anxiety neurosis, 262
APA. See American Psychological
    Association
Apache, 43
Arab Americans, 41
Armenians, 62
Art forms, 101
Artistic style, 202
Asante, 48
Asian Americans and Pacific
    Islanders, 74
    acculturation, 118–120
    "brainiac" stereotype, 159
    census (1990), 57, 60
    culture, 117–118
    ethnicity, 40, 60
    family structure, 143
    indigenous models of therapy,
        256–257
    as major sociracial group, 11
    Marie (person-centered therapy),
        151–152, 159, 179, 310
    mixed racial ancestry, 65
    occupational stereotypes, 210
    and other ALANAs, 65
    Patty (career counseling), 201,
        203, 204, 210, 214–216
    sociopolitical histories of, 60–65
    subgroups, 65
    and White American history, 63–64
    women, 209–210
    See also ALANAs; VREGs
Asian Indians, 60, 62
    indigenous healing, 258–260
    See also Asian Americans and
        Pacific Islanders
Assertiveness, 217

Assertiveness skills training, 234
Assessment
    for career counseling, 218–221
    research in, 304–307
Assimilation, 19, 29, 101
    definition of, 37
    stresses and pressures, 21, 118,
        126–27
    See also Culture
Association of Counselor Education
    and Supervision, 284
At-home culture, 101–102, 107, 111,
    125–126
    and language, 193, 194
Attitudes, 7
Audiotapes, 283
Authority, 117
Authors, 2, 3
    questions and answers, 316–326
Automatic thoughts, 153, 154
Autonomy ego status (White), 91, 93
Autonomy vs. shame and doubt, 141
Avoidance patterns, 144
Avoiding responses, 245
Ayurveda, 258
Aztecs, 57

Backup assertion, 234
Baines, Andrew, 67
Basic social skills, 234, 235
Basic trust vs. mistrust, 141
Beauty standards of White
    Americans, 51
Beck, Aaron, 150, 153
Beck Depression Inventory, 152
Beginning phase of therapy, 158–172
    clarification of expectations and
        education, 168–169
    client assessment, 166–168
    client dynamics, 160–161
    establishing a relationship, 159–169
    intake, 158–159
    problems, 169–171
    the process, 164–166
    therapist dynamics, 161–164
Behavioral patterns in culture
    processes, 106
Behavioral rehearsal, 234
Behavior-focused indigenous therapy,
    260–262
Beliefs, 7
Bemidji State University, 111
Between-group diversity, 16, 17,
    23, 24

Bhuta-preta, 257
Big Eagle, 111
Big Foot, 121
Bigotry versus racism, 325–326
Bilingual backgrounds. *See* Language
Birth to rebirth cycle, 259–260
Blackness and evil, 48, 53, 75
Blacks. *See* African Americans
Blank screen of therapists, 144–146
Blue-collar jobs, 74
Book overview, 2, 4
Books and films on ALANAs, 66
Boundaries, 189, 320
Bradley, Michael, 75–76
Brislin's criteria of culture, 22
Brotherhood, 268
Brown v. Topeka, 16
Buddhism, 117
Bureau of Indian Affairs (BIA), 221
Burial practices, 136

CAB. *See* Cognitive, affective, and
    behavioral responses
California, 56
California Supreme Court, 62
"Calo," 193
Card sorts, 223
Career counseling, 200–225
    assessment, 218–222
    Carter and Cook's model, 213–214
    cultural diversity perspective,
        216–218
    developmental process perspective,
        204–205
    Holland's theory, 202–203
    interviews, 217–218
    modifications for racial and
        cultural perspectives,
        209–218
    occupational distribution, 211
    Patty, 201, 203, 204
    personality and self-concept
        theories, 202–203
    racial and cultural concerns,
        204–209
    racial identity perspective,
        214–216
    Roe's theory, 203
    steps in process of, 222–223
    systems perspectives, 213–214
    traditional theoretical perspectives,
        201–218
    See also Occupations;
        Patty; Therapy

Care giving philosophies, 173
Caribbean, 55, 56
Carter and Cook's model of
    vocational development for
    ALANAs, 213–214
Case notes, 283
Castro, Fidel, 57
Catharsis, 240–241
Caucasians, 62, 74
    See also White Americans
Caucasoid, 76
Center for Holistic Ministry,
    266, 267
Central America, 55, 56
Chanting, 259
Character disorders, 322
Charwood, Angela, 111
Cherokee, 40, 45
Chicanos, 57
    See also Latina/Latino Americans
Chickasaw, 40
Child abuse, 272, 317
Childhood issues, 134, 142
Childhood weaning, 136, 142
Childrearing practices, 136,
    142, 143
Chinese, 60, 117, 210
    indigenous healing, 258
    See also Asian Americans and
        Pacific Islanders
Chippewa, 45, 111
Choctaw, 40, 45
Christianity, 27, 39, 120, 121
    African American, 260
Chumesh, 43
Church auxiliaries, 268
Church-community conferences,
    268–269
Churches, 126
    African American, 207, 265–269
Circumstantial models of racial
    oppression, 76–77
Citizenship eligibility, 208
Civil disturbance, 79
Civil Rights Act (1964), 72
Civil Rights Movement, 53
Civil War, 49–51
Clarification of expectations of
    education in therapy, 168–169
Classic civilizations, 17
Class labels, 24
Clergy, 260
Client-centered therapy. *See* Person-
    centered therapy

Clients
  adjustment themes, 20–21
  beginning phase of therapy,
    160–161, 166–168
  cultural mistrust, 123–124, 147,
    149, 160, 191
  defense mechanisms, 140
  educating about therapy, 168–169
  gift-giving, 186–188, 322–323
  intrapsychic and interpersonal
    styles, 7–14
  language switching, 193–195
  preferences in race, 305
  psychodynamic therapy, 145–148
  racial and cultural history, 8, 220
  religion or spirituality, 189–192
  role in racial and cultural
    sensitivity, 1
  social contact with therapists, 188,
    196, 320, 322
  values, 316–318
  VREG, 43, 175, 178–179, 308
  VREG racist, 325–326
  welfare of, 271, 272
  White racist, 321–322
  in Yalom's therapeutic factors,
    227–242
  See also Transference
Clinton, Bill, 43
Cognitive, affective, and behavioral
    responses (CAB), 244, 245
Cognitive-affective reaction
    behavioral cycle, 152
Cognitive-behavioral therapy, 133,
    150–156, 190, 262
Cohesiveness of ethnic groups, 19
Coining, 136, 271
Collaborating with indigenous
    healers and helpers. See
    Indigenous healers and helpers
Collaborative conflict resolution, 245
Collective identity model, 86
Collectivism, 122
Collectivistic cultures, 21–23,
    101–102, 118, 127–128
  comparison with individualistic,
    105
  other family members, 323
  practices of, 136–137
  social networks as healing sources,
    264–269
  and termination issues, 195
  and work environments, 217
  See also Culture; Extended families

"Color blind," 169
Color-Confrontation Theory, 75
Color inadequacy or albinism of
    Whites, 75
Columbus, Christopher, 44, 56, 111
Columbus Day, 39
Communication styles, 24
Communities (tribes), 43
Community tragedies and disasters,
    268–269
Compensation, 139
Compensatory logic, 75
Conceptions of others in culture
    processes, 106
Conceptions of the self, 104–105
Conceptual barriers in therapy
    research, 300–310
Conceptual nuances of
    psychotherapy, 173–185
  conceptual model, 174
  input, 175–179
  social roles, 180
  therapy interaction process model,
    180–184
  therapy outcome, 184–185
  See also Practice nuances of
    psychotherapy
Confederacy, 49–51
Confidentiality, 188, 266
Conflict resolution, 245
Conformity ego status (ALANA),
    86, 87
Confrontation, 223, 239
Confucianism, 117
Congruence, 202
Consultation, 9
Contact ego status (White), 90, 91
Contact outside therapy, 188, 196
Contraceptive sterilization, 123
Conventional style, 202
Cook, D.A., 265
Corrective recapitulation of the
    primary family group, 232–234
Counseling. See Career counseling;
    Group counseling;
    Psychotherapy; Therapy
Counselors. See Therapists
Countertransference, 21, 159
Covenant Baptist Church, 266
Creek, 40
Criminal activities, 207, 267, 268
Criminals, 39
Criollas, 56
Cronos complex, 76

Cross-cultural conditions, 21, 217
Cross-cultural referrals, 272
Cross-cultural studies, 107, 277, 301
Crossed dyads, 282
Crossed events in therapy, 244
Cross-racial therapy, 147, 149,
    168, 191
Cubans, 56–57
  See also Latina/Latino Americans
Cubberly, Ellwood P., 74
Cultural referent, 303–304
Cultural assimilation, 126
Cultural communities, 264
  See also Social networks
Cultural conceptions of race, 17
Cultural display rules, 107, 108
Cultural distortion, 317
Cultural diversity, 27–30
  in career theory, 216–218
  in research, 299
  See also Diversity perspectives
Cultural issues in therapy
    supervision, 291–295
Cultural labels, 28–29
Culturally sensitive counseling and
    psychotherapy, 1
Culturally skilled therapists,
    175–177
Cultural myths, 254, 255, 269, 271
Cultural paranoia, 140, 160
Cultural racism, 24
  ALANAs and VREGs, 326
  definition, 38
  of Native and African
    Americans, 39
Cultural research in therapy
    supervision, 295
Cultural socialization, 1, 69
  and socioracial socialization, 7
Cultural themes, 1
Cultural values, 316–318
Culture, 19
  American, 19, 21–22
  at-home and marketplace,
    101–102
  criteria of, 22
  definition of, 21–22, 30, 101,
    108–109
  implications for therapy, 22–23
  models of, 101–130
  objective and subjective, 101
  patriarchal, 317
  products of, 101
  and race, 1, 7, 8, 30

Culture, *continued*
  See also Acculturation;
    Assimilation; Collectivistic
    cultures; Individualistic
    cultures
Culture-based socioracial groups,
  55–68
Culture content, 108–118
  African American, 113–116
  Asian American, 117–118
  Latina/Latino, 114, 116–117
  Native American, 110–113
  White, 109–110
Culture of poverty, 23–24
Culture processes, 101–108
  behavioral patterns, 106
  conceptions of others, 106
  emotional expression, 106–108
  the self, 104–105
Customs, 19
Cycle of birth to rebirth, 259–260

Daily life rituals, 7, 101
Dakotas, 43
Darwinism, social, 40, 74
Day, Elizabeth, 111
Death, 241–242
Decline stage, 204
Deculturation, 70, 122
Defense mechanisms, 79, 138–141
Demographic categories, 28–29,
  304, 311
  demographic identities, 8, 16
Demons, 256
Denial, 139
Density of ethnic groups, 19
Dependent, 102, 189, 195
Deportation, 60
Developmental career theory
  (Super), 204–205
Developmental sequences, 138,
  141–142
Deviants or misfits, 39
Didactic instruction, 153, 156
Differential expectations, 7
Directive and nondirective therapy,
  168–169, 178–179
Disasters, 268–269
Discrimination, 20, 28
Discriminitive cue learning, 234–235
Disintegration ego status (White),
  90–92
Displacement, 139
Disposable resources, 26

Dissonance ego status (ALANA),
  86, 87
Distal characteristics (sociological),
  10–11, 175, 184
Diversity perspectives, 9, 19
  See also Cultural diversity
Divination, 255
Dominant groups, 27, 28
  White Americans as, 38–39
Domination and subordination, 17,
  20, 35, 39, 304
Dominican Republic, 56
Draw your culture (exercise), 233
Drug abuse, 267
Dukakis, Michael, 41
Dwayne, 206, 207
Dyad types, 282–283

Earned reputation circumstantial
  model of racial oppression,
  76–77
Educating clients about therapy,
  168–169
Education, 212, 213, 216, 221
  See also Therapy supervision
Ego status themes, 84–89
Elderly people, 264, 267
Ellis, Albert, 150
Emersion ego status (ALANA), 87, 88
Emersion ego status (White),
  90–91, 93
Emotional expression in culture
  processes, 106–108
Empathic understanding in person-
  centered therapy, 148, 190
Empirical studies
  in therapy supervision, 278–283
  See also Research
Encounter-type groups, 237
  See also Group therapy
Enculturation. *See* Acculturation
English language competence, 23,
  41, 60, 124, 155–156, 210
  See also Language
Enmeshed, 102
Enterprising style, 202
Environmental conceptions of race, 17
Environmental racial inferiority
  models of Whites, 75–76
Erikson, E.H., 141
Erotogenic zones, 141
Eskimos, 45
Espiritismo, 116, 257
Espiritistos, 256

Establishment stage, 204
Ethical issues and cultural conflict,
  195–197
"Ethical Principles of Psychologists
  and Code of Conduct,"
  American Psychological
  Association (APA), 196
Ethnic groups, 8, 30
  minorities, 27
  socialization, 1
  White Americans, 19, 38, 40–42,
    124, 126
Ethnicity, 1
  definition of, 19–21, 30
Ethnic matching, 307–308
Ethnocentrism, 20, 24, 28, 65
Etic universalistic perspectives, 73, 83
Euphemisms for race, 19–23, 29, 302
  See also Racial and
    cultural terminology
Europe, 11–12
European Americans. *See*
  White Americans
Evil, 112–113
Evil spirits, 256, 259, 270
Existential factors, 241–242
Experiencing in therapy supervision,
  285–286
Experiential versus objective
  reality, 254
Exploratory stage, 204
Explorers, 38, 44
Extended families, 23, 136, 171,
  187, 264
  See also Collectivistic cultures

Fairchild, Henry Pratt, 74
Faith, 271
Familial history, 19, 20, 220–221
Familialism, 116, 117
Families, 8, 126
  extended, 23, 136, 171, 187, 264
  primary family group, 232–234
  racial and cultural considerations,
    142–144
  in Roe's career theory, 203
  roles in, 137
Family therapy, 9
Fante, 48
Federally-sponsored research, 123
Female genital mutilation, 136
Femininity (expressiveness)
  dimension, 104
Field dependent, 102

Filial piety, 117, 144
"First-generation middle-classdom," 26
Florida, 56
Folk psychology, 75
Fon, 48
Formal ceremonies, 188
Formal conceptions of race, 17
Formal or standard Black English, 194
Franklin, Ben, 57
Fraternities, 126, 264
Freud, Sigmund, 75, 134
    defense mechanisms, 79, 138–141
    psychosexual stages, 141
Frustration-aggression hypothesis, 77–78

Gatekeeper roles, 301
Gender
    in groups, 244
    identity, 1, 8
    identity models, 84
    occupational distribution, 211
    and socioracial/cultural career considerations, 209–213
    See also Men; Women
Generativity vs. stagnation, 142
Generic universalistic perspectives, 73
Genetic color inferiority, 75
Genital stage, 141
Genograms, 222
Genuineness in person-centered therapy, 148
Ghost Dance religion, 121, 190
Gift-giving, 186–188, 322–323
Glacial evolution, 76
Class ceilings, 211
God-figure, 259–260
Goldberg, Whoopi, 94
Governments, 8
Grant, Madison, 74
Group cohesiveness, 239–240
Group leaders, 226–253
    See also Therapists
Groupness, 8
Group nurturing in the Minsitry of Spiritual Nurturing, 267
Group therapy, 9, 226–253
    racial conflict within groups, 243–244
    racial identity and group conflict, 242–252

talking about race, 246–251
therapy implications, 251–252
types of racial identity events, 244–246
See also Therapy; Yalom's therapeutic factors
Guilt
    social-class, 26
    survivor, 26, 43, 242

Half Man, 206
Hall, G. Stanley, 74
Harmonious interpersonal relations, 104
Harmony and disharmony, 112–113, 257
Hawaiians, 61
Healing
    symbolic, 254
    See also Indigenous healers and helpers
Helms, Janet E., "A New Racial World Order," 36–37
Helms's racial identity theory, 84–95, 180
    common themes, 84–85
    expression, 93–95
    People of Color racial identity, 85–89
    White racial identity, 89–93
Here-and-now, 238
Here-and-now focus on racial issues in therapy supervision, 284–287
Hierarchical-collateral relations, 104
Hierarchical relationships, 117, 144, 146
Hierarchy, racial, 40, 70
Higher power, 27, 189, 259, 267
Hill, Howard C., 74
Hindu cultures, 257, 259–260
Hip-hop English, 194
Hispanics, 55–56
    See also Latina/Latino Americans
Hispaniola, 55–56
Historical circumstantial model of racial oppression, 76
Historical and cultural conceptions of race, 17
Histories of socioracial groups. *See* specific groups
HIV/AIDS, 267
Hohokam, 43
Holland, John, 202
Holland's career theory, 202–203

Holocaust, 111
Holocausts in the Americas, 44, 48, 49
Holy books or writings, 259
Homework, 153, 155, 156, 169
Horizontal-vertical collectivism, 104
Hostile work environments, 215
Housing discrimination, 20
Howard University, 67
Hunkpapa Sioux, 121
Hysterectomies, 123

Ibibio, 48
"Ice-man inheritance," 75–76
Identification, 139
Identity vs. role confusion, 141
Igbo, 48
Illness, 112
Illumination in therapy supervision, 286–287
Imani, 122
Imitative behavior, 235–236
Immature, 102
Immersion ego status (ALANA), 87, 88
Immersion ego status (White), 90, 92–93
Immigration, 19, 20, 140
    Asian Americans and Pacific Islanders, 61, 62, 117
    and careers, 208
    Latina/Latino Americans, 57, 58, 60, 114
    White, 86, 124
    See also Old immigrants; Recent immigrants
Imparting information, 229–231
Incas, 57
Incestuous relationships, 317
Inclusion experience (exercise), 232
Independence Day, 111
Indian/Indianer/Indien/Indios, 43, 45, 56
    See also Native Americans
Indigenous Americans. *See* Native Americans
Indigenous healers and helpers, 254–274
    Afrocentric psychotherapy, 262–263
    behavior-focused therapy, 260–262
    medical traditions, 257–258
    Morita therapy, 260–262
    mystical or supernatural beliefs and practices, 256–257

Indigenous healers and helpers,
  continued
  NTU psychotherapy, 262–263
  religious spirituality, 258–260
  social networks, 264–269
  therapy implications, 269–272
  See also Ministry of
    Spiritual Nurturing
Individual differences, 23
Individualism, 39
Individualistic cultures, 21–22,
  101–102, 127–28
  comparison with collectivistic, 105
  See also Culture
Individual nurturing in the Minsitry
  of Spiritual Nurturing,
  266–267
Individual therapy, 9
Industry vs. inferiority, 141
Infantilizing, 26, 148
Information processing strategy
  (IPS), 101
  People of Color ego statuses,
    86–88
  White ego statuses, 89–93
In-group filters, 7, 31
Initiative vs. guilt, 141
Innuit, 43
Instillation of hope, 227–228, 267
Institutional racism, 155, 168
  Asian Americans and Pacific
    Islanders, 61, 62, 65
  and careers, 209
  definition, 38
  Latina/Latino Americans, 56–58
  Native and African Americans, 39
  systemic factors, 206
  VREGs and ALANAs, 326
Integrated autonomous identity, 137
Integrated sense of Self, 8
Integrative awareness ego status
  (ALANA), 87–89
Integrity vs. despair, 142
Intercultural Values Inventory, 103
Interdependence, 117
Inter-generational differences, 20–21
Intermarriage, 49–50, 120, 126
Internalization ego status (ALANA),
  87–89
Internalized racism, 20, 71
Interpersonal learning, 236–239
Interviews for jobs, 217–218
Intimacy vs. isolation, 141–142
Intrapsychic cultural incongruence, 21

Investigative style, 202
Involuntary segregation, 8
Irrational thoughts, 150
Islamic cultures, 257
"I" statements, 104

Japanese, 60, 117, 133, 257
  Morita therapy, 260–262
  See also Asian Americans and
    Pacific Islanders
Japanese Americans, 61, 62
  See also Asian Americans and
    Pacific Islanders
Jargon, 266
Jefferson, Thomas, 120
Jensen, Arthur, 74
Jews, 27, 42, 111
Jikei University (Tokyo), 261
Jinn, 257
Johnson, Charles, 48–49
Journal editors, 300

Kardiner, Abram and Ovesey, Lionel,
  The Mark of Oppression, 79–81
Kongo, 48
Koreans, 60
  See also Asian Americans and
    Pacific Islanders
Kujichagulia, 122
Kuumba, 122
Kwanzaa, 122, 263

Labels, 31
  class, 24
  cultural, 28–29
  negative, 20
  racial, 27–28
Lang, Brenda, 111
Language, 23, 101, 161
  at-home versus marketplace,
    193, 194
  bilingual backgrounds, 24,
    124, 215
  See also English language
    competence; Racial and
    cultural terminology
Latentcy stage, 141
Latina/Latino Americans
  acculturation, 120
  "Calo," 193
  census (1990), 57
  culture, 114, 116–117
  domination within U.S., 58–60
  ethnicity, 40

family structure, 143
folk-healing beliefs, 271
as major socioracial group, 11
occupational distribution, 211
primary reference group, 23
sociopolitical histories, 55–60
Spanish-Mexican and Anglo
  history, 59, 60
Spanish oppression, 55–58
therapy orientations, 133
See also ALANAs; Mexican
  Americans; VREGs
Latin America, 55, 56
Laying on of hands, 259
Libido, 141
Life experiences, 7, 261
Lifespan developmental processes, 141
Life transitions, 267
Lincoln, Abraham, 72
Linda
  in race explicit discussion group,
    246–251
  White Racial Identity Profile, 94, 95
Little Star, 221
Littlewolf, Jamie, 111
Littlewolf, Wenona, 111
Live observation, 283
Los Angeles, 57
Los Angeles riots, 268
Lower class, 24, 25

Machismo, 117
McKenzie, M.A., 122
Mainstream, 27, 29, 30
Maintenance stage, 204
Majority groups, 7, 27, 28
Malcolm X, 67
Mantras, 257
Marianismo, 116–117
Marie (person-centered therapy),
  151–152, 159, 179, 310
Marital assimilation, 126
Marketplace culture, 101–102, 117,
  125–126
  and language, 193
The Mark of Oppression (Kardiner and
  Ovesey), 79–81
Masculinity (instrumentality)
  dimension, 104
Massacres
  African American, 50, 52
  Mexican American, 60
  Native American, 44–45, 121
Materialism, 39

Maxims, 3
Mayans, 57
Meaning-of-life issues, 241–242
Medical traditions of indigenous, 257–258
Medicinal herbs, 258
Meditation, 258, 260
Melting pot, 29, 124
Men
    African American, 206, 207
    occupational distribution, 211
    occupations of ALANAs, 210–213
    White American, 300–301
    See also Gender
Menial labor, 206, 215
    Asian Americans and Pacific Islanders, 61, 62, 65, 208
    Latina/Latino Americans, 60, 208
Mental health agencies, intake process, 8–9
Mental health conceptions, 7
Mental health professions
    acculturation and assimilation, 124
    collaborating with indigenous healers and helpers, 269–272
    and stereotyping, 70, 71
    and White-based standards, 74
    See also Therapists
Merchants, 39
Message matching, 234
Mestizo, 56
Mexican Americans, 57, 58, 60, 193
    See also Latina/Latino Americans
Middle class, 24–26
The Middle Passage, 48
Mind-body-spirit connection, 112–113, 154
Ministry of Spiritual Nurturing, 263–269
    church-community conferences, 268–269
    group nurturing, 267
    individual nurturing, 266–267
    networks, 269
    reaching out/lending a helping hand, 268
Minneconjon Sioux, 121
Minority groups, 7, 27, 28
Minority Identity Development model, 86
Minton, Lynn, 111
Miscegenation, 56
"MmHmm," 178
Modal characteristics or styles, 202

Modeling, 234
Models of oppression and sociorace, 69–100
Monroe, Sylvester ("Vest"), 206
Moors, 56
Morita, Shoma, 261
Morita therapy, 260–262
Mozambique, 48
Mudiwas, 122
Mulatto, 56
Multicultural competencies, 175–177
Multiculturalism, 9, 19, 28, 30
    principle of, 29
    research orientations, 299, 303
Multiple roles of therapists, 188–189
Muslims, 27
Mystical or supernatural beliefs and practices, 256–257
Myths, cultural, 254, 255, 269, 271

Name changes, 41
Narcissistic personalities, 322
Narcotics Anonymous, 267
Nations (tribes), 43
Native Americans, 56, 57, 74
    acculturation, 110, 118–121
    agriculture, 208
    alternative cultural formulation, 104, 105
    assertiveness, 217
    behavioral styles of, 140
    census (1990), 57
    "civilized" tribes, 40
    culture, 110–113
    family structure, 143
    Ghost Dance religion, 121, 190
    gift-giving, 187
    indigenous healing, 257–258, 264, 270
    institutional and cultural racism, 39
    intermarriage, 120
    Little Star, 221
    as major socioracial group, 11
    mixed ancestry, 45, 47, 57
    occupational distribution, 211
    and other VREG groups, 47
    political organizations, 264
    religions, 120–121
    on reservations, 24
    sociopolitical history of, 43–48
    studies of, 304
    and White American intergroup history, 46–47
    See also ALANAs; VREGs

Native-born ethnic groups, 20
Nature, 112
Navajos ("Dine"), 43, 45, 217
Neanderthal man, 76
Necessary conditions in person-centered therapy, 148, 149
Necessary and sufficient conditions of counseling, 307
Negative bias, 43
Negative labels, 20
Negros, 56
    See also African Americans
Negro-to-Black conversion model, 86
Networks in the Ministry of Spiritual Nurturing, 269
"A New Racial World Order" (Helms), 36–37
News Dimensions, 67
Nia, 122
Nominal categories, 16, 303, 308
Nonstandard English usage, 24
Nonverbal communications, 149–150
Normal behavior, 7
Norms, 101
Northern European ethnic groups, 22, 38, 74
Northern Hemisphere, 75
NTU psychotherapy, 262–263
Nuances of psychotherapy, 173–199
    See also Conceptual nuances of psychotherapy; Practice nuances of psychotherapy
Numerical representation in group, 244
Nurses' Aid Society, 268

Objective culture, 101
Object-relations theory, 142
Occupational distribution, 211
Occupations, 8
    See also Career counseling
Office of Ethnic Minority Affairs, American Psychological Association (APA), 175, 197
Old immigrants, 38
    See also Immigration
Open versus closed questions, 179
Oppression, 35, 38, 52
    models of, 69–100
Oral stage, 141
Order theories of racism, 71–72, 77–78
Original socioracial groups, 34–54
Outcome issues research, 309–310

Out-group filters, 7, 31
Outreach services, 9
Overview of the book, 2, 4

Pacification procedures, 258
Pacific Islanders. *See* Asian
    Americans and Pacific Islanders
Paiute Messiah (Wovoka), 121
Paler Hargrove, Lisa, 162–164
Parallel events in therapy, 181–182,
    244–245
Parallel interactions, 282
Parapsychological phenomena, 261
Parents, 190, 196
    in psychodynamic theory, 134,
        136, 141, 145, 147–148
    in Roe's career theory, 203
Passive resistance, 140
Past experiences, 134
Paternalism, 221
Patriarchal cultures, 317
Patronizing, 26, 221
Patty (career counseling), 201, 203,
    204, 210, 214–216
Pawnees, 43
People of Color, 36, 37
    racial identity, 85–89
    See also ALANAs; specific groups;
        VREGs
People v. Hall, 62
Perceptual processes, 7
Personal-experience therapy. *See*
    Morita therapy
Personal or individual racism, 38, 326
Personality career theories, 202–203
Personality development, 138,
    141–142
Personality reconstruction, 134
Personal occupational orientations
    (Holland), 202–203
Person-centered therapy, 133,
    148–152, 190, 191
Phallic stage, 141
Phenotype. *See*
    Physical characteristics
Philippines, 61
Physical characteristics, 7, 15, 175, 304
    Asian Americans and Pacific
        Islanders, 62
    changing, 41
    color inadequacy or albinism, 75
    and cultural assessments, 127
    Latina/Latino Americans, 56,
        58, 60

skin color, 163–164, 325
    and sociopolitical status, 39, 40
    of therapist, 138
    White Americans, 118
Physical contact, 241
Physical punishment, 136
Physiological attributes, 8
Pilgrims, 43
Pilipinos, 60
    See also Asian Americans and
        Pacific Islanders
Pima, 43
Pirs, 257
Plants and animals, 112
Positive bias, 43
Positive and negative emotions, 107
"Post-slavery Syndrome," 67
Post-traumatic stress reactions,
    268–269
Poverty, culture of, 23–24
Poverty level, 213
Power-conflict theories of racism,
    71–72
    White power-conflict models,
        72–78
Power-distance dimension, 102, 104
Practice nuances of psychotherapy,
    185–197
    contact outside therapy, 188
    ethical issues and cultural conflict,
        195–197
    gift giving, 186–188
    language switching, 193–195
    multiple roles of therapist,
        188–189
    religion in therapy, 189–192
    self-disclosure as a therapy tool,
        191, 193
    termination issues, 195
    See also Conceptual nuances of
        psychotherapy
Practice. *See* Therapy
Primary family group, 232–234
Primary reference groups, 23
Principle of multiculturalism, 29
    See also Multiculturalism
Process
    in beginning phase of therapy,
        164–166
    definition of, 180
    research in, 307–309
    See also Therapy
Professional techniques, 8
Professions, 265

Progressive events in therapy,
    183–184, 245
Projection, 139
Protestants, 27, 39, 41
Proverbs, 3
Proximal characteristics (psychosocial),
    10–11, 25, 175, 184
Pseudo-biological characteristics, 303
Pseudo-independence ego status
    (White), 90, 92
Psychoanalytic career theory
    (Roe), 203
Psychoanalytic therapy, 69, 75,
    133–148, 189
    See also Psychodynamic therapy
Psychoculture, 9–11, 21
Psychodynamic therapy, 134–148, 191
    assessment, 138–144
    defense mechanisms, 138–141
    developmental sequences, 141–142
    goals, 134–35
    parents, 134, 136, 141, 145, 147–148
    racial and cultural considerations,
        135–148
    therapy interventions, 144–148
    transference, 134–135, 137–138
    trauma, 136
    See also Psychoanalytic therapy
Psychological adjustment, 8
Psychological attributes, 8
Psychological factors as intrapsychic
    or subjective processes, 9–11
Psychological racial opression models
    of VREGs, 79–81
Psychopathology, 152
Psychoracial, 9–11
Psychoracial studies in therapy
    supervision, 281–283
Psychosexual stages of Freud, 141
Psychosocial stages of Erikson,
    141–142
Psychotherapist's Casebook (Rogers), 149
Psychotherapy. *See* Nuances of
    psychotherapy; Therapy
Public events, 188, 320, 322
Puerto Ricans, 56
    espiritismo, 257
    See also Latina/Latino Americans
Puerto Rico, 56

Quasi-biological criteria, 16, 17
A Question of Color (film), 164
Questions, open versus closed, 179
Questions and answers, 316–326

Race, 30
  and culture, 1, 7, 8, 30
  as demographic category, 8, 16
  euphemisms for, 19 23
  historical and cultural
      conceptions, 17
  implications for therapy, 17–19
  as a social construction, 15–17
  talking about, 246–251, 318–320
  See also Sociorace
Racial attitudes, 7
Racial conflict within groups,
    243–244
Racial and cultural career concerns,
    204–209
Racial and cultural considerations
  in cognitive-behavioral therapy,
      154–156
  in person-centered therapy,
      149–150
  in psychodymanic therapy,
      135–148
Racial and cultural terminology,
    15–33, 302–304
Racial hierarchy, 40, 70
Racial history, 1
Racial identity, 109, 118
  in career theory, 214–16
  expression, 93–95, 316–318
  interactions in therapy
      supervision, 287–290, 296
  models of VREGs, 81–95
  reaction styles, 169–170
  studies of, 282
  of therapists, 161
  types of events, 244–246
  of Whites, 89–93
Racial identity theory, 84–95, 180
Racial inferiority models of Whites,
    74–76
Racial labels, 27–28
Racially sensitive counseling and
    psychotherapy, 1
Racial matching, 307–308
Racial oppression. *See* Oppression
"Racial Oppression Syndrome," 67
Racial preference studies, 304–307
Racial research in therapy
    supervision, 290–291
Racial salience, 215
Racial socialization. *See* Socioracial
    socialization
Racial superiority models of Whites,
    73–74

"Racination," 70
Racism
  cultural, 24
  internalized, 20, 71
  types of, 38
  of VREGs, 325–326
  of Whites, 321–322, 325
Radiation cancer studies, 123
Rationalization, 139
Reaction formations, 75, 139
Real components of therapeutic
    alliances, 159
Realistic style, 202
Reality distortions, 153
Recent immigrants, 21, 40
  See also Immigration
Redskins, 43
Reflection of feelings, 179
Regression, 139
Regressive events in therapy,
    182–183, 245
Reintegration ego status (White),
    90, 92
Relationship establishment in
    therapy, 159–169, 239
Relationship focus, 104
Relative-deprivation hypothesis, 79
Religion in therapy, 189–192
Religious freedom, 39, 121
Religious institutions, 265
  See also Churches
Religious orientations, 1, 8, 19, 29
  socioreligious ethnics, 27
Religious spirituality of indigenous
    healers, 258–260
Remedial groups, 267
Repatriation, 60
Repetitive patterns, 135
Repression, 139
Republic of Haiti, 55
Research
  African American subjects, 123
  assessment issues, 304–307
  conceptual barriers, 300–310
  conceptualization of racial and
      cultural factors, 302–304
  cultural referent, 303–304
  future directions, 310–312
  nominal classification, 303
  outcome issues, 309–310
  process issues, 307–309
  race and culture as psychological
      constructs, 8, 9, 30
  race as nominal category, 16

  racial matching, 307–308
  shared political experiences, 304
  social class as psychological
      construct, 24
  in therapy supervision, 277–283,
      290–291, 295
  VREGs in psychotherapy, 185
Researchers, 300
Research grants, 301
Resistance in therapy, 8, 144–146, 222
Respect for authority, 117
Respeto, 116
Rise-and-drop hypothesis, 79
Rising-expectation hypothesis, 79
Rites of passage, 136, 196
Rituals, 19, 101
Rodriquez, Richard, 58
Roe, Anne, 202
Roe's career theory, 203
Rogers, Carl, 148
  Psychotherapist's Casebook, 149
Role-playing, 153, 155
Roots, 111
Rushton, J. Phillip, 74

Safe environment, 238, 239
Sandler, Kathe, 164
Santee Sioux, 111
Santeria, 260
Santeros, 260
SAT. *See* Scholastic Aptitude Test
Scapegoats, 77
Scholastic Aptitude Test (SAT), 246
School dropouts, 267
Schools, 8
Scientific inquiry. *See* Research
Screening interviews, 239
Segregation, 101
  and ethnicity, 19, 20
  and Social Darwinism, 40
  voluntary or involuntary, 8
Self, integrated sense of, 8
Self-actualization, 148, 150, 189, 262
Self-assessments, 153
Self-concept career theories,
    202–203, 206
Self-conceptions in cultural
    processes, 104–105
Self-defeating behavior, 150
Self-disclosure of therapists, 166,
    191, 193, 236
Self-fulfillment, 107, 202
Self-identification, 20, 28
  Latina/Latino Americans, 57

Self-identification, *continued*
  Native Americans, 45, 47
  White Americans, 37, 57
Self psychology, 142
Self-statements, 154
Seminole, 40
Senegal, 48
Separation and ethnicity, 19, 20
Settlers, 39
Sex-role identification, 143
Sexual intimacies, 196
Sexual orientations, 1, 8
Shadowing jobs, 223
Shamans, 256, 257
Sharing conflict resolution, 245
Shaw, William, 265
Shinkeishitsu, 261, 262
Silent assumptions, 154, 155
Simpatia, 114
Sioux, 45
Sitting Bull, 121
Skin color commentaries, 163–164
Skin color. *See* Physical
  characteristics
Slave mentality, 67
Slavery, 48–51, 74, 76, 113, 208
  See also African Americans
Social class, 1, 8, 19, 23–27
Social-class guilt, 26
Social construction, race as,
  15–17
Social contacts, 188, 320
Social context, 107–108
Social Darwinism, 40, 74
Social environments, 7
Socializing techniques, 234–235
Socially disengaged and engaged
  emotions, 106–107
Social networks of indigenous
  healers, 256, 264–269
Social roles, 107, 180, 244
Social style, 202
Societal institutions, 8
  exclusion from, 213–314
Societal norms, 16
Societies (tribes), 43
Sociobiology, 74
Sociocultural circumstantial model of
  racial oppression, 76–77
Sociological factors as interpersonal
  or systemic processes, 9–11
Sociological racial opression models
  of VREGs, 78–79
Sociopolitical factors, 35

Sociorace, 1, 30
  in groups, 244
  models of, 69–100
  See also Race
Socioracial groups
  culture-based, 55–68
  original, 34–54
Socioracial racial theory, 69–71
Socioracial socialization, 9–11, 69
  and cultural socialization, 7
Socioracial studies in therapy
  supervision, 278–281
Socioreligious ethnics, 27
  See also Religious orientations
Sororities, 126, 264
South America, 56
Spaniards, 56
Spanish-American War, 61
Spanish oppression of Latina/Latino
  Americans, 55–58
Spirit possessions, 256
Spirituality, 120
  in person-centered therapy,
    149, 150
  religion in therapy, 189–192
Standardized assessment tools, 152
Stereotyping, 7, 8
  African Americans, 208, 209
  of Asian Americans and Pacific
    Islanders, 62, 65, 159, 210
  of the client, 26, 140
  and language, 194, 215–216
  and mental health professions, 70
  and therapy, 97, 161–162, 191
  and vocational development, 213
  of White Americans, 71
Sterilization and reproduction
  research, 123
Stigma of emotional problems,
  191, 270
Street English, 194
Structural assimilation, 126
Subcultures, 27
Subjective culture, 101
Sublimation, 139
Suicidal behaviors, 150, 152
Super, Donald, 204
Supernatural and mystical beliefs and
  practices, 256–257, 271
Super's career theory, 204–205, 215
Supervision. *See* Therapy supervision
Support systems, 168, 188, 221
Supreme Being, 113, 189, 190
Supreme Creator, 112

Survivor guilt, 26, 43, 242
Symbolic healing, 254
Syphilis, 123
Systemic changes, 268
Systemic factors, 206
Systems perspectives of career
  counseling, 213–214

Talking about race, 246–251,
  318–320
"Talk therapy," 170
Taoism, 117, 258
Teen pregnancies, 267
Terminal illnesses, 241
Termination issues, 195
Terminology, racial and cultural,
  15–33, 302–304
Territorial behaviors, 76
Texas, 56
Theoretical myth of sameness
  (TMOS), 291
Theories, 133–157
  Afrocentric, 17
  of culture, 101–130
  environmental racial inferiority
    models, 75–76
  frustration-aggression hypothesis,
    77–78
  Helms's racial identity theory,
    84–95
  of oppression and sociorace,
    69–100
  order and power-conflict theories
    of racism, 71–78
  psychoanalytic, 69, 75, 133,
    134–148, 189
  race and culture as psychological
    constructs, 8, 9
  race as nominal category, 16
  socioracial racial, 69–71
  traditional career theoretical
    perspectives, 201–218
  VREG models of racial
    oppression, 78–95
Therapeutic alliances, 159, 239
Therapists
  beginning phase of therapy,
    161–164
  blank screen, 144–146
  and collectivistic perspectives, 22
  countertransference, 21
  culturally skilled, 175–177
  cultural mistrust, 123–124
  gift-giving, 186–188, 322–323

immigration history, 21
intrapsychic and interpersonal
    styles, 7–14
language switching, 193–195
multiple roles, 188–189
in psychodynamic therapy, 145 148
reactions to, 134–135
role in racial and cultural
    sensitivity, 1
self-disclosure, 166, 191, 193, 236
self-exploration, 2, 8, 20, 149,
    162–164
social-class guilt, 26–27
social contact with clients, 188,
    196, 320, 322
techniques of, 175–178
theoretical orientations, 133
training experiences, 133
values of, 316–318
VREG, 43, 48, 176, 178
Whites counseling ALANAs,
    324–325
See also Group leaders; Mental
    health professions;
    Transference
Therapy
    African American, 50–53
    Asian Americans and Pacific
        Islanders, 65–66
    clarification of expectations of
        education, 168–169
    cognitive behavioral, 133,
        150–156
    conceptual nuances, 173–185
    contact outside therapy, 188, 196
    cross-racial, 147, 149, 168, 191
    cultural implications, 22–23
    cultural models in, 103, 126–28
    directive, 168–169
    ethical issues and cultural conflict,
        195–197
    frustration-aggression hypothesis,
        77–78
    gift-giving, 186–188
    Helms's racial identity theory,
        84–95
    Latina/Latino Americans, 65–66
    modalities, 9
    models of oppression and
        sociorace, 96–98
    Native American, 47–48
    outcome, 184–185
    personalized psychological
        reactions, 71–72

person-centered, 133, 148–152
practice nuances, 185–197
psychodynamic, 134–148
race and culture as psychological
    constructs, 8
race and culture as themes, 9 12
racial implications, 17–19, 35
reaction formations, 75
religion in, 189–192
termination issues, 195
theoretical orientations, 133–157
time allowances for, 323–324
White American, 42–43
See also Beginning phase of
    therapy; Career counseling;
    Group therapy; Nuances of
    psychotherapy; Process
Therapy interaction process model,
    180–184
Therapy research. *See* Research
Therapy supervision, 277–298
    cultural issues, 291–295
    different perspective of authors,
        283–97
    empirical studies, 278–283
    experiencing, 285–286
    here-and-now focus on racial
        issues, 284–287
    historical overview, 277–278
    illumination, 286–287
    implications for cultural research,
        295
    implications for racial research,
        290–291
    implications for training, 296
    psychoracial studies, 281–283
    racial identity interactions,
        287–290, 296
    socioracial studies, 278–281
    theoretical myth of sameness
        (TMOS), 291
Thought disorders, 150, 152
Time concepts, 323–324
Tiv, 48
TMOS. *See* Theoretical myth
    of sameness
Toilet training, 136, 142–143
Tools, 101
Traditional cures, 136
Traditions, 19
Tragedies, 268–269
Training programs, 9
Training of therapists. *See* Therapy
    supervision

Transcendence in person-centered
    therapy, 149
Transference, 134–135, 137–138,
    144–145, 147, 159
Trauma, 136
Tribes, 43 44
Tubal ligations, 123
Tuskegee experiment, 123
Twelve-step groups, 267

Ujamaa, 122, 263
Umoja, 122, 263
Uncertainty avoidance, 104
Unconditional positive regard in
    person-centered therapy,
    148, 190
Unconscious motives and needs,
    134, 144
Undoing, 139
Unemployment, 206, 208, 210, 267
United States
    Christian cultures, 260
    dominant ethnic culture, 22
    domination of Latina/Latino
        Americans, 58–60
    explorers, 38
    Indian Bureau, 121
    Latina/Latino population, 56–57
    major socioracial groups, 11, 30
    miscegenation, 15
    patriarchal cultures, 317
    settlers, 39
    Supreme Court, 62
    treaties with Mexico, 58, 59
    work environment, 216
    See also American culture; White
        Americans
Universalistic perspectives of White
    Americans, 73 74
Universality, 229
University professors, 300
Unmada, 258
Unreal components of therapeutic
    alliances, 159
Urban dwellers, 39, 76–77, 268, 269

Values, 7, 101, 103, 166, 189, 316–318
Vasectomies, 123
Vicarious exposures, 283
Videotapes, 283
Vietnamese, 60
    See also Asian Americans and
        Pacific Islanders
Visibility of ethnic groups, 19

Visible racial/ethnic groups. *See* VREGs

Vocabulary. *See* Racial and cultural terminology

Vocational counseling. *See* Career counseling

Voluntary segregation, 8

Volunteer service providers, 266

VREG models of racial oppression, 78–95
  Helms's racial identity theory, 84
  identity models, 81–84
  psychological, 79–81
  racial identity models, 81–95
  sociological, 78–79

VREGs, 24, 28, 30
  as clients and therapists, 43, 48, 175, 176, 178, 291, 308
  and Native Americans, 47–48
  political organizations, 264
  racist versus bigoted, 325–326
  research about, 185
  stereotypic assumptions, 70
  Whites counseling, 325
  See also ALANAs; specific groups

Walters, Eugene, 111

Want-ads, 223

WASPs (White Anglo-Saxon Protestants), 39
  See also White Americans

Wellness, 112

Western culture, 21–22

Western European ethnic groups, 22, 74

Western literature, 2

White Americans
  acculturation, 124–126
  and authors, 2
  beauty standards, 51
  census (1990), 57
  circumstantial models of racial oppression, 76–77
  counseling ALANAs, 324–325
  cultural labels, 29
  culture, 108–110
  as dominant culture, 22, 31
  environmental racial inferiority models, 75–76
  ethnicity, 19, 38, 40–42, 124, 126
  frustration-aggression hypothesis, 77–78
  as major socioracial group, 11–12
  men, 300–301
  occupational distribution, 211
  order models, 77–78
  power-conflict models, 72–77
  racial hierarchy, 40
  racial identity, 89–93
  racial inferiority models, 74–76
  racial superiority models, 73–74
  racist clients, 321–322, 325
  sociopolitical history, 37–43
  stereotyping, 71
  survivor guilt, 26, 43, 242
  universalistic perspectives, 73–74
  See also American culture; United States; WASPs

White people
  definition, 62, 89
  explorers, 38, 44
  settlers, 39

White Rock Baptist Church, 265

Wiley, Christine, 266

Wish lists, 223

Women, 29, 117
  African American, 135
  career development of Asian, 209–210
  female genital mutilation, 136
  occupational distribution, 211
  See also Gender; Marie; Patty

Working poor, 213

Workshops, 267

Worldviews, 154, 167, 185, 220, 233

Worship services, 265

Wounded Knee, 121

Wovoka, the "Painte Messiah," 121

WRIAS Social Attitudes Inventory, 94

Yalom's therapeutic factors, 227–242
  altruism, 231–232
  catharsis, 240–241
  corrective recapitulation of the primary family group, 232–234
  development of socializing techniques, 234–235
  existential factors, 241–242
  group cohesiveness, 239–240
  imitative behavior, 235–236
  imparting information, 229–231
  instillation of hope, 227–228
  interpersonal learning, 236–239
  universality, 229

Yoga techniques, 260

Youth Ministry, 268